The publisher gratefully acknowledges the contributions toward the publication of this book provided by the Society for American Music and by Sukey Garcetti, Michael Roth, and the Roth Family Foundation.

MUSIC OF THE AFRICAN DIASPORA
Edited by Samuel A. Floyd, Jr.

William Grant Still

This man, William Grant Still, is . . .
the only man of his race to abondon
the past on one hand, to cling to it successfully
on the other, and to make a successful and
original artistic cohesion of the two.
                    —*Harold Bruce Forsythe (1930)*

William Grant Still

A Study in Contradictions

CATHERINE PARSONS SMITH

with contributed essays by
Gayle Murchison and Willard B. Gatewood
chronology by Carolyn L. Quin
and
contemporary sources from the 1930s: Verna Arvey,
Harold Bruce Forsythe, Irving Schwerké (edited by Wayne D. Shirley),
and William Grant Still

UNIVERSITY OF CALIFORNIA PRESS
Berkeley   ·   Los Angeles   ·   London

Gayle Murshison's essay, "'Dean of Afro-American Composers' or 'Harlem Renaissance Man': The New Negro and the Musical Poetics of William Grant Still," originally appeared in the *Arkansas Historical Quarterly* 53 (spring 1994): 42–74. Harold Bruce Forsythe's "A Study in Contradictions" and "Plan for a Biography of William Grant Still" are published with the permission of The Huntington Library, San Marino, California, and Harold Sumner Forsythe. Excerpts of letters from Harold Bruce Forsythe to Verna Arvey are published with the permission of The Huntington Library. William Grant Still's "Personal Notes" is published with the permission of William Grant Still Music, Flagstaff, Arizona. Copyright William Grant Still Music. The letters of Irving Schwerké from the Irving Schwerké Collection, Music Division, Library of Congress, are reproduced by permission of the First Church of Christ, Scientist, Boston, Massachusetts. The letters of William Grant Still, examples from Still's sketchbooks, and certain music examples and photographs are reproduced by permission of William Grant Still Music. Music examples from the *Afro-American Symphony,* copyright 1935 by J. Fischer & Bro. Copyright renewed 1962 and transferred to Novello & Co. Ltd., 1970. Reprinted by permission. Music and text example from the opera *Troubled Island* copyright 1976 by Southern Music Publishing Co., Inc. International Copyright Secured. Reprinted by permission. Letters from Alain Locke to William Grant Still are cited with the permission of the Moorland-Springarn Research Center, Howard University. Letter from Arna Bontemps to Verna Arvey is reprinted by permission of Harold Ober Associates, Incorporated, as agents for the Estate of Arna Bontemps. Photograph of Harold Bruce Forsythe is reproduced by permission of Harold Sumner Forsythe.

University of California Press
Berkeley and Los Angeles, California

University of California Press, Ltd.
London, England

© 2000 by
The Regents of the University of California

Library of Congress Cataloging-in-Publication Data
Smith, Catherine Parsons, 1933–
    William Grant Still : a study in contradictions / Catherine Parsons Smith ; with
  contributed essays by Gayle Murchison . . . [et al.], and contemporary sources from the
  1930s, Verna Arvey . . . [et al.].
       p.   cm. — (Music of the African diaspora ; 2)
    Includes bibliographical references (p.) and index.
    ISBN 0-520-21542-7 (cloth : alk. paper). — ISBN 0-520-21543-5 (pbk. : alk. paper)
    1. Still, William Grant, 1895—Criticism and interpretation.   I. Title.   II. Series.
  ML410.S855S65   2000
  780'.92—dc21   99-43232
                                                                              CIP

Printed in the United States of America
08 07 06 05 04 03 02 01 00 99
10 9 8 7 6 5 4 3 2 1

The paper used in this publication meets the minimum requirements of ANSI-NISO Z39.48-1992 (R 1997) (Permanence of Paper) ⊚.

Contents

CONTRIBUTED ESSAYS

Toward a Biography

Sources

Illustrations

MUSIC EXAMPLES

Acknowledgments

I gratefully acknowledge the extensive and varied support I have received in writing and editing this book, the first to establish a critical context for Still's work. Judith Anne Still, the owner of William Grant Still Music as well as the composer's daughter, has been forthcoming and cooperative in supplying copies of rare materials and answering innumerable questions, returning my calls and clarifying many details even as she restrained her impatience with my deliberate ways. It was she who called my attention to her mother's (Verna Arvey's) "Scribblings" and much other invaluable documentation. Moreover, she led me to a major new source on both Still and the New Negro movement in Los Angeles.

I have taken the title of this book from Harold Bruce Forsythe's 1930 landmark essay on Still with the permission of his son, Harold Sumner Forsythe, Professor of History at Rancho Santiago College, Santa Ana, California. Professor Forsythe generously wrote, "I am sure that my father would be honored to finally be recognized as the founder of the critical study of William Grant Still's music." I thank him further for making available the materials in his possession on his father, for answering many questions in the course of interviews on December 21 and 22, 1994, and for subsequently placing his father's surviving papers at The Huntington Library. A celebration of the acquisition of the Forsythe Collection by The Huntington Library in February 1997 was also valuable. Both Judith Anne Still and Professor Forsythe have generously made photographs available as well. I also wish to acknowledge with thanks

the kindness of many other people who have graciously granted interviews, in person and by telephone, including Verna Arvey (long before
I thought to write on Still), Harry Hay, and Annette Kaufman.

Like many another project, this book grew from something else, in
this case a single essay on Still, written for a project that did not come
to pass. Its growth into the present, much more ambitious project also
owes a great deal to interactions with other musicians and scholars interested in Still's music. As these intensified, a rich brew of ideas and
questions developed. Gayle Murchison has been far more helpful than
the contribution of a single essay might suggest. She consistently pushed
me to look further and consider more fully, pointing out additional references and generally sharing the insights of her pathbreaking dissertation research comparing the positions of Still and his contemporary
Aaron Copland. A Still Centennial celebration sponsored by the Department of Music at the University of Arkansas, Fayetteville, organized
by Murchison and Claire Detels in March 1995 stimulated my thought
on Still as well. That meeting made possible lengthy and rewarding conversations on Still's music and some of the issues raised in the course of
his career. Along with Murchison, Carolyn L. Quin, Wayne D. Shirley,
and Jon Michael Spencer were among the major contributors to those
discussions. A larger conference and two concerts of long-unheard works
by Still and his contemporary Florence Price in June 1998 was funded
by a generous grant from Northern Arizona University. This conference
and its performances set in motion new responses to Still's work that can
only be suggested here. I am indebted to Patricia Hoy, Blase Scarnati,
Garry Owens, Jamise Liddell, and Tom Cleman of Northern Arizona University and graduate students David Betancourt, Jennifer Boomgaarden,
Albert Grijalva, and Roger Valencia for the success of that conference,
for which I served as program chair.

Special thanks to the contributing authors and editors, who suffered
many delays in the preparation of this volume while I struggled to find
an appropriate form for the diverse materials that are brought together
in this book. Willard B. Gatewood, Alumni Distinguished Professor of
History at the University of Arkansas, Fayetteville, is a specialist in
Southern history. His numerous books include *Preachers, Pedagogues
and Politicians* (1966), *Aristocrats of Color: The Black Elite 1880–
1920* (1990), and *The Arkansas Delta: Land of Paradox* (1993). Gayle
Murchison is Assistant Professor of Music at Tulane University; she has
written on Mary Lou Williams as well as Still. Carolyn L. Quin, a long-

time student of Still's music, is on the music faculty at Riverside Community College in California. Wayne D. Shirley, Music Specialist in the Library of Congress, is a past editor of *American Music* and has written on many subjects, including Still, George Gershwin, Charles Ives, and George Antheil. Exchanges with many other scholars at professional meetings at which I presented parts of my work on Still and via electronic mail have had an immeasurable value. Lance Bowling, Paul Charosh, Gayle Murchison, Cindy Richardson, and Wayne Shirley all read substantial portions of the manuscript at various stages and gave valuable advice.

Assistance of librarians and archivists is essential to a book such as this, and it was made abundantly available to me. Led by Michael Dabrishus, the staff of the Special Collections Division, Fulbright Library, University of Arkansas, Fayetteville, has been extremely cooperative, dealing with me most graciously in person as well as by telephone, mail, and e-mail. Staff members at the Music Division of the Library of Congress, the Moorland-Spingarn Collection at Howard University, The Huntington Library, the Maryland Historical Society, the Music Division and Billy Rose Collections of the New York Public Library at Lincoln Center, the Schomberg Center at the New York Public Library, and the Beinecke Library at Yale University have been equally gracious and accommodating. The Inter-Library Loan staff at the Getchell Library, University of Nevada, Reno, has long and patiently delivered the goods on my innumerable requests.

I was able to draft early versions of several essays and consult libraries on the East Coast while a participant in a National Endowment for the Humanities Summer Seminar in 1994. The supportive atmosphere and some modest but strategic financial support from the Department of Music, the College of Arts & Science, and the Graduate School at the University of Nevada, Reno, have enabled me to proceed with this project without excessive interruption.

Several readers for the University of California Press have had a major influence on the shaping of this book as well, including but not limited to Rae Linda Brown, Dominique-René De Lerma, and Susan McClary. At the Press, first Doris Kretschmer and then Lynne Withey have been supportive, constructive, and patient throughout, as have Julie Brand, Karen Branson, Sheila Berg, and Suzanne Knott. Of course, I am responsible for the opinions stated, the sources chosen, and the conclusions drawn.

Abbreviations

AM	*American Music*
Amerigrove	Hitchcock, H. Wiley, and Stanley Sadie, eds. *The New Grove Dictionary of American Music.* London: Macmillan, 1986.
Bio-Bibliography	Still, Judith Anne, Michael J. Dabrishus, and Carolyn L. Quin, eds. *William Grant Still: A Bio-Bibliography.* Westport, Conn.: Greenwood Press, 1996.
BMRJ	*Black Music Research Journal*
BPiM	*The Black Perspective in Music*
Du Bois	Du Bois, W. E. B. *The Souls of Black Folk.* Originally published Chicago: McClurg, 1903.
Forsythe Papers	Forsythe Papers, The Huntington Library
Fusion 2	Still, J. A., C. A. Headlee, and L. M. Headlee-Huffman, eds. *William Grant Still and the Fusion of Cultures in American Music.* 2d ed. Flagstaff, Ariz.: Master-Player Library, 1995. 1st ed. Robert B. Haas, ed. Los Angeles: Black Sparrow Press, 1972.

IOL	Arvey, Verna. *In One Lifetime*. Fayetteville: University of Arkansas Press, 1984.
JWJ	James Weldon Johnson Memorial Collection, Beinecke Library, Yale University
LC	Music Division, Library of Congress
MM	*Modern Music*
Spencer, *Reader*	Spencer, Jon Michael. *The William Grant Still Reader*. Special issue. *Black Sacred Music: A Journal of Theomusicology* 6, no. 2 (Fall 1992)
Still-Arvey Papers	William Grant Still and Verna Arvey Papers, Special Collections Division, University of Arkansas Libraries, Fayetteville
WGSM	William Grant Still Music, Flagstaff, Arizona

Introduction

Africa!
Rememb'ring Africa
. . . .
So long, so far away!

> Langston Hughes, *Troubled Island*
> (Act I: Martel's aria)

This book explores aspects of William Grant Still's aesthetic development in the context of the much-contested personal, professional, and cultural landscape in which he worked. Although its focus is on the 1930s—the decade of Still's maturity as a composer—the different voices presented here reflect the conflicts that surrounded Still throughout his dual careers as commercial musician and composer of concert music and opera. Encoded in these different narratives are intersections among the ideas and realities of the Harlem Renaissance, musical modernism, and American musical nationalism. These engage issues involving race, class, musical style and genre, and, to a lesser degree, gender and geography—issues that affected the way Still's music was written and performed, listened to and written about, then as much as now.

W. E. B. Du Bois's famous statement in *The Souls of Black Folk* (1903) about racial doubleness, certainly well known to Still, may serve as the launching point for this study:

> The Negro is a sort of seventh son, born with a veil, and gifted with second-sight in this American world,—a world which yields him no true self-consciousness, but only lets him see himself through the revelation of the other world. It is a peculiar sensation, this double-consciousness, this sense of always looking at one's self through the eyes of others, of measuring one's soul by the tape of a world that looks on in amused contempt and pity. One ever feels his two-ness,—an American, a Negro; two souls, two thoughts, two unreconciled strivings; two warring ideals in one dark body, whose dogged strength alone keeps it from being torn asunder.

> The history of the American Negro is the history of this strife,—this long-
> ing to attain self-conscious manhood, to merge his double self into a better
> and truer self. In this merging he wishes neither of the older selves to be lost.[1]

Du Bois's insight about what he called the "double consciousness" or
the "two-ness" of African Americans struck a responsive chord at the
time and remains a touchstone that frames the lives of many individuals who share the African American experience. It carries a particular
weight when considering creative artists such as Still (as Gayle Murchison points out in her chapter), although explorations of its consequences
by black cultural critics have consistently focused on the other arts more
than on concert music.[2] Certainly Still's desire for a "fusion" of widely
separated musical styles—actually several fusions—plays out Du Bois's
aspiration "to merge his double self into a better and truer self." We are
only beginning to glimpse the process by which Still explored his own
doubleness as a creator of music as well as the multiple contradictions
that surrounded him.

Still's roots were African American, southern, and relatively elite. His
family's lack of wealth was no bar to its social status as, in Willard Gatewood's phrase, "aristocrats of color." Both of his parents were college
graduates, rare among African Americans of their generation. Both followed the teaching profession, highly regarded because formal education,
so long denied, was widely understood as fundamental to race progress.
Still's stepfather (Still's father, a musician, died shortly after his birth), a
postal employee—always referred to as "Mr. Shepperson"—also held a
respected position in the community. The family attended the Allison
Street Presbyterian Church, one of the congregations favored by Little
Rock's African American elite. Still's genteel training, his enduring sense
of high obligation to better the lot of his race, and even his light skin fit
Gatewood's description of an elite African American of his time.[3] His
position of relative privilege made him a member of what Du Bois had
labeled the "Talented Tenth" of the generation of the Harlem Renaissance. Still was well aware of the debate over how African Americans
might best take their full place in American society, for Du Bois's slightly
older rival, Booker T. Washington, was a guest in the Still/Shepperson
home in Little Rock on one occasion.[4] Still's elite affiliation combined
with his creative direction and political conservatism have led to ambiva-

lence about his artistic contributions, for what is usually called the black middle class is "surely one of the most disparaged social groups in all of modern history." [5]

As a child, Still observed all the forms of music making practiced in his community, including traditional religious music sung at home by his grandmother. Yet his musical inclinations lay with the European-influenced African American concert tradition, an often-ignored part of his heritage. His first role model was the Afro-English composer Samuel Coleridge-Taylor (1875–1912), who made several trips to America after the turn of the century. Several older contemporaries were writing concert music that drew from this tradition; Nathaniel Dett, Harry T. Burleigh, and Will Marion Cook all encouraged him and became his friends. His early experience in Harlem included performances of the symphonic repertoire organized by and for African American audiences, as documented in the *New York Age;* such concerts were not unique to New York City. [6] Still's interest in "serious" music, especially opera, seems never to have wavered, although a career as a composer appeared hopelessly out of reach for many years. After all, most "serious" composers in the United States, regardless of race, had (and have) other means of supporting themselves. It is a mark of Still's determination that he was eventually able to devote so much of his time to composition; he created operas, symphonies, and ballets in addition to his commercial work.

In spite of the energy and the complex webs of patronage, audience, and neighborhood that shaped the Harlem Renaissance, the immediate effect of the cultural boom of the 1920s for African American musicians (including Still) was to provide more opportunities to do much as they had earlier done, though at a higher level and with more respect as the popular genres moved from minstrel shows to vaudeville to Broadway revues like *Shuffle Along.* [7] Their new freedom was far from complete, as is especially clear from the perspective of the late twentieth century. Nevertheless, stereotype-driven constraints on blacks as entertainers clearly weakened, allowing the "minstrel mask" to slip and sometimes revealing the creative ferment taking place behind it. Opportunities for new artistic departures that were commercially sustainable remained limited despite the importance of those that were successful. Indeed, many of the black entertainers and artists who achieved substantial fame or success in Still's lifetime did it by performing selected aspects of African American culture to a predominantly white audience. This process necessarily involved continuing mediation and adaptation among black and white cultural and performance traditions and among stereotypes held by both blacks and whites about themselves and each other.

Successful commercial adaptations with which Still was directly involved include the achievement of his mentor W. C. Handy, the "father of the blues," who transcribed and published an existing aural tradition limited to a particular region and group for a wider audience, thereby altering it dramatically and creating the immensely popular "classic" blues; the 1921 musical *Shuffle Along,* which (with Still as a member of its orchestra and a contributor to its orchestrations) initiated a new era of black musicals in the 1920s; and much of his later work in New York as arranger, performer, and conductor. Other adaptations and translations were undertaken by many other artists. White audiences usually accepted them as "black" culture; African American audiences often applauded but sometimes saw them as something else. Collectively, they created new genres and styles that are now seen as quintessential elements of our diverse American culture.

In presenting himself as a composer of concert music, Still chose a path less traveled by members of the race, a path less understood by both blacks and whites to this day. As a composer of concert music, he crossed barriers of class as well as color, forcing him to rethink his racial doubleness in new ways. This move required him to forge new means of communicating and contextualizing his Africanness, taking into account (among other things) the musical language of modernism, with its elements of primitivism and colonialism, that he learned from his teacher Edgard Varèse and the younger white modernists who were his contemporaries. By pursuing his interest in composing concert music, Still had to address the "minstrel mask" directly. It is this challenge that led him to reformulate his long-standing interest in American music away from the modernists' direction of exploring the dissonant, antisentimental "modern." Instead, he sought sophisticated formal constructs that opened the way to and even demanded a truer fusion of European and African American traditions into a genuinely new American voice. That unique and continuing process of rethinking and the circumstances that surrounded it are the underlying theme of this book.

From 1925 on, Still's "serious" works were performed before elite white audiences, making a mark even though they often drew mixed reviews—reviews that turned increasingly on both racial difference and the class-related distinction between concert and popular music. This criticism is frustrating to read and interpret, since it is often couched in oblique terms with coded meanings not only for racial stereotypes but for aspects of musical style and language as well; in these cases the underlying issues are very seldom addressed or explored directly. For example, in Still's 1924 suite for eight instruments and three voices "used instrumentally," *From the Land of Dreams,* performed once (February 8, 1925) and recently rediscovered, a blues gesture appears as a contrasting theme, embedded in a framework of startlingly original instrumental/vocal timbres and chromatic dissonance (Example 1). The *New York Times* critic Olin Downes, not recognizing Still's construct, wrote about it, "One hoped for better things from Still. . . . Is Mr. Still unaware that the cheapest melody in the revues he has orchestrated has more reality and inspiration than the curious noises he has manufactured?" The ultramodern clothing that surrounded the blues theme in the work was clear to his audience, but the blues was not, confounding the expectation of his hearers and probably his intent as well. In May 1931, Downes wrote of the ballet *Sahdji:* "The ballet Sahdji is fully as racial in content as the former work [i.e., *Africa*]. . . . But this is real music, music of a composer of exotic talent and temperament." In addition to the racial stereotypes such as "exotic," with its implication of a difference involving sexuality, the importance of class distinctions drawn between Still's commercial work ("the cheapest melody") and the concert music under review, along with arguments over modernism ("curious noises . . . manufactured"), in these comments appears repeatedly in commentaries on Still's music.[8]

Discussions of commercial theater in the 1920s tend to give a richer perspective for the context in which Still's aesthetic ideas developed and his early performances took place than does published music criticism. The first all-black Broadway dramatic production that attempted to portray African Americans as a collection of diverse humans rather than primarily as clowns was William Jourdan Rapp and Wallace Thurman's *Harlem,* written over several years but not produced until 1929. (Thurman had been a mentor to Still's friend Harold Bruce Forsythe in his pre–New York, Los Angeles days.) *Harlem* drew extensive discussion of racial issues in the press, as well as some acknowledgment of its particular "checker" audience with its implications about class.[9] Some excerpts quoted here are applicable to Still's achievement in music and illustrate the context in which he worked more effectively than do the reviews of

Example 1. Opening, *From the Land of Dreams*. The diatonic passage, hinting at the beginning of a blues, is in bars 6–9, played by the oboe. Courtesy of William Grant Still Music.

his work by music critics.[10] Drama critics waxed most negative when *Harlem* characters failed to act the racial stereotype:

> It is only where the sober realities of life among the negroes are touched upon that the play becomes as forced and absurd and totally lacking in sympathetic insight. Very little of the essential childlike humor and pathos of the colored race is allowed play.[11]

> Most of it is untamed and broad-gauged stuff, full of rowdy jokes and gestures which do somehow catch an authentic jungle note in the brownstone

wastelands of One Hundred and Thirty-fifth street. . . . Since most of the principal actors are negroes, it is stimulated at once by the natural born instinct of that festive race for cutting up monkeyshines.[12]

The authors of *Harlem* responded to the critics' racially directed criticism by laying out the stereotypes they had deliberately avoided:

> Most Negro dramas previous to "Harlem" dealt with what Negroes call "white folks' niggers," while "Harlem" actually presents the Negro as he is.
>
> "White folks' niggers" consist of three distinct categories: the old servant or mammy type known derisively among the Harlemites as "Uncle Toms" and "handkerchiefs," the lazy slow-foot type typified by such vaudevillians as Bert Williams and Miller and Lyles [who starred in *Shuffle Along,* mentioned above], and the superstitious, praying type who is always thrown into abject fear by darkness, lightning and thunder. All these types flatter the white's sense of superiority and it pleases him to believe that all colored people are like this. The dramatist who shows them thusly is bound to be complimented for his keen understanding of the Negro.[13]

Like the authors of *Harlem* and other African American creative artists, Still had to deal repeatedly with the ingrained stereotypes. Blacks and whites alike in many ways remained the prisoners of the old typecasting from the minstrel-vaudeville-variety show tradition. Nevertheless, for racial issues to be discussed so extensively in the white daily papers as well as in magazines intended for African American audiences, at least in the case of *Harlem,* reveals that the subject was at last open for debate.

In Du Bois's terms, Still's achievement was to compose concert music not as represented "through the revelation of the other world" but in a unique African American voice speaking as itself, in its own behalf. By finding his "speaking self," Still took a step toward giving African Americans a direct view of themselves, direct representation in the literate European-derived universe of concert music. From this well-grounded position he was empowered to take the further step of speaking as a "universal" composer, though one who often chose his own form of African American-derived musical speech.

The combination of essays from the 1990s and sources from the 1930s in this book meets the challenge of creating a context that will allow a critical reassessment of Still's music and his place in twenth-century American culture. Its seems more important at this juncture to allow a range of voices to be heard, even at the cost of some repetition, than to attempt a definitive interpretation when so many questions about Still's life and music remain unanswered. The contributed essays by Willard B. Gatewood and Gayle Murchison and the chronology by Carolyn L. Quin collectively provide a launching point. Gatewood begins with a description of the Little Rock of Still's boyhood. He depicts the conditional privilege, located within and dependent on a deeply racist society, enjoyed by Still's forebears and influencing him. Equally important is the reiteration of the theme that Still grew up in a period of increasing racial violence and tension. Along with his family's commitment to racial uplift, his mother's opposition to the growth of Jim Crow laws formalizing racial segregation of public facilities in Little Rock and elsewhere significantly influenced Still's later career decisions. Murchison presents an exposition of the relationship between Still's work and the Harlem Renaissance, particularly with reference to Alain Locke's *The New Negro,* a connection that has not been addressed in Still scholarship until recently. Murchison suggests three style periods for Still's concert music, in keeping with his own statements: "ultramodern," "racial" (from 1925), and "universal" (1932 on). The connection she makes between the Harlem Renaissance and modernism is particularly valuable for understanding Still's position in American music.

Two of the essays focus on close associates and collaborators, Harold Bruce Forsythe (1906–1976) and Verna Arvey (1911–1987). These two associates, friends themselves for many years though enormously different in aesthetic approach and personality, each influenced Still far more than their common role as contributors of librettos might suggest. The biographical sketches of each that form chapters here provide background for their own essays on Still as well as serve to emphasize their personal and professional importance to Still. In their persons as in their writings, they enrich the dialogue on Still and his work that is only now beginning to emerge. These writers stand in striking contrast to each other.

Forsythe, librettist for Still's first opera (*Blue Steel*) and a Los Angeles-based advocate of the New Negro movement, has been virtually an invisible person, one whose very identity has been a source of confusion.[14] The first to write seriously about Still, Forsythe engages emotionally with his music, most notably with the orchestral tone poem *Darker America,* which he argues is the product of Still's essential, African-based sensibility. Through *Darker America,* Forsythe addresses Still's "peculiar isolation from [his] race," which he correctly sees as "only apparent [for] underneath there are significant ties," [15] thus providing an otherwise missing contemporary New Negro view of how Still addressed his racial doubleness in his artistic production during a highly productive period. Forsythe's contribution, published here for the first time, is the more valuable because well-known black intellectuals such as Du Bois and Alain Locke did not address Still's music (or anyone else's) with anything like the level of conviction and forcefulness that they applied to drama, fiction, and poetry.

Forsythe faced the challenge of writing about Still's music without much in the way of usable literary models, a problem analogous to the challenge Still faced in seeking musical models for his compositions. The subtitle of Forsythe's iconoclastic essay is appropriated for this book partly for its continuing aptness to Still research. In addition, it is intended to recognize for the first time that Forsythe is the initiator of Still criticism and to acknowledge the passionate commitment and insight that inform his writing.

Verna Arvey is better known than Forsythe, but she has almost faded from view as an individual despite her position as Still's publicist and collaborator starting in 1934, his wife from 1939 until his death in 1978, and executor of his estate thereafter.[16] Forsythe and Arvey had been friends from their student days in the mid-1920s at Manual Arts High School in Los Angeles. Forsythe, whose family lived on property owned by a Still cousin, met Still in the course of a year's study at the Juilliard School in New York in 1927–1928. Arvey learned about Still several years before Forsythe introduced her to him during his early L.A. visits in 1929–1930. After Still moved permanently to Los Angeles in 1934, a romantic triangle developed among the three, leaving a residue of hostility that both influenced the course and skewed the record of Still's career.

George Fischer, Still's major publisher, was dubious when Arvey approached him in 1937 with her plan for a biography (actually a ghosted autobiography in one of its drafts) but presently changed his mind and cut her text sharply to fit into a series of promotional booklets for the American composers whose work he championed.[17] The resulting monograph, republished here, comes close at times to Still's earlier exposition in his "Personal Notes" but nevertheless entails considerable filtering through both Arvey's eyes and those of its publisher. The restrained, formal prose of her monograph contrasts sharply with Forsythe's flamboyant, unapologetically personal style.

"Toward a Biography" forms the core of the book. The biographical essay on Still in Los Angeles clarifies numerous points with regard to

Still's state of mind at the time of his "expatriation" from New York City as well as his activities before and after the move, including his less-than-satisfying adventures in Hollywood. Still's most famous concert work, the *Afro-American Symphony*, completed within months of his return from his prolonged early sojourn in Los Angeles, is the central paradigm for the working out of the "fusion" aesthetic he had struggled over for nearly a decade. It was the success of this symphony that really launched Still on his career as a composer of concert music and carried his reputation far beyond the reach of those 1920s "new music" concerts, with their limited audiences and self-consciously modernist posture.

The "great truth" Still wished to convey through the *Afro-American Symphony* had to do not only with his religious convictions but much more directly with the creative synergy possible among American cultures as the African American influence took the position he desired for it, as an equal contributor, "another American voice," in his words. In his quest to achieve this goal he went far out of his way to avoid stereotypical portrayals of African American culture, most obviously through his creative uses of the blues. Still's concern with the blues is in fact analogous to that of many African American artists and writers of the mid-twentieth century, though that commonality has been little recognized by theorists of black culture.

One often unspoken issue for Still is his role in the anticommunist movement of the late 1940s and early 1950s, seen here as a dim reflection of his disillusionment at the failure of the dream embodied in his first symphony. Perhaps the cultural necessity for the supposed antimodernism of Still's *Afro-American Symphony* and the contradictoriness of his late political activity is summed up, however obliquely, in Forsythe's perception: "The intellectualism of modern music is more psychopathic than has been generally understood." [18]

Still's voice is heard directly in the first two of the sources. In 1933, Still produced several pages of autobiographical material in response to a request from Harold Bruce Forsythe. In addition to Still's own evaluation of his concert music up to 1933, these notes offer a key that leads toward the documentation and assessment of Still's little-known, apparently substantial contributions to Harlem's commercial music scene through his New York years (1919–1934). His correspondence with a Paris-based critic, Irving Schwerké, who arranged for performances of Still's music in Europe and otherwise encouraged him, shows him in relation to a supportive white critic.

Although Still's concert music had begun to attract critical attention from the mid-1920s, all of it was in the form of brief coverage of individual performances. The sources presented here, most of them never published until now, were the first to consider his music in any depth. Hence, they are important to an understanding of one of the mid–twenth century's most prominent American composers of concert music and opera, and a major contributor to popular music of the 1920s and 1930s. The contradictions with which Still struggled shaped his remarkable creative output in ways we need to understand, as much today as during his lifetime.

NOTES

1. W. E. B. Du Bois, *The Souls of Black Folk* (1903; reprint, New York: Fawcett, 1961), 16–17.

2. For examples, Kwame Anthony Appiah, *In My Father's House: Africa in the Philosophy of Culture* (New York: Oxford University Press, 1992); Houston A. Baker, Jr., *Modernism and the Harlem Renaissance* (Chicago: University of Chicago Press, 1987) and other titles; Henry Louis Gates, Jr., *The Signifying Monkey: A Theory of Afro-American Literary Criticism* (New York: Oxford University Press, 1988) and other titles; Paul Gilroy, *The Black Atlantic: Modernity and Double Consciousness* (Cambridge, Mass.: Harvard University Press, 1993). African Americans in jazz and blues have attracted far more literary attention than those in other fields of music.

Baker's scheme, intended to apply to literary figures but appropriate as well for composers such as Still, involves complex and continuing negotiation among the "minstrel mask," the "mastery of formation," and presently the "deformation of mastery" in all fields of music. These categories generally refer to the portrayal of African Americans as European Americans wished or wish to see them and the mastery of the white formal languages by blacks and the consequent adjustment of the formal language to accommodate and express the creator's intention. These stages of expressiveness are not necessarily sequential; they may well overlap in ways as various as the creative artists involved.

3. See Willard Gatewood's chapter in this volume; also Gatewood, *Aristocrats of Color* (Bloomington: Indiana University Press, 1990); and Du Bois.

4. Du Bois's visit is reported in Verna Arvey, "Scribblings," longhand notes on Still (no date, no page number). Gatewood is unable to confirm a visit to Little Rock by Du Bois; most likely Arvey was in error and the visitor was Booker T. Washington. (See Gatewood's chapter below.) Still's brief interest in becoming a chicken farmer was probably inspired by Washington's visit and his writings.

5. Andrew Ross, *No Respect: Intellectuals and Popular Culture* (New York: Routledge, 1989), 76, quoted in Ingrid Monson, "The Problem with White Hipness: Race, Gender, and Cultural Conceptions in Jazz Historical Discourse,"

Journal of the American Musicological Society 48 no. 3 (Fall 1995): 396–422.
See also Imamu Amiri Baraka [LeRoi Jones], *Blues People: Negro Music in
White America* (New York: William Morrow, 1963), 231, 130, and passim, for
expressions of concern about the integrity of the "autonomous blues" in the face
of [Monson] "conformist and assimilationist demands of a black middle class
that has dictated an 'image of a whiter Negro, to the poorer, blacker Negroes.'"

6. *New York Age,* February 12, 1921, 3, "In the Realm of Music," reports
that Still was a member of the New Amsterdam Musical Association orchestra
that gave a concert at the New Star Casino on 107th Street on Sunday evening,
February 5, 1921, at 10:00 P.M. Dancing followed the formal program, a variation not modeled on symphony concerts downtown. Hall Johnson, later director of a black choir famous for its performances of spirituals, was among the
violas. The program included music by Rimsky-Korsakov, Samuel Coleridge-
Taylor, Montague Ring, Sarasate, Ethelbert Nevin, and Elgar. (Coleridge-Taylor
and Ring had African ancestors.)

Michael W. Harris, *The Rise of Gospel Blues: The Music of Thomas Andrew
Dorsey in the Urban Church* (New York: Oxford University Press, 1992). See
chap. 5, "Old-Line Religion and Musicians, 1920–1930," esp. pp. 106 ff.
Harris documents a vigorous, widespread musical practice, although he regards
it negatively as part of a borrowed middle-class culture that attempted to suppress indigenous African American musical customs. It is likely that most of
these had features, like the dancing that followed the Star Casino performance,
designed to accommodate both the location and the audience.

7. The nexus of blackface entertainment that provides part of the background from which the black musicals of the Harlem Renaissance is treated in,
among other places, Robert Toll, *Blacking Up* (New York: Oxford University
Press, 1974); David Nasaw, *Going Out: The Rise and Fall of Public Amuse-
ments* (New York: Basic Books, 1993); and Eric Lott, *Love and Theft: Blackface
Minstrelsy and the American Working Class* (New York: Oxford University
Press, 1993). For discussions of the need for more broadly based and perceptive
musical analysis, see Katherine Bergeron and Philip V. Bohlman, eds., *Disciplin-
ing Music: Musicology and Its Canons* (Chicago: University of Chicago Press,
1992), especially Don Michael Randel, "The Canons in the Musicological Tool-
box," and Gary Tomlinson, "Cultural Dialogics and Jazz: A White Historian
Signifies."

8. Still reacted to this incident by suppressing *From the Land of Dreams.*
His experience raises the question of whether his next work to be performed at
a similar concert, *Levee Land,* was intended as a practical joke. *Levee Land,* discussed in Murchison's essay, uses a blues singer and mixes "ultramodern" ges-
tures with blues chord progressions. The performance of the work by the well-
known blues singer Florence Mills, then appearing in a show with which Still
was involved (*Runnin' Wild*), created a sensation, but the connection between
Still's self-styled "stunt" and the response to *From the Land of Dreams* went unremarked.

9. Francis R. Bellamy, *Outlook and Independent,* undated clipping in Wallace
Thurman Papers, James Weldon Johnson Memorial Collection, Beinecke Li-

brary, Yale University. Bellamy wrote, "One of the most interesting things about 'Harlem,' the new negro play at the Apollo, is its audience. For it is a prize-fight audience, a spectacle audience, and is fairly representative, we should say, of the element of American society among which the negro in real life has to make his way. . . . The white audience may seem more sinister to you than the colored play."

10. Wallace Thurman (1902–1934) spent several years in Los Angeles (ca. 1922–1925) before going to New York City and earning a reputation as a fine editor. There he met the younger Bruce Forsythe and published some of his early essays in a short-lived journal, so far unlocated, the *Outlet*. Thurman's influence on Forsythe's thinking about race will become clear in the separate chapter on Forsythe. For a recent study on Thurman, see Eleonore van Notten, *Wallace Thurman's Harlem Renaissance* (Amsterdam and Atlanta, Ga.: Rodolphi, 1994). See also n. 7, p. 110. The clippings quoted below are in the Wallace Thurman Papers, James Weldon Johnson Memorial Collection, Beinecke Library, Yale University.

11. Francis R. Bellamy, *Outlook and Independent*.

12. John Anderson, *New York Evening Journal*, February 21, 1929. Clipping in Wallace Thurman Papers.

13. William Jourdan Rapp and Wallace Thurman, "The Negro Made Human: Two Authors Defend Their Play," unlabeled clipping, Wallace Thurman Papers.

14. In "Chosen Image: The Afro-American Vision in the Operas of William Grant Still," *Opera Quarterly* 4, no. 2 (Summer 1986): 1–23, Donald Dorr confuses Forsythe with Richard Bruce [Nugent], a writer, artist, and actor from Washington, D.C., who wrote the initial sketch for *Sahdji* that appears in *The New Negro* (1925). (Bruce's sketch was expanded by Locke for *Plays of Negro Life* two years later; the expanded version became the source for Still's ballet.) Several years later, Locke wanted to recruit Bruce, not Forsythe, to write a libretto, for which Locke had constructed an outline, on the subject of Atlantis. Dorr cites a "Dear Bruce" letter from Locke, in the Department of Special Collections at Howard University. From its contents, the undated letter was written between the premiere of *Sahdji* in May 1931 and Locke's departure for Europe on June 13, 1931. Many of Locke's letters to Still begin "Dear Still," suggesting that Locke addressed males by their last names in his letters.

Although Locke claimed in the same letter to have registered the title and outline for "Atlantis," no record of it now exists in the Copyright Office. I am grateful to Wayne Shirley for making the copyright search and for pointing out that the material submitted by Locke for copyright, if it was in outline form, would probably have been rejected.

15. Forsythe's letter dated "1933" by a hand that is probably Still's is reproduced as an addendum to Forsythe's monograph. This letter elicited Still's "Personal Notes," also reproduced here.

16. Edward R. Reilly's remark that "widows of composers can have a considerable effect on the posthumous images we have of their husbands" surely applies to the Still-Arvey relationship. Quoted in "Snapshots," *Nineteenth Cen-*

tury Music 20, no. 2 (Fall 1996): 199, referring to Herta Blaukopf, ed., *Gustav Mahler, Richard Strauss: Correspondence, 1888–1911,* trans. Edmund Jephcott (Chicago: University of Chicago Press, 1984).

17. In April 1937, Fischer wrote to Still, "Frankly speaking, I am of the opinion that it would seem rather premature to now already publish an extended biography relating to yourself. In my opinion, this ought to be postponed for yet a few years until your name as a composer is still better known in every musical household." Two other letters from George Fischer to Still, September 24 and November 1, 1937, reveal his change of mind. Box 18, Still-Arvey Papers. The Fischer correspondence takes up more than one full box. Fischer handled several of Still's most successful publications in the late 1930s and promoted them assiduously.

18. Forsythe, "Frailest Leaves," undated typescript [ca. 1935], p. 445. Forsythe Papers, The Huntington Library.

A Brief Chronology

Carolyn L. Quin

1895	Born May 11, Woodville, Mississippi, to William Grant Still (1871–1895) and Carrie Lena Fambro Still (1872–1927). Moved with his mother to Little Rock, Arkansas, after his father's death.
1911	Graduates as valedictorian from M. W. Gibbs High School; matriculates at Wilberforce University (Ohio).
1912	Hears Victor Red Seal recordings of opera excerpts.
1915	May, leaves Wilberforce before graduating; October 4, marries Grace Bundy.
1916	Summer, to Memphis to play in W. C. Handy's (1873–1958) bands and arrange for them; earliest arrangements published by Pace & Handy.
1917	Begins music study at Oberlin.
1918	U.S. Navy, serves on shipboard as mess attendant and violinist.
1919	Returns to Oberlin briefly; goes to New York City to work for Handy.
1920s	Arranges or orchestrates for Will Vodery, Eubie Blake, Earl Carroll, Sophie Tucker, Donald Voorhees, Paul Whiteman, and others.

1920   Leaves Handy's band to play in a Clef Club orches-
            tra; joins Hall Johnson's band.

1921   Joins pit orchestra as oboist for Noble Sissle
            (1889–1975) and Eubie Blake's (1883–1983) all-
            Afro-American revue, *Shuffle Along,* to which he
            contributes arrangements as it plays 504 New York
            performances before going on tour; later plays in
            other shows and conducts at the Plantation Club
            until he can support himself as an arranger.

1922   In Boston with *Shuffle Along,* studies composition
            privately with George Whitefield Chadwick (1854–
            1931), director of the New England Conservatory,
            for four months. Returning to New York City, works
            for Harry Pace's Black Swan Phonograph Company
            until some time before it fails in 1925.

1923   Begins two years of study with Edgard Varèse (1883–
            1965).

1925   February 8, first performance of Still's concert music,
            by the International Composers' Guild, the result of
            his study with Varèse (*From the Land of Dreams*).

1928   *Darker America* score published (composed 1924,
            performances in 1926 and 1927).

            Wins Harmon Award for Distinguished Achievement
            among Negroes in Music.

            Charter member, Pan American Association of
            Composers.

1929–1930   May–May, contracted by Paul Whiteman (1890–
            1967) as arranger for his weekly radio show, the
            "Old Gold Hour," broadcast from Los Angeles;
            renews friendship with Harold Bruce Forsythe,
            whom he had met in New York in 1927; meets
            Verna Arvey.

1930   Returns to New York, completes the ballet *Sahdji,*
            revises *Africa* again, composes the *Afro-American
            Symphony.*

April 6, *Africa* premieres in a version for reduced orchestra by the Barrère Little Symphony in New York; October 24, version for full orchestra, Rochester Philharmonic, Howard Hanson (1896–1981) conducting.

1931   May 22, first performance of the ballet *Sahdji*, Eastman Ballet and Rochester Civic Orchestra, Hanson conducting.

October 28 and 29, first performances of the *Afro-American Symphony*, Rochester Philharmonic Orchestra, Hanson conducting.

Late in the year, hired to arrange for orchestra on "Willard Robison and His Deep River Hour" radio show; for a time conducts the orchestra as well.

1932   Grace Bundy and their four children go to Canada.

1934   Fellowship from the John Simon Guggenheim Memorial Foundation to compose an opera.

Leaves the "Deep River Hour" and moves permanently to Los Angeles in May. *Blue Steel* completed 1935 (unproduced).

1935   Works for Columbia Pictures for six months as composer and orchestrator; credits include *Pennies from Heaven* with Bing Crosby and *Theodora Goes Wild* as well as miscellaneous film cues for Columbia's files.

November 20, *Afro-American Symphony* played by the New York Philharmonic, Hans Lange conducting.

1936   Becomes a member of ASCAP (American Society of Composers, Authors, and Publishers); conducts the Los Angeles Philharmonic at the Hollywood Bowl. The Philadelphia Orchestra plays the fourth movement of the *Afro-American*

	Symphony on a coast-to-coast tour, including a performance in Los Angeles at the Pan-Pacific Auditorium.

1937   *Lenox Avenue,* commissioned by the CBS radio network, broadcast on May 23; first performance of *Symphony in G Minor;* begins working on the opera *Troubled Island* with Langston Hughes as librettist (completed in 1941); the first works to be published by J. Fischer & Bro. appear.

1939   Divorces Grace Bundy and marries Verna Arvey; wins the first of his two Rosenwald Fellowships.

1940   June 23, *And They Lynched Him on a Tree,* choral ballad to a libretto by Katherine Garrison Chapin, performed by New York Philharmonic; arranges "Frenesi" for Artie Shaw, whose recording of it becomes a best-seller; collaborates with Zora Neale Hurston on *Caribbean Melodies.*

1941   *Plain-Chant for America,* commissioned by the New York Philharmonic for its centennial, premiered October 23.

late 1942–   Brief stint at Twentieth Century–Fox studio; quits
early 1943   production of *Stormy Weather.*

1949   March 31, April 10, and May 1, *Troubled Island* is produced by the New York City Opera.

After   Lives quietly in Los Angeles, filling a decreasing number of commissions. Continues to compose operas: *Bayou Legend* (produced November 15 and 17, 1974, by Opera South, Jackson, Miss.; PBS broadcast June 15, 1981), *A Southern Interlude* (revised as *Highway 1, U.S.A.,* produced May 11, 1963, by University of Miami Opera), *Costaso* (produced 1991 by NANM, Altadena, Calif.), *Mota, The Pillar, Minette Fontaine,* and numerous other works; honorary degrees from Wilberforce (1936), Howard (1941), Oberlin (1947), Bates (1954), University of Arkansas (1971), Pepperdine University (1973), New England Convervatory (1973), University of Southern California (1975).

1978   December 3, dies in Los Angeles.

CONTRIBUTED ESSAYS

The Formative Years
of William Grant Still

Little Rock, Arkansas, 1895–1911

Willard B. Gatewood

Late in 1895 Carrie Fambro Still, a talented, well-educated, and strikingly handsome African American woman, left her home near Woodville, Mississippi, with her infant son headed for Little Rock, Arkansas. Within little more than a year after her marriage in 1894, the twenty-three-year-old Carrie Still had become a mother and a widow. Shortly after the sudden death of her husband, she decided to move to Little Rock where her mother and sister lived. She and her son moved into the house on Fourteenth Street occupied by her mother, her sister, Laura, and her brother-in-law, Henry Oliver, a barber. Carrie Still acquired a teaching position in the public schools within a year and quickly became self-supporting.[1] It was in the capital city of Arkansas—very much a city of the "New South"—that she made a new life for herself and her son, William Grant Still, who would become known as the "dean of Afro-American composers."

The Little Rock in which Still spent his first sixteen years was a bustling center of the cotton trade located on the Arkansas River. Served by five rail lines in 1900, the city boasted thirteen miles of paved streets, a seven-story "skyscraper," a Grand Opera House, numerous handsome residences, commodious hotels, a public library with 3,200 volumes, sixty-odd social clubs, seventy-five churches, public high schools for blacks and whites, and a profusion of gardens and flowers that accounted for its being known as "the City of Roses." But no amount of roses or booster rhetoric could obscure the existence in the city of numerous saloons, houses of prostitution, gaming parlors, and "low life dives," patronized by a substantial proportion of its population.[2]

The city, however, exhibited a cosmopolitan character unusual in Arkansas and much of the South. In addition to native-born white Southerners, its population included transplanted Northerners, African Americans, and an assortment of foreign immigrants. Conspicuous among the latter were the Irish and Germans who, along with a few Poles and Italians, were responsible for a substantial Catholic presence in the city. Jews were sufficiently numerous to support a synagogue. A few other nationalities such as Slavonians, Italians, Greeks, and Syrians arrived around the turn of the century and like other groups perpetuated their identity through a wide variety of organizations. But by all odds the largest racial minority in Little Rock in 1900 were African Americans, who constituted more than 38 percent of its total population of 38,307.[3]

If African Americans benefited from the diverse composition of the population, the city's distinctive political complexion also promoted their interests. Unlike most of Arkansas, which was solidly Democratic, Little Rock possessed something approaching a two-party system. Such a political environment was advantageous to black citizens, who traditionally supported the Republican party, the party of Lincoln and Emancipation, and helped to explain why they were able to influence city decision making and to obtain public schools of a quality absent in other areas of Arkansas.[4]

Although Little Rock was a racially segregated city when William Grant Still and his mother settled there, the lines had not yet been rigidly drawn. Interracial association still existed to an extent that had virtually disappeared in the rural districts of the state. Not until 1903 did segregation on streetcars go into effect, and even after that date racial mingling persisted in various areas. Nor did residential patterns yet conform to a rigid color line. In many sections of the city blacks and whites lived in close proximity in what were known as "mixed neighborhoods." Isaac Gillam, Jr., a member of an old and highly respected black family and a well-known educator, was a neighbor and friend of a German immigrant family. That Gillam, a Howard University alumnus who had also attended Yale, spoke fluent German undoubtedly facilitated the friendship. Still himself grew up in one of the city's mixed neighborhoods, and his playmates were white boys. In fact, his best childhood friend was white, the son of a railroad engineer. But Still, unlike his white friend, did not have access to the city's public library, and beginning in 1903 the two could not sit together on the streetcar.[5]

Still's residence in Little Rock from 1895 to 1911 coincided with the climax of a movement that substantially altered race relations—from a flexible to a fanatically rigid system of segregation, involving both legal and extralegal proscriptions imposed on African Americans. Contributing significantly to the shape of the new order in race relations in Arkansas was the flamboyant, freewheeling Jeff Davis, who after serving a term as an active, highly visible attorney general, occupied the governorship from 1901 to 1907. Few other southern political demagogues of the time were more adept than Davis in exploiting the racial fears of whites. Embracing the myths of white supremacy, he invoked incredibly crude racist rhetoric that often appalled those whites whom he called "the high collared roosters" of urban Little Rock but that made him the darling of rural "rednecks," a term that he used as one of endearment.[6] For black Arkansans, as for black Americans in general, it was a time of shrinking opportunities, increasing discrimination, and what has been termed the "withering of hope." The Mississippi Way in race relations was rapidly becoming the American Way.

In 1903, when Still was eight years old, the state legislature in session a short distance from where he lived enacted measures that appeared to translate Governor Davis's racist rhetoric into legal reality. One measure required the segregation of state and county prisoners. Because the statute did not apply to city prisoners, Little Rock continued for some years what has been described as its "topsy-turvy arrangements" in dealing with black and white inmates in the city jail. More relevant to Still's family and most of the city's African Americans was a law requiring segregation of the races on streetcars, a measure that encountered opposition from blacks and some whites. Little Rock's most prominent black citizens vigorously protested the law and organized a boycott of the streetcars. One can easily imagine that the proud, fiercely independent Carrie Still was deeply offended by the Jim Crow streetcar law and participated in the "We Walk League." On an earlier occasion when a white streetcar conductor called her "Carrie," she had rebuked him for such familiarity and had given him a lecture on proper conduct and manners. Neither the boycott by African Americans nor the grumbling of some whites failed to deter the implementation of the streetcar law.[7]

Despite the enactment of such measures, old patterns of race relations in Little Rock, the only place worthy of being described as urban in the state, adjusted only gradually to the new order. Racially mixed neighborhoods persisted as long as Still resided in the city. The city's police force continued to employ African Americans at least until 1920. Few policemen, white or black, were held in higher esteem than Samuel Speight, a black detective who served on the force from 1879 to 1905, when he left to open his own private detective agency.[8] That the color line did not become entirely inflexible while Still lived in Little Rock was also demonstrated by the fact that Dr. James H. Smith, a well-to-do black dentist with an office on Main Street, possessed "a large and lucrative practice among the wealthy white class."[9] African Americans still figured prominently in the state's Republican party despite mounting pressures from white members who embraced the philosophy of "lily-whitism." Among these were two of Little Rock's best-known black citizens, Mifflin W. Gibbs and John E. Bush. Elected municipal judge in Little Rock in 1873, Gibbs was reputedly "the first Negro elected to such office in the United States." Thereafter, until his death in 1915, he was active in Republican party affairs and received a succession of federal appointments.[10] More than thirty years younger than Gibbs, Bush was also prominent in Arkansas's Republican circles. He served as receiver of public monies in the United States Land Office in Little Rock from 1898 until 1913 and constantly waged war on the lily-white forces in the party.[11] Other African Americans in Little Rock were the recipients of federal appointments, including Still's beloved stepfather, Charles B. Shepperson, whom Carrie Still married in 1904. As a clerk in the Railway Mail Service, Shepperson had an income that placed him among the city's most affluent blacks.[12]

Notwithstanding such evidences of continuing interracial association and the access of a few blacks to federal government jobs, African Americans in Arkansas, including those in Little Rock, witnessed a steady erosion of rights, privileges, and opportunities. During the decade preceding the enactment of the two segregation measures in 1903, new election laws had rendered blacks politically powerless and eliminated them from public office. The "separate coach" law of 1891 had required racial segregation of railroads a dozen years prior to the streetcar law.[13]

Confronted by the white majority's Jim Crow mentality that was evident in the increasingly rigid color line and diminishing options for the black minority, African Americans sought without success to arrest the assault on their rights, privileges, and even humanity. The new order in race relations prompted them to accelerate the withdrawal into a world of their own that was separate and distinct from the society of whites. The result was a more formalized dual society in Little Rock. Experienced in institution building as evidenced by the existence of their own cemetery, fraternal orders, churches, and home for destitute elderly women,

blacks followed the advice of Booker T. Washington, the premier spokes-
man for African Americans, by launching their own business enterprises
that increasingly catered to a black clientele. In fact, Little Rock had a
thriving chapter of the National Negro Business League, an organization created in 1900 and headed by Washington until his death fifteen
years later. In 1903, Gibbs, a loyal disciple of the Tuskegean, launched
the Capital Savings Bank, the second black-owned bank in Arkansas.
The bank thrived for five years but failed, for various reasons, in the
wake of the Panic of 1907. Other enterprises lasted much longer and
even expanded beyond Little Rock.[14]

One such enterprise was the Grand Mosaic Templars of America, organized in 1882 by Bush, Chester W. Keatts, and a dozen other prominent individuals. Much more than a fraternal order of "men of good
character regardless of occupation or class," the Mosaic Templars operated an insurance company, a loan association, and a newspaper. It also
owned extensive real estate throughout Arkansas. By the mid-1920s the
organization had assets of a million dollars and one hundred thousand
members in twenty-six states and six foreign countries. Just as young
William Grant Still left Little Rock for college in 1911, the Mosaic Templars headquarters building, a three-and-a-half-story brick structure,
opened on the corner of Ninth and Broadway streets.[15]

By the opening of the twentieth century, West Ninth Street was already emerging as the center of black Little Rock. Blacks had long been
present in the vicinity of Ninth Street, but their number vastly increased
after Emancipation in 1863. The Union Army constructed a hodgepodge
of log shanties in the area to accommodate the freed slaves who crowded
into Little Rock. By the turn of the century, black-owned businesses,
mostly small, service-oriented enterprises, had substantially increased on
Ninth Street, interspersed among establishments operated by people of
Italian, Irish, and German descent. While Still was growing up on West
Fourteenth Street, the black presence on Ninth Street increased even
more. Not only did the street include the headquarters of the Mosaic
Templars and other fraternal and mutual aid societies, it also had an assortment of tailors, grocers, barbers, boot makers, jewelers, confec-
tioners, and other small businesses.[16] Among these was the Spot Cash
Drug Store owned by F. B. Coffin, a graduate of Meharry Medical College and for some years the only black registered pharmacist in Arkansas. Although Coffin made his living as a druggist, his first love was
poetry. In 1897 a volume entitled *Coffin's Poems* was published and sold
for $1.00.[17]

By the 1920s Ninth Street had become virtually all-black and indisputably the economic, social, and political heart of Little Rock's black community. Black professionals—physicians, attorneys, clergymen—were found in this city-within-a-city. As one authority has observed, here African Americans could find everything from medical services and spiritual nourishment to Saturday night entertainment and excitement. Blacks often referred to Ninth Street as "the Line," because it functioned as the demarcation between black and white Little Rock.[18]

This demarcation was evident in an article by John E. Bush chronicling the "progress" of African Americans in Little Rock that appeared in 1905 in the *Colored American Magazine* published in New York. Despite his boast about the absence of race friction "of any kind," Bush did not deny the existence of a racially dual society in which "the Negro has his own churches, his own schools, his own secret societies, and his own social functions." But within the racially segregated society of Little Rock, he declared, Negrophobia was "very far in the background" when it came "to trade and commercial relation." Certain white businesses such as the department stores owned by Gus Blass and M. M. Cohn, in fact, did assure black consumers that they were welcome and would be shown "uniform courtesy." The white owner of a jewelry store proclaimed the absence of any "colorlines" in his establishment.[19] The optimism expressed by Bush was to be expected of one who was Booker T. Washington's chief lieutenant in Arkansas and who subscribed to his accommodationist, self-help philosophy. When Washington visited Little Rock in November 1905 at Bush's invitation and delivered an address at the Opera House, he had an opportunity to observe the degree to which his host and other blacks in the city had succeeded in implementing his self-help philosophy. His visit was "the occasion of a public holiday by the Negro people," thousands of whom crowded into Little Rock to get a glimpse of "the Sage of Tuskegee."[20] It seems reasonable to assume that young William Grant Still and his mother and stepfather were among those who packed the Opera House to hear Washington's address, just as they had been on hand to greet President Theodore Roosevelt earlier the same year.[21] Washington's visit in 1905, followed by another in 1911 when his National Negro Business League met in Little Rock, thoroughly convinced him that Bush had not exaggerated in his assessment of the economic progress made by the city's black citizens. "The Business League meeting in Little Rock," Washington confided to a friend in 1911, "was by far the best we have ever held. You would have been surprised at the high type of the delegates and especially pleased with the many beautiful homes owned by our people in Little Rock." [22]

Of special importance in the life of the city's African American community while Still was growing up there were its churches and schools. As elsewhere in the South, the black church was a multifunctional institution that served as an agency of education, social control, and economic cooperation and as a refuge from a hostile environment. Of the thirty-nine black churches in Little Rock in 1910, seventeen were affiliated with various Baptist denominations and fifteen were Methodist, including African Methodist Episcopal, African Methodist Episcopal Zion, and Colored Methodist Episcopal congregations. Other blacks in the city worshiped at Protestant Episcopal, Catholic, Presbyterian, Congregationalist, and Holiness churches. The largest black church was the First Baptist with a membership of 1,100 and a sanctuary that seated 3,000, followed by Bethel A.M.E. Church with a seating capacity of 1,000.[23]

No less than churches, educational institutions were centers of African American social and cultural life. Particularly important were Little Rock's black colleges—Arkansas Baptist, Philander Smith, Williams Industrial, and Shorter (located in North Little Rock)—and the public schools. According to Bush, the public school system was "the pride of the city." Of the approximately ninety teachers employed in the city school system, thirty were black, including Still's mother, who was a teacher of English in the high school. This school, first known as Union, was moved and renamed Capitol Hill School in 1902. Moved again two years later, it was known as the Mifflin W. Gibbs High School. The high school was, in many respects, the centerpiece of black education in Little Rock and was undoubtedly the best black public school in the state. Although it included a vocational department, the emphasis was on a college-preparatory, classical curriculum that included literature, foreign languages, science, and social science taught by a highly qualified faculty.[24] Here William Grant Still received his secondary education, and his mother, a graduate of Atlanta University, served for many years as a faculty member who not only introduced hundreds of students to Chaucer and Shakespeare but also wrote and directed dozens of plays.[25] In addition to Still and Florence Smith (Price),[26] the daughter of Dr. James H. Smith, both of whom achieved renown in the musical world, a host of other graduates of Little Rock's black high school demonstrated throughout their careers the high quality of the education they received there. Among these was William Pickens of the class of 1899 who graduated, Phi Beta Kappa, from Yale and later won fame as an educator, writer, and official of the National Association for the Advancement of Colored People.[27] In 1909, two years before Still departed for college, two other products of the same high school graduated from college: Jefferson Ish from Yale and his brother, George Ish, from Harvard Medical School. Both returned to Little Rock, one to become a teacher and later a businessman and the other to practice medicine in the city for a half century.[28]

Such conspicuous achievement did little to eliminate the prevailing white perception of African Americans as a homogeneous mass without significant differences in background, attitudes, culture, behavior, and prestige. Whites in Little Rock, no less than those elsewhere in the United States, were rarely inclined to think in terms of a stratified black society across the color line. Reluctant to move beyond vague generalities about the black class structure, whites tended to classify African Americans as "good Negroes" or "bad Negroes" or to designate, for one reason or another, certain individuals and families as exceptional. Even though whites obviously knew that not all blacks were alike, no matter how often they voiced such a sentiment, they undoubtedly would have expressed dismay, even disbelief, at any suggestion that a well-defined class hierarchy existed in Little Rock's black community. Such a suggestion, on the contrary, would have come as no revelation to William Grant Still's parents.

Income, education, occupation, and other indices traditionally used to define the white class structure have proved to be inadequate in explaining the social hierarchy that evolved among African Americans in the decades after Emancipation. More subjective considerations related to historical experience and traditions and to a color-conscious, dominant society figured significantly in determining the contours of the black class structure. Much of what accounted for status and prestige in the black community had no counterpart in white society, because status and prestige among blacks were in large part bound up with their experience with slavery—their particular place in the slave system, their role in opposing it, and the extent to which their families had been free from it. In parts of the antebellum South, especially along the Atlantic and Gulf coasts, there developed elites made up of free mulatto families who in some cases were slave owners. Such elites as flourished in Charleston, Savannah, Pensacola, Mobile, and New Orleans did not exist in antebellum Arkansas or its capital city.[29]

The black upper class that emerged in post–Civil War Little Rock consisted largely of two groups: one was made up of those who had occupied the status of favored slaves in the city, such as the Andrews, Wallaces, Rectors, and others who came to be considered the "old families"; and the other was composed of talented, often well-educated émigrés including Mifflin W. Gibbs, Dr. J. H. Smith, and the Ish and Gillam families, who settled in the city during or shortly after Reconstruction. A member of the city's postwar black elite whose forebears enjoyed the status of "privileged" slaves in antebellum Little Rock recalled that "class distinction" existed among slaves "perhaps to a greater extent than among white people." Slaves of the highest stratum, she pointed out, cultivated good manners, proper speech, and "good form" in receiving guests, attributes perpetuated by their descendants.[30] The Andrews, Rectors, and others who could claim to be "old families" easily combined with the more recent residents such as the Ishes, Gillams, and Smiths to form Little Rock's small black elite whose behavior bore all the earmarks of gentility, super-respectability, and refinement. Reflecting their concerns with social ritual, E. M. Woods, the principal of a black school in Little Rock, lectured widely on etiquette and in 1899 produced a full-length etiquette guide, *The Negro in Etiquette: A Novelty.*[31] Alongside this elite that functioned as cultural brokers who spoke to blacks and for blacks to whites, a black middle class drawn in large part from small entrepreneurs, such as those along Ninth Street, began to emerge and figure prominently in the public life of the city's black community.[32] The vast majority of black citizens in Little Rock during Still's years were unskilled, uneducated, and low-income people who were largely employed as day laborers and domestics. This group formed the lower class in the black community. As elsewhere at the time, the city's black class structure resembled a pyramid: a broad base rapidly narrowing as it moved upward and culminating in a minuscule elite at the apex.

The black upper class in Little Rock always exhibited a degree of flexibility that allowed admission to those who, unable to claim old-resident status, possessed other essential qualifications. Recent émigrés such as Carrie Still, who was a college graduate and adhered to the "genteel performance," were readily incorporated into what was termed the "upper tens" of black society. Although wealth was a stratifier, it alone did not ensure one a place at the top of the class structure. For example, John E. Bush, perhaps Little Rock's wealthiest black citizen, made his lofty status secure by marrying the daughter of Solomon Winfrey, a highly respected building contractor and old resident of Little Rock. To a remarkable degree the city's black upper class constituted an educational elite, composed of those possessing a tradition of literacy or advanced education. Various members of the Ish, Rector, Gillam, and Andrews families were identified at some point in their careers with either the colleges or the public schools in the city. Conspicuous among this educational elite was Charlotte Andrews Stephens, an Oberlin graduate who was a teacher in Little Rock for seventy years. She, along with Mary Speight, the wife of the detective, Marietta Ish, Carrie Still Shepperson, and various other teachers and school administrators, possessed enormous prestige and influence in black Little Rock.[33]

Church affiliation in Little Rock's black community also reflected the prevailing class structure, and association with certain denominations provided an index of social preferment. Although members of the city's black upper class were found in the congregations of the oldest and most prestigious Baptist and Methodist churches, perhaps the largest number of such people belonged to the First Congregational Church, where the Ishes, Winfreys, and "many of the best people of the city" worshiped. Dr. Smith's family was active in Allison Presbyterian Church, while many of their friends were communicants at St. Philip's Episcopal Church, which, according to a black observer in 1901, consisted largely of "the blue veins," a term used to refer to African Americans who were so near white in complexion as to reveal their blue veins. Although many of those in Little Rock's black upper class were fair-skinned, the linking of skin color with social status does not appear to have created the mischief in the city that it did elsewhere. But that such a connection was not entirely absent is suggested by the fact that the *New Handy Map of Little Rock,* published in 1905, cited St. Philip's Episcopal Church as "blue-vein, col[ored]."[34]

There is little evidence to suggest that Still's family was particularly religious or that the church was the focal point of their lives. The family appears to have worshiped at Allison Presbyterian Church with the Smiths, their daughter, Florence, and other members of the black "upper crust." Attracted to St. Philip's because of the "glorious music" sung by the Episcopal choir, Still briefly attended services there and even joined the choir. But wearying of the constant kneeling and rising, he left the "glorious music" of St. Philip's behind to concentrate "on the violin, without calisthenics."[35]

Much of the social life of Little Rock's black upper class was home-centered; therefore, attention was focused on securing commodious homes in respectable residential areas. The white reporter of the *Arkansas Gazette* who interviewed Frederick Douglass in 1889 at the home of Dr. J. H. Smith was surprised at the elegance of the Smith residence. The extensive library, oil paintings, and a variety of musical instruments in the Smith home reflected the family's wide cultural interests. Dr. Smith himself was not merely a dentist but also a successful inventor, a talented artist, and a novelist. One of his paintings was exhibited at the Columbian Exposition in Chicago in 1893, and his lengthy novel about miscegenation, *Maudelle,* appeared in 1906.[36] The Smiths, as well as their friends, entertained mostly at home with small, selective affairs such as teas, receptions, dances, card parties, and musicales. William Grant Still later recalled such social gatherings at the Shepperson home, which was also the meeting place on occasion for the various literary and musical clubs to which his mother belonged.[37] The Sheppersons, like other members of the city's black elite, often entertained out-of-town guests, especially when fraternal, church, and other organizations met in Little Rock. Because of the absence of enough black hotels considered "respectable," the homes of the upper class tended to be the stopping-off place for those of comparable status from elsewhere who were en route to other cities such as Hot Springs, the famous Arkansas spa.

William Grant Still's mother and stepfather moved in the highest circles of the city's black community and actively participated in the rich intellectual and cultural life of its black upper class. Charles Shepperson, a strikingly handsome, fair-complexioned man, whom everyone black and white addressed as "Mr. Shepperson," shared his wife's love of "good" music. It was his stepfather's sizable collection of Victor Red Seal phonograph records that introduced young Still to the world of operatic music. A doting, even indulgent father, Shepperson often took Still to the theater to see stage shows such as *Ben Hur, The Wizard of Oz,* and *Robin Hood.* On other occasions the two journeyed to theaters on Ninth Street to attend performances by Cole and Johnson, one of the most famous African American troupes in the country. Young Still was also exposed to performances by well-known black artists, including a violin concert by Clarence Cameron White, a vocal recital by Mme Azalia Hackley, and a Shakespearean reading by Richard B. Harrison. The Sheppersons encouraged their son to learn to play the violin and employed a white teacher to provide private lessons.[38]

Although Still's maternal grandmother, Anne Fambro, an illiterate former slave, scarcely fit into the cultured, sophisticated circles in which her daughter and son-in-law moved, she nonetheless exerted a profound influence on "Baby Will," as she called her beloved grandson. "Grandma" Fambro more than compensated for her daughter's lack of culinary skills and delighted Still with pastries and other delicacies from her kitchen. When he was a young child his grandmother took over management of the household, including "Baby Will." On trips to Georgia with his grandmother he visited his mother's birthplace and became acquainted with his Fambro relatives. His grandmother told him endless stories from the days of slavery, relating in minute detail the "weather portents" just prior to the Civil War and the nocturnal activities of slave patrollers who tried to keep slaves under tight control. Young Still reciprocated by reading books to his grandmother. Anne Fambro not only introduced him to black folk music with her regular singing of spirituals, hymns, and other songs but also connected him to an important aspect of his heritage with her repertoire of stories.[39]

The central figure in Still's life in his formative years was his mother, a person of wide-ranging interests and enormous energy. A serious student of literature, music, and drama, Carrie Shepperson won prizes for her embroidery and other needlework, painted fine china, was an accomplished pianist, and possessed sufficient business acumen to acquire substantial real estate, including the house in which her mother and sister lived. A strict disciplinarian who was a stickler for proper manners and "good taste," she tolerated no use of what was called "dialect" and constantly reminded her son that he "*must* amount to something in the world."[40]

Like others of her station, Carrie Shepperson was committed to a mission of service and racial uplift so that disadvantaged African Americans could also make something of themselves. For example, one summer she, accompanied by Still, traveled to a rural community to teach black children who otherwise had no access to schooling. She labored to correct their speech and personal habits, which she considered "uncouth," and to provide them with the rudiments of education. The children of poor black sharecroppers no doubt looked upon Carrie Shepperson, an educated woman with impeccable manners, as the quintessential lady, a paragon of knowledge and a perfect role model. In Little Rock, Still's mother found time to engage in various civic and social activities. Deeply concerned that African Americans were denied access to the city's public library, she organized and staged performances of Shakespearean plays to raise money for a library of their own. The proceeds from these annual performances purchased books that formed the nucleus of a library for blacks established at Capitol Hill High School. A founding member of the Little Rock chapter of the Phyllis Wheatley Club and active in the Lotus and Bay View Reading clubs, two women's literary organizations, she supported the M. W. Gibbs Home for Elderly Women, wrote a book-length manuscript dealing with women's rights, and later helped to organize a local chapter of the National Association for the Advancement of Colored People.[41]

Reared in a comfortable home filled with books, musical instruments, and all the attributes of what was simply termed "culture," Still lived in a world far removed from the black masses, and, in view of the strong discipline imposed by his mother, he undoubtedly lacked any direct knowledge of the seamier or "lowlife" aspects of life in Little Rock. "I grew up," Still later recalled, "in an atmosphere of literary clubs, lectures, musical recitals [and] stage shows, Red Seal operatic recordings, lots of homework, and violin lessons."[42] He could scarcely have been unaware that he and his family were indeed different from the vast majority of blacks in the South who in the early years of the twentieth century suffered from poverty, ignorance, and daily encounters with racial prejudice. Indicative of his class consciousness were references to "our group," a term he used to identify friends and associates whose social life conformed to all the prevailing canons of polite society. Furthermore, his reaction to the black residents of the rural community in which his mother conducted a summer school can only be described as cultural shock. The product of a relatively affluent, sheltered environment in an urban setting, Still was appalled at the "primitive" life of these rural blacks— their appearance, living condition, speech, and even worship services.[43]

Notwithstanding the proliferation of Jim Crow contrivances directed against all black Arkansans, both Carrie Shepperson and her son considered Little Rock a center of racial enlightenment and "open-mindedness." In view of the racial climate in rural Mississippi, where Still's mother had lived immediately before settling in Little Rock, such a view scarcely seems unreasonable. As for Still himself, he remembered his boyhood in the city as a time of happiness in which he had white playmates, including several who remained his lifelong friends, and strong, loving parents who shielded him from the grosser forms of racial prejudice to the best of their ability, maintained high standards and ideals, and provided a home in which, as Still later observed, "we were not accustomed to think along racial lines."[44]

By the time Still graduated from high school at the head of his class in 1911, his primary interest was clearly in music. He had long since abandoned the fleeting idea of attending Booker T. Washington's Tuskegee

Institute in Alabama to learn how to raise chickens. If Carrie Shepperson found such an idea repugnant, the prospect of her son embarking on a musical career was scarcely more appealing. For her, Still recalled late in life, "the majority of Negro musicians of that day were disreputable and were not accepted into the best homes." That her son would be unwelcome in "the best homes" was unthinkable to Carrie Shepperson. Her plans for Still to attend college with a view toward studying medicine prevailed, and at her insistence he entered Wilberforce University in Ohio. An institution supported by the African Methodist Episcopal Church and often the scene of fierce ecclesiastical politics, Wilberforce was especially well known for its strict discipline, military science training, and premedical curriculum. In the fall of 1911, William Grant Still left Little Rock to begin the protracted process of preparing to become a physician. Instead, he became a world-renowned musician and composer.[45]

Reflecting on his early years in Little Rock from the perspective of almost six decades, Still described his boyhood there as "a typically American one, far removed from the ordinary concept of a little colored boy growing up in the South."[46] Because his family neither possessed the substantial wealth of some whites and a few blacks in the city nor experienced the grinding poverty of most of its African American residents, Still described himself as a product of the "middle class," who had enjoyed the luxuries and amenities characteristic of that class at the turn of the century.[47] His reference to his "middle-class" origins was a case of using generic terminology to describe what was actually the upper-class status of his family within the black community of Little Rock more than a half century earlier. But Still's intention was not to provide an accurate analysis of the city's black class structure; rather it was to underscore the fact that, given the time and place in which he grew up, he had possessed extraordinary advantages.

Those of the class to which Still belonged were keenly conscious of their family background and often viewed themselves as heirs to a legacy that commanded authority, bestowed prestige, and imposed responsibility within the black community. Such people, according to an African American journalist in 1902, dealt "heavily in family trees." Other blacks ridiculed the pretensions of these so-called thoroughbred families. There is no evidence that Still's family drew up elaborate genealogical charts that included an assortment of African kings, Indian chieftains, European noblemen, and white American statesmen, as some upper-class black families did,[48] but Carrie Shepperson and her mother possessed intimate knowledge of their ancestry. Still clearly understood that he represented a "mingling of several bloods"—Negro, Native American, Scotch, Irish, and Spanish.[49] Such blending was obvious in the physical appearance of Still and his mother no less than his stepfather, all of whom possessed light complexions, but not as light as some of their African American acquaintances in Little Rock who chose to "pass" for white.[50] Regardless of his "mixed-blood" ancestry and light complexion, Still grew up in an era in which whites adhered to the "one drop" rule that classified all persons with any black ancestry whatsoever as Negroes and subjected them to Jim Crow proscriptions.[51] Although his parents never encouraged him to "think along racial lines," Still was fully aware that he was a Negro and was painfully reminded of the fact by the occasional slurs and insults directed at him by whites. On a trip to Georgia with his grandmother he witnessed a frenzied mob of whites "out for the blood of a Negro accused of rape." Such early experiences with racism could have easily created within him an enduring bitterness toward whites in general, but they did not for a variety of reasons. His pleasant association with whites, especially those in his neighborhood, coupled with efforts of his parents to impress on him the necessity of evaluating others in nonracial terms, enabled him to conduct himself "as a person among people instead of as an inferior among superiors."[52] The "mingling of several bloods" in his ancestry meant that the notion of proud hybridization also figured in his sense of himself, making it all the easier for him later to characterize his extraordinary musical achievements in terms of a fusion of diverse cultural traditions.

Still repeatedly insisted that "Negro music" per se was not an important part of his youth in Little Rock and noted that during the summer when he accompanied his mother to a rural community to conduct a school, he laughed at the shouting and singing of the black residents during religious services. "The thought that I was hearing 'authentic Negro music at its source,'" Still recalled, "never entered my irreverent little mind."[53] But "Grandma" Fambro's continual singing of "Negro songs" as she worked, coupled with her seemingly endless supply of stories about black life both before and after the Civil War and the performances of Cole and Johnson and other black troupes that Still witnessed in Little Rock, became elements in a memory bank that, either consciously or unconsciously, must surely have figured in the musical compositions that later won him wide acclaim. By the time Still left Little Rock in 1911, he had been exposed to both black vernacular and classical musical traditions that he used to produce a music that expressed the rich diversity that is America.

NOTES

1. Judith Anne Still, "Carrie Still Shepperson: The Hollow of Her Footsteps," *Arkansas Historical Quarterly* 62 (Spring 1983): 41–42; Verna Arvey, *In One Lifetime*, 13; *Little Rock City Directory, 1897–98* (Little Rock: R. L. Polk & Co., 1897), 437, 532.

2. *Little Rock City Directory, 1900–1901* (Little Rock: Press of Arkansas Democrat Co., 1900), 56–58, 67–79; Ira Don Richards, "Little Rock on the Road to Reunion, 1865–1880," *Arkansas Historical Quarterly* 25 (Winter 1966): 328–329; John William Graves, *Town and Country: Race Relations in An Urban-Rural Context, Arkansas, 1865–1905* (Fayetteville: University of Arkansas Press, 1990), 114–115; C. Allan Brown, "The Legacy of the 'City of Roses,'" *Pulaski County Historical Review* 31 (Summer 1983): 22–28.

3. Graves, *Town and Country,* 104–106; Carolyn Gray LeMaster, *A Corner of the Tapestry: A History of the Jewish Experience in Arkansas, 1820s–1990s* (Fayetteville: University of Arkansas Press, 1994), 3–96 passim.

4. Graves, *Town and Country,* 108–109.

5. Ibid., 106–107; William Grant Still, "My Arkansas Boyhood," *Arkansas Historical Quarterly* 26 (Autumn 1967): 285–286.

6. For a sophisticated analysis of Jeff Davis's appeal, see Raymond Arsenault, *The Wild Ass of the Ozarks: Jeff Davis and the Social Bases of Southern Politics* (Philadelphia: Temple University Press, 1984).

7. Fon Louise Gordon, "The Black Experience in Arkansas, 1880–1920" (Ph.D. dissertation, University of Arkansas, 1989), 199–200; August Meier and Elliott Rudwick, "The Boycott Movement Against Jim Crow Streetcars in the South, 1900–1906," *Journal of American History* 55 (March 1969): 773–774; Graves, *Town and Country,* 218–225.

8. Adolphine Fletcher Terry, *Charlotte Stephens: Little Rock's First Black Teacher* (Little Rock: Academic Press of Little Rock, 1973), 107.

9. D. B. Gaines, *Racial Possibilities as Indicated by the Negroes of Arkansas* (Little Rock: Printing Department of Philander Smith College, 1898), 95.

10. On Gibbs, see Tom W. Dillard, "Golden Prospects and Fraternal Amenities: Mifflin W. Gibbs's Arkansas Years," *Arkansas Historical Quarterly* 35 (Winter 1976): 307–333.

11. On Bush, see C. Calvin Smith, "John E. Bush of Arkansas, 1890–1910," *Ozark Historical Review* 2 (Spring 1973): 48–59; G. P. Hamilton, *Beacon Lights of the Race* (Memphis: P. H. Clarke & Brother, 1911), 139–151.

12. Arvey, *IOL,* 27–28.

13. These measures are explored in detail in Graves, *Town and Country,* chaps. 8, 9, and 10.

14. Fon Louise Gordon, "From Slavery to Uncertain Freedom: Blacks in the Arkansas Delta," in Jeannie Whayne and Willard B. Gatewood, eds., *The Arkansas Delta: Land of Paradox* (Fayetteville: University of Arkansas Press, 1993), 116–117, 119; Tom W. Dillard, "Perseverance and Black History in Pulaski County, Arkansas—An Excerpt," *Pulaski County Historical Review* 31 (Winter 1983): 64.

15. See A. E. Bush and P. L. Dorman, eds., *History of the Mosaic Templars*

of America: Its Founders and Officials (Little Rock: Central Printing Co., 1924); Berna Love, "A Proposal to Preserve and Rehabilitate Two Historical Landmarks on Ninth Street, the Mosaic Templars of America Headquarters Building and the Taborian Hall" (typescript in possession of the author).

16. I am indebted to Berna Love, Curator of Anthropology and Director of Social Science Education, Arkansas Museum of Science and History, Little Rock, for information on black businesses on Ninth Street; see her "Proposal" and "The Victory Chicken Shack: A Business History of West Ninth Street" (typescript in possession of the author).

17. Gaines, *Racial Possibilities,* 37–38; F. B. Coffin, *Coffin's Poems with Ajax' Ordeals* (Little Rock: The Colored Advocate, 1897); fifty years later Coffin published *Factum Factorum* (New York: Haven Press, 1947).

18. Love, "The Victory Chicken Shack," 5.

19. John E. Bush, "Afro-American People of Little Rock," *Colored American Magazine* 8 (January 1905): 39–42; Gordon, "Black Experience in Arkansas," 205.

20. "An Account by Emmett Jay Scott of a Speech in Little Rock," in Louis R. Harlan et al., eds., *The Booker T. Washington Papers,* 14 vols. (Urbana: University of Illinois Press, 1972–1989), 8:440–443.

21. Arvey, *IOL,* 29.

22. Booker T. Washington to Robert Russo Moton, August 21, 1911, in Harlan et al., *Booker T. Washington Papers,* 11:296–297.

23. *Little Rock City and Argenta City Directory, 1910* (Little Rock: Polk's Southern Directory Co., 1910), 44–46; Gaines, *Racial Possibilities,* 121–126.

24. Bush, "Afro-Americans in Little Rock," 39–41; Faustine C. Jones, *A Traditional Model of Educational Excellence: Dunbar High School of Little Rock, Arkansas* (Washington, D.C.: Howard University Press, 1981), 12–14; Dillard, "Golden Prospects and Fraternal Amenities," 331n.

25. Still, "My Arkansas Boyhood," 289–290; Arvey, *IOL,* 24.

26. On Florence Price, see Barbara Garvey Jackson, "Florence Price, Composer," *BPiM* 5 (Spring 1977): 29–43; Rae Linda Brown, "Selected Orchestral Music fo Florence B. Price (1888–1953) in the Context of Her Life and Work" (unpublished Ph.D. dissertation, Yale University, 1988); Rae Linda Brown, "William Grant Still, Florence Price, and William Davison: Echoes of the Harlem Renaissance," in Samuel Floyd, Jr. (ed.), *Black Music in the Harlem Renaissance: A Collection of Essays* (Knoxville: University of Tennessee Press, 1933), pp. 71–86; and Rae Linda Brown, The Heart of a Woman: The Life and Music of Florence B. Price (Urbaba: University of Illinois Press, forthcoming).

27. See William Pickens, *Bursting Bonds; Enlarged Edition of the Heir of Slaves: The Autobiography of a "New Negro,"* ed. William L. Andrews (Bloomington: Indiana University Press, 1991); Pickens's autobiographical *Heir of Slaves* appeared in 1911 and was reprinted as the first nine chapters of an autobiographical account entitled *Bursting Bonds* which was originally published in 1923.

28. Frank L. Mather, ed., *Who's Who in the Colored Race, 1915* (Chicago: n.p., 1915), 149; Marla Manor, "The Ish House and the Doctor," *Arkansas Democrat Sunday Magazine,* June 9, 1968, 1–3.

29. Generalizations about the African American class structure are drawn from my *Aristocrats of Color: The Black Elite, 1880–1920* (Bloomington: Indiana University Press, 1990).

30. Paul D. Lack, "An Urban Slave Community: Little Rock, 1831–1862," *Arkansas Historical Quarterly* 41 (Autumn 1982): 264, 268.

31. E. M. Woods, *The Negro in Etiquette: A Novelty* (St. Louis: Baxton and Skinner, 1899).

32. This emerging entrepreneurial class is treated in E. M. Woods, *Blue Book of Little Rock and Argenta, Arkansas* (Little Rock: Capital Printing Co., 1907).

33. Gatewood, *Aristocrats of Color,* 93–95; Gaines, *Racial Possibilities,* 61–75; see also Terry, *Charlotte Stephens.*

34. E. M. Saddler in (Indianapolis) *Freeman,* September 12, 1901; "The 1905 'New Handy Map of Little Rock,'" *Pulaski County Historical Review* 34 (Winter 1986): 91; Michael J. Beary, "Birds of Passage: A History of the Separate Black Episcopal Church in Arkansas, 1902–1939" (M.A. thesis, University of Arkansas, 1993), 15–16.

35. Jackson, "Florence Price," 32; Arvey, *IOL,* 31.

36. Willard B. Gatewood, "Frederick Douglass in Arkansas," *Arkansas Historical Quarterly* 41 (Winter 1982): 303–315; Gatewood, *Aristocrats of Color,* 94; Jackson, "Florence Price," 32.

37. Still, "My Arkansas Boyhood," 290.

38. Ibid., 278; Arvey, *IOL,* 28–29, 37.

39. Arvey, *IOL,* 20–21, 25.

40. Judith Anne Still, "Carrie Still Shepperson," 37–46; Arvey, *IOL,* 17–20; Still, "My Arkansas Boyhood," 288.

41. Still, "My Arkansas Boyhood," 288–289; Fon Louise Gordon, "Black Women in Arkansas," *Pulaski County Historical Review* 35 (Summer 1987): 28–29; Benjamin G. Edwards, "The Life of William Grant Still" (Ph.D. dissertation, Harvard University, 1987), 49–50; Judith Anne Still, "Carrie Still Shepperson," 42–43.

42. William Grant Still, "Remembering Arkansas," in Claire Detels, ed., *William Grant Still Studies at the University of Arkansas: A 1984 Congress Report* (Fayetteville: University of Arkansas, 1985), 44.

43. Still, "My Arkansas Boyhood," 288–290.

44. Ibid., 285, 286; Edwards, "William Grant Still," 53.

45. Arvey, *IOL,* 36–37; Still, "My Arkansas Boyhood," 291; William Grant Still, "A Composer's Viewpoint," in *Fusion 2,* 65–66.

46. Still, "My Arkansas Boyhood," 286.

47. Ibid.

48. Gatewood, *Aristocrats of Color,* 69, 73, 123, 205.

49. Arvey, *IOL,* 1–12; Still, "A Composer's Viewpoint," 134; Judith Anne Still, "Carrie Still Shepperson," 41.

50. On "passing" in Little Rock, see Arvey, *IOL,* 34; Gordon, "Black Women in Arkansas," 34.

51. On the "one drop" rule, see Joel Williamson, *New People: Miscegenation and Mulattoes in the United States* (New York: Free Press, 1980).

52. Still, "My Arkansas Boyhood," 286.

53. Ibid., 289.

"Dean of Afro-American Composers" or "Harlem Renaissance Man"

The New Negro and the Musical Poetics of William Grant Still

Gayle Murchison

Often referred to as the "Dean of Afro-American Composers," William Grant Still has been credited with pioneering the way and establishing a place for the African American composer of twentieth-century art music. Despite the recent increase of publications on Still and the issuance of numerous new recordings and re-releases of his music, there is still a need for critical study of his career and musical works. Still remains in many ways an enigma, both musically, as the figure he represents in African American art music, and historically, as an individual who lived during sweeping changes in American social history. The title "Dean of Afro-American Composers" is Still's due. Yet it does not aptly describe his accomplishments or the artistic and aesthetic ideals he pursued in his work. Such a title is easily bestowed on Still, who crossed many racial barriers during a period in American history when the achievements of African Americans were measured by *firsts* as a marker of racial progress and improvement in race relations. But to see him in this way is to accord him a place in American music history largely on the basis of his race and to consider only one facet of his accomplishments.

A more complete understanding of Still and his music results from situating him in music history and intellectual history based on other criteria. He participated in three musical trends in art music during the first half of the twentieth century. One of these was American musical modernism. During the period between the two world wars, young American composers, like their European counterparts, sought independence

from the aesthetics and conventions of nineteenth-century German ro-
manticism and explored new musical styles and modes of expression.[1]
The second trend reflected American musical nationalism; American
composers were engaged in a self-conscious attempt to create an art music that would be of an artistic quality equal to that of Europe and also
reflective of American culture. The third was the cultural movement
known as the Harlem Renaissance, which engaged a number of African
American artists and intellectuals. The Harlem Renaissance, or New
Negro movement, took place during a period of self-conscious African
American culture definition lasting from approximately 1919 to 1934
and found expression in literature, art, music, theater, and the performing and plastic arts.

A deeper understanding of Still's position in American art music
history begins by considering his position in African American art music history. Still should be viewed as a composer who reached artistic
maturity in New York during the Harlem Renaissance. He can be
deemed appropriately a Harlem Renaissance composer: throughout his
career, his musical works and professional activities reified the visions
of the leaders of the movement; his aesthetics, as voiced through his
writings, amplified the mission of the figures associated with the Harlem
Renaissance.

THE HARLEM RENAISSANCE

The Harlem Renaissance is conventionally perceived primarily as a literary movement, one that began toward the end of World War I and
flourished during the 1920s and 1930s.[2] *The New Negro,* a collection
of essays, poetry, and graphic art edited by Alain Locke, a professor of
philosophy at Howard University, in 1925, served as a cultural manifesto, expressing the aspirations and visions of the movement. Locke
identified New York's Harlem as a cultural and social mecca for African
Americans, or the race capital. Attracting blacks from throughout the
world, Harlem represented a place where "Negro life [was] seizing upon
its first chances for group expression and self-determination."[3] Thus it
symbolized the progress made by blacks from slavery through the mid-
1920s. In his foreword, Locke described his efforts as presenting the
"first fruits of the Negro Renaissance."[4] As such his book provides an
important piece of the literary and philosophical background against
which Still's work may be viewed. It contains poems by Countee Cullen,
Claude McKay, Jean Toomer, James Weldon Johnson, and Arna Bon-

temps; short fiction by Zora Neale Hurston, Jean Toomer, and Richard Bruce (Nugent); essays on African American visual and graphic art, literature, legitimate and musical theater, and comedies; and a play by Willis Richardson. Music figured prominently in *The New Negro*. Locke contributed an essay, "The Negro Spirituals," and J. A. Rogers wrote "Jazz at Home." The book surveyed more than the arts. There were also essays on the life and culture of the African American in general, ranging from E. Franklin Frazier's "Durham: Capital of the Black Middle Class" to essays by Walter White and Melville Herskovitz on the new urban culture of the African American as reflected by Harlem.

The works of numerous writers—novels, poems, plays—were produced and published during this period, as were journals, newspapers, and magazines. These literary products served as vehicles for the ideas and aspirations of the exponents of the movement. Foremost among the writers who expressed the visions of the Harlem Renaissance were Locke, Johnson, Hurston, Cullen, W. E. B. Du Bois, Sterling Brown, and Langston Hughes. However, the movement was not confined to literature, for the artistic life of Harlem outside of literature was very rich. African Americans found opportunities in other arts such as painting, sculpture, and legitimate theater. Black vernacular music—jazz, blues, and musical theater—thrived. The all-black musical *Shuffle Along* (1921) sparked an interest in African American culture among white Americans. The music of artists such as Duke Ellington and Bessie Smith reached beyond the African American community and emerged on the local New York cultural scene, and into American popular culture. The decade of the 1920s was the heyday of black revues at Harlem theaters such as the Apollo and the Lafayette.[5]

Recently there has been a move toward a more inclusive conceptualization of the Harlem Renaissance, broadening its scope to view it as an intellectual and cultural movement as well as a literary movement. Although it was not specifically political, there were political dimensions to its vision. The chronology has been extended beyond the 1920s and 1930s. Samuel A. Floyd, Jr., considers the Harlem Renaissance as beginning before the end of World I and extends the movement even beyond the location of Harlem itself, viewing it not as an isolated period in African American literary history but as part of a continuum. Reviving Locke's term and referring to it as the Negro Renaissance, Floyd locates its origins in towns and cities across the country before the turn of the century and links it to changes in African American life and intellectual history. He links the Negro Renaissance to the trends of nineteenth-century African American nationalism, the movement of African Americans "from slavery to freedom" and their migration from "rural to city living." [6]

Not only was the Harlem Renaissance concerned with literature and popular music, but art music was a significant part of Harlem musical culture during the 1920s and 1930s. The watershed in art music and the Harlem Renaissance, according to David Levering Lewis, was tenor Roland Hayes's December 1923 Town Hall concert, where he performed both lieder and spirituals. Hayes, and other concert artists such as Marian Anderson and Paul Robeson, demonstrated that African American musical artists were more than capable of performing the classical repertoire. By performing spirituals on the same programs with Italian arias and German lieder, these soloists elevated the African American spiritual to the same artistic level.[7] Performers were not the only figures in African American art music who gained prominence: composers created a body of large- and small-scale works—symphonies, operas, solo and chamber music—many of which were programmed and performed by leading figures and musical institutions in American music.

STILL AND THE HARLEM RENAISSANCE

The biography of William Grant Still allows us to situate him *chronologically* within the framework of the Harlem Renaissance. Still was born in 1895 in Woodville, Mississippi, was raised in Little Rock, and came to maturity during the early years of the Harlem Renaissance. Still was also *geographically* in the midst of the Harlem Renaissance. Eileen Southern first drew attention to the fact that Still's move to New York coincided with the traditionally understood start of the Harlem Renaissance.[8]

Not only was Still in New York during this period, he also participated in the musical life of Harlem. Throughout his residence in New York, Still took part in myriad musical activities that ranged from jazz and popular music to art music to musical theater. During the earliest stages of his career, he was involved in popular music as a performing musician on oboe and cello and as an arranger. He was first drawn to New York by W. C. Handy with an offer in 1919 to work in the Pace & Handy Publishing Company, one of the earliest black-owned and operated publishing companies, and to play in Handy's band. After leaving Handy's band in 1920, he performed with numerous Harlem jazz and popular music ensembles such as the Clef Club orchestras.[9] In 1921 Still was involved in the black musical revue *Shuffle Along,* in which he played the oboe and did several of the show's orchestrations. Later he worked for the Pace Recording Company (the Black Swan label), the first black-owned and operated record company, whose recordings included concert music. Still also performed art music, playing oboe in the Harlem Orchestra, a classical music organization. Following his departure from Pace Recording Company, Still turned more and more to orchestrating and arranging professionally, spending the second half of the twenties working not as a performing musician but as an arranger for several musical shows, such as *Rain or Shine* (1928), *Earl Carroll's Vanities of 1926,* and the black revue, *Dixie to Broadway* (1924).[10]

Still's involvement in the Harlem Renaissance extended beyond merely "being in the right place at the right time." He maintained close personal and professional relationships with several prominent novelists, poets, and playwrights. In his most publicized and documented collaboration, he composed the opera *Troubled Island,* a setting of Langston Hughes's libretto of his play *Drums of Haiti,* which was based on the story of Haiti's first emperor, Jean-Jacques Dessalines. Still wrote the opera between 1937 and 1939, completing it five years after his move to Los Angeles (Verna Arvey made minor changes to the libretto in 1941).[11] His collaborations with Harlem Renaissance literary figures began much earlier in New York. During the late twenties Still, desiring to write an opera, had approached several Harlem Renaissance writers and requested librettos from them, including in addition to Langston Hughes, Arna Bontemps and Countee Cullen.[12]

In late 1927 Cullen began to collaborate with Still on an opera originally entitled "Roshana" (later changed to "Rashana"). Cullen was enlisted to provide poetry for Grace Bundy Still's outline. In 1928 Cullen received a Guggenheim Fellowship and in June set sail for France. With Cullen less than enthusiastic about the project, their collaboration came to an end.[13] Another collaboration with a Harlem Renaissance artist during the thirties produced a completed work. A short story by the playwright and actor Carlton Moss provided the basis for the opera *Blue Steel,* and Harold Bruce Forsythe, a Los Angeles writer and musician whose work appears elsewhere in this volume, supplied the libretto.[14]

Still was an artistic collaborator with Alain Locke. Locke first became aware of Still in the twenties and heard at least two of Still's early works.[15] Taking an interest in Still's career, Locke listed his compositions in the "Bibliography of Negro Music" in *The New Negro.* He brought several texts to Still's attention, one of which would serve as the basis for a major theater work. In 1927 Locke sent Still Richard Bruce's brief fiction, "Sahdji," which had appeared in *The New Negro,* suggesting it as the basis for an African ballet: "Frankly I would like to see you try your hand at this. Will you? Does it interest you?" [16] Locke was persuasive, and contributed to the final version of the scenario. Following the failure of the Still-Cullen collaboration on "Rashana," Locke suggested to Still that he should write an opera with Bruce as librettist. Though the proposed project ("Atlantis") never materialized, Locke remained interested in Still's career, attending performances of his music and corresponding with him. [17]

Locke recognized Still's importance as one of the few African American art music composers and as someone who could contribute to his program for the promotion of African American culture and race relations. Following the first performance of Still's second symphony, on December 20, 1937, Locke wrote to Still encouraging him to continue his work of composition. Seeking to dispel the sting of negative reviews of the *Symphony in G Minor,* Locke offered his views on the future forms and styles of African American art music. Locke supported Still's musical ideas—his departures from conventional musical forms and musical language—and urged him to continue in the same direction. In addition, Locke expressed concern about the lack of interest among many African American musicians in art music: "It is so strange that nowhere among Negro musicians do you find any really intellectual interest in new works and experimenting." [18]

Thus Still may be situated within the context of the Harlem Renaissance on the basis of chronology, location, and his association with prominent artists and intellectuals. However, Still's involvement with the movement and its influence on his thinking and musical style is much more extensive. The depth of Still's participation in the Harlem Renaissance can be measured by first considering Locke's purpose in publishing *The New Negro.* Examining Still's own writings and his musical works reveals not only how they accord with those of Locke on aesthetic and philosophic points but also how they reflect the visions set forth by Locke and speak the voice of the Harlem Renaissance art music composer.

First appearing in an issue of the *Survey Graphic* dedicated to Harlem, Locke's cultural manifesto was expanded to become a book. In the foreword Locke described the purpose of the book: "to document the New Negro culturally and socially,—to register the transformations of the inner and outer life of the Negro in America that have so significantly taken place in the last few years."[19] Recognizing progressive changes in African American life such as the migrations from the rural South to the urban North and Midwest, Locke constructed the metaphor of the "New Negro." The "New Negro" of 1925 embodied the progress made by blacks since slavery and Reconstruction. These northward migrations produced not only a change in the geography of the black population, or outer life, but also a new psychological outlook and sense of self-awareness, or inner life, which awakened racial identity and racial pride. Locke also sought to show the progress that African Americans had made since the appearance of an earlier work that *The New Negro* evokes, Du Bois's *The Souls of Black Folk*.

In his book, Du Bois laid the intellectual foundation for Locke's volume and Still's intellectual aspirations. Examining the African American condition in 1903, almost a half century after Emancipation, and discussing problems facing the United States, Du Bois defined racism as *the* problem of the twentieth century and addressed issues of social, economic, and political inequality of African Americans. In the opening essay of his book, "Of Our Spiritual Strivings," Du Bois directly refers to the "Race problem" with the question, "how does it feel to be a problem?"[20] Denied the opportunity to speak for themselves and viewing themselves through the eyes of others, blacks lacked a "true self-consciousness."[21] Rather, they possessed a "double-consciousness," which arose from the complex of knowledge of the racial self and knowledge of the American self. The tensions between American democratic ideals, which declared all men equal, and American racism, which denied individuals social, political, and economic parity, resulted in the irony of being both American and black.

Du Bois wrote about racial progress or uplift in "Of the Strivings of Men," which dealt with the black man's striving to merge his two selves. Advancement could be achieved partly through education, artistic culture, and the efforts of the best members of the Race, which he called the "Talented Tenth." In the essay "The Training of Black Men," Du Bois discusses the role higher education could play in the economic progress of the Race by giving blacks the "key to knowledge" and a chance to become professionals rather than laborers or tradesmen.[22] Educated, cultured black individuals could contribute to advancement through the education of other blacks, to their social regeneration by teaching them about life, and to the solution of the race problem through contact and cooperation with whites.[23] These educated individuals would be the new leaders of their communities and would play a role in the future development of the South in improving race relations by promoting racial understanding and working to empower blacks.

In Du Bois's view, music and the arts played an important role in race progress and race relations. In the first essay, where Du Bois speaks of the African American as being handicapped, he wrote about the double bind of the black who desired to compose music. Du Bois described the artistic aspirations of blacks who, wanting "to be a co-worker in the kingdom of culture, to escape both death and isolation, to husband and use his best power and his latent genius," had lacked the opportunity to realize this potential. Speaking of music, he said that though black music was appreciated by blacks, if a black musician composed or performed black music, it was scorned by the "larger audience" outside the race. Without extensive musical training, a black artist had no chance to express his musical art in the concert hall; the black artists of the past "could not articulate the message of another people."[24] In "Of the Sorrow Songs," he described the gift and beauty of black music, specifically the spirituals, noting that they had long been "neglected, . . . half despised, . . . persistently mistaken and misunderstood." These songs were more than just music; they were the voice of the slave through which he spoke of his experience, through which he expressed the conditions of his life and messages of hope.[25] Du Bois considered them the "singular spiritual heritage of the nation and the greatest gift of the Negro people."[26] These "sorrow songs" were also part of America's musical heritage and were America's true cultural gift to the world.[27] For Du Bois, in achieving full participation in American culture, African Americans should be allowed to develop and create their own artistic forms.

Du Bois believed education, the arts, and the Talented Tenth would not only achieve progress in the life and condition of the lives of blacks; together they would also be factors in promoting racial understanding. Locke continued the same themes in his 1925 volume. He described a new generation in his own contribution, "The New Negro."[28] The New Negro was the Young Negro—urban, educated, with poetry, art, and a new outlook that promised a new leadership after fifty years of freedom.[29] The northward migrations then under way were a marker of two types of progress, one economic and the other of ethnic identity. "In the very process of being transplanted," he wrote, "the Negro is being transformed." The changes in African American culture and psychology that accompanied the migration resulted in the development of a new outlook, or a new consciousness. The most important change in the life of

African Americans, as represented by the New Negro, was, in Locke's terms, "spiritual emancipation." [30]

Music was central to Locke's beliefs about the cultural strivings of the New Negro. Locke concurred with Du Bois that the spirituals were truly American, the gift of the Negro to American music, and were expressive of African American life, culture, history, and condition. In addition to their beauty and special position as a folk form to be treasured and preserved, the spirituals contained "the richest undeveloped musical resources anywhere available." [31] Thus, in Locke's view, the spirituals held promise for contemporary art music—a potential that had only been touched on by composers such as Dvořák. For Locke, it would not suffice to merely preserve the spirituals; they must also be cultivated. [32] Although Locke acknowledged that the masses were on the vanguard of change in African American life (e.g., migrations, vernacular music such as folk traditions, jazz and blues, and other vernacular culture), it was not folk or popular music that would be redemptive in his vision of artistic culture. Rather, it was a genius, or a member of the Talented Tenth, who should use the spirituals and other black vernacular musical idioms as a resource to create the foundation for an African American art music. Locke cast Still in this role. [33]

Referring to the "voluminous literature" written by others about the Negro, Locke intended to encourage blacks to represent themselves and to view themselves not as a "problem in common" but as a "life in common." In this respect, the arts had more than entertainment, religious, or creative purposes. By allowing the New Negro to speak in his or her own voice, the arts could serve a social purpose beyond individual creative self-expression: the arts were redemptive, serving the strivings of African Americans to develop an ethnic identity. The arts were useful in achieving the Negro's inner objectives as he or she attempted to repair a damaged group psychology and reshape a warped social perspective. By writing about themselves, these New Negroes were "shedding the old chrysalis of the Negro Problem." [34] Through their writings, paintings, poems, plays, ballets, and music—through the creation of a body of artistic works that were expressive of African American thought, history, and contemporary life—African Americans were actively forging a new self-image and ethnic identity other than that of the slave past or of socioeconomic despair. The arts also had a place beyond the African American community in reinforcing the democratic ideals on which America was founded. By means of self-representation achieved through the arts, this younger generation of African Americans could promote racial understanding by combating the myth of the "Negro" and present a more accurate picture of the African American. Locke was not so naive as to believe that racism could be successfully combated by the arts acting alone. Rather, he recognized the need for mutual understanding between the races as a basic prerequisite for furthering race relations in America. The arts could be used to promote greater knowledge among blacks and whites by contributing to a "revaluation by white and black alike of the Negro in terms of his artistic endowments and cultural contributions, past and retrospective." [35]

Still's musical poetics reflect the ideals of the Harlem Renaissance. Throughout, his writings resonated with many of the themes expressed by Du Bois and Locke and amplified them. Still also moved the ideals of the Harlem Renaissance in his music from the realm of abstract thought about the role of music to the aural realm of musical composition and performance. Though the Harlem Renaissance is considered to have ended in the early 1930s, Still continued these themes until his death, attesting to their enduring mission.

Still and his musical compositions fully realized Locke's ideals in two respects. Still created a substantial body of music, composing primarily large forms such as symphonies, operas, ballets, and choral works. Endeavoring to create both an *African American* art music and an *American* art music, Still drew on black vernacular musical traditions for his art music compositions.

Still grouped his mature musical output into three broad stylistic periods. The first spans the early to mid-twenties prior to his studies with the avant-garde composer Edgard Varèse and his modernist period during which he explored modernistic techniques; this period ends in 1925. During the second, 1925 to 1932, Still adopted what he described as the "racial idiom." These dates correspond to the appearance of Locke's book and the accepted end of the Harlem Renaissance. The third began in 1932 when he turned from the specifically racial idiom toward the "universal idiom."

Still's earliest pre-Varèse compositions can be counted among the earliest works of the Negro Renaissance. Orchestral music and opera greatly appealed to Still. He first attempted to combine popular musics such as jazz and blues with modernistic techniques in these idioms when he arrived in New York and participated in jazz and popular music ensembles. The work *Three Negro Songs* for orchestra has movements entitled "Negro Love Song," "Death Song," and "Song of the Backwoods," all three composed in 1921 in New York. An early work, it nonetheless shows Still incorporating African American melodic idioms in an orchestral work that predates the publication of *The New Negro*. Still had an interest from the beginning of his career in composing art music on Negro themes.[36]

THE ULTRAMODERN IDIOM

During his study with Varèse, Still composed several "ultramodern" works in which he attempted to assimilate experimental techniques of the New Music into his own musical language.[37] He sought to combine traditional African American music with the atonal harmonies of modern music. *Darker America,* a work for orchestra composed in 1924 and one of the few surviving works from Still's study with Varèse, is discussed in several other places in this book.[38] Still used melodic types found in African American music such as the descending melodic curve, the pentatonic scale of the spirituals, and the "blues scales" of the blues. The primary harmonies used were the tonic, subdominant, and dominant harmony of the spirituals. Rhythmically, the "Theme of the American Negro" features syncopation, or if viewed in another way, additive rhythm.[39] Structurally, this theme uses the call-and-response that reflects the choral tradition of the spirituals.[40] Combined with African American musical traits are the dissonant harmonies of modern music, which Still used to dramatic end.

Though in his Varèse period works Still found ways of integrating modernist techniques with traditional African American music, he decided to limit the use of what he referred to as the ultramodern style: "Experiments proved to me that the Negroid idiom tends to lose its identity when subjected to such treatment. I wanted to employ an idiom that was unmistakenly Negroid because I wished to do my part in demonstrating to the world that the American Negro is capable of making a valuable contribution in the field of symphonic music, and I wanted to write a Negroid idiom, music that would help build more harmonious race relations."[41] The two musical idioms were not always compatible and when used together produced what he saw as incongruous results. Still felt limited by the dissonant style of Varèse and after ending his studies, began to change his style. He desired to show the beauty of black music and realize its possibilities in the concert hall by example. Dissonant modern music met with great resistance from audiences. If he was to show the beauty and worth of black music, he would have to turn away from dissonant music and compose in an idiom to which audiences would be more receptive. Furthermore, though he had leaped at the chance to study with Varèse, Still was not very comfortable assimilating this style. Still's musical aesthetic placed an emphasis on melody and music that an audience could find easily accessible.

Following his study with Varèse, Still sought a style that would reflect his racial background. He moved away from overt attempts to be modern and concentrated on realizing in an art music context the potential inherent in African American traditional music. By his own account, Still committed himself to black music during the mid-twenties: "After this period, I felt for a while that I wanted to devote myself to writing racial music." [42] In his first efforts at writing "racial music," Still turned to jazz. He had experimented with jazz earlier but had destroyed many of those works. His first mature jazz work was *Levee Land,* a suite for chamber orchestra and soprano soloist in three movements, composed in 1925 in New York City on texts by Still. "This was one of the very first efforts toward a symphonic treatment of jazz motifs." [43] Still used instrumentation suggestive of a jazz or popular music orchestra of the twenties. Melodically, harmonically, and rhythmically, the style of the work resembles various types of popular jazz from the twenties. Carol Oja has identified the manner in which Still combined modern dissonant harmonies with standard blues harmony and vocal and instrumental techniques. [44] *Levee Land* has additional experimental features, particularly the text and the way in which Still uses the voice. The voice is used not in a narrative fashion but instrumentally, repeating a text consisting mostly of short phrases such as "hey" and "baby" that were inflected to express different emotions ranging from sadness to humor and surprise. (This is in contrast to the use of three untexted voices in *From the Land of Dreams,* another work from the same period.) [45]

Aside from the limited use of modernistic techniques, *Levee Land* can be considered modern in the context of African American music and culture; it was a departure from Du Bois's and Locke's concept of "traditional music." Both Du Bois and Locke felt that African American folk materials of the spirituals and other "sorrow songs" could be used to build a great African American and American art music. Other proponents of the movement differed in their views on the use of folklore. Writers such as Sterling Brown, Langston Hughes, and Zora Neale Hurston held the view that the "folk" materials of jazz and blues, the vernacular of African Americans, were the substance of African American art. Their creative efforts used the expressions of African American speech, folktales, and the lyric forms of the blues. Forms such as the spirituals were rooted in pre-twentieth-century, rural African American history. The musical forms of jazz and blues, when Still began using these, were associated primarily with urban centers such as Memphis, New Orleans, Chicago, and New York and with the "city blues," or singers such as Ma Rainey and Bessie Smith, respectively. Just as Locke had documented the New Negro as urban, Still was expressing the contemporary African American, the urban black, of the mid-twenties, not the Negro of the slave or rural past. Still was also attempting in *Levee Land* to show the beauty of jazz and its usefulness as a basis for modern art music by integrating it within an experimental work.

THE RACIAL IDIOM

In the early 1930s Still, desiring to demonstrate the worth of an African American music that was denigrated by both whites and middle-class blacks, expressed his views in a typescript that may have been an early version of his earliest published essay, "An Afro-American Composer's Point of View."

> I feel that it is best for me to confine myself to composition of a racial nature. The music of my people is the music I understand best. It offers the medium through which I can express myself with greater clarity and ease. Then too, I am convinced that the time has arrived when the Negro composer must turn from the recording of Spirituals to the development of the contributions of his race, and to the work of elevating them to higher artistic planes.[46]

Still thus shifted his musical aesthetic from an objective modernistic one toward a proactive one that aligned more directly with Locke's aesthetic of redemptive culture but differed from it in one important respect.

The change in aesthetic resulted in a change in Still's musical style. He curtailed the use of dissonance but continued to create new forms, frequently drawing on folk forms and modifying them. Among his early compositions in his "racial" idiom were songs such as "Winter's Approach" and "Breath of a Rose" (composed in New York City in 1926–1927), settings of poems by Paul Laurence Dunbar and Langston Hughes, respectively. Analysis of both these songs reveals that Still combined African American vernacular musical forms such as the eight-bar blues with suggestions of modern dissonant harmony. Although Still continued to compose art songs, he was never completely drawn to the genre. He wrote, "Frankly, this art form has never appealed to me sufficiently for me to devote much thought to it." [47]

Still also turned to sources other than jazz or the spirituals. In the *Afro-American Symphony,* composed in New York City in 1930, Still turned to the blues, explaining, "I wanted to prove conclusively that the Negro musical idiom is an important part of the world's musical culture. That was the reason I decided to create a musical theme in the Blues idiom and develop it into the highest of musical forms—the Symphony." [48] Still had extensive experience with the blues during his tenure with W. C. Handy in Memphis. He assimilated elements of the idiom into his personal style. The first theme of the *Afro-American Symphony* displays essential features such as the "blues scale" of the lowered third and seventh scale degree, a falling melodic contour, and the call-and-response structure. He integrated African American musical elements into the formal aspects of the piece, basing parts of the first movement's internal sections on the twelve-bar blues form. These internal divisions were incorporated into a modified sonata form, a conventional form used in the Western European art music genres of symphony and sonata. Thus Still embedded a local form within a global form. By composing original music in an African American idiom, Still began to realize Locke's vision. By example, Still demonstrated that folk music could migrate from the dance hall to the concert hall. African American folk and vernacular music could be transformed into high art.

Still reified the Harlem Renaissance ideals not only aurally but also philosophically and historically. Many of his works bear programs. Considered by themselves, several of his works present a slice of African American life in music; considered as a group, they present a varied picture of the history, culture, and psychology of blacks in America. *Darker America* operates on multiple levels as Still's representation of his own culture and history. The themes taken in sequence depict the history of the American Negro, or the triumph over sorrow through prayer and hope.[49] At the end of the piece, Still constructed a musical profile of the psychology of the American Negro by presenting the three principal themes in counterpoint, using the dense texture of interwoven melodic lines to represent a complex psyche, or racial Self. The complex inner life of the American Negro is further expressed through Still's use of dissonance. Introduced after the first statement of the "Theme of the American Negro," the modern dissonances following the consonant "spiritual" melody illustrate irony—or double-consciousness, after Du Bois—the irony of being an American Negro in the United States, or a member of Darker America. The *Afro-American Symphony* was also meant to be a psychological or emotional portrait of the Negro, as spelled out more fully elsewhere in this volume.[50]

Pairing the *Afro-American Symphony* and the *Symphony in G Minor* further reveals the nature of Still's historicism. *The Symphony in G Minor* was subtitled "Song of a New Race" by Leopold Stokowski, who suggested Still add subtitles that expressed what feeling or thought had inspired him to each movement in order to "help [the] public to enter more intimately [the] mood of each movement."[51] Still considered this symphony, composed in 1937 in Los Angeles, an extension of and companion piece to the *Afro-American Symphony*.[52] "The principal theme of the first movement of the G Minor is allied, indeed derived from, the thematic material in the final movement of the 'Afro-American.'"[53] Still described his intentions in composing the symphony: "It may be said that the purpose of the Symphony in G Minor is to point musically to changes wrought in a people through the progressive and transmuting spirit of America."[54] The two works are analogous to the *Souls of Black Folk–New Negro* pair that documents the progress of blacks from the nineteenth-century rural "Old Negro" to the urban, educated New Negro of the twentieth century. As a pair, Still's symphonies reflect this race progress, documenting the life and culture of blacks, in musical terms, in much the same way that both Du Bois and Locke set about to describe the condition of the Negro in letters. Outlining the program, Still wrote that "the *Afro-American Symphony* represented the Negro of the days not far removed from the Civil War."[55] He described the *Symphony in G Minor* as "represent[ing] the American colored man of today."[56] The first symphony expressed emotional longing, sorrow, humor, and aspirations; the second symphony expressed more immediate optimism and the self empowerment of a people who could now take action.[57] Still continued to write a history of African Americans in music, tracing various stages from origins in Africa through slavery to the twentieth century. In composing his history in music, Still drew largely on musical styles of the urban New Negro and was actively expanding the range and scope of African American art music.

Still's output was not limited to musical composition. He also spoke and wrote extensively on music. In his earliest published articles, such as "An Afro-American Composer's Point of View" in Henry Cowell's *American Composers on American Music* (1932), Still wrote as a representative of the race.[58] Subsequent articles written by Still, and those on which he collaborated with Verna Arvey, addressed various subjects ranging from music to interracial marriage and politics. Still also gave numerous addresses before various groups: professional and student music organizations, college audiences and faculty, church groups, and schools. Since his days in New York, Still had spoken on music. On May 5 of the same year his first article was published, Still delivered the address "Modernism in Music." He spoke during the session "Modern Trends in Music," one of the events held during the Ninth Annual Music Week in Harlem, sponsored by the New York branch of the National Association of Negro Musicians and the West 135th Street branch of the YMCA.[59]

Throughout his writings and speeches on music, Still revealed his personal musical aesthetics, addressing modern music, American musical nationalism, African American music, and the African American musician. While his writings expressed his own ideas, within them resonate the philosophies of the Harlem Renaissance. After the public success of his *Afro-American Symphony,* Still began to occupy a prominent position from which he could speak with authority on African American music. He addressed musicological questions such as the history and stylistic features of African American vernacular music and aesthetic questions such as their value and position in African American culture and American music at a time when American art music was seeking to define itself. His writings and speeches served a twofold purpose: (1) they articulated the voice of the black composer on his own music, and (2) they educated others, black and white, about black music.

In his articles and speeches on the spirituals, jazz, and blues, Still sought to do in words what he had done in music. Since most of his writings appeared in the mainstream press, Still was addressing primarily a white audience. He dissociated black vernacular music from its negative stereotypes by explaining its style and history. Expounding on its beauty and virtues, he defended its importance and place in American art music and culture.

The promoters of the Harlem Renaissance, James Weldon Johnson and Alain Locke, had an uneasy position on jazz. They thought it could be useful in building a great art music, but by itself, it was not art.[60] Sterling Brown and Langston Hughes maintained a more amiable position toward the vernacular, basing many of their poems on the blues. Many middle-class blacks disapproved of jazz and blues, associating them with nightclubs and brothels. Still often pointed out that during his younger days, the blues were considered immoral. This he attributed to their association with barrooms and brothels and to the belief that they expressed only, in his own words, "sexual cravings." The nightlife origins of these musical forms went against black middle-class propriety and also reinforced negative white stereotypes of black sexuality. Still attempted to free both jazz and blues from their negative associations by emphasizing their beauty, their unique musical qualities, and their overall value to American music.

Still departed from Locke in recognizing the inherent value in jazz and blues. His experience touring with Handy and his blues band as a performer and arranger during 1916 and 1919 created a lasting impression on him: "I learned, for example, to appreciate the beauty of the blues, and to consider this the musical expression of the yearnings of a lowly people, instead of accepting it superficially as being immoral and sexy, as so many other people did." [61] He sought to educate others about the music, distinguishing between two distinct types of blues—rural or country blues and urban or city blues. The first was the "traditional blues," or rural folk blues, which he "associated with emotional expression." The second type was the "sophisticated blues," or city blues, which was usually associated with dancing. [62] For Still, the primary value of both types lay in their unique musical features. Assuming the role of music theorist, he noted that the blues used both a special scale and a unique form, the twelve-bar blues, neither of which was found in any other type of music.

The second redeeming feature of the blues was their emotional expressiveness. Still believed that the "emotional content of Blues springs from a deeper and worthier source than mere sexual desire." "I refer specifically," he wrote, "to the traditional type of Blues which seems to me to express a yearning for unattainable happiness." [63] Du Bois considered the spirituals to be expressive of the emotions or the inner life and strivings of the Negro during slavery. As a type of syncretic music in which African melody, rhythm, and musical structure were combined with Western musical elements such as functional harmony, they embodied the twoness of the Negro in that they were both African and American. Still's ideas on the blues as expressive of blacks' longings and desires and their unique African American features parallel those of Du Bois. The emotional content of the blues expressed the history and consciousness of African Americans in the United States as they fought slavery and racial discrimination.

Still held a similar position on jazz, which represented to him an important development in American music: "It appears to me that any form of expression which has spread over America and from there all

over the world, which has (after many decades of public recognition) retained the power to interest intelligent thinkers like Mr. [Winthrop]
Sargeant and which has found its way, in some form, into serious American music of all types, is a vital force that cannot be pushed aside
lightly." [64] Like blues, jazz was rich in emotional expressiveness: "Negro
music has given to those who create it, who interpret it and who merely
enjoy it a sincerity and an emotional freedom that provides a release for
pent-up feelings. The sensuous Jazz as well as Negro folk music and the
serious, sophisticated music created by Negroes, partake of this sincerity." [65] Still recognized the contributions that jazz musicians had made
to American music, particularly in the areas of instrumental technique,
orchestration, and rhythm.[66] In addition to its musical value as a vernacular art form, Still held the view that jazz should also be used in creating art music and believed further that all American composers should
familiarize themselves with the idiom and use it as one of many musical
resources.

Still also sought to dispel myths about jazz. The great misconception
was that jazz was the African American's sole contribution to music.
Having begun his career performing popular jazz, Still greatly valued this
type of music; however, he sought to counter any judgments of black
musicians that limited them to jazz or popular music and to bring attention to the endeavors of black composers of art music. Still did not
seek to denigrate vernacular music but to clarify the public's understanding of the range of African American musical activity. He also valued the
spirituals highly, considering them perhaps the African American's single
most important contribution to the music of the nation. Addressing the
controversy over the origins of the spirituals—whether they were of black
origin or merely paraphrases of white Protestant hymn—he staunchly
defended their African American origin. He addressed more than their
history. The spirituals were greatly esteemed because of their history and
redemptive power: "Long before the advent of Jazz, Negro Spirituals had
made a large dent in the public consciousness on more than one continent, and their wide dissemination also was a contribution to good race
relations." [67] The spirituals were also valuable for the composer. This
repertory presented the musician, in Still's estimation, with "a large
amount of new and untouched musical material—material that will, in
fact, always be new and untouched because it is constantly being re-born,
just as the folk music in other lands." [68] African American vernacular
music, sacred and secular, rural and urban, could be used by American
composers, black and white, as a musical resource for art music.

Although Still consistently and strongly advocated positioning African American vernacular music within the American musical heritage, he believed that African American music should not be limited to vernacular music. In effect, he was a Talented Tenth Race leader, demonstrating that it was possible for a black man to be active as a composer of art music and encouraging young, aspiring black musicians. Still believed that art music was a new field open to African Americans. That black art music was welcomed in the concert hall was, for Still, proof of "America's basically democratic spirit" and emblematic of an improvement in race relations.[69]

Still was quite aware of the dilemma faced by the black composer. Aware that Americans patronized popular music more than they did serious music, Still advised the black composer to go into popular music if his or her goal was to become wealthy, but to resist being arbitrarily shunted into popular music. As he pointed out, "Another reason [black composers could become wealthy in popular music] is that a Negro in this field conforms to many people's idea of where a Negro ought to stay."[70] But Still encouraged other African Americans who were interested and possessed the talent to enter art music. Although not as financially remunerative as popular music or jazz, art music had greater social value for the Race. "In serious music, a Negro can be a pioneer and thus contribute to racial advancement and to inter-racial understanding, and he can have the satisfaction of doing something eminently worthwhile."[71] In the philosophy of redemptive culture, an African American working in art music served the Race both as a leader and role model and as a cultural ambassador to whites. These individuals were not merely artists but cultural activists—promoters of race relations. In the aesthetics of redemptive culture, works created by these composers were not merely artistic products but rungs in the ladder of racial uplift and racial progress.

Still directly addressed racism and race relations in his writings. Aware of racism from his own painful experiences, Still knew that though he was an accomplished man, there were obstacles facing him in society. Publicly, he tended to downplay racism, frequently stating that racial prejudice had not greatly hindered his progress and career as a composer. In his diary and in personal correspondence, however, Still frequently expressed sentiments to the contrary. For example, in a letter to Irving Schwerké, his friend and Paris-based American music critic, Still confided his frustration: "It is unfortunate for a man of color who is ambitious to live in America." At a moment when he had been unemployed for some months, he spoke of those "who are opposed to placing a colored man in any position of prominence." [72] Still expressed these sentiments in 1931, within a month after completing the *Afro-American Symphony*.

Views presented in "Are Negro Composers Handicapped?" in the November 1937 issue of the *Baton* are representative of his public statements. There, Still addressed whether the African American art music composer was denied opportunity and success because of his or her race. Though Still admitted that he had experienced racial prejudice and segregation, he did not believe that race presented a problem to the black composer. In music a composer could not succeed solely by virtue of his or her race; talent was the great determining factor. "Thus musically, the colored man is handicapped solely by the extent of his own capacity— or his lack thereof—of advancement." [73] Still did concede that African Americans faced difficulties, but these were not specific to any particular field: "No, the handicap of the Negro composer has nothing to do with music; it is one that must be faced not only by the composer but also by every person of color in America." [74] Despite incidents of racism, Still remained optimistic, believing relations between the races were improving and prejudice was being gradually replaced by racial understanding: "These and other handicaps of similar nature would probably grieve me greatly were it not that I find them gradually but steadily being displaced by better understanding and more harmonious relationships." [75] He believed that it was ignorant, "ill-bred" people who were racially prejudiced and that "cultured people in the country are those who are free from racial antipathy." [76] Through education and culture, people could overcome racism.

Music could play an active role in Still's vision of racial understanding and progress in race relations. Black art music could redeem the nation and aid in fulfilling the promise of democracy in America. A profound believer in American democracy, Still accorded the African American artist in the United States special significance: "The Negro artist is important in American society because he demonstrates that achievement is possible in our democracy." [77] The black artist was the Talented Tenth Race leader who, through the arts, dissolved the Du Boisian irony of being both black and American by merging the two selves and fulfilling the longing of being a "co-worker in the kingdom of culture." The African American artist promoted good public relations. African American composers and African American art music were powerful embodiments of the Lockeian vision of redemptive culture: "Negro music is also important to the *world* as well as to the nation, for as we place emphasis on our worthy cultural products, we also further the cause of better human relations, as well as better race relations. In a concrete way, we are helping to negate the bad effects of the actions of delinquents and others who are publicized in such a way as to give the Race a bad name. *Everything* we can do to help propagandize our *good* points should be done at this time, and also in the future." [78]

THE UNIVERSAL IDIOM

Though Still spoke specifically as a "Race Man," articulating the Harlem Renaissance/New Negro themes of racial progress and racial understanding, his vision was not limited to African Americans. He believed that each ethnic group had something to contribute musically, and therefore culturally and socially, to the fabric of the United States. The contribution of various groups to the artistic culture of the nation would unite the nation across racial boundaries. He expressed himself in what he referred to as the Negro idiom because of his desire to show the beauty of the music. However, his style was not limited to the racial idiom. During the early 1930s, he turned to what he later called his universal idiom. In addition to black vernacular music, he also drew on other American and New World folk music sources, such as cowboy songs, Latin American and Caribbean traditions, music suggestive of Native Americans, and Hispanic missionary music from pre-statehood California. The race issue was not limited to just blacks and whites but encompassed all racial and ethnic groups. Still believed that "when we all awaken to the fact that each group has something important and worthwhile to contribute to the culture of the entire country, then we will have a society that is well integrated—in which all of us will be working for the common good." [79]

Yet Still was not a political activist; he was a composer. Though his compositions bear racial titles, such as the *Afro-American Symphony* and *Darker America,* for the most part these works were not overtly political. They depict abstractions of the history or the psychology of blacks. As he put it, "Some people have tried to work through legal or political means, but I have sought to work through friendship and music, expressed in my own way and according to my personal beliefs." [80] In this respect, two works stand out in that they directly addressed racial violence and racial injustice. The composition *And They Lynched Him on a Tree* (1940), a setting of the poem by Katharine Garrison Chapin, confronted the issue of racial violence. Still employed two choruses as personae in the lynching drama: the white chorus assumed the role of an angry, unruly, hate-filled mob; the black chorus assumed the role of the victims and opposers of racial hatred. The soloist sang the role of the mother.[81] At the end of the work the choruses joined together to plead for racial tolerance and the brotherhood of man. Wayne Shirley has established that Still was composing the piece as an antilynching bill was passed by the House of Representatives and was being argued before the Senate.[82] Once again, Alain Locke played a major role in the genesis of a Still composition, sending Still a copy of the poem and recruiting him to compose the music. Locke described the poem as "really an epic indictment but by way of pure poetry not propaganda."[83] Following its first performance, Locke applauded its success in a review in the pages of *Opportunity*. The review read, in part, "[It] universalizes its particular theme and expands a Negro tragedy into a purging and inspiring plea for justice and a fuller democracy." A work such as this was a prime example of Locke's aesthetic of redemptive art: "When, on occasion, art rises to this level, it fuses truth with beauty, and in addition to being a sword for the times it is likely to remain, as a thing of beauty, a joy forever."[84]

During World War II, Still, like many other composers, turned to patriotic themes. His music, however, took on dual significance. *In Memoriam: The Colored Soldiers Who Died for Democracy* carried an ironic subtext. The work was dedicated to black soldiers who were facing discrimination both in the segregated units in the armed forces and at home yet were fighting "to make the world safe for democracy." It signified both the double-consciousness of the Negro and the incongruousness of democracy, racism, and war. It, like *And They Lynched Him on a Tree,* served a social end through artistic means.

The writings and music of William Grant Still are suffused with the ideals and spirit of the Harlem Renaissance. Resonating with Still's writings and music are central themes raised by Locke, Du Bois, and Hughes (with whom he later worked): the creation, preservation, and cultivation of African American music—art music primarily but also vernacular music; progress of the race from slavery to the early twentieth century;

and redemptive culture, or the aesthetic that the arts could serve to combat racial discrimination by promoting racial understanding. Still believed that the African American composer should not be limited only to black musical idioms—to expressing only his or her racial background. All styles were open to the African American who could compose in any genre, form, or style of music he or she chose. Still himself eventually chose to move beyond a racial idiom, turning to what he described as the "universal idiom" in the 1930s. In his writings and works that specifically address issues of race relations and racism, one can hear the philosophies of Du Bois and Locke and their ideas on how art could be redemptive and serve as one tool to bring about progress in race relations and racial understanding. Although committed to using his efforts in the field of art music to serve this purpose of promoting better race relations, Still saw his work as not just serving America and African Americans. He approached his compositions with great spirituality and believed that his music should serve all of humanity and promote universal brotherhood. Despite Still's move toward the universal idiom, he remained a strong advocate for African American music. The Harlem Renaissance came to an end in the early thirties, but for Still, who came to artistic maturity at about this time, the spirit and visions of the Renaissance endured.

Still's work in African American and American art music should be reassessed at least partly on the basis of his participation as a modernist and his participation in the Harlem Renaissance. He should be seen not as the "Dean of Afro-American Composers" but more suitably as a "Harlem Renaissance Man." Like Du Bois and Locke and his other contemporaries, he was a Race Man, advocating progress of the Race and progress in race relations so as to fully realize the democratic ideals of the nation. Indeed, his ideas about the rise of modernism and twentieth-century American musical nationalism were dominated by his position as a Race man.

Still left a substantial body of music—nearly two hundred works. In many of these, just as he sought to realize the aesthetics of the Harlem Renaissance, he also sought to create a style of music that was expressive of America. Perhaps the years following the 1995 centennial of Still's birth will bring about a renaissance of Still studies and result in a deeper understanding of Still as a man of letters and as a man of music. Perhaps he will be seen, more properly, as "Still, American Composer of American Music."

NOTES

1. See Carol J. Oja, "'New Music' and the 'New Negro': The Background of William Grant Still's *Afro-American Symphony*," *BMRJ* 12, no. 2 (Fall 1992): 145–169, for a study of Still's involvement in modernist music circles in New York during the mid-twenties.

2. See Nathan Irvin Huggins, *Harlem Renaissance* (London: Oxford University Press, 1971); David Levering Lewis, *When Harlem Was in Vogue* (New York: Oxford University Press, 1979); Cary D. Wintz, *Black Culture and the Harlem Renaissance* (Houston: Rice University Press, 1988); and George Hutchinson, *The Harlem Renaissance in Black and White* (Cambridge, Mass.: Belknap Press of Harvard University Press, 1996).

3. Alain Locke, *The New Negro* (1925; reprint New York: Atheneum, 1968), 7.

4. Ibid., xvii.

5. Huggins, *Harlem Renaissance*, 291.

6. Samuel A. Floyd, Jr., ed., *Black Music in the Harlem Renaissance* (New York: Greenwood Press, 1990), 173.

7. Lewis, *When Harlem Was in Vogue*, 163.

8. Eileen Southern, "William Grant Still—Trailblazer," in Claire Detels, ed., *William Grant Still Studies at the University of Arkansas: A 1984 Congress Report* (Fayetteville: University of Arkansas–Fulbright College of Arts and Sciences, 1985), 2.

9. The Clef Club functioned as a booking agency or business organization active in securing employment for black musicians, sometimes fielding several orchestras simultaneously.

10. Arvey, *IOL*, 60.

11. Letter, William Grant Still to Ralph McCombs, March 30, 1949; William Grant Still, "Highway 1, U.S.A.," typescript of speech, p. 3, Still-Arvey Papers.

12. Still, "Highway 1, U.S.A.," 2.

13. Donald Dorr, "Chosen Image: The Afro-American Vision in the Operas of William Grant Still," *Opera Quarterly* 4, no. 2 (Summer 1986): 1–23, reprinted in *Fusion 2*, 144–161.

14. Moss was one of the organizers and one of three African American men named to direct the Negro Theater Unit of the WPA Federal Theater Project in New York City. The others were Harry Edwards and Augustus Smith. "Three Colored Men Are Named to Direct the Negro WPA Theater," unidentified clipping, Scrapbook, 1935–1936, n.p., Still-Arvey Papers. *Blue Steel* has never been performed.

15. Alain Locke to William Grant Still, July 8, 1927, Still-Arvey Papers.

16. Locke to Still, July 8, 1927, Still-Arvey Papers.

17. Dorr, "Chosen Image." Dorr erroneously interprets Locke's "Bruce" as Harold Bruce Forsythe. In his correspondence, Locke regularly referred to other males by their last names; he wrote to "Dear Still" and signed himself "Locke." Neither Richard Bruce, who eventually dropped his family name (Nugent), nor Forsythe, who was almost certainly unknown to Locke, is an exception.

18. Locke to Still, December 20, 1937, Still-Arvey Papers.

19. Locke, *The New Negro,* xv.

20. Du Bois, 44.

21. Ibid., 45.

22. Ibid., 136.

23. Ibid., 138.

24. Ibid., 47.

25. Ibid., 270.

26. Ibid., 265.

27. Ibid. Still turned beyond the spiritual to the blues as having absorbed less Caucasian influence than the spiritual, however. See "The *Afro-American Symphony* and Its Scherzo," below.

28. The preferred term to refer to persons of African descent dwelling in the United States is "African American," though "black" is also currently used. Throughout this article, the term "Negro" is employed as a metaphor, either as Locke used the term in *The New Negro,* to refer to an ideal, or as an abstraction of myths or stereotypes.

29. Locke, *The New Negro,* 5.

30. Ibid., 4.

31. Ibid., 200.

32. Ibid., 210.

33. Ibid., 15.

34. Ibid., 4.

35. Ibid., 15.

36. The manuscript for this work resurfaced in 1995, since the original publication of this article, and is in the possession of WGSM. Future study of this work promises to illuminate Still's style prior to study with Varèse. I am grateful to Catherine Parsons Smith for allowing me to examine a copy of this manuscript.

37. For further discussion of Still's "ultramodernism" during his Varèse period, see Oja, "Still." For Varèse's opinion of Still, see his letter to Dane Rudhyar, March 7, 1928, quoted below in "Finding His Voice."

38. See below in this volume, "Personal Notes," "William Grant Still and Irving Schwerké," and the essays by Forsythe and Arvey, for more discussion of *Darker America.*

39. For the musical themes in *Darker America,* see "William Grant Still and Irving Schwerké," below.

40. Call-and-response is a structural pattern in which a melodic phrase or call, sung by a leader, is answered by another phrase or response, sung by another voice or by a group.

41. William Grant Still, "American Art and Culture: The Negro's Contribution," October 24–27, 1966, typescript of speech, p. 5, Still-Arvey Papers. [Editor's note: Another of his "ultramodern" works, *From the Land of Dreams,* described in the introduction, certainly helped to precipitate this decision, since it is even more dissonant than *Darker America,* and its use of blues much less obvious. *From the Land of Dreams,* however, was neither published nor given a second performance, and was unknown to critics and commentators on Still's music until the rediscovery of its score in 1997 by Carolyn L. Quin.]

42. William Grant Still, "The Contemporary Composer and His Audience," June 15, 1964, typescript, p. 6, Still-Arvey Papers. Still's move away from modernism was probably more difficult because he admired Varèse as a musician and a man.

43. William Grant Still Thematic Catalog, n.d., p. 7, Still-Arvey Papers.

44. Oja, "Still," 157.

45. *From the Land of Dreams* is discussed in the introduction.

46. William Grant Still, untitled essay, [Ladies and Gentlemen], n.d., typescript, p. 4, Still-Arvey Papers.

47. Letter, William Grant Still to William Treat Upton, n.d. [ca. 1925], Upton Collection, LC.

48. William Grant Still, untitled speech, delivered February 2, 1968, at Honors Luncheon, Association of the Presentation and Preservation of the Arts, 1968, typescript, p. 1, Still-Arvey Papers. See "The *Afro-American Symphony* and Its Scherzo," for two other statements by Still, both much closer to the time of the symphony's composition, that strongly reinforce this view.

49. Throughout this paragraph, the term "Negro" is used metaphorically.

50. Still, untitled speech on the *Afro-American Symphony,* n.d., typescript, p. 1, Still-Arvey Papers.

51. Leopold Stokowski telegram to Still, December 2, 1937, Still-Arvey Papers.

52. William Grant Still Thematic Catalog, 27.

53. Letter, Still to Rudolph Dunbar, December 1, 1945, Still-Arvey Papers; also discussed in Arvey, "William Grant Still" in this volume.

54. Letter, Still to Irving Schwerké, December 20, 1937, Still-Arvey Papers.

55. Ibid.

56. Ibid.

57. Ibid.

58. William Grant Still, "An Afro-American Composer's Point of View," in Henry Cowell, ed., *American Composers on American Music* (Stanford: Stanford University Press, 1932), 182–183.

59. Program for the Ninth Annual Music Week in Harlem, May 2–7, 1932, Still-Arvey Papers.

60. Huggins, *Harlem Renaissance,* 198.

61. William Grant Still, "A Composer's Viewpoint," *Fusion 2, 64.*

62. Still, speech, "The Composer's Creed," May 29, 1963, and January 22, 1964, for Dr. Karl With's class, University of California, Los Angeles, typescript, p. 5, Still-Arvey Papers.

63. Ibid., 6.

64. Letter, Still to Joseph W. Ferman, September 23, 1943, Still-Arvey Papers.

65. William Grant Still, "The Music of My Race" (English translation of "La Musica de Mi Raza,"), p. 2, Still-Arvey Papers.

66. Ibid.

67. Still, speech, "Negro Music," July 22, 1969, typescript, p. 6, Still-Arvey Papers.

68. William Grant Still and Verna Arvey, "Negro Music in the Americas," *Revue Internationale de Musique* (Brussels) 1 (May–June): 283. In his early writ-

ten remarks about the *Afro-American Symphony*, however, he argued in favor of using the blues in preference to the spirituals because the blues was the black music least influenced by the European tradition. See "The *Afro-American Symphony* and Its Scherzo," below.

69. William Grant Still, "Serious Music: New Field for the Negro," *Variety* 197 (January 5, 1955): 227.

70. William Grant Still, "Can Music Make a Career?" *Negro Digest* 7 (December 1948): 82.

71. Ibid., 82.

72. Letter, Still to Schwerké, January 9, 1931, quoted fully below in "William Grant Still and Irving Schwerké."

73. Still, "Are Negro Composers Handicapped?" *Baton* (November 1937): n.p.

74. Ibid.

75. Ibid.

76. Ibid.

77. Still, interview, ed. Edward Kamarck, *Arts in Society, Special Issue: The Arts and the Black Revolution* (n.p.: Research Studies and Developments in the Arts, University Extension, University of Wisconsin, 1968): 222.

78. Still, speech for the installation of new officers of the Los Angeles Chapter of National Association of Negro Musicians, 1963, p. 2, Still-Arvey Papers.

79. Letter, Still to Richard Bardolph, October 15, 1955.

80. Still, speech, "The Composer's Creed," p. 4, Still-Arvey Papers. This becomes particularly important given Still's opposition to communism, for the Communist party took the position that music was indeed a political expression. He obviously wanted it to serve the cause of racial equality, however.

81. William Grant Still Thematic Catalog, 32.

82. Wayne D. Shirley, "William Grant Still's Choral Ballad *And They Lynched Him On a Tree*," *AM* 12 (Winter 1994): 425–461.

83. Letter, Locke to Still, August 9, 1939, Still-Arvey Papers.

84. As quoted in Dorr, "Chosen Image," 9.

TOWARD A BIOGRAPHY

Finding His Voice

William Grant Still in Los Angeles

On May 22, 1934, a few days after his thirty-ninth birthday, William Grant Still arrived in Los Angeles, completing a cross-country trip that signaled a new departure in his career.[1] Until then, he had pursued two parallel careers in music. He had established himself as a brilliant and facile commercial arranger and orchestrator who had quietly helped W. C. Handy shape the "classic" blues, contributed to a series of Broadway musicals such as *Runnin' Wild, Rain or Shine,* and *Earl Carroll's Vanities of 1928,* then worked on radio shows like Paul Whiteman's "Old Gold Hour" and "Willard Robison and His Deep River Hour." There may have been as many as a thousand such arrangements.[2] In the world of concert music, Still was among the most prominent and promising American composers of his generation. Three major works premiered over fifteen months in 1930 and 1931 convincingly demonstrated three ingenious new ways to express his African American heritage. "*Africa* was [a] sensation," he wrote of its first performance for full orchestra in Rochester in late 1930,[3] and the critics agreed. The ballet *Sahdji* and then the *Afro-American Symphony,* now his best-known and most widely performed composition, followed in 1931. This achievement, which drew on what he had absorbed from each of his two professional paths, was significant both for the history of American music and for his own career. It marked a major step in his emergence from the world of Broadway and early radio into the rarefied but less lucrative world of concert music, a difficult transition that he was among the

first of any race to negotiate. Indeed, the informal title, Dean of Afro-
American Composers, was both a recognition of the wide appeal his art
had attained and an intimation of the racial barriers he challenged but
never fully overcame.[4]

When he left Wilberforce University in 1915, Still's prospects for any
sort of career in music seemed gloomy. A connection, possibly through
his late father, with the well-known Memphis-based bandmaster W. C.
Handy helped him along. Handy hired him for the summer of 1916 and
published at least ten early Still songs and arrangements.[5] Through his
work with Handy, Still absorbed the blues tradition that the black elites
of his boyhood had largely rejected; his playing and his arrangements
for Handy in turn contributed something to the blues' widespread commercial appeal.

After his year of navy service Handy rehired him, this time in New
York, for about two years (1919–1921). There, after World War I, Still
became part of the blossoming world of black music and theater. He was
soon working with such musicians as Eubie Blake, Luckeyth Roberts,
Will Vodery, and other members of the Clef Club, a combination union/
booking agency for African Americans organized in 1914 by the late
James Reese Europe.[6] In 1921–1922 Still was an orchestral musician in
Sissle and Blake's landmark all-African American revue, *Shuffle Along*,
featuring the African American blackface entertainers Miller and Lyles.[7]

Will Vodery, an early African American orchestrator of Broadway
shows, musical director at the Plantation Club, and later the first African American to work as an arranger and orchestrator in Hollywood,
gave Still's commercial career a major boost by introducing him to the
bandleader Donald Voorhees.[8] Through Voorhees, Still found himself
orchestrating *Earl Carroll's Vanities* and, presently, the radio shows that
confirmed his reputation as an innovator in the commercial field. The
"Personal Notes" show him to have been as active and arguably as influential an arranger as Don Redman or Ferde Grofé, both now much
better known in that capacity. By early 1925 he was described in the
New York Times as "orchestrator of much of the music for negro revues
and other theatrical attractions."[9] Still may well have contributed the
arrangements that drew this comment from the *Times* drama critic
Brooks Atkinson in his review of the *Vanities of 1928*: "Stung by the jazzy
lash of Dan [*sic*] Voorhees and his squealing band, the music sweeps like
a breaking wave."[10] The distinctive and widely admired style of arrang-

ing Still developed in the course of this apprenticeship is audible in a few surviving aluminum recordings of the "Deep River Hour."[11] There is much more to be learned about Still's influence on popular music in the 1920s, hinted at in Sigmund Spaeth's 1948 comment that "he continues to command respect as a creative musician, and it is impossible to estimate the extent of his anonymous contributions to the lighter music of America."[12]

At the same time that Still was leaving his imprint on commercial music, he was finding entrées into the exclusive world of concert music. Even in 1923, as he was musical director, arranging and conducting for the short-lived Black Swan record label, orchestrating shows, and composing commercial songs like "Brown Baby" to suggestive lyrics over the pen name "Willy M. Grant," Still was going against the grain by studying composition in the European-based tradition. While he played in *Shuffle Along* during its Boston run, he studied with George White-field Chadwick, a prominent composer at the time and director of the New England Conservatory. Chadwick imparted the ideal of a "characteristic" American concert music to complement the ideas Still was already forming.[13] Later, in between Clef Club gigs and summer stands in Atlantic City, Still studied with Edgard Varèse. Varèse gave him the tools to express his musical ideas with greater freedom and introduced him to the avant-garde composers of the day and to conductors who would champion his concert works, then and in later years.[14]

After his two-year apprenticeship with Varèse, and after several of his concert works had been performed, Still came to understand that (1) he wanted to write concert music whose African American character was clearly recognizable to white audiences and (2) a "serious" African American style could not, by its nature, use much of the ultramodern dissonance to which Varèse had introduced him and at the same time reach the audience with which he sought to communicate. Still therefore decided to limit his use of "modernist" techniques to those that contributed to his own goals as a composer, an important step in developing his distinctive musical speech. The most important of the techniques imparted by Varèse to his further development was more subtle—the creative use of musical form.[15] The three works completed or revised after his 1930 visit to Los Angeles (the ballet *Sahdji,* the *Afro-American Symphony,* and the suite for orchestra *Africa*) exemplify his racial style, as do the operas *Blue Steel* and *Troubled Island.* The shift away from Varèse's more obvious influences implied an eventual break with the insurgent white modernists of the day, a break based on culturally derived aesthetic considerations and one with heavy long-term consequences. Still was clearly influenced in this move by the New Negro movement, even though his association with it was often more a matter of geographic and social proximity than direct, self-conscious intellectual participation.

In 1929, the bandleader Paul Whiteman sought out several African American arrangers for his enormously popular band.[16] Still, whom Whiteman judged the most successful of these, was signed as the band departed for Hollywood to make *King of Jazz* (released 1930). Still was hired, not to work on the movie, but to provide orchestrations for Whiteman's regular weekly radio broadcasts.[17] While the band was in Los Angeles, the broadcasts originated from the studios of Earl C. Anthony's KFI, the local NBC affiliate. Under the terms of his employment, he was expected to produce three arrangements—about thirty pages of orchestrated score—for each broadcast. He considered that rather substantial amount a light load. "Since I am a pretty fast worker, that gave me a great deal of time to myself," he said later.[18]

On his 1930 trip to Los Angeles, Still revived his friendship with Harold Bruce Forsythe, whom he had met in New York several years earlier, and met Verna Arvey for the first time, probably when Forsythe recruited her to read Still's music at the piano. Forsythe was already an enthusiastic advocate of Still's work; he played an important role in stimulating Still to complete the major works of his racial period. Soon after Still returned to New York City, the twenty-two-year-old Forsythe wrote about Still's early tone poem *Darker America* in some detail in "A Study in Contradictions"; his slightly later monograph on the ballet *Sahdji* is the product of considerable thought about contemporary literary treatments of African myth as well as familiarity with Still's score. It seems likely that Forsythe's ideas about the representation of Africa and of African Americans were especially valuable to Still, not so much because Still had not thought about them before (he clearly had) or because he agreed with Forsythe (he didn't, especially about the "dark-heart"), but because with Forsythe he could talk about how these cultural issues might be represented in the technical language of music. Considering Forsythe's loquacity and Still's usual reserve, one imagines Forsythe doing a lot of the talking and Still sifting Forsythe's ideas in keeping with his own experience, his artistic sensibility, and his goals as a composer—including both the projects at hand and future projects, such as opera. Verna Arvey's role expanded as Forsythe withdrew after the completion of *Blue Steel;* their separate contributions and Still's relationship with each is considered more fully in their separate chapters.

The short-term sojourn in Los Angeles while he worked for Whiteman was a productive one, as it turned out. Still planned out his ballet *Sahdji,* on an African subject by Richard Bruce (Nugent) that Alain Locke had proposed to him two or three years earlier.[19] He decided to add a prologue to be written by Forsythe, even creating a title page acknowledging his friend's contribution.[20] Still may also have thought about the *Afro-American Symphony.* The conception of a trilogy of symphonic works, portraying first the African roots, then the voices of African Americans, and finally the integrated, equal society for which he hoped, seems to have emerged here. *Africa* (1930), the *Afro-American Symphony* (1931), and finally, the second symphony, *Song of a New Race* (1937), eventually became the trilogy. At first Still had thought of *Darker America* (composed in 1924) as its first element. By the time Forsythe completed "A Study in Contradictions," though, Still had developed doubts about the work.[21] Though he disagreed with Forsythe on *Darker America*'s aesthetic value, Still remained interested in his friend's potential as an opera librettist.

Away from the tumult of New York and the turmoil of a failing marriage, Still found the time and the serenity in those months to think about his future as a composer. As one considers later developments in his career, it is clear that Still's early visit to Los Angeles affected him profoundly and that he hoped to return after his contract with Whiteman ended. Even as he worked on *Sahdji* and thought about the *Afro-American Symphony* and searched for operatic subjects, he was moving toward what became the next step in his stylistic development. He came to the conclusion that he would retain the range of characteristically African American expressions but that these would henceforth be among the wider variety of styles he might use, depending on the specific circumstances of a given composition. This developing "universal" aesthetic represented a further step, an understanding that he could compose with integrity without being self-consciously "racial." This was neither a retreat from his modernist experiments of the 1920s nor a rapprochement with the white modernists. It was, rather, a statement of his mastery of the musical language. He wanted his musical utterance to become one of many possible authentic American voices, and to write music that would communicate with all Americans. In his universal style, he asserted his freedom to speak in his music as the individual he was.

He settled into this style, or rather cluster of styles, after he returned to Los Angeles permanently.

One later example of his universal style is the music he composed for the New York World's Fair of 1939. His private response to winning the World's Fair commission reflected his pleasure in not feeling obligated to deal in stereotypically racial expression: "It seems to me that this must be the first time, musically speaking, that a colored man has ever been asked to write something extremely important that does not necessarily have to be Negroid, and I must admit that I can't help but be proud of the distinction." [22] In that same year, of course, his major compositional energies were directed toward a much larger African American-oriented project, his collaboration with Langston Hughes on the opera *Troubled Island*, based on a story from the revolution that ended slavery in Haiti.

Still understood that his first California stay coincided with his artistic maturity: "I think 1930 marked my real entry into serious composing. . . . [M]ost of the major works began in 1930 with that ballet, *Sahdji*, and the *Afro-American Symphony*." [23] He wrote in his successful Guggenheim application of 1934, "I should like to go to California . . . for there I find an atmosphere conducive to creative effort." [24] In the later interview he remarked, "After I went back to New York from here, I was never satisfied. . . . California did something to me. . . . When I came here, it was like coming home." [25] No wonder, then, that Still sought an opportunity to return to Los Angeles to pursue his chosen goals.

Still apparently made two attempts to provide music for Verna Arvey to perform after his 1930 visit to L.A. and before his return in 1934. A two-piano version of *Africa* (the first movement only) exists in the Still-Arvey collection, with "Verna," "Arvey," "Bruce," and "Forsythe" used to label certain repeated measures. Still attempted to adapt another work for Arvey to perform. *Four Negro Dances,* for solo piano and large dance orchestra, was commissioned by Paul Whiteman, most likely while Still was under contract with him or soon afterward. [26] The same work, under the title "The Black Man Dances: Four Negro Dances for Piano and Orchestra," exists in a pencil draft score in the Still-Arvey Archive. At the start of the pencil score is pasted in: "Acknowledging with gratitude the helpful suggestions of Miss Verna Arvey concerning the preparation of the piano part." At the head of each dance is pasted a four-line stanza, each one signed "Bruce Forsythe."[27] The pasted-in texts appear to be an afterthought. Still's longhand note at the end of the score, "He can't dance any more," probably reflects his frustration that Whiteman would not release the work for Arvey to perform.[28]

From the time he turned away from the self-consciously "modern" in the interests of his creative integrity as an African American, Still characterized himself as "conservative," although his urge to work the various aspects of his life and his music into a coherent strand made him an innovator in spite of himself. The decision to leave New York was agonizingly personal as well, for he was under considerable pressure to emigrate to France. A letter from his wife, Grace Bundy Still, to Countee Cullen, dated December 9, 1929 (while Still was in Los Angeles with Whiteman), remarks, "I am eagerly awaiting the summer to make my first visit to France. I feel quite as you do about letting the children grow up there and as soon as possible after this proposed visit plan to begin looking about for permanent quarters for the family."[29] June 1930 found Still back in New York, unemployed and determined to use his time to carry out the projects he had developed in the course of his Whiteman contract. There is no evidence that he made a move toward a visit abroad. The declaration in his letter to Irving Schwerké of January 9, 1931, after six months without steady work and (ironically) just a few days after the *Afro-American Symphony* was completed, that he must soon either abandon music or "go where such conditions [of racial discrimination] do not exist" reflects his ambivalence about which geographic direction to take. The truncated journal of 1930 demonstrates that his marriage to Grace Bundy was very severely stressed after his return. We cannot follow this thread, for Still's journals over the next few years have not been found. We do know that before Bundy emigrated to Canada in September 1932 with their four children, Still had made his first application for a Guggenheim fellowship—to work in Los Angeles, not Paris.

Still's choice of Los Angeles over Paris carried implications that, whatever their personal dimension might have been, relate to the aesthetic choice embodied in his achievement of a racial style and his determination to develop it further, into a more universal speech. In large measure, the modernists had sought the "new" and learned their trade abroad; he had learned his trade with Handy in Memphis and on Broadway. The "new" he sought was developed from the African American folk traditions he had set out to absorb and fuse into an "American" concert voice. From this point of view, his exodus to Los Angeles, grounded in an aesthetic choice, was a form of expatriation, not across the Atlantic, but westward, within his own country. In Los Angeles he intensified his efforts to bridge the gap that had developed between high modernism, based in New York City, and the traditional concert audience, which he wanted to expand across lines of race and class. Thus Still bucked a trend of stratification by genre through much of his career.[30] His decision may also have predisposed his critics to dismiss his work thereafter as no longer modern but merely commercial. To be sure, the commercial opportunities there made his personal decision easier.

"Serious" New York-based white composers often came to work in Hollywood in the 1930s and 1940s (Copland is but one example). They tended, however, to separate this financially necessary movie work from their concert vocations geographically as well as aesthetically, marking the "seriousness" of their purpose by retaining their eastern residences. (That many of them had spent time in Paris and elsewhere in Europe in the 1920s was a further geographic credential.) European composers came to America, and to Los Angeles, to escape the horrors of Hitler's Europe and to carry on as best they could. Although the racial situation in Los Angeles had deteriorated after 1920, as it had elsewhere, members of the race nevertheless came to take advantage of the relatively less oppressive racial climate and the availability of commercial work, both factors in Still's decision to relocate there.[31]

In addition, Still had personal connections with some of the area musicians, some of whom were probably members of the segregated Los Angeles Musicians' Association, Local 767.[32] Before she joined the Fisk Jubilee Singers and eventually settled in Los Angeles, Sadie Cole had sung in a pageant written by Still's mother, back in Little Rock. Still may have heard Cole's daughter, Florence Cole Talbert, when she concertized in New York City (sometimes with Roland Hayes) in his Harlem years.[33] The success of Will Vodery, who had given Still arranging opportunities in New York and who had already broken the color barrier for arrangers in the movie studios, must have encouraged Still. There were family associations as well. Still's first residence in Los Angeles when he returned was on Thirty-fifth Street, where his near neighbors included both his cousin Charles Lawrence, a part-time musician whose music Still had orchestrated some years earlier, and Harold Bruce Forsythe, who was Lawrence's tenant for many years.[34]

Once in Los Angeles permanently, Still reached out to the African American music community and beyond.[35] A gift of fifty scores and books on music to the Gray Conservatory and a talk, "Writing Music for Films," followed a concert at the Twelfth Street YWCA in which John A. Gray accompanied Leola Longress, soprano, in a group of Still songs, and Verna Arvey, the future second Mrs. William Grant Still, played piano reductions of *Africa, Kaintuck'*, and *La Guiablesse.*[36] *Kaintuck'* was soon repeated for a predominantly white audience at a Pro Musica concert. Arvey, a diligent publicist, succeeded well in calling the attention of local white composers and regional music journals to Still's ability; Mary Carr Moore, for example, wrote of *Kaintuck'* as a work of "real power and splendid proportions" and became a regular at his performances.[37] Still's work was clearly perceived by much of the preémigré European American musical community in Los Angeles as not strongly associated with musical modernism, a plus from their point of view. The (mainly) white composers of the first Los Angeles school partook of the community's embedded racism but were nevertheless far more receptive to Still's aesthetic orientation than were the better-known modernists, many of the film composers, or the famous émigrés who began to arrive shortly after him.[38]

Still's first appearance at the Hollywood Bowl was at the head of the all-white, all-male Los Angeles Philharmonic on July 23, 1936. The Bowl had been a Los Angeles landmark since its founding in 1919 by an idealistic group of Theosophists, community activists, and real estate developers.[39] So it was appropriate that when Still became the first of the race to conduct a major symphony orchestra, it should have been there. As it turned out, his share of the program was relatively small. The unusually long first half of the concert consisted of standard European fare, an overture by Weber and a Brahms symphony, conducted by Fabien Sevitzky. After a late intermission, the advertised "American Music Night" began. Still conducted two excerpts from his own works: "Land of Romance" from *Africa* and the Scherzo from the *Afro-American Symphony*. His old friend and sometime rival Hall Johnson then led his own choir, the Hall Johnson Singers, in fourteen numbers, divided into three groups: songs from *The Green Pastures,* secular songs, and spirituals.[40] The fullest review, which appeared in the weekly *Los Angeles Saturday Night,* recognized that Still's share of the evening represented something less than half of the proverbial loaf:

Mr. Still very clearly demonstrated his ability as a composer in the two numbers which he conducted. The works are sincere, dignified utterances, written in a straightforward style. They present "an American Negro's concept of the land of his ancestors, based largely on African folklore, and influenced by his contact with American civilization." His orchestration is colorful, yet trickery has not been employed to achieve it. One cannot escape the feeling that the merit of these compositions warranted a performance in their entirety. As it turned out, we heard only "Land of Romance" from the *Africa* Suite, and "Scherzo" from the *Afro-American Symphony*.[41]

Forsythe subsequently wrote an essay on Hall Johnson and Still in which he celebrated the importance of this concert as a breakthrough for race relations in the concert music field.[42]

Still's music soon reached an even wider audience than that provided by the Bowl's popular concerts. Appropriately for a composer who had earlier contributed to the developing art of arranging for radio orchestra, schoolchildren and home audiences began to hear Still's serious music over the radio, thanks to the Standard School Broadcasts (sponsored by Standard Oil of California) that originated in Los Angeles. Between 1939 and 1955, more than thirty performances of Still's music, including perhaps twenty different works, were given on the Standard broadcasts. This led to broadcasts of music by other African American composers and, presently, to programs devoted to discussions and performances of jazz. These school broadcasts of jazz were said to be "the first radio-sponsored attempt to grant jazz a serious place in the musical world."[43]

More quietly, Henry Cowell's New Music Edition published the orchestra score of Still's tone poem *Dismal Swamp*, one of the early works composed in Los Angeles, thus giving him the imprimatur of at least one branch of the "ultramodern" movement.[44] The publication was supervised by the young Gerald Strang, then one of Schoenberg's composition students. There is no formal record of Still meeting Arnold Schoenberg, but if he did, it would have been at the symposium of new music organized by Arvey at the Norma Gould Studio in 1935.[45]

A vignette of Still and his family a few years after his arrival is given by Pauline Alderman, a member of the University of Southern California's music faculty. In 1942, her musicology seminar met every other week in her home.

Since three of the class members were working on American music projects, I had invited William Grant Still to come and lead an informal discussion on what he thought were the present needs of the American composer. . . . The

Stills came promptly, bringing their two small children whom they put to bed in my bedroom and we had just settled down for his introductory lecture when there were sounds of a siren and shouts along the street—"Lights out. An air raid." After the shock of the first moment we hurriedly blacked out the room, as all householders had been instructed to do, and Mr. Still went on with his well-prepared lecture.[46]

Although Still had lectured at Eastman at Howard Hanson's invitation in 1932, this would appear to be one of the few times he spoke at a southern California university. Later on, in the 1960s, there were numerous presentations at middle schools and high schools, both public and private.

Still had hoped to put his radio and theater arranging skills to work in Los Angeles, and he presently got his opportunity in Hollywood. In 1936, after the first Guggenheim stipend had run out, Still was signed to a six-month contract as a composer-orchestrator for Columbia Pictures by Howard Jackson, the studio's music director. With this chance for a good income came some in-house manipulations that unsettled Still. Jackson was fired on the day the contract was signed; Morris Stoloff was hired in his place. Still said of the incident, "That was some of the unclean practices in the studio, . . . politics and so on that got him out. . . . Stoloff, who was not a composer at all, . . . had never conducted."[47] Nevertheless, things went well for a time. He worked on several films, including *Theodora Goes Wild* and *Pennies from Heaven,* then produced a series of "sketches for the catalog." These consisted of short bits of music composed to support stock situations and kept on file to be used as needed. As was the case for film composers in general, Still himself did not have any way to know what was done with his sketches after he left the studio, but to judge from his ASCAP list, quite a few of them found their way into films.[48]

Columbia was best known for the numerous "B" movies that were its stock-in-trade. A prominent exception to its usual policy, the main feature *Lost Horizon* (released 1937) was filmed during Still's tenure there. Frank Capra, the director, hired Dimitri Tiomkin to compose the music; then, bypassing the inexperienced Stoloff, he hired a second experienced film composer, Max Steiner, to conduct and back up Tiomkin. Eight outside orchestrators were brought in to work alongside Still to speed up the project.[49] Still had seen nothing remotely like this musical overkill in his radio days. Given the lack of confidence in his skills that

Figure 1. Still at the piano, probably at Columbia Pictures. Courtesy of
William Grant Still Music.

this extravagance implied, he was sure that his contract would not be renewed once his six months were over. As a sort of desperate joke, he
penciled into a section of quiet background music an inappropriate
trumpet solo, "The Music Goes Round and Round," intending that
it be erased after the rehearsal. The studio moguls, who wanted their
swollen musical forces to work at white heat to keep their costs down
and were doubtless worried about the change in policy represented by
Lost Horizon, did not see anything funny about it. Later, Still said, "I
was let go . . . [because] it doesn't look well to have a composer in the
organization [and then] to go out and bring in people." [50] Columbia may
have fired Still, but both Steiner and Tiomkin recognized his talent.
Soon after leaving Columbia, Still completed a short job for Steiner at
Warner's. Tiomkin sent orchestrations his way several times later on.

A few years after his stint at Columbia, Still took part in a published symposium about music in films, along with such composers as
Marc Blitzstein, Paul Bowles, Benjamin Britten, Aaron Copland, Henry
Cowell, Hanns Eisler, Karol Rathaus, Lev Schwartz, Dmitri Shosta-
kovich, and Virgil Thomson. The symposium was conducted by mail;

Still's increasing conservatism would likely have led him to avoid a gathering of these liberal-to-leftist men, several of whom he had come to distrust. The remarks he wrote for this symposium constitute his most extensive statements about composing for film. What he had to say also reflects his short and tenuous relationship with the studios, his awareness of his position as the only African American in the group, and, indirectly, his grasp of the possibilities of film music. The unpretentious directness of his remarks contrasts sharply with the posturing of some of the other respondents. Unlike his fellow composers, who claimed compositional autonomy for their film music, Still wrote that he had worked only on the music director's orders, from the completed film sequences, thus frankly admitting that he never had any control over the overall product:

> I never took into account the level of musical understanding of the film audience, but from the instructions given me by the musical director it was my opinion that he did. . . .
>   The difference in the music for a film and for any other dramatic medium is great; in the former, quality does not count so much as cleverness and perfection of the time-element. . . . Yes, the future cutting of a film makes it more difficult to write good music for films, as one is never sure whether or not a carefully worked out form or balance will be destroyed in the final cutting. . . . There are no more special facilities of sound-recording for films than there are in radio; personally, the resources in modern radio appeal to me more. . . . I have long felt the need for drastic changes in the conditions under which most film music is composed, and most other serious composers who have been momentarily attracted to this work agree with me, but such changes would involve changing the film industry itself, and this is impossible. . . . [T]he serious composers therefore have no recourse but to adapt themselves to Hollywood—they early learn that they cannot expect an industry to adapt itself to them.[51]

Still's best opportunity in films came late in 1942, when he was asked to be music director on a film with an all–African American cast, *Stormy Weather,* at Twentieth Century Fox. It was his biggest contract ever, for $3,000, but he walked out on it a few weeks after he was hired, apparently over the issue of how African Americans and their music should be represented in film. Although Still was never able to persuade the studios to use his concert music, it appears that, probably in the early 1950s, he produced a "Laredo Suite" from which excerpts were used as fillers in television series such as "Gunsmoke" and "Perry Mason."[52]

One of Still's projects after completing *Blue Steel* was a musical portrayal of Central Avenue, the center of African American life in Los

Angeles, probably intended for a film production.[53] Something of a mystery surrounds this score. Forsythe agreed to provide a scenario in 1935; the original idea was very likely his.[54] Still offered it to Howard Hanson for a ballet production at Eastman and then withdrew it. Not long after this, Still became one of six composers commissioned by the CBS radio network to compose a work specifically designed for radio orchestra.[55] *Central Avenue* was quickly revised into a suite specifically for broadcast, becoming New York's *Lenox Avenue* and scoring one of a series of national successes that came to Still in the first fifteen years of his Los Angeles residence. Later, *Lenox Avenue* became a ballet, with a new scenario by Arvey.[56]

Still applied for the Guggenheim and moved to Los Angeles to compose an opera, or possibly two of them. By the time he stopped composing in the late 1960s, he had completed eight operas. Only the second, *Troubled Island,* had a major production in his lifetime. That disappointment did not prevent him from continuing to compose them. Still's commitment to opera went back to his days as a teenager in Arkansas when he was enthralled by the early Victor Red Seal opera recordings his stepfather brought home. Donald Dorr details several of his unsuccessful early attempts to find or develop a libretto, the most serious (discussed above) involving an unpublished novel by Grace Bundy Still, his first wife, and Countee Cullen.[57] One result of the 1930 visit to Los Angeles was that Still was able to complete several symphonic works; a second result was that he began to seek out the long-term financial support necessary to compose an opera. In 1931–1932 he applied to the Guggenheim Foundation: "I am planning two operas. The scene of the first is to be laid in Africa, and its music will, in as far as artistically possible, reflect the primitive and barbaric nature of the African savage. The scene of the second opera is to be laid in the United States, and its musical idiom will be that of the American Negro."[58] This first proposal was not funded, but a second application two years later was successful. Thus his drive to become an opera composer was what enabled him to make the move away from New York City. A single scene by Forsythe, "The Sorcerer: A Symbolic Play for Music," which Still set as a ballet in 1933 and discarded later, may have been intended as part of the "primitive," "barbaric" African opera. By the time of his second application, he had chosen the second of his two ideas as the primary project and proposed a third as his backup.[59] He chose to set *Blue Steel,* a short story on an American Negro subject by his friend Carlton Moss, a writer just getting started in radio.[60] From the story, he developed his own very detailed dramatic outline for his setting, almost a libretto in itself, for Forsythe, his inexperienced librettist, to work from. Still intended his outline to present "roughly and concisely the gist of the lines which are to be given each character, and the stage directions."[61] Forsythe apparently accepted Still's working conditions, making his own notes on the outline and supplying language to suit the composer's specifications. Still annotated the libretto liberally, writing down motives and their variants. After *Blue Steel* was finished in 1935, Forsythe signed a contract to write a libretto for a full-length "Sorcerer," but he probably never completed it, and the second opera was not composed.[62]

Although both Arvey and Judith Anne Still came to regard the occasionally dissonant musical language of *Blue Steel* as the reason the composer rejected this first opera, it was not withdrawn until several years after it was completed, when Still, who was unable to convince the country's major opera companies to look seriously at it, had a newer one to promote.[63] Sadly, *Blue Steel* remains unperformed. The next opera, *Troubled Island,* set in Haiti to a libretto by Langston Hughes (with additions by Verna Arvey), eventually achieved a pinnacle of success for an American opera, a professional production by the New York City Opera. This production and its aftermath formed a major turning point in Still's life; so troubled was it, and so troubling for students of Still's life and works, that it will be treated at some length in another chapter.

Still did not allow his unhappiness over the treatment of *Troubled Island* to interfere with his commitment to opera; in fact, he continued to complete them at a remarkable rate. *A Bayou Legend* and *A Southern Interlude* were completed before the New York production of *Troubled Island* ever came about. Another opera, perhaps his best work, was composed entirely in 1949, the traumatic year of the *Troubled Island* production. Still worked out the outline for *Costaso* in the two weeks before he went East for the rehearsals and premiere of *Troubled Island.* Within a year he completed the entire score, down to extracting the orchestral and choral parts, then proceeded without a pause to the next project, *Mota,* on which he worked just as expeditiously. Once he was well settled in Los Angeles in his quiet domestic life with Arvey, it appears that Still purposefully embarked on a long-term project to use the various cultures of the Americas that were a part of his racially mixed background and his life in the Southwest as settings for operas. Arvey became his librettist for this project mainly by default, after Forsythe

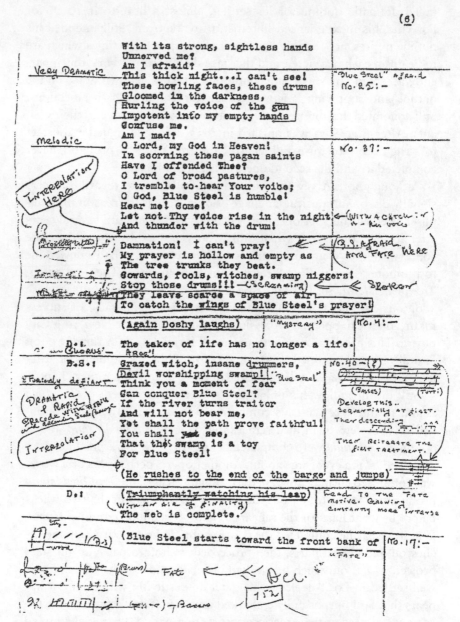

Figure 2. Page from Forsythe's libretto to *Blue Steel,* with Still's annotations. Library of Congress. From the collections of the Music Division, Library of Congress. Courtesy of Library of Congress.

and Langston Hughes (for different reasons) dropped out of the picture. (Still had always wanted his librettists close at hand, where they could write words to fit his music rather than the other way around.⁶⁴) *A Bayou Legend* (1941) and *Minette Fontaine* (1958) are set in Louisiana and draw on voodoo practices. *Costaso* (1950), reportedly Still's own favorite, is set in a Hispanic town in an isolated, austere southwestern desert. *Mota* (1951) is set in Central Africa; *The Pillar* (1955), in a Native American pueblo; and *Highway 1, U.S.A.* (begun in 1942 as *A Southern Interlude* and revised into a one-act opera in 1963), in the eastern United States, where it portrays a family whose culture is generally "American" but not racially specific.

Since the 1949 production of *Troubled Island,* none of Still's operas has been produced by a major company, although most have had regional productions of varying quality. By the late 1960s, when regional opera companies and university opera departments began to produce new American works more frequently, Still was no longer in a position to take much advantage of this new and fruitful trend. At this writing, *Mota* and *The Pillar,* like his first opera, *Blue Steel,* remain entirely unknown to operatic audiences.

Los Angeles gave Still a relatively relaxed racial climate, a friendly aesthetic atmosphere, and just enough support so he could pursue his career as a composer. His choice to remain there, away from the center of things musical, represents a going against the grain for composers of symphony and opera. His decision to turn down the opportunity (in 1941) to become a "university composer" at Howard University (at Alain Locke's urging) affirmed his decision to turn away from the worlds of both the modernists and the Harlem Renaissance, a kind of expatriation in his own country. Over the years the defeats added up alongside the successes, partly because Still aimed so high and attempted so much: his firing from Columbia Pictures, the summary dismissals of *Blue Steel* and *Troubled Island* by the Metropolitan Opera, the years of struggle before *Troubled Island* was produced at the New York City Opera and then its equivocal reception, the debacle at Fox Studios over *Stormy Weather,* the lapse of fifteen years before another opera got a hearing (*Highway 1, U.S.A.,*1964, on public television), the obscurity and poverty of the 1950s and 1960s. The quiet domesticity of his second marriage gave him extraordinary freedom to compose, a freedom he used for almost unceasing work, but the relative isolation it brought may have stimulated the feelings of suspicion and distrust that he displayed in his

later years. One remembers Carlton Moss's description of him as a din-
ner partner at the Harlem YMCA in his youthful New York days:

> This was as I saw it, Still's personality. The only time I saw him was at the
> dinner table at the YMCA in Harlem, which was the only really decent place
> to eat. He would sit there, and he had this habit of tapping his foot. He never
> talked about anything else but that music. Later on I always felt that, I was
> just an interlude. That I never talked to him about this lynching, or this prob-
> lem, or what the NAACP was doing. I just listened to his loyalty to his mu-
> sic, and I got the impression that when he left me, wherever he went, he'd sit
> down and mess with that music. . . . [He was] very attractive. But he was al-
> ways off, in another world.[65]

On his first visit to Los Angeles, Forsythe described him as "the most
original and gifted negro composer ever to be in circulation," and wrote
"there are few artistic paradoxes to compare with the artless simplicity
of his personality and the uncanny complexity of his art creations." [66]

In the late 1920s and especially in the 1930s, Still had attracted substantial attention as a composer of art music, with numerous readings
of his works by major symphony orchestras. This continued for some
fifteen years and more after he moved to southern California. For example, Still's concert music had no fewer than ninety-eight performances
nationwide in 1942.[67] A succession of commissions and first performances by major symphony orchestras around the country, the Hollywood Bowl appearance conducting the Los Angeles Philharmonic, the
CBS broadcast of *Lenox Avenue,* the Perisphere commission, were more
than most composers could hope for in a lifetime. Many of these works
seem to be the product of the repeated challenges, personal and cultural,
that he had faced in his early years, that confronted him anew as he
made his way in New York, and that led him to leave New York for Los
Angeles. To some extent, these challenges changed as he moved from his
early struggles to his successes in commercial music, to his career as a
"classical" composer, and to the conflicts of his later years. But the underlying themes remained and can be followed in his best-known work,
the *Afro-American Symphony,* in his relationships with Forsythe and
Arvey, and even in the development of his late political activism.

NOTES

1. This chapter is extensively revised from an earlier essay intended for an
exhibition, "The Musical Renaissance of Black Los Angeles," originally scheduled for 1991 and opened in February 1995.

2. Still's arrangements are widely scattered. Some early arrangements published by Pace & Handy in Memphis have been located at the Hogan Jazz Archive at Tulane University. Approximately one hundred are in the Paul Whiteman Archive at Williams College. About half that number of arrangements for Robison's Deep River Orchestra have been identified in the Ellington Collection at the Smithsonian Institution. Some arrangements of spirituals were published. A few other arrangements are in the Eubie Blake Collection at the Maryland Historical Society. Many others are lost or unlocated.

Judith Anne Still has counted some four hundred such arrangements listed by title in Still's diaries, which are only known for 1929–1930 and 1937—and thus do not include many of his busiest years. The estimate of one thousand is mine, based on this admittedly incomplete information. Research on Still as an arranger and composer of popular music is in its infancy; copyright deposits are one example of a major source that remains virtually untouched.

3. Diary, October 24, 1930.

4. According to Thomas Warburton, "Still, William Grant," in *Amerigrove*, 4:544, Howard Hanson, the major champion of Still's music, coined this phrase. Intended as high praise, its limiting function soon became evident.

5. W. C. Handy's (1873–1958) importance to the history of the blues is well established. Biographical information appears in print as early as 1908, in G. P. Hamilton, *The Bright Side of Memphis: A Compendium of Information Concerning the Colored People of Memphis, Tennessee, Showing Their Achievements in Business, Industrial and Professional Life and Including Articles of General Interest to the Race* (Memphis, 1908). He published an autobiography, *Father of the Blues* (New York: Macmillan, 1941). Most of Handy's surviving correspondence, business records, and music are in a closed private collection.

The songs were published in band arrangements by Pace & Handy, Memphis. I am indebted to Dr. Bruce Boyd Raeburn, Curator, Hogan Jazz Archive, Tulane University, for pointing out the existence of eight of these arrangements in the John Robichaux Collection. One, "No Matter What You Do," sets lyrics by his first wife, Grace Bundy, whom he met at Wilberforce; the lyrics are not included in the arrangement. Several other of Still's early stock band arrangements have been located by Gayle Murchison in a private collection.

6. For information on the enterprising Europe, whose untimely death interrupted the development of a distinctively African American symphonic tradition, see Reid Badger, *A Life in Ragtime: A Biography of James Reese Europe* (New York: Oxford University Press, 1995); also Robert Kimball and William Bolcom, eds., *Reminiscing with Sissle and Blake* (New York: Viking Press, 1973). Eubie Blake, who composed most of the music for *Shuffle Along* and was a longtime friend of Still, was Europe's assistant conductor. The Blake Collection contains folders of music used by Europe's band. Luckeyth [Luckey, Luckyeth] Roberts (1887–1968) was a pianist, bandleader, and composer of musical comedy.

7. For information on *Shuffle Along*, the Clef Club, and the influential James Reese Europe, whom Still probably did not meet, see Kimball and Bolcom, *Reminiscing with Sissle and Blake*.

8. There is surprisingly little information on Vodery despite his prominence. See Mark Tucker, "In Search of Will Vodery," *BMRJ* 16, no. 1 (Spring 1996):

128–182. A collection on Donald Voorhees (1903–1989) is located in the New York Public Library at Lincoln Center.

9. Olin Downes, review of International Composers' Guild concert of February 8, 1925, that included Still's *From the Land of Dreams,* published February 9.

10. J. Brooks Atkinson, review of show opening August 6, 1928. Arrangers worked under pressure of time with little thought beyond the immediate production or performance. Since they worked on an ephemeral product in collaboration with composers, conductors, performers, and perhaps authors and directors as well, the evidence about their contributions is often anecdotal in nature.

11. See Wayne D. Shirley, "Religion in Rhythm: William Grant Still's Orchestrations for Willard Robison's 'Deep River Hour,'" *BMRJ* 18, no. 2 (forthcoming). Archival tapes of air checks from the "Deep River Hour" are at WGSM. Still's later comments on arranging and composing for radio, along with his ideas about "American" music, appear in an interview done by Forsythe, now in the Forsythe Papers.

12. Sigmund Spaeth, *A History of Popular Music in America* (New York: Random House, 1948), 478–479.

13. No formal record has been found of Still's study with Chadwick, who was in ill health by 1921. See Steven Ledbetter, "William Grant Still, George Whitefield Chadwick, and the New England Conservatory," paper read at "A Tribute to William Grant Still," Flagstaff, Arizona, June 25, 1998.

14. See Still's "Personal Notes," below, for his log of these performances and critical responses.

15. Still expressed his admiration for Varèse several times. A letter from Varèse to Dane Rudhyar, listing his best students and describing them, gives his teacher's view of Still:

7 March 1928

. . .

William G. Still—A Negro, my student since 1922, lyrical nature, typical of his race. I handle him with care, not wishing that he should lose these qualities, but not wishing that he should keep the banalities of the whites that was inculcated through the course he followed at the New England Conservatory. . . . These [i.e., Edouardo Fabini, Adolf Weiss, Colin McPhee, Sam Reichmann, and Still] are the students who do themselves credit and for whom we await with confidence and hope what the future will allow them to achieve.

William G. Still nègre—mon élève depuis 1922—nature lyrique—et typique de sa race. Je le pendle avec précaution—ne voulant pas qu'il perde ses qualités—mais ne voulant pas non plus qu'il garde les poncifs "des blancs" qui lui ont été inculquè par les cours qu'il a suivi au New England Conservatory. Ceci. . . . Faites lui crèdit et attendez avec confiance et espèrè ce que le futur leur permettre de réaliser.

Rudhyar Collection, Department of Special Collections, Stanford University Library, Stanford University.

16. Thomas A. DeLong, *Pops: Paul Whiteman, King of Jazz* (Piscataway, N.J.: New Century Publishers, 1983), 102. According to DeLong, Whiteman decided to improve the quality of his already popular group by adding some Afro-

American musicians. Dissuaded by the argument that a racially mixed group would create insuperable problems with accommodations when it traveled, he settled for hiring some Afro-American arrangers, of whom Still was the most successful. Don Redman also made a few arrangements for Whiteman.

17. Ferde Grofé (1892–1972) was hired to work on the film. His orchestrations for *King of Jazz* are in the Grofé Collection, LC.

18. Eileen Southern, "Conversation with William Grant Still," *BPiM* 3, no. 2 (May 2975): 165–176.

19. Bruce, a native of Washington, D.C., was a prominent Harlem Renaissance poet and artist who published relatively little. Locke published his two-page sketch of "Sahdji" in his 1925 *The New Negro*.

20. The title page, an isolated single page, is at WGSM.

21. See "Personal Notes," Arvey's "William Grant Still," and "William Grant Still and Irving Schwerké," all in this volume, for evidence of Still's dissatisfaction with *Darker America*.

22. Letter, William Grant Still to Alain Locke, August 6, 1938, Moorland-Spingarn Research Center, Howard University.

23. "William Grant Still: Negro Serious Music," interview by R. Donald Brown, November 13 and December 4, 1967, Oral History Program, California State University, Fullerton.

24. Application to the John Simon Guggenheim Foundation, "Plans for Study" (1934). Courtesy of the Guggenheim Foundation.

25. "Negro Serious Music," interview, 1967.

26. A condensed score and set of parts are in the Whiteman Collection at Williams College.

27. This may be the work that Forsythe invited Arvey to read for Still in 1930, the occasion of their first meeting. The poems are lacking in the Whiteman materials.

28. Neither the Whiteman materials, which do not include a full score, nor the pencil score is dated. The interpretation given here is confirmed by Arvey in a "Scribbling." Arvey reports that Whiteman had reserved the right of first performance but not exercised it. Still then composed *Kaintuck'* as a vehicle for her. In *Fusion 2*, 175, Carolyn L. Quin lists "The Black Man Dances" as a movement of *A Deserted Plantation*, another work composed for Whiteman; this is an error. The incipit listed in the same source in the composer's catalog as edited by Celeste Anne Headlee belongs to some other work.

Still experimented with his new music typewriter with *The Black Man Dances*. Although he prepared only part of a page of this score on the typewriter, he used the clumsy device regularly thereafter.

29. Letter, Grace Bundy Still to Countee Cullen, December 9, 1929, Countee Cullen Papers, Amistad Research Center, Tulane University. Cullen, a prominent poet of the Harlem Renaissance, was involved in an opera project with Bundy and Still under the title "Rashana" which did not come to fruition. At this point, Cullen was continuing to express interest in completing the project.

30. Efforts to bridge the cultural gap between elite U.S.-born white audiences and urban working-class audiences that included many European-born immigrants are documented in the early chapters of Claire R. Reis, *Composers,*

Conductors and Critics (New York: Oxford University Press, 1955; reprint 1974); and Catherine Parsons Smith, " 'Something of Good for the Future': The People's Orchestra of Los Angeles," *Nineteenth-Century Music* 16 (1992): 147–161. Michael W. Harris, *The Rise of Gospel Blues* (New York: Oxford University Press, 1992), chap. 5, describes performances in black churches in the early 1920s of European and African American concert music. Still had participated in a similar tradition as a member of the Amsterdam Musical Association; see the introduction, n. 6.

31. See Mikel Garcia, "Adaptation Strategies of the Los Angeles Black Community, 1883–1919" (Ph.D. dissertation, University of California, Irvine, 1985), for the coping strategies developed by L.A.'s relatively small African American population before World War I.

32. C. L. Bagley Collection, Regional History Center, University of Southern California, Box 4, includes copies of Bylaws for the Musicians' Association from 1925 and 1940, as well as a directory of the members from 1944. Local 767 was integrated into Local 47 in 1953.

33. Eileen Southern, *The Music of Black Americans,* 3d ed. (New York: Norton, 1997), 278. Sadie Cole Talbert toured in Europe after her New York debut and taught at Tuskegee, Fisk, and elsewhere before retiring to Los Angeles. Verna Arvey, *IOL,* reports her connection with Mrs. Shepperson. Florence Cole Talbert had graduated from Los Angeles High School, the only African American in her class, studied at the University of Southern California and later in Chicago, and retired to Los Angeles after an extensive career as a singer and voice teacher. I am grateful to Phyllis Panhorst for providing evidence of Sadie Cole Talbert's New York concerts from the weekly *New York Age.*

34. December 22, 1994, Smith interview with Harold Sumner Forsythe, who pointed out that in the early 1930s there were only two neighborhoods where blacks could live in Los Angeles, Central Avenue and the smaller area near Jefferson, where Lawrence, Still, and Forsythe all lived. Latinos, Asians, and African Americans lived in proximity to one another, since all three groups experienced discrimination in housing.

35. For more information on Still's Los Angeles, see Betty Yarbrough Cox, *Central Avenue—Its Rise and Fall (1890–c.1955), Including the Musical Renaissance of Black Los Angeles* (Los Angeles: BEEM Publications, 1996).

36. "Writing Music for Films," typescript prepared by Verna Arvey "from an address delivered at the John Gray Conservatory of Music on December 13, 1937," at WGSM, was probably for this occasion. (See below concerning Still on film music.) Clippings from the Still-Arvey Papers. Many African Americans in Los Angeles had their musical training from either the Wilkins Conservatory or the Gray Conservatory.

37. Mary Carr Moore, "Los Angeles News," *Music and Musicians,* September 1935.

38. Such composers would have included Charles Wakefield Cadman, Fannie Charles Dillon, Homer Grunn, Mary Carr Moore, and Elinor Remick Warren. Many of them were women, who often had much less access to the lucrative commercial field and who were also marginalized and stereotyped, though collectively they formed an important part of the audience for the opera, the

Philharmonic, and the touring virtuosi of the day. See Catherine Parsons Smith and C. S. Richardson, *Mary Carr Moore, American Composer* (Ann Arbor: University of Michigan Press, 1987), especially the chapters "The First Los Angeles School" and "The Ultra-Moderns"; also Catherine Parsons Smith, "'A Distinguishing Virility': On Feminism and Modernism in American Concert Music," in Susan C. Cook and Judith Tsou, eds., *Cecilia Reclaimed: Essays on Music and Gender* (Urbana: University of Illinois Press, 1994). Among the prominent émigrés were Igor Stravinsky, Arnold Schoenberg, Ernst Krenek, Ernst Toch, and Eric Zeisl.

39. See Catherine Parsons Smith, "Founding the Hollywood Bowl," *AM* 11 (1993): 206–242. A concert by several all-African American choruses was one of the earliest performances in the Bowl, probably in 1920, even before the Philharmonic began its regular summer series there. The Philharmonic began playing there in 1922. African Americans did not attend Bowl concerts in large numbers, however. The Bowl's sponsors wished its audiences to be integrated, but the community of Hollywood itself was not. See Isabel Morse Jones, *Hollywood Bowl* (New York: G. Schirmer, 1936), 24.

40. Program, Hollywood Bowl, Thursday, July 23, 1936. Courtesy of Lance Bowling. Later, when he was director of the Indianapolis Symphony, Sevitzky conducted Still's music.

41. *Los Angeles Saturday Night* 43, no. 45 (August 1, 1936): 10. William K. Purves, a substitute for the regular reviewer, Francis Kendig, wrote the review.

42. Harold Bruce Forsythe, "Johnson and Still," unpublished typescript, Forsythe Collection. The typescript was intended for *California News,* an unidentified periodical.

43. Paul Eduard Miller in *Esquire* magazine. Quoted in Adrian Michaelis, "Still Music on the Western Air," *BPiM* 3, no. 2 (May 1975): 177–195. Conductors included Werner Janssen, John Barnett, Paul Lemay, Henry Svedrofsky, Alfred Wallenstein, Pierre Monteux, William Steinberg, Maurice Abravanel, Vladimir Bakaleinikoff, Meredith Willson, Carmen Dragon, and Still. In fact, many of Still's arrangements, including some for Whiteman and others for the "Deep River Hour," attempted to treat jazz in a serious manner.

44. *Dismal Swamp* was composed in 1935 and published in 1937. The League of Composers, based in New York City, commissioned a work from Still in the late 1930s. Still offered *Dismal Swamp,* written in a style that retained traces of his "modernist" idiom and the more populist *Kaintuck'*. Claire Reis chose *Kaintuck'* as the piece to be dedicated to the league, which in fact did not perform either piece. *Kaintuck',* however, found performances in Cincinnati and elsewhere. See "*they,* Verna and Billy," below, for more on *Kaintuck'*.

45. See "*they,* Verna and Billy."

46. Pauline Alderman, *We Build a School of Music: The Commissioned History of Music at the University of Southern California* (Los Angeles: Alderman Book Committee, 1989), 198.

47. Interview, "William Grant Still: Negro Serious Music."

48. A few of these sketches are in the archives of Columbia Pictures. Judith Anne Still kindly allowed me to look at Still's ASCAP list of film and television cues.

49. William H. Rosar, "*Lost Horizon*—An Account of the Composition of the Score," *Filmusic Notebook* 4, no. 2 (1978): 42. The orchestrators, in addition to Still, were Robert Russell Bennett, Peter Brunelli, Hugo Friedhofer, Herman Hand, Hugo Kaun, Charles Maxwell, George Parrish, and Max Reese. Jester Hairston, who continued to collaborate with Tiomkin, made the arrangements used by the Hall Johnson Choir in the film. (The Hall Johnson Choir was hired at Still's suggestion.)

See also Tony Thomas, *Film Score: The View from the Podium* (South Brunswick: A. S. Barnes, 1979), 93. Tiomkin assembled the largest orchestra ever at Columbia (45–65 pieces).

50. Interview, "William Grant Still: Negro Serious Music."

51. "Music in Films, a Symposium of Composers," *Films* 1, no. 4 (Winter 1940): 5–18. See "*they,* Verna and Billy," below, for a discussion of how Still's response was produced. The 1937 typescript "Writing Music for Films" (see n. 36 above) explains the process and pitfalls of composing music for films; it serves as something of an introduction for the remarks quoted here.

52. The hypothesis of a "Laredo Suite" incorporating these elements was offered in informal conversations between Clifford McCarty, author of several books on film music, and Lance Bowling of Cambria Records and Archives, July 1994.

53. Letter, George Fischer to Still, September 22, 1936, Still-Arvey Papers.

54. The Forsythe Papers contain a one-page outline for "Central Avenue," undated. Forsythe's unpublished novel, "Frailest Leaves," uses Central Avenue as a metaphor for the African American community in Los Angeles.

55. The others were Aaron Copland, Louis Gruenberg, Howard Hanson, Roy Harris, and Walter Piston.

56. *Lenox Avenue* was broadcast over CBS radio on May 23, 1937. Still wrote to Schwerké that it was a new work. Wayne Shirley has ascertained that it is a revision of *Central Avenue* in which the second half is essentially recomposed ("*Central Avenue* and *Lenox Avenue,*" paper presented at "A Tribute to William Grant Still," Flagstaff, Arizona, June 26, 1998). There were also changes in scoring between the radio and ballet versions. For more on *Central Avenue/Lenox Avenue,* see "An Unknown 'New Negro,'" this volume.

57. Donald Dorr, "Chosen Image: The Afro-American Vision in the Operas of William Grant Still," *Opera Quarterly* 4, no. 2 (Summer 1986): 1–23. Dorr is wrong in identifying Forsythe as a potential librettist for "Atlantis" on the basis of a 1931 letter from Alain Locke to Still; in accordance with his practice of using last names (for example, "Dear Still" rather than "Dear William" or "Dear Billy"), Locke referred not to Bruce Forsythe but to Richard Bruce (Nugent).

58. Still, application to the John Simon Guggenheim Memorial Foundation. This application was initiated in June 1931, but the "Plans for Study" is dated 1932. A second application filed in June 1933 was successful; this time, *Blue Steel* was to be the primary project. Still's Guggenheim was renewed for six months in 1935; another application for *Troubled Island* was funded in 1938.

59. Still refers to "A NEGRO ETUDE, text by Mr. Trask." Mr. Trask is not further identified. He might be Sherwood Trask (b. 1890), author of *The Interweaving Poetry of American History: New Frontiers* (New York: Pageant Press,

1967), a volume of poetry; or more likely Willard Ropes Trask (b. 1900), editor of *Classic Black African Poems* (New York: Eakins Press, 1971) and *The Unwritten Song: Poetry of the Primitive and Traditional Peoples of the World* (New York: Macmillan, 1966). For more on *The Sorcerer*, see "An Unknown 'New Negro,'" below.

60. Moss attempted to return the favor during World War II, when he was working for the Office of War Information and was involved in making the film *The Negro Soldier*. Although Still was hired to compose the music, presumably at Moss's behest, his score was not used. Moss (1909–1997) was an important African American figure in early radio, the Federal Theatre Project, and film. See obituary, *Los Angeles Times*, August 15, 1997.

61. Forsythe Papers. A copy of the libretto, with Still's musical annotations, is in the Library of Congress along with a draft piano-vocal score. WGSM has both the full score and the finished piano-vocal score. Still and Bundy had prepared a similar scenario for Countee Cullen to work from for their proposed "Rashana," but the scenario is unlocated.

Copyright materials at the Library of Congress consist of a piano-vocal score in which Act I is copied on transparent sheets for duplication using a blueprint process; the remaining two acts are incompletely sketched in pencil. These suggest that Still abandoned this opera before he completed a fair copy. However, William Grant Still Music has his hand-copied full score and a version of the piano-vocal score done on Still's music typewriter, acquired in 1935. From this it is clear that he abandoned the hand-copied transparent sheets (a) to make further revisions and (b) to produce the piano-vocal score on the music typewriter, a more technologically advanced but still very laborious method. Thus he had no intention of discarding the opera at this time.

62. Much later, *Mota*, with a libretto by Arvey, had an African setting unrelated to *The Sorcerer*.

63. See Arvey's "William Grant Still," below, for her enthusiastic discussion of *Blue Steel*.

64. Katherine Garrison Chapin, who supplied several choral texts, was the exception.

65. Carlton Moss, interview with the author and Lance Bowling, February 21, 1993.

66. Forsythe, "W. G. Still: A Study in Contrasts," undated two-page typescript in the Forsythe Papers.

67. Benjamin Griffith Edwards, "The Life of William Grant Still" (Ph.D. dissertation, Harvard University, 1987), 242.

An Unknown "New Negro"

Harold Bruce Forsythe's training as a musician made him both an enthusiast and a wonderfully insightful commentator on Still's concert works, which were generally ignored by better-known writers of the Harlem Renaissance/New Negro movement. None of what eventually emerged from them comes close to matching the now-unknown Forsythe's vivid perceptions. I supplement his "Study in Contradictions" and "Plan for a Biography of Still" with this biographical study because of the quality of Forsythe's work, because of the significant artistic collaborations he undertook with Still, and because of his influence on Still's personal life.

Indeed, Forsythe's artistic and personal impacts on Still are not fully separable. To begin with, he was a powerful advocate and facilitator for the Africanist aesthetic position he read in Still's music. During Still's 1929–1930 sojourn in Los Angeles, Forsythe arguably served as a catalyst for several works Still produced at the end of his "African" period, immediately after his return to New York City. Forsythe played a role in stimulating Still to clarify his conceptions of the ballet *Sahdji* and the *Afro-American Symphony,* and probably also *Africa,* the suite for orchestra that Still completed in Hollywood in February 1930. An early title page for *Sahdji* in Still's hand acknowledges Forsythe as the author of a prologue, now missing.[1] Forsythe's availability as a librettist was a major reason for Still's return to Los Angeles in 1934. Indeed, Forsythe wrote the libretto (to Still's detailed specifications) for *Blue Steel,* Still's first completed opera, and he provided the start for a second, which turned into a ballet, *The Sorcerer,* later withdrawn. Moreover, it was Forsythe who introduced Still to his future wife and later artistic collaborator, Verna Arvey. The romantic triangle that developed in 1934—discussed below—was the immediate cause of his estrangement from Still and Arvey, although there were underlying aesthetic issues as well. The complications of these personal relationships probably influenced the way in which Still's "universal" aesthetic developed, and possibly its timing. More concretely, they may have affected Still's decisions to withdraw or alter certain of his works composed around 1935.[2] Forsythe's importance may thus be even greater than "A Study in Contradictions" suggests. Before the gifted, vulnerable librettist/ scenarist/ poet disappeared from view he had played a major role in the lives of both Still and Arvey.

Forsythe was born in Georgia (July 14, 1908) and taken to the Los Angeles area when he was about five years old, possibly earlier.[3] He attended Manual Arts High School, where he was an older contemporary of Verna Arvey. The two established a friendship that lasted almost fifteen years, longer than his association with Still. Several years before he went to New York City to study, Arvey wrote about him in the Manual Arts weekly paper:

> Harold Forsythe . . . not only composed one piece of music, but many. Music was his natural mode of expression; and as Miss Rankin says, "His music is beautiful thoughts, lovely ideas. While he is able to speak and write in exquisite language, he has also the happy faculty of explaining himself in music." His compositions, on first sight, have an almost disarming simplicity. One imagines that they are easy to perform, but in reality they are most difficult. He is indeed a sensitive soul, responsive to all musical impressions.
>
> Although he has composed many songs, short piano pieces, a string quartet and a fantasia for violin and piano, he is remembered in particular here for several of his works which were performed in assembly.[4]

About a decade after Arvey's article, Forsythe wrote this self-description for the *Hamitic Review,* a short-lived Los Angeles literary magazine:

> Whether I'm a writer-musician or a musician-writer is a matter that doesn't trouble me. I've always kept the two functions in separate psychic compartments. My musical education was received from Prof. C[harles] E. Pemberton of U.S.C., and Dr. Rubin Goldmark of the Juilliard in New York. Since one disastrous venture into public taste, my music has been held in reserve. Have composed an opera, a symphonic poem, a monody and various works for small orchestra, string quartet and voice. Adolf Tandler, Nicolas Slonimsky, Leonard Walker, Fannie Dillon and others have spoken of this music. Be-

Figure 3. Harold Bruce Forsythe. Courtesy of Harold Sumner
Forsythe.

ing a peculiar cuss, Verna Arvey and Gladys Mathonican alone play and sing it. My literary studies have been entirely independent and secretive. I have written about a dozen books covering the field of novel, biography, poetry, drama, scenario, libretto, metaphysics and criticism. Much interested in Negro history, art, religion, magic. Associated with the composer, William Grant Still in an effort to articulate the subtler currents of ethnic sentience. First published stuff in W. Thurman's old *Outlet,* and his *Looking Glass.* Did some bad articles for the *California Eagle.* Wrote during its lifetime for the stormy *Flash,* a sharp little publication. Am more than happy to be associated with the *Hamitic Review,* and have in mind a series of articles that might be of interest.[5]

His sensitivity in response to a rather well-received recital and the "secretive" character of his writing suggest, at least in hindsight, his extreme shyness and vulnerability.[6] The references in this biographical sketch and other of his writings also suggest a chronicle of the African American intellectual connections he made in his midteens. Wallace Thurman, later a prominent Harlem Renaissance literary figure, attended the University of Southern California in about 1922, then published his *Outlet,* to which Forsythe contributed, while working in the post office alongside Forsythe's uncle around 1922–1923.[7] Thurman boarded with Forsythe's family for a time and was at least indirectly a mentor. Forsythe later wrote, "You see although never a 'friend' he's closely bound up in my life. He was a friend of my brother and boarded in our house when i [sic] was a stripling. Nietzsche, Hearn, Flaubert, all came into my life from the books Thurman left about the house."[8] Arna Bontemps, later a poet and novelist of the Harlem Renaissance, was in Los Angeles at roughly the same time; it is very likely that Forsythe knew Bontemps as well.

Bontemps's 1941 letter to Arvey, giving biographical information for one of her articles, describes his own Los Angeles background and gives a rationale for his family's westward migration that very likely parallels Forsythe's:

When I was three, my parents moved to Los Angeles [ca. 1905, from Louisiana; 1912 or 1913 for Forsythe]. The following year they entered me in the kindergarten of the Ascot Avenue school. I believe I was the only colored child in the room (and perhaps in the whole school at that time), and I still remember how amused and pleased my mother seemed when she visited the school and found me completely integrated into the group. . . . Kindergarten turned out to be an epitome of all my schooling. I am a product of neighborhoods in which relatively few Negroes lived and of schools in which we were always greatly in the minority. The same is true, I believe, of a good

many Negroes who grew up in Los Angeles in those days. . . . My parents
were always anxious to put the South (and the past) as far behind as possible. . . . One by one, however, our relatives migrated to Southern California during my childhood, and a link with the past was established for me in
spite of all efforts to the contrary.[9]

Coming to Los Angeles was in fact an old tradition for African American
musicians, who were visiting regularly by the 1890s and often performing to mixed audiences in white-run theaters. Flora Batson, the Original
Nashville Students, and Sissieretta Jones were among those who had
concertized there before the turn of the century.[10] Forsythe might have
heard Will Marion Cook's American Syncopated Orchestra in Los Angeles shortly after World War I. In Forsythe's teen years, the city was the
launching point for bands of both races that formed in the West and
traveled East as well, contributing to the development of jazz. Freddie
Keppard played in Los Angeles just before his successful move East, as
Paul Whiteman also had. Keppard's Olympia Orchestra, including New
Orleans bassist Bill Johnson, later became "the first black dance band,
and the first from New Orleans, to make transcontinental tours, as the
Original Creole Band. . . . It was this band . . . that carried the jazz of
New Orleans to the rest of the nation."[11]

Many African American musicians had come to Los Angeles to live
before Forsythe arrived. The vigorous classical music activities of the
African American community are chronicled most fully in the weekly
California Eagle to which Forsythe briefly contributed. Music making
in African American churches was very well established.[12] Forsythe may
well have heard groups like the choir of one hundred white-clad African
American women, choral singers from local churches, who joined several hundred more of their white sisters in a formal greeting to President
Theodore Roosevelt in 1912, as he campaigned in Los Angeles for election on his third-party Bull Moose ticket and women prepared to vote
for the first time.[13] The African American community was relatively small
but well educated. John A. Gray operated a conservatory and wrote a
weekly column in the *Eagle*. Arkansas-born and Los Angeles-trained
William T. Wilkins, in whose conservatory Forsythe first studied piano,
began presenting his students in recitals in 1914. Forsythe, according to
his son, hung out at Wilkins's conservatory. His piano teacher there was
Nada McCullough, a graduate of the University of Southern California.[14] After several decades of teaching, Wilkins's and Gray's students

would number well into the thousands.[15] Thanks to the work of Gray, Wilkins, and others, many of L.A.'s jazz musicians were, like Forsythe, classically trained, which means that they did more reading from arrangements and less improvising than was done in New Orleans or Chicago.[16] Later, Charles Mingus was among the products of this tradition.[17]

Forsythe must have known about Still from an early age, for a Still cousin, Charles Lawrence, also a musician, lived in the same close-knit African American neighborhood around West Jefferson and Thirty-fifth Street in Los Angeles where Forsythe spent part of his childhood. Still had orchestrated a piece by Lawrence in the early 1920s.[18] (Later on, Forsythe and Lawrence shared living quarters in New York City.) It is quite likely that Forsythe had begun to learn about the possibilities of the Harlem Renaissance and the "New Negro" by then and that he introduced Arvey to its new intellectual currents while they were high school students. (Perhaps they read Alain Locke's 1925 The New Negro together, discovering among its treasures the first sketch of Richard Bruce Nugent's "Sahdji.")[19] Their friendship suggests the likelihood that Arvey became aware of Still and his work much earlier than she might have otherwise and that her meeting with Still in 1930 carried more weight than one might think from her later statement that she had barely met him in 1930. It is at least likely that Arvey is the "'not much praised but altogether satisfactory lady'" of Forsythe's essay who already in late 1930 "has become sweet on him [i.e., Still]." The chronology as well as the dynamic of Still and Arvey's relationship began earlier than previously thought because of this friendship, a matter of considerable import. This hypothesis is strengthened by H. S. Forsythe's report that his father's friendship and working relationship with Still ultimately foundered over Arvey.

Forsythe was a gifted pianist, as Arvey recognized and as is confirmed elsewhere.[20] He may have been among the student pianists that Arvey, whose own skill is well documented, recognized as a superior performer. His training in piano and composition was in the European concert music tradition, a background he shared with Still as well as with many other African American musicians of his time. The training in composition he received (after leaving Manual Arts High School and the Wilkins Conservatory) from Charles E. Pemberton, who had been a working musician in Los Angeles since the late 1890s, would have been very much in a conservative nineteenth-century German tradition. Forsythe's relatively early short piano compositions at William Grant Still Music, his graduation gifts to Arvey, are in the European tradition (character-ized by him as French-influenced) and testify to his pianistic ability. Many songs now among the Forsythe papers reflect his conservative training in Pemberton's hands.[21] However, Forsythe later made arrange-ments of one or more spirituals "with a jazz flavor," according to the re-port of his and Arvey's friend Harry Hay, who sang the arrangements on several occasions in Los Angeles. Forsythe lists other now-lost composi-tions, including an opera and a lengthy symphonic poem. He wrote to Arvey about them,

> I have been looking over my long Symphonic Poem, the Opera and a small pile of songs. All done three or four years ago. I THINK MY BEST WORK IS BEHIND ME. So I've another balm. Deaf like Beethoven and Franz, stoop shouldered like Mencken, I do my best stuff early, like Mendelssohn, Poe. (Don't tell me that's the only resemblance with such guys. Ah knows!!!)
>
> But art is Not technique, knowledge, . . . it is inspiration. And as I look at the pages of the Symphonic Poem, a work NOBODY has read and studied but me mahsehf I get broody and sad as the devil. That Spring was gor-geous . . . the months of its composition. Each morning I awakened with mu-sic bubbling and trembling in the head . . . could hardly get dressed before dashing for pencil and paper. . . . Never will forget the glorious day the cli-mactic section was written . . . and that strange passage where the theme rises, like a phoenix from fire, in the trumpets from a rumbling chaos of poly-tonal trombones, cellos and contrabassi and fiddles, sul. G portamento.[22]

Forsythe's impulsiveness seemingly contrasts with his interest in neo-classicism, his general distrust of the modernism of which neoclassicism was a major aspect, and his respect for the training he received at the hands of the German-trained Pemberton. With some of his contempo-raries, he formed a club whose sole remnant is a letterhead bearing the heading, "The Iconoclasts: 'Down With Tradition,'" dating from the 1920s.[23] In the early 1930s he produced a lengthy novel, "Frailest Leaves," which contains a short and highly imaginative lecture on the historical values of counterpoint. His profound ambivalence about mod-ernism is clear from this extract. The lecturer, a gifted but floundering young artist trying his hand at teaching younger students indifferent to both his brilliance and the expressive power of music—transparently Forsythe himself, perceives the ambivalence of modernism's claims to objectivity. A few excerpts:

> The perfectly worked contrapuntal exercise was the nearest thing to absolute communism we will ever witness. That is true, but it is at the same time the

more aristocratic of the arts. Everything is part of the whole, yet nothing is subordinated to it. Its parts have all the characteristics of the best among men. They have character, charm, purpose. They must vary their tendencies, yet remain true to their own destiny, they must be strong, yet not inflexible. And most important, and this is where most of us fail, in life as well as in art; the parts conduct themselves with courtesy, respect and regard, each for the other. This is the most stringent note in our art. We admit here no percussive discords, no appoggiaturas, but only prepared discords of suspensions.[. . .]

[. . .] It is not my purpose to denounce contemporary music, but to encourage you in a fuller understanding of it by drinking deep of these purer, more intellectual fountains. The intellectualism of modern music is more psychopathic than has been generally understood.[. . .] Above all, do not regard this as the study of a dead language.[24]

The unreconciled, conflicting currents in Forsythe's thought are complicated by his anger about the race barrier. He was acutely aware of his distance from his white friends, including Arvey, but did not hesitate to tackle prominent African Americans who did not agree with his opinions, including Clarence Muse, the prominent actor, singer, and composer, then a Hollywood fixture:

So darned mad at a Negro that for the moment I hate all of them. Clarence Muse. The most blankety-blankest idiot the Devil ever tossed upon the poor, long suffering Nig.[. . .]

Tomorrow I will be calm and contemptuous again. Today I'm rip snorting, and hating, and furious.[. . .] I could whoop for the Ku Klux Klan, if an equally asinine white man hadn't irritated me before C.M. got started.[25]

On recommendations from both Pemberton and Wallace Thurman, Forsythe was awarded a fellowship to the Juilliard Graduate School in New York City for 1927–1928.[26] There he studied composition briefly with Rubin Goldmark and theory with another, unidentified teacher. He withdrew from Juilliard on March 18, 1928, before completing a full year of study.[27] Harold S. Forsythe reports that Forsythe wrote to his mother from New York that he was having trouble with his hearing, something that he seems to have kept from his friends. Whether he was in New York City before the fellowship began and how long he was able to remain in New York City afterward are not known; his mother's letters to him reflect her taking on extra work and making other sacrifices to send him money. The fictional but autobiographical hero of his "Frailest Leaves" describes a brief, disastrous affair with the woman

designated by Goldmark to teach him; one of the few letters from his
New York sojourn confirms a brief engagement.[28] His later letters from
New York used as their return address the location of Thurman's *Fire*
commune on 135th Street, suggesting both that he lived or worked there
and that he had some association with Harlem Renaissance literary activity. Yet his self-descriptions listing a lengthy series of short-term jobs
do not include a connection with the short-lived, flamboyant *Fire*. Likewise, his claim in the sketch quoted above to have studied with Varèse—
Still's teacher—has not been verified and is not repeated in other places.

Forsythe and Still renewed their acquaintance during Still's sojourn
in Los Angeles in late 1929 and early 1930, just before "A Study in
Contradictions" was written. The implication is very clear that they
discussed future projects; perhaps Arvey even participated in some of
the discussions about whether Forsythe and/or Still were really more
"African" than "Afro-American," and if so, how that quality should be
reflected in Still's compositions. The later evidence is that they talked
about subjects for operas and that Still acted on some of these discussions. One of Forsythe's proposals that Still did not accept or even acknowledge (so far as is known) was Forsythe's offer to complete the libretto of *Roshana,* the project Still had begun in collaboration with his
wife, Grace Bundy.[29]
      Forsythe had a hand in the sequence of events that brought Still back
to Los Angeles permanently in 1934. In his first application to the
Guggenheim Foundation for funding (rejected in 1932 but awarded for
use in 1934), Still wrote that he planned two operas, one about black
Africans set in Africa, the other about African Americans in the United
States. He wrote, "The librettist has already completed a portion of the
first act, and his work is well done." [30] From this it is plain that Still had
decided on the subjects of his operas and on his collaborator before he
applied in 1931 and probably earlier, before he returned to New York
in 1930. The first of the two operas was to be *The Sorcerer,* for which
Forsythe produced a one-scene libretto. In 1933, while Still was in New
York, he composed a ballet to *The Sorcerer,* whose scenario resembles
the libretto scene and is attributed to Forsythe. Four years later, Still sent
the manuscript to Howard Hanson for a possible reading at an American music symposium in Rochester, scheduled for fall 1937. After
expressing doubts about its value, Still withdrew it, not even allowing
an orchestral reading in a closed rehearsal, then sent his orchestrated

version of his song "Summerland" from *Three Visions* (for piano) instead.[31] Still did not destroy this manuscript, which exists in the form of a seventeen-page piano score, but the orchestration is so far unlocated.[32]

The second opera, on an American subject, was to be *Blue Steel.* The libretto fleshed out a short story by Carlton Moss.[33] This is the project that Still chose to work on in Los Angeles. In keeping with the composer's manner of working on opera, Forsythe stayed obligingly close to hand, providing new or changed text as Still worked.[34] It is likely that at this time (1935) he wrote the essay on Still's ballet, "The Significance of Still's *Sahdji,*" which appeared in the *Hamitic Review,* probably in the same April 1935 issue for which he provided the self-description given in full above. Forsythe's essays on *Sahdji* show that he became deeply involved with the work; in the longer essay he claimed to have suggested that Still rewrite the final dance, something that Still later seems to have done.

There seemed every intention of continuing the collaboration following the completion of *Blue Steel.*[35] On May 21, 1935, Still and Forsythe contracted to collaborate on an opera called *The Sorcerer* and a ballet called *Central Avenue.*[36] In the first case, Forsythe was to provide a libretto for a story already "invented" by Still, no doubt an expansion of the earlier sketch/ballet or a movie short. In the second, Forsythe was to complete the scenario, already partly "invented" by Still, for a ballet. There is no evidence that the opera *The Sorcerer* ever went forward beyond the ballet Still had composed in New York. *Central Avenue* was composed and, according to some sources, discarded. Much of it resurfaced as the suite for radio orchestra and later ballet, *Lenox Avenue,* for which Arvey supplied the scenario. Letters from Howard Hanson and Thelma Biracree, who had directed and choreographed performances of *Sahdji* and *La Guiablesse* at Eastman, indicate that Still sent them *Central Avenue* and that Biracree and Hanson were very eager to perform it. Before it could be produced, Still withdrew it in favor of *Lenox Avenue,* whose scenario Biracree regarded as much less satisfactory for the resources available at Eastman. *Lenox Avenue* remained unperformed at Eastman, and the mystery of *Central/Lenox Avenue* remains unresolved.[37]

On the basis of their common interests in composition, the piano and its literature, and music criticism, Verna Arvey had maintained a longstanding, warm friendship with Forsythe that peaked in the eight or nine

months after Still's arrival. In August 1934 she wrote with unusual eloquence to Carl Van Vechten, a major patron and champion of the
Harlem Renaissance, in behalf of Forsythe's literary production:

Aug 6, 1934

My dear Mr. Van Vechten:

. . . For the past ten years, I have known and written to Bruce Forsythe, a
young Negro intellectual, writer and composer-friend of Langston Hughes,
William Grant Still, Wallace Thurman, Richard Bruce, etc. His letters to me
have been impersonal, yet filled with a most interesting view of the race situation in America today, various musical and literary thoughts which may
or may not prove of value, comments on those famous colored people he
has known and anecdotes, his own personal history, etc. Because they extend over a long period of time, the later letters are necessarily more mature. All of them are beautifully written.

   I have compiled these letters into a book (with Forsythe's permission
and approval)—and now I wonder whether you would be interested
enough to read it, pass judgment and to suggest a possible outlet for it?
For the last few years I have been writing articles and criticism of my own
(mostly on music and dance subjects) for various and sundry publications.

   If you *are* interested, may I call on you when I come to New York, or
would you prefer that I mail it to you? . . . Sincerely yours, Verna Arvey[38]

Given this prodding, Forsythe put aside his earlier opinion of Van
Vechten (expressed in "A Study in Contradictions") as "a mere surface
polisher and wise-cracker" and wrote his own letter describing something of his life and his work as a composer and writer. He revealed his
own shyness and vulnerability in the process:

[August 24, 1934]

Mr. Carl Van Vechten

Dear Sir:

Letters of this sort, which assume an enormous amount of importance to
the writer, are very difficult to write. But after having postponed the writing
of this one for several *years* I have at last reached a sort of serenity and perspective; and from this little perch I do not feel so much of my former fear
of thus addressing you.[. . .]

   It is simply that having never mailed a book or a piece of music to a
publisher; having never really contacted a first-rate critic, and having, at 26,
lived a sufficiently peculiar life devoted to such pastimes as dish washing on
a diner, office boying, elevator operating, night watchmaning, janiting, soda
jerking, shipping clerking, private secretarying, ditch-digging, editing a tiny
magazine, studying harmony, counterpoint, orchestration, composition,
with Goldmark among others, piano pounding in sweet houses, ditto on a
steamer, ditto in jazz bands, ditto in vaudeville, book reading, and having

found time during this to compose with a minimum of exhibitionism a symphonic poem, an opera, innumerable smaller stuffs, and having loved and studied the [European art] Song. Hallelujah to Wolf, Franz, Debussy, van Dieren and composed three volumes of it . . . as well as about fourteen literary slices, many of which have been burned by this hand. . . . At last comes the urge to a more practical view of things, and a genuine view of what I have done. Since it is an axiom about starting at the highest perch I approach you in this manner. . . .

In all seriousness now, I have now a book. . . . In some respects a biography of my dear friend William Grant Still, that most brilliant (Musically) of all Negro musicians. This is not a conventional biography, but one told through a *figure* of personal and ethnic experience. The book not only places an entirely fresh evaluation of the "Spiritual" but takes a somewhat strange view of Jazz. At the same time it serves to throw into relief the work of a man known by few (if any). He has composed beautiful music . . . music of a far deeper spiritual and mental significance than any other Negro composer ever heard of. I am a musician. I compose. I am a Negro composer. Yet I approached this book with a beating heart for at last a composer of my blood spoke with something other than bilgewater spiritual derivations or sloppy sentimentality.[. . .]But Still's music is rooted in the Dark-heart. How deeply I show in the book.[. . .]

Very sincerely yours, Bruce Forsythe [39]

Within a few days, he wrote to Jean Toomer, expressing his great admiration ("you are not so much the finest but the *only* writer partaking of the Blood, in this country") for Toomer's novel *Cane* (1923) and its hero, Kabnis, and asking permission to quote from it in his own work.[40]

Forsythe busied himself with revision of the material he had agreed to send to Van Vechten, while Arvey prepared for her lecture-recital at the New School in early December and the warm-up performance in Los Angeles a month earlier. Perhaps it was the growing tension as her travel date drew nearer that led to the warmth of his letter to her, following her Los Angeles recital:

And since you are going away I do want to step outside everything, Verna. And say a final word. You may imagine perhaps, that to have known one person for many years, and to value them highly, and to almost live looking forward to their brief visits, and then when a stranger comes to town, to have that old friend suddenly cease . . . bingo! Do you realize you haven't set foot in my house since Bill came to L.A. Do you wonder that this hurt me, and caused me to say and do rude things. For I say for the final time; I have no utilitarian bone in my body. I love a few people very strongly and

for themselves alone. And am acutely sensitive where they are concerned.
But tho it now is a matter of no importance, I still think as highly of Verna
as ever since M.A.H.S. and suppose I always will in years to come when the
silly causes of my foolish losing of your friendship have vanished, and you
move in an entirely different group.[41]

Upon receiving a postcard reporting on her call on Van Vechten, Forsythe
sent off not one manuscript but three, and enclosed a small snapshot of
himself for good measure:

Dec 13, 1934

Dear Mr. Van Vechten:

[. . .]This novel, biography and romance are dear for several reasons,
(none literary). They were largely composed in a fine old house in San
Gabriel where I was attended to by my sister-in-law Irene, so lovely a person and so rare. I had no job then; and had only to write all day and drink
and talk all night. At that time I had no thought of publication or of large
minds. I wrote for the sheer love of it and because Irene wanted me to.
There is no page in "Rising Sun" or "Maron-Mutra" that has not been discussed and rewritten, re-written and discussed by us for days on end. It was
Verna A., however, who encouraged and insisted upon the revision of the
novel when I disgustedly almost gave it up. . . . As in my first note to you I
tried hard to explain my position and the peculiar way such colleagues as
Wallace [Thurman] have always looked at me. I think that Still and I are a
little more Negro than they are, a little more *African*. I do not remember
ever showing anything to Langston Hughes who has had highballs with me
several times. . . .
    . . . Five feet eight, very thin, with an "agnostic stoop" (Moore?) Pale
yellow face, . . . gray eyes, large mouth and heavy mustache (now). Much
stronger than look. Played quarterback as kid and was handy with boxing
gloves. Very shy at times and very pugnacious at others. Given to silence
among strangers and wild monologues among friends. Like beer, port and
scotch, and since 1928 have repudiated gaudy wearing and use only black
from head to foot.[. . .]
    I praise heaven that my work on Still's opera is largely if not completely
finished. . . .

Gratefully, Bruce Forsythe[42]

Van Vechten's answer, unlocated, stunned him to the point of in-
coherence:

Jan 15, 1935

I come just this once again with much humility, for I thank you deeply for
your courtesy. And yet although I have boasted that I could take it, the air

is very bleak from the hint of doom in your letter. A year or two ago it would have thrilled . . . or even a year ago, for then I felt bursting with books and music, and the suggestion that these things are yet thin, and Future yawned brighter would have been terribly encouraging. But now . . . Many more lonely years ahead, and those years no doubt filled with the errors and foolishness of the past ones. This letter shouldn't be written of course, for it is just after reading yours, but I think a man who fears his emotions, or better, fears his fear is in some ways a coward, and of all virtues that is the least.[. . .]

Sincerely yours, Bruce Forsythe

P.S. If it were possible to explain the real reason for this sudden passion, after years of indifference to opinion and publication, I'm sure you would agree that it is not all mere ego and self-seeking.[43]

Van Vechten must have queried Arvey after receiving this letter, for she reported back to him:

2/5/35

When I returned, Harold seemed to be as he was, and showed me your letter. Strangely enough, and unlike the warlike old Harold, he seemed very meek and was constantly studying your suggestions to see where he could use them and thus help himself. More, he was *very* grateful to you for your frankness. He is going to revise "Frailest Leaves" now, according to your suggestions. In other words, (though this is small consolation for all the time and trouble you took in reading the mss., seeing me and writing to us) I think you have done Harold a far greater service by doing exactly what you did than if you had followed out your first idea, and, as a matter of fact, I think perhaps that is what I hoped for all along. Because a little personal triumph is relatively unimportant when it comes to making finer human beings of people! In the long run, I am sure Harold will profit more.[44]

Although Arvey tried to put a good face on it, Forsythe must have been devastated by what he saw as his failure, especially in combination with the loss of Arvey's friendship after Still's arrival in Los Angeles. Even without the sexual aspects of this triangle, Arvey had supplied him with a one-person audience and with knowledgeable encouragement for his creative work; now she focused these attentions on Still and away from him. We cannot know more ramifications than this unless Still's diaries, missing for 1931–1937, the period of his collaboration with Forsythe, are recovered, and perhaps more of Forsythe's materials. Arvey's annual datebooks are likewise lost, subsumed into five-year summaries that do not give sufficient information to make things clearer. The loss of Forsythe's letters to her, except for the half dozen from late 1933 and early 1934 (just before Still's arrival) that are quoted here, becomes even more poignant in this circumstance.

Still family tradition has it that Forsythe was unable to live up to his side of the contracts for *The Sorcerer* and *Central Avenue* because of his alcoholism and that Still's piano piece, "Quit Dat Fool'nish," was initially intended as a bit of unsolicited advice for Forsythe.[45] We know now that the unusual contracts to supply librettos were somehow tied to the literary disaster that Arvey precipitated through her overture to Van Vechten as well as, perhaps, to the alcoholism. Arvey never lost her anger at what she perceived as Forsythe's self-destruction, and perhaps her guilt at having had a role in precipitating it. Later, in one of her "Scribblings," she acknowledged his early deafness (while he was studying with Pemberton, before he went to New York in 1927) and her belief that he had tuberculosis. In private, she summed him up this way:

> HBF was a marvelous, strange character. He wrote wonderful letters. I admired them and compiled them into a book, only to discover afterward that he was a drunkard, that he lied about me, that he didn't like the book merely because I had arranged it journalistically. He had whitewashed himself in his letters to make me know him as he wanted me to! One of the finest things in his life was his love for Irene, but even she grew disgusted after a time.[46]

Irene Forsythe, the sister-in-law who had encouraged him to write and allowed him to live in her comfortable house in San Gabriel, died in 1938, another severe blow. One imagines Forsythe destroying his manuscripts as he retreated noisily from his literary and creative friendships into the grinding poverty that was his family's lot.[47] Would he have continued as a musician? Although his name does not show up in the directories of Local 47, or in the surviving directories of Local 767, the segregated African American local that was abolished only in 1953,[48] Forsythe had once found employment as pianist on Prohibition era gambling ships anchored outside the three-mile limit, where they were free to sell alcoholic beverages.

The denouement to Forsythe's story told by his son is different: Forsythe, the loser in a classic triangle, broke with Still over Arvey.[49] He did not, and could not, continue his career as a musician. His deafness, apparently a congenital condition shared with other family members, advanced inexorably to the point that by 1940 he sought and received retraining from the county as a horticulturalist. Thereafter he learned the botanical names for thousands of plant species and worked steadily, six days a week, at the Enchanted Way Nursery at La Tijera and Slauson. On the seventh day, he often got drunk. In 1945 he married the former Sara Turner, a onetime Cotton Club showgirl. Their two sons were born in 1947 and 1955. By 1950 the piano had disappeared, Forsythe being too deaf to play it. The family, which included Turner's daughter, lived in the cramped cottage Forsythe had first rented as a bachelor when he returned from New York. In the 1960s his health deteriorated further; the family subsisted on the earnings of the two older children. He died in 1976, within a few days of Paul Robeson, to whom he had a family connection. He is remembered by his son as an unhappy man, often depressed.

When he wrote to Van Vechten, Forsythe can hardly have imagined how thoroughly he would find himself "retreating to the shadows whence [he] came." Even in this rediscovery of his work, his initial importance lies in the manner in which his shadow throws the life of his role model, friend, and rival into a richer perspective.

NOTES

1. Title page at WGSM. "The Rising Sun," a lengthy manuscript now at The Huntington Library, may have been intended as the prologue.

2. See "*they,* Verna and Billy," below, for the alterations and more on this triangle.

3. Forsythe's death certificate shows his parents to have been Sumner Forsyth and Elizabeth Smith of Georgia; that he had lived for sixty-two years in Los Angeles County; that his surviving spouse was Sara Turner; that he had worked for twenty-three years as a horticulturalist in a nursery; that he died February 2, 1976, of a brain tumor. His school records are not open; an obituary notice in the *California Sentinel* contains no biographical information. Harold S. Forsythe reports that Sumner Forsyth came to Los Angeles in 1912 and his family followed the next year. Sumner Forsyth was a Pullman porter; he later was divorced from Elizabeth and lived in San Gabriel, California, east of Los Angeles. Family letters among the Forsythe Papers show that Sumner Forsyth did not help his son financially during his New York sojourn. Forsythe added the "e" to the family name.

4. "Song composer gains laurels writing lyric . . . ," undated clipping in Arvey Scrapbook #49, Still-Arvey Papers. Except for some songs and piano music, none of the compositions listed here or later in this chapter has been located.

5. "Introducing a New Contributor," *Hamitic Review* (April 1935). Except for the clippings and one later issue, this journal is unlocated outside the Still-Arvey Papers. The *California Eagle* was a weekly African American newspaper

published in Los Angeles. *Flash* was a weekly African American newsmagazine published in Los Angeles briefly, ca. 1930–1931. Several copies, none containing Forsythe's byline, are in the Forsythe Papers.

6. March 20, 1931, Baldwin Hall, 810 South Broadway. The program reads, "Mr. Charles E. Pemberton presents the original compositions of his pupil, Harold Bruce Forsythe." Performers included Arvey for the piano solos; Neyneen Farrell, soprano; Victor Boggis and Dewey Johnson, baritones; and Charles Lawrence, accompanist. The concert was favorably reviewed in the *California Eagle* and the *Los Angeles Examiner*.

7. For more on Thurman, see Phyllis I. Klotman, "Wallace Henry Thurman (1902–1934)," in *Afro-American Writers from the Harlem Renaissance to 1940,* ed. Trudier Harris, vol. 51 of *Dictionary of Literary Biography* (Detroit: Gale Research Co., 1987), 260–293; see also p. 13, n. 10.

8. Letter, Forsythe to Verna Arvey, March 15, 1934, Forsythe Papers.

9. Letter, Arna Bontemps to Verna Arvey, December 29, 1941, Still-Arvey Papers.

10. This information is taken from albums and scrapbooks containing theater programs and newspaper clippings in the L. E. Behymer Collection at The Huntington Library. See also Robert Stevenson, "Los Angeles," in *Amerigrove,* 3:107–115.

11. Eileen Southern, *The Music of Black Americans,* 2d ed. (New York: Norton, 1983), 343.

12. See Jacqueline Cogdell Djedje, "Gospel Music in the Los Angeles Black Community: A Historical Overview," *BMRJ* 9, no. 1 (1989): 35–79; and "Los Angeles Composers of African American Gospel Music: The First Generations," *AM* 11, no. 4 (1993): 412–457.

13. This event is described in the pages of the Progressive weekly, the *California Outlook,* over several issues in the fall of 1912. A report in the *Outlook* after the fact remarks that the African American women sang "surprisingly well." Theodore Roosevelt campaigned actively for the votes of African American women and men in this campaign. Women got the vote in California in 1911, nine years before the Nineteenth Amendment was approved.

14. I am grateful to Josephine Blodgett Smith, who volunteered this information after I spoke at "The Musical Renaissance of Los Angeles, 1890–c. 1955," Los Angeles, February 17, 1995. She suggested that it was probably McCullough who sent Forsythe to study with Pemberton at USC.

15. I am grateful to Miriam Matthews for locating several sources on Wilkins and on the younger John S. Gray, both of whom operated private conservatories, primarily for African American students. Wilkins graduated from Polytechnical High School and studied at the pre–World War I Von Stein Academy in Los Angeles, which in those years offered excellent European-style conservatory training to as many as seven hundred (mainly white) students at a time.

16. Interview with Jack McVea, by Michael Bakan, reported by Bakan in "Way out West on Central: The African American Jazz Scene in Los Angeles, 1917–1929," paper read to the Society for Ethnomusicology, November 7, 1990. McVea was a saxophonist who began his career in the 1920s in Los Angeles.

17. Charles Mingus, *Beneath the Underdog,* ed. Mel King (New York: Knopf, 1971).

18. Listed in *Fusion 2,* 231, as "What Makes Me Believe You?" from the "early 1920s."

19. Alain Locke, *The New Negro* (New York: Albert & Charles Boni, 1925), 112–114. See Murchison's numerous references to Locke's *The New Negro* in "'Dean of Afro-American Composers' or 'Harlem Renaissance Man,'" above.

20. Interviews with Harry Hay, 1993–1994. Hay, a sometime musician, actor, and writer who became a Communist party member and later was a founder and activist in the Gay Rights movement, first called my attention to Forsythe. Hay was part of a circle that included Arvey, John Cage, and various dancers and theater people; he sang Forsythe's arrangements of spirituals on several occasions in the early 1930s. He describes a brief homosexual relationship with Forsythe in the same period. I am grateful to him for supplying information and answering my questions. For more on Hay, see Stuart Timmons, *The Trouble with Harry Hay, Founder of the Modern Gay Movement* (Boston: Alyson, 1990); and Harry Hay, *Radically Gay: Gay Liberation in the Words of Its Founder,* ed. Will Roscoe (Boston: Beacon Press, 1996).

21. Now in the Forsythe Papers.

22. Letter, Forsythe to Arvey, March 7, 1934, Forsythe Papers.

23. The members listed may be a key to identifying members of the New Negro movement in Los Angeles in the 1920s: Theodore Banks, Roy Johnson, William Middleton, Eardly Gauff, Forsythe, Haven Johnson, David Floyd, Lawrence Johnson, Ronald Jefferson, Clifford Gantt, Marvin Johnson, Lawrence Lassiter.

24. Harold Bruce Forsythe, "Frailest Leaves," undated typescript [ca. 1935], 442–445, Forsythe Papers. It is listed in the finding aid as "Masks."

25. Letter, Forsythe to Arvey, October 19, 1933, Forsythe Papers. In the quotations that follow, the present author's ellipses are bracketed to distinguish them from Forsythe's.

26. The letter from Pemberton is in Forsythe's Juilliard file; Forsythe's son reports Thurman's recommendation. The value of the fellowship is put in question by the letters from Forsythe's mother to Forsythe while he was in New York, and even one from her to Goldmark, promising to put together the money for her son's lessons.

27. Information from the Archives of The Juilliard School. The reason for his early departure is unknown.

28. Letter, Eardly Gauff to Forsythe, November 4, 1927, Forsythe Papers. This is the letter on "Iconoclast" letterhead.

29. Forsythe writes of making this offer to Still and Still's failure to acknowledge it in "A Study in Contradictions" (29). The following journal entry may relate to this issue: "Letter from Harold Forsyth. Grace angry because of it" (Still, Diary, July 23, 1930), Still-Arvey Papers.

30. Letter of application to the Guggenheim Foundation, stamped "received 6/12/1931." Courtesy of the Guggenheim Foundation, with permission from Judith Anne Still.

31. Wayne Barlow to Still, July 7, 1939; July 27, 1937; September 7, 1939. Barlow wrote in Howard Hanson's behalf; the letters are filed under Hanson, Box 21, Still-Arvey Papers.

32. The piano score carries the notation "This ballet was later rejected" on the front cover. (Courtesy William Grant Still Music.) Arvey, *IOL,* 15, reports its role in Still's recycling of rejected works: "'Dance of Love' (played over the radio many times) was put into the 'Sorcerer Ballet' which has itself been scrapped and its themes used in other compositions." One section of this ballet surfaces later as the "Orator" scene in *Lenox Avenue.*

33. A copy of the libretto, heavily annotated by Still, is in the Library of Congress. A copy of a contract among Moss, Still (both of New York), and Forsythe (of Los Angeles) to collaborate on *Blue Steel* is dated June 19, 1933. Still-Arvey Papers.

34. A typescript of Forsythe's libretto, with additions in Forsythe's hand and extensive annotations in Still's, is in the Library of Congress. A second copy, also annotated, is in the Forsythe Papers.

35. In "Chosen Image: The Afro-American Vision in the Operas of William Grant Still" (*Opera Quarterly* 4, no. 2 [Summer 1986]: 1–23), Donald Dorr reports that Alain Locke proposed an opera under the title "Atlantis," mistakenly identifying Bruce Forsythe as the librettist. Nothing seems to have come of this project.

36. No other such contracts between Still and librettists are in the Still-Arvey Papers. On the same day that Forsythe signed the contracts for *The Sorcerer* and *Central Avenue,* he witnessed a contract drawn up between Still and Ruby Berkely Goodwin of Fullerton, California, in which Still agreed to provide arrangements for voice and piano of the following spirituals, to appear as part of a book, *Great Day,* already written, a collection of stories built around these spirituals: "Great Day"; "Lis'en to de Lam's"; "Camp Meetin' Peter, Go Ring Dem Bells, Mah Lawde Says He's Goin' to Rain Down Fishes"; "Good News"; "Didn't Mah Lawd Deliver Daniel"; "Ah Got a Home In-a Dat Rock"; "All God's Chillun Got Wings"; "Keep Me F'om Sinkin' Down"; "Gwinter Sing all Along De Way"; "Lawd, Ah Wants to be a Christian." See n. 37, below, for more on *Central Avenue.*

37. In a paper on *Lenox Avenue* given to the American Musicological Society in 1996, Gayle Murchison mentions a contract with Columbia Pictures for *Central Avenue.* Although the film was not made, the movie studios were protective of their copyrights; the Stills may have feared claims of copyright infringement from the studio. Wayne D. Shirley compared the two scores in "*Central Avenue* and *Lenox Avenue,*" in a paper presented at A Multicultural Celebration of Diversity in Music: A Tribute to William Grant Still, Flagstaff, Ariz., June 26, 1998.

38. Verna Arvey to Carl Van Vechten, August 6, 1934, autograph letter on Arvey's stationery. Carl Van Vechten Papers, JWJ.

39. Letter, Bruce Forsythe to Mr. Carl Van Vechten, postmark August 24, 1934, JWJ.

40. Letter, Bruce Forsythe to R. Jean Toomer, August 29, 1934, Jean Toomer Papers, JWJ.

41. Undated typed letter, Forsythe to "Dear Verna," Still-Arvey Papers. The concert in question was given on November 4, 1934.

42. Letter, Harold Bruce Forsythe to Mr. Carl Van Vechten, December 13, 1934, JWJ.

43. Letter, Forsythe to Van Vechten, January 15, 1935, JWJ.

44. JWJ. There are no pre-1940 letters from Van Vechten to Arvey or Still in the Still-Arvey Papers.

45. In *IOL*, Arvey reports "Quit Dat Fool'nish" as dedicated to Still's dog Shep. Arvey suggested the alternative story in her 1985 interview with Smith.

46. Verna Arvey, "Scribblings," undated entry from notebook at WGSM. In a postcard to Van Vechten dated March 6, 1944, she wrote more succinctly: "No, Bruce Forsythe is not related to Cecil Forsyth and we do not see him anymore. He is still in Los Angeles, and not overly popular with hosts or hostesses." Arvey to Van Vechten, JWJ.

47. Arvey's "Scribblings" reports a series of such incidents. The poverty is confirmed by his mother's letters while he was in New York as well as Harold Sumner Forsythe's account of his own youth.

48. The C. L. Bagley Collection, Western History Center, University of Southern California, includes a run of directories for Local 47, the white union, and only a few for Local 767, the black musicians' union. (The two locals merged in the 1953.) Forsythe's name does not appear in any of these.

49. Arvey, "Scribblings": "He was in love with me, he said, and I was on a high pedestal in his home. . . . His jealousy when I was writing to Still flamed out in disagreeable remarks."

The *Afro-American Symphony* and Its Scherzo

He who develops his God-given gifts with [a] view to aiding
humanity, manifests truth.
    Afro-American Symphony (1930)

LP08082
LP14511
LP32309

Most of this volume deals with the cultural, biographical, and aesthetic
issues that surrounded Still's career. I have chosen to discuss only one
work in any detail, the *Afro-American Symphony,* emphasizing specifically its third movement, the Scherzo, whose score is now included in
the latest edition of a widely used anthology.[1] The completion of the *Afro-
American Symphony* in 1930 marks the crowning achievement of Still's
self-consciously "racial" period. As Still's best-known work, it is the one
most readily available on records, the one most likely to be heard on
classical music stations, and the one that has drawn critical examination
in any detail from more than one writer.[2] Thus it is and has been the
single most influential expression of his aesthetic of racial fusion. In it,
he brought one genre, the symphony, to another, the blues, and transformed both in the process.[3] The extreme polarization of these two
genres in 1930—by musical language, medium of performance, presence or absence of text, social class, race, audience, implicit moral value,
even, arguably, gender—reflects the societal polarizations that Still challenged in this symphony. Newly available sketch materials and notes on
the symphony, along with Still's long-available diaries and other published writings, make it possible to reconsider the whole symphony and
the Scherzo's pivotal role in it. The quotation of George Gershwin's
"I Got Rhythm" and speculation on Still's reasons for citing it make the
Scherzo all the more attractive as the locus for a discussion that moves
in a concrete way toward an increased understanding of the cultural

interactions that pervade Still's boundary-blurring enterprise. As one
follows the composer in his choice of materials and his handling of
them, one may detect the voice of the satirist in the Gershwin quotation,
or perhaps the fabled West African trickster figure who practiced irony
or misdirection to make his point. One may also perceive the cold and
merciless logic on which Still, along with other modernists of his time,
depended.[4] All three are arguably present in the Scherzo, although only
the third of these attitudes is suggested in his several written descriptions
of the work, three of them included in the Sources section of this book.

One analytical study, written four decades after the symphony, provides musical detail but no overview.[5] Four more recent discussions
deal significantly with the symphony's cultural and historical context. In
"'New Music' and the 'New Negro,'" Carol J. Oja insists on the work's
double life: "Alongside its preeminent position among black concert
works of the early twentieth century, the *Afro-American Symphony* belongs with a group of pivotal pieces by white composers written in 1930
and 1931, especially Aaron Copland's Piano Variations, Ruth Crawford's String Quartet, and Edgard Varèse's *Ionisation*. . . . Still led a dual
existence, part of which involved treading the same path as young white
concert composers of his day and part of which kept him in step with his
own people." She points out that his "ideological link" with the white
modernists was "fraught with powerful tensions" and that it became
"increasingly more tenuous" as he pursued his career as a concert composer. She discusses two concert works (*Levee Land* and *Darker America*) that preceded the *Afro-American Symphony* as formal experiments
leading to various "imaginative" solutions to "the conflict between a
more dissonant—or 'ultramodern'—musical style and an identifiably
black one." She shows that *Levee Land* is composed on two planes;
one with "conventional blues-derived melodies and harmonies" and another with "chromatic-third relationships that play off a basic trait
of the blues." *Darker America,* however, is sectional, moving between
blues-derived harmonies and moments of "intense chromaticism." The
contrasting affects are combined in the symphony's finale. Oja concludes
that "in the *Afro-American Symphony*, conventional, blues-derived harmonic practices prevail" and that, overall, "no other composer, either
black or white, claimed quite the same turf [as Still]."[6]

Rae Linda Brown takes up the *Afro-American* as one of three symphonies dating from the early 1930s by three different African American
composers. She says, "Although Still was not a conscious participant
in the Negro renaissance, his music speaks of the essence of the New

Figure 4. One-page outline of the *Afro-American Symphony*, "Rashana" sketchbook. Courtesy of William Grant Still Music.

Negro." She points out that the primary theme of the first movement of the *Afro-American Symphony* is accompanied by a "typical blues progression" in a standard twelve-bar blues pattern and that the second movement is built on a related theme in a spiritual style. The third movement's "syncopated cross rhythms [are] clearly rooted in Afro-American dance." [7] Orin Moe's contribution is to begin exploring the nature of the "tension" in the symphony between its "black musical characteristics and those from the Euro-American tradition." His discussion of the symphony amplifies those of Brown and Oja because of his observation that "the black materials fundamentally alter the inherited shape of the symphony" and that "Still juggles . . . with considerable success" the confrontation he has created between the historical symphonic structure and "the stanzaic variation structure of the blues." Oja speaks of the *Afro-American Symphony*'s aesthetic conservatism from the perspective of contemporary white modernism. Moe remarks further that its "surface conservatism" has prevented it from being seriously considered by critics and prompted its exclusion from surveys of twentieth-century music.[8] Samuel A. Floyd, Jr., develops Moe's ideas and explores the symphony in terms of recent black cultural criticism. He points out that Still's thematic treatment may be heard as employing the practices of African-derived call-and-response and "signifying" as well as European compositional techniques. He argues that Still participated in three contemporary movements, adding nationalism to the avant-garde and the Harlem Renaissance in which the others place him. Floyd correctly identifies Still's avant-garde style as neoclassical. "After rejecting the avant-garde, Still eventually triumphed in the nationalist and Harlem Renaissance realism with the *Afro-American Symphony,* a work that blended African-American and European elements more successfully, in my opinion, than those of any other composer of the period." [9]

In hindsight, late 1930 was the right moment for Still to attempt his first symphony.[10] He had learned something new, it seems, with each of the new works of the previous fifteen years. Still's earliest-known multi-movement work for orchestra is an early *American Suite* recently located in the archives of the Chicago Symphony Orchestra. It was composed no later than early 1916. Not until that summer, when he first worked for W. C. Handy, was Still immersed in African American popular music and converted to its advocacy; at that point he apparently also achieved basic technical competence as an arranger.[11] Given Still's later interests, this suite is remarkable for its lack of reference to African

American popular music making. Its Native American reference ("Indian Love Song") hints of the turn-of-the-century Indianist movement, widespread among American composers; this may be suggestive of MacDowell or even of Dvořák, whose sojourn in the United States in the 1890s acted as a catalyst for the nationalist movement in American music. These are the other known multimovement instrumental works that preceded the *Afro-American Symphony,* with their dates of composition:

American Suite (1916 or earlier)

Three Negro Songs (1921) (orchestral despite its title)

From the Land of Dreams (1924) (includes three voices used "instrumentally")[12]

From the Journal of a Wanderer (1925)

From the Black Belt (1925)

Log Cabin Ballads (1926)

Africa (1928–1930)

Like the single-movement *Darker America* (1924; discussed at length by Harold Bruce Forsythe elsewhere in this volume), all of these works after the *American Suite* used African American musical materials, and all received performances, with generally increasing success. (*Three Negro Songs* was probably performed for an African American audience in Brooklyn; the others were heard by generally white audiences in New York or elsewhere. *From the Land of Dreams,* believed lost for decades, is discussed briefly in the introduction.)

On the basis of this achievement and of a generally supportive critical response, couched in stereotyped language though it was, Still's confidence in his skill as a composer was at a high point. His diary gives not only a time frame for the composition of the *Afro-America Symphony* but also a sense of Still's state of mind, his manner of working, and his other activities. When he began it, he had just returned from Rochester, New York, where he heard the first stunning performance of *Africa* with full orchestra on October 24, 1930. His diary entry reports the performance: "God sent me success today. Africa was a sensation."[13] On the same trip, Still conferred with Harry Barnhart, a well-known choral conductor then at Rochester, about his ballet *Sahdji,* completed three months earlier and scheduled for its premiere in Rochester the following spring.[14] His yearlong contract with Paul Whiteman had expired four months earlier, and Whiteman was not in a financial position to rehire him. Although he had no steady job, a well-received new orchestration for the "Deep River Hour" radio show a few weeks earlier (October 9) may have encouraged him in his search for regular work and suggested that the window of opportunity to work on another large-scale composition might not last too long.[15] As we shall see, the opening of Gershwin's show *Girl Crazy* on October 14 may also have triggered a sense of urgency about this long-contemplated project.

In spite of all this, the diary shows that Still started work on his new symphony in a mood of discouragement. Both the difficulty of finding regular work as an arranger and domestic problems outweighed the satisfactions of his compositional achievements, even the recent triumph of *Africa*. These are the entries that record his work on the symphony, complete for the days in which he reports such work:

> Oct. 30. Start working on Afro-American Symphony. Things look dark. I pray for strength that I may do just as God would have me. Would that I never did anything to displease him. I believe that he will straighten out conditions. I must not lose faith. I must not complain.

religious element

> Nov. 5. Raining. Gloomy. Thanks to God I received some splendid ideas for the Afro-American Symphony last night.

> Nov. 20. Rehearsal. My arrangement did not sound well. But who knows how it will sound on the air [;] tonight tells the tale. God's will be done.
>
> Completed sketch of Afro-American Symphony's first movement. May God grant it succeeds.

> Nov. 28. Praise God. Well along in 3rd movement of Symphony. Call from Willard Robison.[16]
>
> Dance of Wilberforce Univ. Club.[17]

> Dec. 2. Cold today. Worked on Symphony. Thank God for the inspiration He gives me. I am so unworthy. To think that God in His majesty would take thought of such as me! Let me seek to draw closer to Him. Let my greatest desire be that of doing His will in all things.

> Dec. 5. Was able to accomplish much today in scoring of "Afro-American Symphony."

> Dec. 6. Completed scoring 3rd Movement of Afro-American Symphony today.

> Dec. 26. Nothing of unusual interest. Symphony progressing rapidly.[18]

As several of these and other entries suggest, Still was heavily involved in seeking paying work as the symphony progressed. Given that distraction, the speed with which he worked on the new symphony is even more impressive. In a letter to Irving Schwerké dated January 9, 1931, Still remarked the completion of the entire project shortly after New Year's, about ten weeks after he had begun.[19] (Other remarks in that letter—his most forthright discussion of the racial obstacles he faced, and his only known mention of leaving the United States as a serious possibility—reinforce the notion that this was a period of great personal stress.)

Two early notebooks in Still's hand at William Grant Still Music give a great deal more information concerning the creation of the symphony than has previously been available. I will describe them here and return to them as needed later in this chapter. The first, its front cover deco-rated with cigar bands, is actually a theme book. It is labeled on the cover "Still 1924," one of the years when Still was studying with Varèse. Its thirty-eight unpaged leaves contain 444 numbered themes, many of them labeled with one-word "affect" suggestions (e.g., "voodoo," "lament," "spiritual"). The first forty-three appear in a consistent fair hand, in ink, seemingly copied all at once from an earlier source. Thereafter the themes are written in a less consistent script and sometimes in pencil; these are most often in the hand that Still used for the fragmentary sketches that fill blank pages and margins in many drafts and fair copies of his own scores. Some earlier themes (as late as #178) are marked "good" or "better" in Still's hand. Sketches having to do with the uncompleted opera from the late 1920s, "Rashana," fill much blank space to the right of the shorter themes. That Still returned to this theme book for some time after it was begun in 1924 is evident, for the composer took themes from it for many works of the late 1920s and early 1930s (such as *Africa* and *Blue Steel*); one was used as late as 1938 or 1939, when he was working on the opera *Troubled Island*. Several themes used in the *Afro-American Symphony* (only one of them so labeled) are among them. Several that suggest Gershwin's "I Got Rhythm" raise the old question about the ultimate source of Gershwin's melody, to be discussed below. In the last few pages are sketches of other works either destroyed or not completed. There are unlabeled, partially harmonized sketches on three staves, a numbered group of "chords," a verbal outline of "Ode to the American Negro: For the Oppressed" (very likely a program sketch for *Darker America,* composed in 1924), a pasted-in, typed sketch for the ballet *La Guiablesse* (dated 1927 in the thematic catalog), and a page too damaged to read labeled "Material for *From the Black Belt*" (dated 1926 in the composer's thematic catalog). "From the Land of Blues," labeled a "melodic outline" and filling about a half-page, is one item to which I will return. While it is likely that Still began to use the theme book during his study with Varèse, it is not at all clear when he stopped using it as a place to notate his melodic ideas. Nineteen twenty-seven, the last year for a work known and completed that is referred to by name, may be a reasonable cutoff date.

The other notebook bears the label "Material for Rashana" on the cover and is stamped "DEC 1926" on the inside.[20] It is somewhat shorter than the 1924 theme book. After a sketch of *Africa,* it is paginated in Roman numerals by the composer. A series of numbered themes, now classified by affect (e.g., "Passionate Themes"), some with references to numbered themes in the 1924 theme book, follow. These seem to have been organized with a view toward the aborted opera. Some notes on orchestration suggest that this book, too, was started during Still's study with Varèse. Most of this book was left blank at that time. Still returned to it to sketch out the *Afro-American Symphony* in late October or early November 1930, as noted in the diary. Starting approximately in the middle of the book, he began with a one-page outline of the symphony (see fig. 4), then an outline of the first movement, from which he methodically began to compose, writing out a series of "treatments" of his thematic material for each movement. The first two movements occupy the last part of the book; then Still returned to his starting point and worked steadily forward as he composed the last two movements. From the diary entries cited above, these sketches can be dated quite accurately as between October 30 and early December, when the diary shows him occupied with scoring the work. The "Rashana" sketchbook includes Still's draft foreword to the symphony (see fig. 5):

> I harbor no delusions as to the triviality of Blues, the secular folk music of the American Negro, despite their lowly origin and the homely sentiment of their texts. The pathos of their melodic content bespeaks the anguish of human hearts and belies the banality of their lyrics. What is more, they, unlike many Spirituals, do not exhibit the influence of Caucasian music. The Afro-American Symphony, as its title implies, is representative of the American Negro. In it I have placed stress on a motif in Blues idiom. It is employed originally as the principal theme of the first movement. It appears also in various forms in the succeeding movements, where I have sought to present it in a characteristic (style) manner.

Greatly I acknowledge and humbly I thank God, the source of my inspiration.

Wm. Still[21]

Both Still and (later) Arvey provided a series of typed, undated descriptions and program notes for the work, one of them in the Arvey monograph later in this volume, that address his intentions in composing the symphony.[22] One of these begins, "The 'Afro-American Symphony' is based on an original theme in the 'Blues' idiom, employed as the principal theme of the first movement, and reappearing in different forms in the course of the composition." After a sizable quotation from the draft foreword (see above), these continue:

> I seek in the 'Afro-American Symphony' to portray not the higher type of colored American, but the sons of the soil, who still retain so many of the traits peculiar to their African forebears; who have not responded completely to the transforming effect of progress. Therefore, the employment of a decidedly characteristic idiom is not only logical but also necessary. . . . In a general sense, one may apply to the movements the following titles:
>
> 1. Longing   3. Humor (expressed through religious fervor)
> 2. Sorrow   4. Aspiration.
>
> When judged by the laws of musical form the A.A.S. is somewhat irregular in its form.[23]

Example 2 shows Still's blues theme as it appears in the "Rashana" sketchbook and as it is used at the opening of the first movement in the finished score, both as the introductory figure and as the principal theme. The introductory figure, played by the English horn without accompaniment and in an improvisatory style, suggests the early folk blues that became the basis for the twelve-bar "classic" blues of the 1920s. Still's main theme, as many commentators have noted, is a "classic" blues, and is harmonized as such. Frequently varied in the first two movements, it is radically transformed in the third, as I will show.

At the end of the sketches in the "Rashana" notebook is the poetry Still copied out from the work of the turn-of-the-century dialect poet Paul Laurence Dunbar (1872–1906), one excerpt for each of the four movements. Still did not identify the excerpts by title in the sketchbook or in either edition of the published score. Like many a nineteenth-century tone poet and even some of his modernist contemporaries who wanted

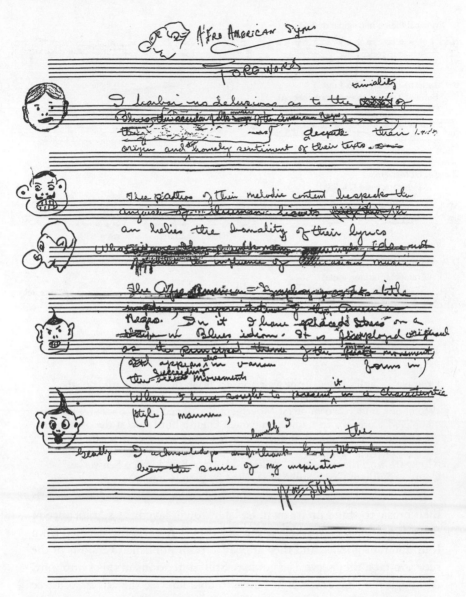

Figure 5. Still's draft foreword for the *Afro-American Symphony,* "Rashana" sketchbook. Courtesy of William Grant Still Music. From top to bottom the sketches are Still, Donald Vorhees, Paul Whiteman, Still, and the Li'l Scamps (popular cartoon characters of the day).

A   Principal theme in original outline

B   **Moderato assai - (Più Lento)**
    "Form of 1st Movement" (sketchbook)
    Oboe

Score
C Intro. 1st Movement
    Moderato assai (♩ = 88)
    English horn

legato   poco accel.   ritard.   a tempo   riten.

D Principal theme
    Trumpet (Harmon mute)

Example 2. Still's blues theme as it appears (a) in the initial outline of the symphony ("Rashana" sketchbook) "depicting pathos and power"; (b) in the sketchbook under "Form of 1st Movement," assigned to the oboe; (c) in the completed score as a free, unaccompanied English horn solo at the opening of the first movement; and (d) in the completed score as the primary theme in the first movement, a twelve-bar "classic" blues played by the solo trumpet. (Compare with the themes in "William Grant Still and Irving Schwerké.") Courtesy William Grant Still Music. Used by permission.

their music to stand on its own, he later downplayed the significance of these quotations. Nevertheless, the excerpts were carefully selected from four different poems, and they appear in both published versions of the score. In fact, they serve as a guide to Still's intentions in this symphony. Although the single words he chose to characterize the affects of three of the four movements seem to reflect the meaning of the poetry directly, the couplet and the affect word he chose ("Humor") for the Scherzo movement have a far richer meaning than an audience unfamiliar with Dunbar's poetry (as white concert audiences would generally have been) might have supposed.

Consider, then, all four of the excerpts Still selected for epigraphs in the context of longer quotations from Dunbar's poems. The poems used as epigraphs for the first two movements refer to the dreams and sorrows of the former slaves. The opening stanza of "Twell de Night Is Pas'," prefacing the opening movement with its blues theme, reads:

All de night long twell de moon goes down,
Lovin' I set at huh feet,
Den fu' de long jou'ney back f'om de town,
Ha'd, but de dreams mek it sweet.

Still quotes the close:

"All my life long twell de night has pas'
Let de wo'k come ez it will,
So dat I fin' you, my honey, at last,
Somewhaih des ovah de hill."

The first stanza of "W'en I Gits Home" is attached to the slow movement, with its spiritual-like melody:

It's moughty tiahsome layin' 'roun'
Dis sorrer-laden erfly groun',
An' oftentimes I thinks, thinks I,
'T would be a sweet t'ing des to die,
An go 'long home.

The final movement, with its hymnlike, modal opening hardly changed from the initial one-page outline in figure 5 and its lively finale, was first assigned the final stanza from Dunbar's "Ode to Ethiopia":

Go on and up! Our souls and eyes
Shall follow thy continuous rise;
Our ears shall list thy story
From bards who from thy root shall spring,
And proudly tune their lyres to sing
Of Ethiopia's Glory.

Both printed editions of the score bear this rather better known stanza from the same poem:

Be proud, my Race, in mind and soul,
Thy name is writ on Glory's scroll
In characters of fire.
High 'mid the clouds of Fame's bright sky,
Thy banner's blazoned folds now fly,
And truth shall lift them higher.

The only quotation not in dialect, either stanza is appropriate to the apotheosis of the finale that follows the final transformation of the blues theme in the Scherzo.

For the Scherzo movement, the situation is more complicated. The poem, "An Ante-Bellum Sermon," from which the quoted couplet is drawn, signals that the movement is about much more than "humor (expressed through religious fervor)." It plays on the meaning of the word "scherzo" as a joke, revealing Still in the role of Trickster. The whole of Dunbar's poem shows how effectively Still used the "minstrel mask" to reflect his sense of racial doubleness. However trivial the lines quoted, the poem is in fact about Emancipation and citizenship, matters not at all trivial, thus pointing to the Scherzo as the crux of the symphony. Here are some longer excerpts from the poem; the quotation used by Still appears in italics.

> We is gathahed hyeah, my brothahs,
> In dis howlin' wildaness,
> Fu' to speak some words of comfo't
> To each othah in distress.
>
> . . . .
>
> So you see de Lawd's intention,
> Evah sence de worl' began,
> Was dat His almighty freedom
> Should belong to evah man,
>
> . . . .
>
> But when Moses wif his powah
> Comes an' sets us chillun free,
> We will praise de gracious Mastah
> Dat has gin us liberty;
> *An' we'll shout ouah halleluyahs,*
> *On dat mighty reck'nin' day,*
> When we'se reco'nised ez citiz'—
>
> Hun un! Chillun, let us pray![24]

This "Ante-Bellum Sermon" is delivered in the voice of a black preacher, himself a slave. As the sermon proceeds, the biblical references allude more and more pointedly to his and his listeners' intolerable situation. Asserting that "de Lawd will sen' some Moses / Fu' to set his chillun free," he cautions "I'm still a-preachin' ancient, I ain't talkin' 'bout to-day," and admonishes his listeners "Now don't run an' tell yo' mastahs / Dat I's preachin' discontent." He further reminds them "Dat I'm talkin' 'bout ouah freedom / In a Bibleistic way." At the climax of the poem, which includes the couplet Still uses as his epigraph, the full contemporary application of the sermon comes out, only to be stopped in midword—"citizens"—one imagines by fear of being overheard.

The "Rashana" sketchbook contains Still's working plan for the entire symphony (see fig. 5). His original plan calls for a key scheme from movement to movement of A-flat to F to A-flat and to G-flat for the fourth movement, which would presumably have finished either in A-flat or in F minor. In fact he followed this plan until the final movement:

Movement 1 ("Longing"): A-flat major tonal center. The blues theme introduces modal chromatic alterations. An excursion to G major in a slower section provides a contrast in tempo that elaborates on the blues theme but is not confrontational, as formulaic nineteenth-century prescriptions for first movements of symphonies often require.

Movement 2 ("Sorrow"): F major tonal center, with many chromatic alterations in keeping with the blues theme.

Movement 3 ("Humor"): A-flat major tonal center, moving toward and mixing with A-flat Dorian.

Movement 4 ("Aspiration"): F minor tonal center. The movement begins with a lengthy slow section that establishes E major from an unlikely modal beginning on C-sharp minor before moving triumphantly to its jubilant ending in F minor.

In the *Afro-American Symphony*, Still uses simultaneous contrasting stylistic levels as well as alternation and blending of contrasting European- and African-derived styles, refined from his earlier experiments (described above by Oja) in *Levee Land* and *Darker America*. The "double consciousness" of W. E. B. Du Bois permeates the work.[25]

To represent the European-derived style, Still chooses not the chromatic harmony of the modernists but a system of very clear if somewhat irregularly used key relationships. This choice is a technical reflection of his often-mentioned departure from the ultramodernist aesthetic of his teacher Varèse and others, made partly in reaction to his discovery (starting with *From the Land of Dreams*) that audiences could not recognize his fusion practice if they were occupied with puzzling over elements of European-derived modernist expressiveness. It also provides a framework in which Still can portray both his nominal subject—the "old" post–Civil War Negro (rather than the "New" one of the Harlem Renaissance)—and his underlying aesthetic purpose—to demonstrate through his music a "great truth," the profound and continuing influences and borrowings between two parallel but racially divided cultures.

Still uses the major-minor system to supply a modal framework rather than a rigidly functional harmonic one. He uses the major scale to represent the Euro-American culture, while the Dorian minor, built on the same tonic but using the minor third and the lowered seventh degree, serves for the African-derived blues scale. Such chromaticism and harmonic tension as arises comes most commonly from the interaction between the major and minor thirds (and less often the sevenths) that result from the simultaneous use of these scales. This interaction is clearest in the Scherzo, where A-flat major and its parallel Dorian are superimposed on each other; I will discuss it further below. This is of more than technical interest because it reverses the standard European symphonic practice, involving the progression from minor to major.[26] In the course of all four movements, Still's symphony moves from A-flat major to its relative minor on F, something of a musical pun on the major-minor relationship of his third movement. The modal usages and the play on motion from major to minor are technical realizations of Still's purpose as he stated it in his draft foreword—to use the idiom of the blues specifically because "it does not exhibit the influence of Caucasian music."

The dominant-to-tonic (V–I) relationship, which permeates the European tradition as a way to define sections and set up rhetorical confrontations, is downplayed in Still's scheme, though it is not entirely absent. (For example, a dominant pedalpoint introduces both movements 1 and 3, and there is a contrasting section on the dominant key in the final F minor section of the last movement.) Leading tones and perfect authentic progressions (i.e., affirmations of dominant-to-tonic harmony) are relatively rare as elements of the work's macro-structure. They are abundant, however, within small melodic units, especially in the Scherzo. In the more "African" second movement with its strong blues coloring, the melodic and harmonic materials are both more chromatic and less functional, evading a commitment to a Western drive-to-cadence. The absence of formal authentic cadences and the avoidance of even a suggestion of modulation in the slow, spacious opening of the final movement create a strongly modal sense, leaving the listener with a certain ambiguity about the tonic. (See fig. 4, the theme associated with movement 4.) In this movement, the slow section appears three times, each time followed by a contrasting section on F minor, the movement's destination and the overall tonal center of the symphony. The climactic final Allegro is remarkable not only for the absence of any dominant-to-tonic progression but also for the virtually complete absence of the leading tone, in this case, E natural. The earlier slow, modal sections centering on E (as a tonic) literally preempt that note from its leading-tone function, so essential for the traditional nineteenth-century Western sense of closure. In the coda, the bass line moves from F up a minor sixth to D-flat, avoiding the customary European move from V to I to the very end while at the same time providing (along with the English horn solo in the first movement) a subtle homage to the Dvořák of the *New World Symphony*.[27]

Table 1 is a diagram of the Scherzo; example 3 shows its themes. As we saw from the poetry that Still chose as an epigraph for this movement, the Scherzo's "humor" is weighted with meaning; it supports the high seriousness of Still's privately stated comment to Forsythe about "presenting a great truth" through this symphony.[28] This "Hallelujah" is no mere celebration of innocents mimicking their own "primitive" religion, as Still had initially intended and white audiences might have been led to assume. It wears the minstrel mask and bears the weight of the human comedy as fully as any other moment in the symphony, and perhaps in Still's entire output. No one can doubt that the poem's narrator intends the biblical assurances of freedom for Moses' people to apply to his own people as well. The meaning of the scherzo/joke is thus doubly played. The "clever fox trot" (as one hapless critic described the Scherzo)[29] that began with a lighthearted minstrel tune (theme 1A) not only gains depth from its exposure to a more authentic African American influence, it is transformed by the declaration in theme 2A to imply a progression from superficial white minstrel representation to a statement of aesthetic and political emancipation.

Changes of tonal center are entirely missing from the Scherzo in Still's realization, a highly unusual procedure for any movement that pretends to be the product of the European tradition, and the only movement in this symphony for which this is true. This absence heightens the importance of the motion from major to Dorian minor that takes place

Table 1.
Afro-American Symphony
Form of the Scherzo

A. *Major mode dominates, containing the mixed mode area; symmetrical phrases, Eurocentric position strong.*

	Intro	Prin Theme 1A ("Hallelujah!") ("I Got Rhythm" cite)	Prin Theme 1B	Prin Theme 1A
		8	16	24	32
	Dominant pedal	major mode	major/Dorian mix (contained on either side)	major mode

B. *Blues/Dorian dominates, containing the "development"; irregular phrases, African American position strong.*

Secondary themes 2A 2B			1A and 2B fragmented; slurred, chromatic passages "development"—tonality briefly destabilized		2A 2B
32	35		47	63	65	69
"Emancipation" (on I)	12-bars, theme fragmented		Euro-style (contained on either side)	"Emancipation" (on V)	

A.¹ *Major and blues/Dorian modes sounding simultaneously; phrases less irregular; affirmation of fusion.*

Recap. 1A transformed	2A	"Emancipation" (on I)	1A	Coda
69	77	84	88	96	100
Major and blues modes	Major and blues modes (no longer contained)	most exuberant synergy		modal "leading-tone" cadence minor 3rd to major 3rd Tonic pedal

Example 3. Themes from the Scherzo. Theme 1A, "Hallelujah!" is given as it appears the first and last times. Three forms of theme 2A and two forms of theme 2B are given. Used by permission.

without any change of tonal center. (A brief barbershop passage in measures 51–53 is the one moment when there is any doubt at all about the key center.) Still outlined the Scherzo in multiple sections identified by their themes. The principal theme, labeled 1A, is transformed in the course of the movement from a straightforward, lively statement in the major mode to a richer and more exuberant mix of major and minor. Theme 1B, which usually follows 1A, mixes the two modes from the start.

These two themes (especially 1A, with its tenor banjo afterbeats) carry the "minstrel show" affect. Theme 2A, orchestrated for trombones and other low-pitched instruments, contrasts sharply with themes 1A and 1B in its driving, fanfarelike affect, its off-beat accents, and its irregular length, different in each of its three statements. So different is the affect of 2A that it seems to appear on an expressive plane separate from the other themes in the movement. Appearing shortly before the midpoint of the movement, it provides a strong contrast to 1A, the "Hallelujah!" that Still intended in his initial description of this movement as portraying a "janny sect," the "old-time" African American religion in which motion is an essential part of worship.[30] This theme, unequivocally in the Dorian (minor) mode, depends entirely on melodic action for its cadences. This interrupting, "Emancipation" theme (my characterization) is derived from the most clearly African-derived idea in the symphony, the haunting English horn solo that opens the first movement. (See examples 2c and 3 above.) Theme 2B, "Emancipation," is the one theme that is stated first on the tonic, then a fifth higher, on the dominant, and finally on the tonic, but its appearance on the dominant does not change the tonal center of the movement even temporarily. With its repeated high notes and emphasis on the descending fifth, theme 2A presents a radical transformation of the "classic" blues statement of the first two movements, a transformation that logically must accompany the disappearance of the minstrel mask.

The stanzalike "treatments" of themes that lead to the sectional contrasts-with-continuity characteristic of the work's individual movements are particularly clear in the third movement. The constantly changing statements, especially of themes 1A and 2A (see ex. 3 above) are reminiscent of both older New Orleans improvisatory practice associated with the beginnings of jazz and very long-standing European-derived variation practice.[31] Figure 6 shows a series of such treatments in the sketchbook, and figure 7 is the beginning of Still's melodic outline for the movement, showing varied treatments of theme 1A. In his scheme, the "treatments" involve variations in instrumentation and accompaniment figures as well as small melodic decorations and changes.

The sectionality of this movement is strongly rooted in African-derived practice as well as in the theatricality of the minstrel show; its key structure is likewise, as Still said of the entire symphony, "somewhat irregular in form." Thus it is awkward to describe the Scherzo in Euro-

Figure 6. Melodic "treatments" of theme 1A, Scherzo, "Rashana" sketch-book. Courtesy of William Grant Still Music.

pean-derived terms. Even though Still attached the term "development" to some of his "treatments," suggesting a sonata form of sorts, the Scherzo could just as well be characterized in several other ways. Although the detailed outline shows it as a ternary form, the movement could also be thought of as a large-scale barform suggestive of the aa¹b form of the classic twelve-bar blues, as a rounded binary form, or

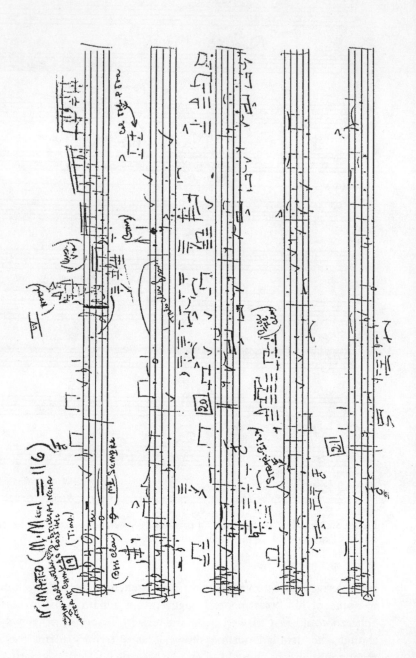

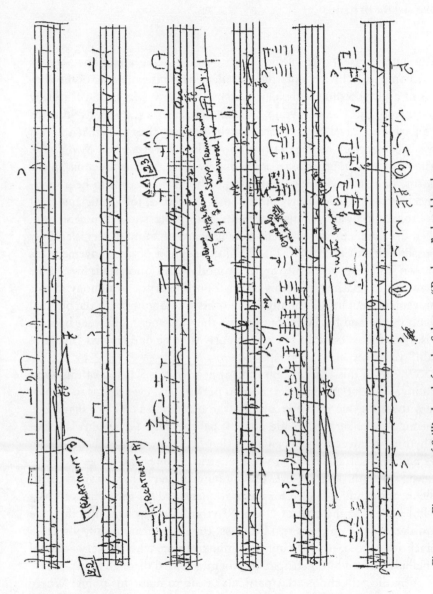

Figure 7. First page of Still's sketch for the Scherzo, "Rashana" sketchbook. Courtesy of William Grant Still Music.

maybe even two rather simple ABA forms that happen in sequence. More simply, it might also be seen as revealing some formal, trickster-like sleight of hand.

The initial presentation of the minstrel tune (theme 1A) in the Scherzo is accompanied by a countermelody identical to the opening of the chorus of a hit pop tune of the day. Gershwin's show *Girl Crazy,* featuring the infectious "I Got Rhythm," opened October 14, 1930, as Still was preparing to travel to Rochester for the performance of *Africa* and just two weeks before he began to compose the *Afro-American Symphony.* The quotation appears once, immediately after the introduction, in the horns, in a spot where it is intended to be heard, meant to be a reference listeners would clearly understand. A second, following statement is broken up by octave displacements and changes in instrumentation; then the fragment of this catchy tune is heard no more. It seems entirely possible that Still changed his initial conception of this movement (as shown in fig. 4) specifically to accommodate this quotation. Indeed, he made more revisions from his original outline of the symphony in this movement than he did for any of the others, scrapping both the original main theme and his initial outline for the movement. He went back to his 1924 theme book to borrow an early tune he had labeled "Hallelujah!" years earlier.

Why does this current pop tune appear in the Scherzo of this symphony? The question puzzles modern performers, even seems to embarrass them; in one recent recording, the quotation is all but inaudible, seemingly deliberately made so.[32] I believe that Gershwin's "I Got Rhythm" reinforces the meaning of that first statement of theme 1A, in its major/minstrel form in which the African American presence is perceived solely through the eyes of white interpreters, thereby speaking to the meaning Still intended for the movement and for the symphony as a whole. We hear the start of "I Got Rhythm" intact only once; then the movement goes on to its real business, the transforming shift toward a black-influenced, modally inflected minstrel tune with the very political "Hallelujah" and "Emancipation" themes folded through it.

Why did Still choose this particular tune to make his point? Where did the "I Got Rhythm" melody come from in the first place? Here the answer grows more speculative. Modern listeners more familiar with Gershwin's song than Still's work assume that Still borrowed Gershwin's melody, but some older African American musicians believe it was Still's

Example 4. Scherzo, first statement of theme 1A, with countermelody in the horns and afterbeats in the tenor banjo. Used by permission.

Figure 8. Theme 48, "Hallelujah," used as theme 1A of the Scherzo, "Rashana" sketchbook. Courtesy of William Grant Still Music.

to begin with. Evidence from the theme book supports them—partly.
The story about Still, Gershwin, and "I Got Rhythm" also draws on
anecdotal evidence, all collected well after the fact. There are several
versions. Judith Anne Still tells of her father walking down a New York
City street with Eubie Blake and hearing the tune as they walked past an
open door. Blake asked wasn't that Still's tune from *Shuffle Along* days,
and Still acknowledged that indeed it was. Blake expressed anger at the
theft; Still's response was more sanguine. In a published interview from
1973, Blake went into much greater detail:

> Do you know William Grant Still? . . . He's a personal friend of mine. [Eubie
> darts to the piano.] Do you know this tune? [He plays Gershwin's "I Got
> Rhythm."] . . . All of the fellows in my orchestra would be playing around,
> having a good time, but Still would be playing this little tune over and over.
> [Eubie hums the melody.] So I heard the darn thing so much that one day I
> said to him (not while we were playing in New York, but later when we were
> in Boston), "What's the tune you're playing?" Still answered me, "One day
> you'll hear it in a symphony, an American symphony!" . . .
>
>   Now, one day Dooley Wilson . . . comes up to me and says, "Boy, have I
> got some music; this is swell music!" I played the music for him—it was all
> Gershwin music—and when I got to the piece "I Got Rhythm," I didn't have
> to look at the music. I knew it! You know, once I hear a tune—if it's a good
> tune—I don't forget it. . . . Now, one day I was walking down 56th Street,
> and I saw Still standing in front of the Carnegie Hall entrance. . . . I said,
> "You know that tune you used to play?" I hummed it for him. "Is that your
> tune?" He looked at me but didn't answer. So I said, "I saw the music to 'I
> Got Rhythm' and it's the same as your tune." Still said, "Yeah? Well, I'll see
> you later." He would not say that Gershwin stole the tune; he is just that kind
> of man.
>
>   [Interviewer] How do you explain it?
>   Oh, that's easy. Still used to teach Gershwin orchestration. He had to go
> to Gershwin's place on Park Avenue to give the lessons, and while he was
> waiting for Gershwin to come down—Gershwin was always late—he would
> play this darn tune on his oboe. Gershwin heard the tune and took it. Now
> Gershwin probably didn't mean to take it or steal it because he didn't have
> to. The man was a genius! But that tune was Still's tune. It could happen to
> anyone.[33]

Blake's version is demonstrably inaccurate on at least one point. In a
section of the interview not cited here, he has Still conducting his
own symphony at Carnegie Hall. Actually, the New York premiere of
Still's symphony (which must have been the *Afro-American*) took place
in late 1935, long after *Girl Crazy* had closed. Still did not conduct, nor
did he conduct any of his concert works in New York City. (He was living in Los Angeles by then and probably did not attend the perfor-

mance.) In fact, Blake's association of the theme with the Boston run of *Shuffle Along* argues against Gershwin having heard it in the theater, for Gershwin is much less likely to have attended performances outside of New York.[34]

In October 1996, Dominique-René De Lerma wrote of interviewing Still about this when the two met in 1969:

> Still told me (I was also an oboist) that he doodled from the pit before Shuffle Along performances [i.e., in 1921 or 1922] with this little figure—. . . and knew that Gershwin was in the audience. The figure, of course, generates the Gershwin tune. . . . The same figure with the same rhythm appears in the third movement of the Afro-American Symphony in the horns, with the statement of the theme. Still had an expression on his face when we talked about this which clearly suggested he felt Gershwin had appropriated his doodle. I don't think it is extended enough to justify a copyright violation, but it is a strange coincidence and Still's reaction might be symptomatic of his vigilance.[35]

Gershwin was well known to seek out performances by black musicians, and *Shuffle Along* would have been an obvious show for him to have attended, maybe more than the one time Still mentioned to De Lerma.[36] Affirming once more that Gershwin was interested in Still's work, Verna Arvey notes that Gershwin attended the performance of Still's *Levee Land* at a concert presented by the International Composers' Guild at Aeolian Hall, January 24, 1926. In the same essay, probably from the late 1960s, she wrote of Gershwin's attendance at a performance of *Shuffle Along*.

> One Negro musical show which took New York by storm in the early Twenties was Shuffle Along. George and Ira Gershwin and most of the other Broadway celebrities attended it, some more than once. . . . As the show went on and on, the players in the orchestra began to get tired of playing the same thing over and over again, so very often they would improvise. Most of them had a special little figure that they added, as they felt so inclined. Still's figure was melodic. Later, when he was composing the Afro-American Symphony, he used the small little figure, wedded to a distinctive rhythm which he had originated in the orchestration for a soft-shoe dance in the show, Rain or Shine.[37]

Arvey was reporting what Still had told her. The awkwardness of her telling betrays her unfamiliarity with a milieu outside her own experience, but it also reflects a struggle to get the story as Still remembered it. Her words seem to amplify De Lerma's report about what happened. Later, Still wrote generally about musical borrowings in American music, though not in detail about his own experiences. In "The Men Behind

Example 5. Numbered themes from the 1924 theme book suggestive of the "I Got Rhythm" motif. All are lightly crossed out, meaning that Still had used them. Themes 249 and 251 are marked "Good—Negroid"; 260 is marked "Good for Land of Blues." Courtesy of William Grant Still Music.

American Music" (1944), Still writes with a certain ambivalence, mainly about plagiarism in commercial music:

> As for George Gershwin, who wrote so much in the Negroid idiom, there are many Negro musicians who now claim to have done work for him, arranging or composing. I have no way of knowing whether any of these claims are justified. I do know that Gershwin did a great deal of unconscious borrowing from several sources (not always the Negro) and that he did some conscious borrowing which he apparently was generous enough to acknowledge, for he gave W. C. Handy a copy of the "Rhapsody in Blue," autographed to the effect that he recognized Handy's work as the forerunner of his own. . . .
>
> Quite often colored musicians claim to have had their creations or their styles stolen from them by white artists. In many cases these tales may be dismissed as baseless rantings. But there have been so many instances in which they are justified that one cannot ignore all of them. I have learned this from my own experience and from the experiences of my friends in the world of music.[38]

In support of his statement, he describes hearing an arrangement of his own over the radio that was ascribed to another arranger.[39]

Still never claimed "I Got Rhythm" for himself, at least in writing. Yet the 1924 theme book and the 1926 "Rashana" sketchbook offer evidence that partly supports the claims to precedence made in his behalf. The theme book shows several themes that begin with the tune's opening four pitches, *sol, la, do, re* (see ex. 5). In every case, the opening melodic contour is similar, but the tempos are slower, syncopation is not notated, and the melodies go off in other directions rather than (or before) turning back on themselves. Most memorable is its use as shown in figure 9, "From the Land of Blues," the "melodic sketch" in the "Rashana" sketchbook not otherwise identifiable.

Gershwin's "I Got Rhythm" depends for its impact on three musical elements in addition to its text: a four-note gap-scale figure that turns back on itself, a syncopated rhythmic pattern, and a drive to a cadence that rounds it off. Still's themes, as they are notated in the examples we have, all lack the syncopation that is associated with Gershwin's tune. A handwritten notation on a draft of the Arvey essay quoted above, very likely made at Still's behest, reinforces Arvey's reference to the 1928 musical *Rain or Shine* as the place where Still, in one of his orchestrations, used both the melodic pattern and the syncopated rhythmic figure.[40] At least for now, this clue leads to a dead end. Only two songs from *Rain or Shine* are deposited in the Library of Congress; six more were returned to the claimant several years after they were deposited for copyright, and another six were never deposited.[41] One cannot know which (if any) of the fourteen might have quoted the "soft-shoe dance" to which Arvey refers, or whether the pattern occurred only in a section that never reached print or copyright. We are left with what appears to be Still's word—which is reliable in other cases but which cannot be verified in this one. Blake, who seems to have embroidered his story in order to make his broad point about unacknowledged borrowing, went out of his way to acknowledge that Gershwin's use of Still's idea was inadvertent: "it could happen to anybody."

It is obvious that the ascending gap-scale figure (*sol, la, do, re,* or *do, re, fa, sol*) fascinated Still. How Still improvised on it from the orchestra pit during the run of *Shuffle Along* (or in Gershwin's living room), we cannot know. Comparison of Still's and Gershwin's treatments of it shows both their similarity and where they parted company. Still's failure to claim the song as his own may simply represent his acknowledgment

Figure 9. Melodic sketch, *From the Land of Blues*, 1924 theme book. Courtesy of William Grant Still Music.

Example 6. Still's and Gershwin's themes compared. Used by permission.

that he used it differently from the way Gershwin did, and/or that the distinction between something improvised and something written down was very important to him. Perhaps he feared that any serious claim on his part would be dismissed as "baseless ranting." Since the melodic motive we know about is not used in the same way by both composers, at least in the surviving written versions, the question of primacy becomes less relevant. The difference in their use of the same basic melodic material seems far more interesting than the similarity. For Still, it was a brief blues gesture to be extended at will; for Gershwin, a snappy, open-and-closed eight-bar song-and-dance phrase. The contrast points to the operation of different sensibilities powerfully influenced by the cultural position of each composer, the specific tasks in which each was involved, and the unpredictable vagaries of individual talents and predilections.

Despite his lack of action, Still must have known that, one way or another, he had helped Gershwin reach that melody. Perhaps Still could see the interaction on a broader scale. For him the melodic figure belonged to the blues, and to the African American past. By quoting Gershwin's version where he did, as part of the whites-in-blackface minstrel representation with which the Scherzo begins, he suggested where Gershwin's tune fitted into his fusion aesthetic with a subtlety appropriate to the mythical Trickster. Moreover, the appearance of "I Got Rhythm" along with *Girl Crazy* in mid-October 1930—assuming that dates when Still first heard it—must have pushed Still to begin writing the symphony he had contemplated for so long.[42] It might even have provoked him to re-think the Scherzo, to abandon for something far richer his initial idea of portraying the "janny sect" that he had laughed at when his mother had taken him along during the summers she taught rural African Americans without access to regular schools. One imagines his thought that Gershwin's use of that material aptly demonstrates the "minstrel mask" of the past, the one imposed from "outside." His own treatment pointedly addresses the "real" past: slavery, Emancipation, the blues. He felt secure, perhaps, in his own sense of the "authenticity" of his own application, with the scale, with his constantly changing thematic "treatments" that modern commentators may think of as "signifying." If Still stimulated Gershwin from the pit in the *Shuffle Along* production or as the orchestrator of *Rain or Shine,* Gershwin's commercial adaptation in turn provoked Still to sit down and compose the symphony he had contemplated for so long, and even to add this tricksterish layer of meaning.

In one of her "Scribblings," Verna Arvey records an anecdote about Still's friend Harold Bruce Forsythe and the *Afro-American Symphony.* She writes that when Forsythe heard about Stokowski's telegram announcing that the fourth movement would be performed on a lengthy 1936 Philadelphia Orchestra tour, he visited Still's home and asked to see the score of the symphony, which was unfamiliar to him. He looked at it for a while and announced that he would write to Stokowski supporting the performance, remarking that he was the only one who knew what the symphony was about. Arvey took this as another symptom of Forsythe's insufferable arrogance; yet Forsythe may have been right in his judgment that most audiences would have listened to the symphony without seeing the complexity of the cultural message Still had inscribed in it, much less the topicality of the Gershwin reference, a seemingly minor point in the overall work.

It is clear enough that given the abyss that separated whites and blacks in Still's America, no composer who identified as European-American or "white" would or could have composed with the sensibility revealed in this or others among Still's self-consciously racial works. Still's symphonically treated blues decentered the expected neat enclosure of the African by the European for white concert audiences.[43] Whether his actual audiences were prepared to receive his work as he intended it to be interpreted is another question entirely, and may explain his own comment, "This symphony approaches but does not attain to the profound symphonic work I hope to write; a work presenting a great truth that will be of value to mankind in general."[44]

While the symphony itself is successful as a work of art that continues to be performed regularly, neither it nor later works by Still had (or could have had, given the relatively small general audience for concert music in the United States) an impact comparable to that of the blues' entry into popular music with its mass audience. Moreover, the racial barrier in concert music remained higher than for popular music. Two decades after he composed the *Afro-American Symphony,* Still himself acknowledged that there was not yet parallel recognition for African Americans in concert music and opera, that "the serious Negro musician who is said to have 'arrived' today still is confronted with all sorts of preconceived notions."[45] Certainly no single work could revitalize or restore in 1930 the black concert audiences that had existed in the early 1920s, nor could it create the genuinely integrated audience to which his fusion aesthetic ultimately looked forward.

Still conducted his quest to find a speaking subject position in concert music and opera with unique persistence and skill over his long creative career. Though his first concert works came almost sixty years after Abolition, the need to establish and redefine the status of African American musicians by composing in the elite genres of symphony and opera remained critical in a society where blacks were overwhelmingly confined to "popular," that is, "lower-class," music making. He went to great lengths to fight his way into the world of high musical literacy, to find a place as a speaking subject in the world of concert music. The *Afro-American Symphony* stands as a landmark in this project.

NOTES

1. Claude Palisca, ed., *Norton Anthology of Western Music,* 3d ed. (New York: Norton, 1996), 822–838.

2. J. Fischer and Bro. published the complete score in 1935; two years later,

the same publisher brought out the Scherzo, arranged for small orchestra. In some unlabeled, typed notes on the symphony supplied through the courtesy of Judith Anne Still, there is a reference to three such reduced versions:

A. flute, oboe, 2 char, bassoon, 2 horns, 2 trp, trb, perc, pf, strings.
B. 2 alto sax, tenor sax, trb, 2 trp, perc, of, 1 or more violins, bass, tenor banjo.
C. 5 woodwinds, 3 sax, 2 hn, 2 trp, trb, perc, pf, tenor banjo, strings.

In other typewritten material, Arvey lists 56 performances through February 14, 1953, and 52 more of the Scherzo alone through September 3, 1951. Several of these were conducted by Donald Voorhees, Still's old employer, on the NBC Telephone Hour.

3. Still's "racial" aesthetic, expressed in his concert music especially between 1925 and 1932, is described in Murchison's chapter above. As shown in this chapter, it implies a fusion of African American folk music, especially the blues, and the European concert tradition. Its centrality to Still's work is affirmed by the title *William Grant Still and the Fusion of Cultures in American Music,* a collection whose two editions were prepared under Still's and his daughter's supervision, respectively. But this is hindsight; the primacy of the *Afro-American Symphony* in Still's oeuvre was not established until some years after its composition. In his compositions from 1924 on, he tried several techniques to achieve this fusion. We are reminded of that by the fact that Still's contemporary and friend Forsythe was entirely unfamiliar with this symphony until about 1936.

4. Guthrie Ramsey made this suggestion in the discussion that followed my presentation, "Transforming the Blues: Doubleness of Race, Genre and Geography in the Music of William Grant Still," American Studies Association, Kansas City, October 25, 1996. The trickster figure is exploited in relation to the efforts of the African Diaspora to enter the written, European language by Henry Louis Gates, Jr., in *The Signifying Monkey: A Theory of African-American Literary Criticism* (New York: Oxford University Press, 1988).

5. Paul Harold Slattery, "A Comprehensive Study of the *Afro-American Symphony,*" *Fusion 2,* 101–127, is described by Orin Moe (n. 8 below) as "schoolmasterish." Assembled many years after the symphony was composed under the eye of the composer, Slattery's 1972 description and analysis includes charts and phrase-by-phrase descriptions of all four movements. The charts refer to "expositions" and "development" areas and otherwise follow the terminology used for analysis of sonata forms in the European concert tradition. Still also used this terminology. I have taken Slattery's numbering of the Scherzo's themes (1A, 1B, 2A, 2B).

6. Carol J. Oja, "'New Music' and the 'New Negro': The Background of William Grant Still's *Afro-American Symphony,*" *BMRJ* 12, no. 2 (Fall 1992): 145–169.

7. Rae Linda Brown, "William Grant Still, Florence Price, and William Dawson: Echoes of the Harlem Renaissance," in Samuel A. Floyd, Jr., ed., *Black Music in the Harlem Renaissance* (New York: Greenwood Press, 1990), 71–86.

8. Orin Moe, "A Question of Value: Black Concert Music and Criticism," *BMRJ* 6 (1986): 57–66.

9. Samuel A. Floyd, Jr., *The Power of Black Music: Interpreting Its History from Africa to the United States* (New York: Oxford University Press, 1996), 109–110, 152–154, 253–254. This quotation is from p. 153. White critics are more likely to award Gershwin's *Rhapsody in Blue* this status even as they remark negatively on its sectional construction.

10. Ultimately there were five symphonies and many more suites.

11. My dating, based on several aspects of the work. They include its uncharacteristic style features, its technical clumsiness, and its impractical notational style. An undated postmark (Columbus, Ohio) on a letter of inquiry suggests that the manuscript was submitted after Still had left Wilberforce (May 1915). See also pp. 5–6 and 222–223.

12. This work has been known only by its critical reviews and Still's description. It was thought lost until it was located at WGSM in September 1997. See also pp. 5–6 and 222–223.

13. The *Bio-Bibliography*, W1, 45–50, gives substantial information about the eleven-year evolution (1924–1935) of this work, which had a number of partial performances between 1930 and 1938. It was consistently well received by critics. A revival, this time of cut versions of the first and third movements, by the Centennial Celebration Orchestra, conducted by Ronnie Wooten, at Northern Arizona University on June 25, 1998, leads one to wonder about the eclipse of this remarkable work, arguably a twentieth-century masterpiece. Two explanations suggest themselves. One is that *Africa* was overshadowed by the eventual success of the *Afro-American Symphony* and that Still was too busy composing to promote it. The second is more likely. Still contracted with Robbins Music Corporation to publish his concert music between 1934 and 1936. Robbins did not promote his music; moreover, the company retained the rights to *Africa* until 1947. In 1937 Still signed with J. Fischer and Bro., a firm that vigorously promoted the *Afro-American Symphony* and other Still works for several years before the untimely death of George Fischer, the "Bro." who was the firm's driving force. I am grateful to Wayne D. Shirley for calling my attention to Robbins's and Fischer's roles.

14. The contact with Barnhart is noted in his diary on October 22, 1930.

15. There was, however, considerable freelance work. A list at the front of the diary reports his arranging work, all of which follows the end of his contract with Whiteman on May 30:

> Glow-worm—delivered Aug. 25 $95
> Deep River—delivered (radio) $95
> Rumba Rhythm—delivered (Remick) (radio) $115.50
> Kentucky Home (24 pages)—scoring $84
> Composing interlude $20 (bill in) $104
> Suwanee River (28 pages) $98
> Peg O' My Heart (28 pages) $95.50
> Ol' Man River, 42 pages [Probably the "Show Boat Medley" done for Paul Whiteman.]
> Chinese Lullaby $80
> Blue—(Reisman) $50

Aunt Hagar's Blues (Reisman) $50
Waters of Perkiomen $80
Sunshine of Your Smile $80
2 numbers for woodwind $15

Most of these cannot be associated with specific employers, though "Ol' Man River" was probably for Paul Whiteman (who discussed a 52-week contract at one point but couldn't deliver) and the radio arrangements were almost certainly for Willard Robison. Other musicians with whom he had contact, according to the diary: Sam Lanin (Oct. 29), [Nathaniel] Shilkret (Oct. 31), John Rehauser (Nov. 4), Hugo (Leo?) Reisman(n?) (Nov. 14), Paramount Studios (Nov. 15), [Irving] Weill (Nov. 15), Don Voorhees (Nov. 26).

16. Willard Robison, singer, songwriter, pianist, and bandleader, organized the Deep River Orchestra in the late 1920s. Still worked as arranger and sometimes conductor for Robison's radio show, the "Deep River Hour," from 1931 to 1934. Some of Still's arrangements for Robison have surfaced in the Ellington Collection at the Smithsonian. See Wayne D. Shirley, "Religion in Rhythm: William Grant Still's Arrangements for Willard Robison's 'Deep River Hour,'" *BMRJ* 18, no. 2 (forthcoming).

17. Still attended Wilberforce University from 1911 to 1915. His wife, Grace Bundy, graduated from Wilberforce in 1915. This was probably a social engagement rather than a working one.

18. This is the first volume of Still's diary that survives. It runs from July 7, 1930, through the end of that year. No further diaries are known until the one for the year 1937.

19. "The first of this week saw the completion of my latest effort. Its title, Afro-American Symphony, is self explanatory." See "William Grant Still and Irving Schwerké," below, for the full text.

20. "Rashana" (earlier entitled "Roshana") was to be an opera, but it was never completed.

21. "Rashana" sketchbook. See figure 5. The final sentence, reduced to "With humble thanks to God, the source of inspiration," appears at the end of all Still's scores after the *Afro-American Symphony*. Of the caricatures drawn by Still in figure 5, he represents himself twice. The two upper figures are probably Donald Voorhees and Paul Whiteman. The lower figures are not identified; they could be two of his children.

22. See three different accounts by Still in Arvey's "William Grant Still," the "Personal Notes," and the Still-Schwerké correspondence below.

23. Courtesy of Judith Anne Still. The paragraph was typed on Still's typewriter. Some of it is written in longhand in the sketchbook described below. In that source, parts of the poems are given as well. Ellipses in the original.

24. All of Dunbar's poetry quoted here is from Joanne M. Braxton, ed., *The Collected Poetry of Paul Laurence Dunbar* (Charlottesville: University Press of Virginia, 1993), 243, 195, 13–15, 15–16 (includes *The Complete Poems of Paul Laurence Dunbar* [New York: Dodd Mead, 1913]). I am grateful to Wayne Shirley for calling my attention to the meaning of the third of these quotations.

Only one of the two holograph scores in the Library of Congress bears this stanza.

25. See the introduction and Murchison's chapter for Du Bois's famous paragraphs.

26. The European practice is exemplified in the single best-known work in the entire symphonic repertoire, Beethoven's Fifth Symphony, which "progresses" from C minor to C major.

27. I am grateful to Craig Russell for pointing out the resemblance to Dvořák's music in this passage. After a presentation based on the "Politics of Race and Class" at the Northern and Southern California Chapters meeting of the American Musicological Society, April 26, 1997, Russell suggested that Still's fondness for the oboe and English horn, shown both in his selection of the oboe as his major performing instrument and in his use of it in his scores, was an acknowledgment of Dvořák's use of these instruments in the New World Symphony.

For a discussion of the controversy around Dvořák's use of "American" melodies in that symphony, see Adrienne Fried Block, "Dvořák, Beach, and American Music," in Richard Crawford, R. Allen Lott, and Carol J. Oja, eds., *A Celebration of American Music: Words and Music in Honor of H. Wiley Hitchcock* (Ann Arbor: University of Michigan Press, 1990), 256–280.

28. See the "Personal Notes," below.

29. Robert A. Simons, "Music Events: Three Native Composers, Many Orchestras, and a Few Virtuosi," *New Yorker* 11 (November 30, 1935): 55. Quoted in *Bio-Bibliography*, WB2.13, 54–55.

30. See Chadwick Hansen, "Jenny's Toe Revisited: White Responses to Afro-American Shaking Dances," *AM* 5 (1987): 1–19, for an etymology for Still's term, "janny."

31. In the course of his 1916 summer in Memphis playing, traveling, and arranging for W. C. Handy, Still almost surely heard and absorbed echoes of older New Orleans improvising style that involved varying the melody but not necessarily composing new melodies as later improvisers did.

32. Detroit Symphony, Neeme Järvi, conductor, Chandos CHAN 9154, 1993. The tenor banjo is also almost inaudible on this otherwise excellent recording. The horns, which are assigned the first "I Got Rhythm," and banjo are very clear, however, in the performance by the Cincinnati Philharmonia Orchestra, Jindong Cai, conductor, Centaur CRC 2331, 1997.

33. "Conversation with Eubie Blake (continued): A Legend in His Own Lifetime," ed. Bobbi King, *BPiM* 1–2 (1973): 155–156.

In a 1977 interview, Blake lists this among unacknowledged white "borrowings" from black musicians. Eubie Blake, taped interview with Lorraine Brown, Research Center for the Federal Theater Project (George Mason University), January 9, 1977, Eubie Blake Collection, Maryland Historical Society.

34. Judith Anne Still reports that her father and Blake went at least once to Gershwin's apartment to help him with orchestration. But in his 1973 interview Blake was probably confusing Still with Will Vodery, who orchestrated for Gershwin, most notably Gershwin's 1922 one-act opera, *Blue Monday*.

35. Manuscript Reading Report, Dominique-René De Lerma to University of California Press, September 29, 1996. De Lerma and Still met at a conference organized by De Lerma at Indiana University, June 18–21, 1969. Subsequently De Lerma edited a collection that included a Still speech drawn from the conference: *Black Music in Our Culture: Curricular Ideas on the Subjects, Materials and Problems* (Kent, Ohio: Kent State University Press, 1970).

36. Still's recollection of Gershwin in the audience of *Shuffle Along* (De Lerma, n. 35 above) dates Gershwin's acquaintance with African American jazz and blues earlier than assumed by Charles Hamm in "A Blues for the Ages," in Crawford, Lott, and Oja, *A Celebration of American Music,* 346–355. Hamm was unable to document Gershwin's acquaintance with African American music making before 1925, the year of Gershwin's *Concerto in F.*

37. Verna Arvey, "Memo for Musicologists," reprinted in *Fusion 2,* 21–25. This essay first appears under this title in the first edition of *Fusion* (ed. Robert Bartlett Haas; Los Angeles: Black Sparrow Press, 1972, 88–93). To judge from the citation in the *Bio-Bibliography* (A30), which quotes a sentence reproduced in the quotation here, it is probably an expansion of Arvey's "Afro-American Music Memo," *Music Journal* 27 (November 1969): 36, 68. Arvey goes on to discuss Dvořák's use of "national American melodies" in the symphony *From the New World,* so strongly influenced by the singing of "Plantation songs and Hoe-downs" by Harry T. Burleigh.

38. William Grant Still, "The Men behind American Music," *Crisis* (January 1944): 12–15, 29. Reprinted in Spencer, *Reader,* 114–123.

39. In June 1938 Still wrote to Willard Robison to complain, "While listening to a local radio station last Thursday night, I heard some transcriptions [implied: from Robison's "Deep River Hour," for which Still had arranged] made by the Associated Music Publishers Inc. [Still was later to correct this to "Associated Recorded Program Service"] . . . All of them sounded like my own arrangements, although they were credited to Walter Remson. Do you think that it is fair to me to do a thing like that?" In a later letter he notes that the Associated Record Program Service had informed him that " 'Walter Remsen' [*sic*] is a pseudonym for Willard Robison." Carbon copies of letters, Still to Robison, June 12, 1938, and August 1938, Still-Arvey Papers.

Still also wrote very generally about white borrowings of the music of African Americans, distinguishing again between unconscious borrowings and conscious imitation, in "A Symphony of Dark Voices," *Opera, Concert and Symphony* (May 1947): 18–19, 36, 38–39 (reprint, Spencer, *Reader,* 136–143).

40. Unsorted biographical papers at WGSM.

41. Wayne D. Shirley to the author, June 24, 1997. Short excerpts from the choruses of four of the returned songs appear on the back covers of the two deposited songs. None shows the characteristic rhythm.

42. Still was not the only musician to quote "I Got Rhythm," although he was probably the first to use it in concert music, in a written score. Richard Crawford, in *The American Musical Landscape* (Berkeley and Los Angeles: University of California Press, 1993), devotes a chapter to "I Got Rhythm." He describes its subsequent use as a song, as a jazz standard, and as a chordal structure for jazz improvisation. His table, listing seventy-nine recordings of "I Got

Rhythm" and contrafacta between October 1930 and January 1942 indicates the song's enormous popularity. Still's artistic intention and his relationship to the tune were clearly different from the uses examined by Crawford.

43. Lawrence Kramer, "Powers of Blackness: Africanist Discourse in Modern Concert Music," *BMRJ* 16, no. 1 (Spring 1996): 53–70, shows how white modernist composers often used quotations of African-derived music in ways that contain it, reflecting the prevailing societal power structure in their music.

44. See Still's "Personal Notes," below.

45. "Fifty Years of Progress in Music," *Pittsburgh Courier,* 11 November 1950, 15. Reprinted in Spencer, *Reader,* 177–188.

"*they,* Verna and Billy"

Verna Arvey would be known only as a minor figure in Los Angeles's pre-émigré world of music and dance were it not for her long association with William Grant Still. She learned of Still's work as early as the mid-1920s but met him only in 1930, when she came to his attention as a lively young musician and writer with commitments to both the "new" and the New Negro movement that in many ways paralleled his own. Her interest in musical modernism emerges clearly in January 1926, in a review for her school newspaper of a concert that included music by Henry Cowell.[1] As will be seen, Cowell encouraged her career in several significant ways, as he did that of many others, including Still. Arvey's awareness of Still and the Harlem Renaissance (elsewhere the New Negro movement) came through Harold Bruce Forsythe, an older contemporary, longtime friend, and inspired correspondent since Manual Arts High School days. Forsythe's developing advocacy of an eclectic modernism influenced her strongly.[2]

Arvey followed Forsythe's model in placing her skills in the service of Still's career. She began soon after Still's arrival in Los Angeles in 1934 by serving as his secretary, rehearsal pianist, publicist, and sometime performer of his music. After the break with Forsythe, which probably occurred in late 1935 or early 1936, she committed herself much more fully to Still, abandoning her own aspirations as a recitalist and turning down an offer of a teaching position in New York City. Thereafter she displaced Forsythe as Still's collaborator and friend, eventually becom-

Figure 10. Verna Arvey. Courtesy of William Grant Still Music.

ing his librettist, editor, and archivist as well as, from 1939, his spouse. Arvey's early bohemian persona was so fully subsumed in her commitment to Still that one recent commentator, finding it virtually impossible to separate out her contribution, wrote that "in many respects, *they, Verna and Billy*, were William Grant Still."[3]

The picture of Arvey in her teens and early twenties that emerges from her scrapbooks, five-year diaries, and other memorabilia is of someone almost unimaginably different from the later images. In particular, the forbidding self-image projected by *In One Lifetime* (1984), Arvey's late personal memoir/biography of Still, separates her from this early identity; it serves, if anything, to intensify the urgency of the questions about the nature and extent of her influence on Still.[4] These questions tend to place a heavy burden on Arvey, in some cases diverting attention away from the difficult aesthetic issues that Still faced, even tending to shift responsibility for decisions that were clearly his. For example, Arvey's role in Still's increasing isolation after 1939 is challenged, and even Still's aesthetic approach indirectly questioned by the remarks of two of his acquaintances, who said in separate interviews that Arvey had "protected" Still from his proper source of inspiration, the everyday lives of African Americans.[5] The quality of Arvey's librettos for all of Still's operas after *Troubled Island* has been directly attacked, perhaps with more justification, by Donald Dorr.[6] Beyond Arvey's private statement that she was the author of an anticommunist speech delivered by Still in 1951, questions have arisen about the extent of her influence as the typist or editor or perhaps even the writer of many of his letters, articles, and speeches, and as the "manager" of his domestic and professional life. It becomes important, then, to sort out something of Arvey's identity and to explore what her contributions to Still's career were.

Arvey was born in Los Angeles in 1910 of working-class Jewish parents, both of whom had emigrated as children from Russia to Chicago. She was the second of three children, the older of two sisters. She skipped two grades in elementary school, then was made to sit out a year to rest her eyes. That year she got interested in practicing the piano, learned to sight read music printed in old issues of the *Etude,* and worked as a volunteer reader in a kindergarten. Although the family identified themselves as Jewish, they were not observant. They were enthusiastic members of a spiritualist church while Verna was in middle school and high school. She served as the congregation's pianist, playing hymns and becoming thoroughly disillusioned as she observed some obvious fakery. Remembering this experience, she was disappointed to learn of Still's deep interest in the occult. Later, however, she accepted the integrity of his purpose and participated with him willingly in an informal spiritualist circle.[7]

An inspiring middle school teacher helped Arvey become fluent in Spanish and stimulated her interest in Hispanic culture; later on she won a prize in a citywide high school competition for her skill. Her early desire to pursue journalism as a career led her to Manual Arts High School. There her extracurricular activities included Girls' Self-Government, Press Club, the debate squad, and a stint as feature writer for the *Manual Arts High School Weekly:* "I went out on my own and interviewed a lot of musical celebrities for the paper. In consequence, ours was one of the few high school papers carrying interviews with such artists as Joseph Lhevinne, Tito Schipa, Lucrezia Bori, Lawrence Tibbett (one of our own graduates) and others."[8] Interviews remained a favored journalistic genre for her long after Manual Arts.

When Arvey graduated from high school in 1926, she was four months beyond her sixteenth birthday. In the same year, her parents divorced and her mother became a chiropractor. Her older brother was already an undergraduate at the University of California at Los Angeles, studying zoology, but the teacher training course in music offered there did not appeal to her. She aspired, according to a graduation brochure, to attend a "musical conservatory or University of Southern California—music course."[9] She continued her piano study for several years and developed a studio of her own, but her hopes and plans to go to college or to a conservatory never materialized.

Arvey's scrapbooks, assembled between about 1922 on, reflect her eclecticism, for they include her writings on film, theater, and dance as well as music.[10] They also reveal her efforts to learn and write about concert music by composers of Latin American and African American heritage. Her ideas about the use of music in movies developed soon after she left high school. Finding it impossible to gain the access to the studios she sought, she asked for help from her paternal uncle, Jake Arvey, whose name occasionally surfaces in books on machine politics in Chicago, where he was already a prominent alderman. Uncle Jake's connections with the distribution side of the movie business were no help.[11] Her interest in music for the movies continued, during this period of transition from silent to sound film, and eventually resulted in what is apparently the first "serious" magazine article about movie music, published in the *Etude* in January 1931.[12] That article—the first of many for that magazine—reflects her journalistic approach, which continued to depend on interviewing prominent people and reporting their remarks. For it, she queried the heads of the music departments at RKO, MGM, Fox, and Universal, respectively, as well as Los Angeleno Lawrence Tibbett.[13]

After leaving high school, Arvey found work accompanying dance classes (which she preferred to accompanying singers), and by the early 1930s she was well known locally as an accompanist for dance recitals. Los Angeles was a spawning ground for modern dance; Ruth St. Denis and Ted Shawn had begun their company there in 1913, presently giving Martha Graham and Doris Humphrey their early opportunities. These dancers had left by the time Arvey became active in the field, but there was still wide interest and a lot of activity in modern dance. (In Los Angeles, modern dance was said to have a quality of naïveté that distinguished it from its New York counterpart.)[14] She reported extensively for the *American Dancer,* founded locally by Ruth Howard in 1927, especially after Howard moved it to New York in 1932.[15]

Arvey developed strong practical ideas about how to accompany the dance: "In playing dance accompaniments, one follows the *dancer*, not the *music*. It is a new musical language. The accompanist must forget all he has learned about music and learn anew." [16] At the end of her book, *Choreographic Music: Music for the Dance* (1941), she wrote:

> A good accompanist for the dance will play the music just a little differently. . . . That is, there is a lift: a rise and fall in each phrase that is almost indescribable. At least, it is not possible of description with ordinary crescendo and diminuendo marks. A curve of the hand or a rising gesture will occasion this "lift." It follows that a successful composer for the dance will have in his music that indescribable something that gives to choreographic music, on the whole, that strange, unrigid, rhythmic, living character! [17]

As for her music, especially her interest in the piano, Arvey told an interviewer, "My family was a music-loving family, although they were not performers in any way. I don't know where I got that from." [18] At Manual Arts, she took courses in harmony, music history, and composition, at a time when such courses were widely available in Los Angeles high schools. She gave up her own interest in composition only after Still's arrival in 1934. Over the years, she worked with five different piano teachers, none of them especially prominent. She left the last one, Ann J. Eachus, a student of the locally illustrious Thilo Becker, some time after giving a recital in Eachus's studio in 1932.[19]

What was she like as a pianist? Her one surviving recording, of Still's *Seven Traceries,* made for Co-Art Turntable in 1940 or 1941, is of rather poor quality. The written evidence, like the recording, is equivocal. There were positive reviews, mainly in connection with her work with dancers. For example: "A masterly accompaniment for the exacting program was supplied by Miss Verna Arvey at the piano. Her dynamic power and musical understanding not only afforded a flawless support for the dancer, but in five solos of diverse moods [she] proclaimed herself a young virtuoso of great promise." [20] A 1933 radio performance by the Raymond Paige orchestra on the program "California Melodies," in which she was the soloist, was noted by the *New York Daily News:* "[Paige's] orchestra gave a brilliant performance of Gershwin's 'Concerto in F.' A Pacific Coast crew that should visit the East." [21] Still heard the broadcast and reacted with surprising warmth:

> I must pause in the midst of the mad rush to tell you of my reaction. . . . I was more than repaid for my eagerness. You are an artist; a soul through whom higher beings speak to mortals. Under your fingers the piano sang, then spoke

in caressing tones tinged with sorrow, and then spoke in more authoritative tones. . . . I hope I may hear you again, many times.[22]

In her own estimate of her skill, Arvey was not so flattering. She wrote that she was chosen to play a piano solo at her high school commencement "despite the fact that I actually was not the best concert pianist then in school."[23] For three consecutive years (1930–1932) she auditioned unsuccessfully for the position of pianist with the Los Angeles Philharmonic. "Musicians always thought I was a good writer; writers always thought I was an excellent pianist," she wrote in a "Scribbling." Eventually she took an empirical approach to exploiting her talents:

> Countless times I decided I'd never try for anything again. Each time I changed my mind. For, on the instant, it seemed as if there was always an open life beyond, instead of a door closing off the life behind. . . .
>   There came a time when I resented being dubbed a dance accompanist forever, and wanted to strike out for myself in other lines, but luckily decided to capitalize on what knowledge I had and gave recitals of dance music and wrote books on the subject. ("Scribblings")

One of the few surviving letters from Forsythe gives another view of her thinking in early 1934:

> Would like to hear a more detailed idea of what you will put into the projected "Without Bitterness." . . . I remember the poem you will base it on. It sounds like a good idea: but can it be done Without Bitterness? That's the problem! . . . I will wait impatiently for it, for it will be emmensely [*sic*] interesting to see how you have reacted to this America . . . can't remember ever reading anything of the sort. . . . Africs are almost moaning in print on the subject, but the story of the young Jewish intellectual must be told in your book. . . . Do it well, and don't spare America![24]

While still at Manual Arts High School, Arvey demonstrated an interest in "the new" as it was developing in Los Angeles, shown both by the connection she cultivated with Cowell and by her work in behalf of modern dance. By the early 1930s, her "modernist" acquaintances in L.A. included John Cage and Harry Hay. Arvey was sufficiently interested in Cage's ideas that she arranged for him to perform at the Mary Carr Moore Manuscript Club.[25] Forsythe was on the periphery of this circle, mainly through Hay. Whether Arvey had met Wallace Thurman or Arna Bontemps in her early high school days is unknown, but her "Scribblings" include a description of an inebriated Thurman at a party given by Still in his honor in 1930 and attended by Forsythe. Arvey's acquaintance with musical modernists expanded in the early thirties; in late 1933 and early 1934, she spent some weeks in Mexico, interviewing composers and listening to as much music as she could. With help from Carlos Chávez, she gave a concert in Mexico City in January 1934.[26] An unpublished novel, "Beware of Bandits, Señorita," also resulted from this trip.

After several seasons of increasing prominence, Arvey attempted her most ambitious public performances, beginning with a concert in Los Angeles on November 3, 1934, and continuing with a tour that took her to New York City, Cuba, and Colombia. The Los Angeles performance was sponsored by Norma Gould's Dance Theater Group, for which Arvey frequently played, and was given at Gould's dance school. It was labeled "A program of Idealized Dance Music" and included music by Galuppi, Bach, José Rolón, Castelnuovo-Tedesco, Neupert, Chopin, Ravel, Friedman-Gaertner, Arvey, Smetana, Still, Milhaud, and Handy.[27] A publicity item and a review give a picture of her.

> Small, dark-eyed, nervous—they call Verna Arvey a revolutionary pianist. The night of Nov. 4 she will show Los Angeles a new approach to music, . . . piano idealizations of dance compositions.
>
> "To go beyond the notes, clear through technique, to the spirit, to summon dancing images in the mind of each individual in an audience more true to the music than any interpretation by a flesh-and-blood dancer, that is my desire," she says.[28]

Rob Wagner's Script, a local weekly, carried a review that gives a visual description of her playing:

> When she gets to the piano she starts in with the serious business of playing and saves her calisthenics for the privacy of her bedroom, a very agreeable change! Her work with dancers has given Miss Arvey a sense of dramatic values not possessed by most pianists. At a concert, one not only hears, but sees as well, and her use of lights was sufficient to hold audience interest so that nothing marred the enjoyment of a nicely balanced program.[29]

About the colored lights, a realization of the color-sound associations that were a feature of early modernism, Arvey commented in a "Scribbling": "My use of colored lights—perhaps superficial, when considered in the light of all those detailed treatises on color and sound combinations, but really more fundamental than all of them."

A few weeks later, she performed at a symposium sponsored by Henry Cowell at the New School in New York. No program survives, and there is no indication in Arvey's diary as to what she played. There is very little evidence about her reception at that concert. Two months after the performance, Cowell wrote that she had "made good" at the New School.[30] But no review has been located in any of the papers or journals listed by Cowell as having sent critics.[31] A letter from Hedi [Korngold] Katz, the founder of the Music School of the Henry Street Settlement, becomes the most revealing report.[32] It addresses Arvey as an artistic personality with teaching potential rather than as a pianist:

> My dear Miss Arvey: I have heard you last Friday at Henry Cowell's forum at the New School. . . . What I would like to know is, do you plan to return to New York, and, if so, would you be interested in teaching at our school? Also, what subjects would you care to teach? I would like very much to have you connected with the Music School, after the impression I got that evening. Would you kindly let me know? Sincerely yours, . . .[33]

No further comment about this trip has been found.

Influenced by the overall success of Cowell's New School symposia, Arvey determined to attempt something similar in Los Angeles. Her symposium differed from Cowell's model in several ways. It was held in a dance studio, reflecting not only what was readily available to Arvey but also her sense of what was appropriate. She invited both established and new composers, with the idea of seeking common ground between old and new. The established composers included Mary Carr Moore and Charles E. Pemberton. The "new" ones, including those new to Los Angeles, were Joseph Achron, Hugo Davise, Gilberto Isais, Richard Drake Saunders, Arnold Schoenberg, William Grant Still, and George Tremblay. Artie Mason Carter, the founder of the Hollywood Bowl (long departed from the Bowl's administration by 1935), remained an enthusiast of the "new," and was invited to moderate the discussion that was to follow. The event presented a Los Angeles-specific window on the "new," with its mix of local composers and teachers, film composers and émigrés. Several letters report the proceedings; they suggest that the event failed to create rapport among the factions and that "common ground" remained, to say the least, unlocated. Artie Mason Carter's sets the tone:

> Dear Verna: I can't bear your great disappointment after all your sincere effort, altho I feel you are wrong to feel the evening was a failure. To me it was

truly interesting and I don't want you to promise never to attempt it again!
We must have leaders for the cause of contemporary music and you are an
excellent one. . . .

You played beautifully—gave a fine impression of a charming work—that
and the Schoenberg songs (*The Book of the Hanging Gardens*) were worth
coming a long distance to hear. . . .

Don't be discouraged. You are too young and too valuable. Bless you my
dear! Faithfully, A.M.C.[34]

A fuller (and less positive) account comes from the shaky hand of another of the old guard. Charles E. Pemberton, once Forsythe's composition teacher, had been a Los Angeles resident for at least thirty-five years
and was still active as a teacher at the University of Southern California
in 1935.

My dear Miss Arvey:

. . . it was kind of you to think it necessary to apologize for the affair not
turning out as you had planned. It was not your fault and you did everything you could to make it a success. . . .

I suffered horribly during those 15 Schoenberg songs. (Was it 15? they
seemed endless.) I lost count, breaking out in a cold sweat. It was poor
taste upon the part of this Rogers lady to sing all those songs upon a program of such a character. . . .

[When] I peeped behind the scenes, . . . I thought I heard this charming
Arvey lady say, "My God what have I got into." . . .

It was of course to be regretted that the lateness of the hour the program
closed left no time for discussion. But again, that was no fault of yours.

I expect you are going to think me "horrible" for writing so frankly, but
it's just between us, and somehow it relieves my mind, like escaping steam
from an engine relieving the pressure on the boiler.[35]

Arvey reported further complications. The genial Cowell failed to appear at the last moment, although they delayed the start for him. The
less genial Schoenberg did not receive his invitation in timely fashion,
even though his songs were scheduled and he had coached the singer in
advance. Calista Rogers, his singer, stretched out her part by reading
English translations before each song, helpful in the absence of program
notes but serving to prolong the agony of Professor Pemberton (and perhaps others).[36]

Arvey did not repeat this experiment; in fact its failure seems to have
encouraged her to withdraw from the battlefield between modernists
and traditionalists entirely. Increasingly, she immersed herself in her work

on Still's behalf, although she continued to play for dancers and write about the dance. How fully she withdrew will become clearer presently.

Forsythe made a deep and lasting impression on the young Arvey, and she on him. His present for her high school graduation, manuscript copies of several of his own songs, is by far the most personal among the handful of modest presents she listed in her graduation program.[37] He could hardly have resisted telling Arvey about Still well before he introduced them, given the unbridled enthusiasm and openness of his few surviving letters.[38] She may well have read his "William Grant Still: A Study in Contradictions" at the time it was written, or even helped him edit it, soon after Still returned to New York in the summer of 1930.[39] Thus she was aware quite early of the contrast between Forsythe's zealous theorizing on racial matters and Still's methodical focus on practical applications in music.[40] Her relationship with him was already strained before Still's arrival in 1934:

> My dear friend Verna:
>
> As I write to you now, all the years during which I loved you as a dear and cherished friend stand congealed on the pin-point of the moment.
>
> Just how anything entered into our lives that could change this feeling a bit is extremely difficult to say, but ever since a few months ago I have felt that I was losing Verna . . . the Verna that had meant so much to me . . . the Verna who meant beauty . . . not so much piano playing, but the loveliness of music written for the piano. I don't think that I thought of Schumann's beautiful Fantasie, or Rachmaninov's 2nd Concerto, or Beethoven's Hammerclavier Sonata, or Mozart's C minor . . . without thinking of the Verna . . . MY Verna, as the executent [*sic*], and the catalyst.[41]

The melodramatic "farewell" with which this letter ends is defused by a postscript: "Next morning: Dear Verna: All is true, save the goodbye. Don't say goodbye, Verna! Hello is so much nicer a word!!!!!!!" An undated letter from Arvey to Forsythe, now known only in Arvey's transcription, may well have been in response to this letter:

> It just occurred to me that you have a very wrong idea of me. I'm not deep or profound or intellectual. I may be intelligent, but not intellectual. And I don't like to read philosophic things. I want things with a human side. And I don't like to study technicalities and big words. And I don't like to write un-understandable stuff just because it is arty. And I don't want to be a famous artist, I want to do my work and do it well. . . . [And] anyway, the

adjectives you use in describing me aren't true. I'm just myself, that's all. Don't idealize me.[42]

Even if the two letters are not directly connected, they reveal the developing conflict between Arvey and Forsythe that was exacerbated by Still's arrival.

The transition from the rather enterprising, adventuresome early Arvey and the Arvey of *In One Lifetime* is both remarkable and sad. At one point, probably later on, she commented on her decision to remain in southern California and not seek further education in this way:

> I was born in a section of the country which has spawned some important creative minds, as well as some outstanding ideas. It has also routinely absorbed many of the "greats" from other parts of the nation and of the world at large. So many came to live and work in the friendly climate of Southern California that it was always a surprise to find that many Easterners still considered us "provincial" and still thought that we on the West Coast were in dire need of their superior "leadership"! . . .
>
> At any rate, right at hand were so many big "names" in so many professions, so many interesting artistic projects and so much to absorb that I soon decided to cast down my bucket where I found myself. It came up loaded with nuggets of knowledge."[43]

Likewise, she recognized the loss of further systematic study indirectly in one of her "Scribblings": "The transition from a bright youngster with exceptional promise to an artist in competition with all the mature minds of the artistic was terribly hard."

It seems that Arvey's public means of maintaining her equilibrium during those "exasperating years" was humor. One of the dancers she accompanied wrote about her:

> She whose humor unfailing
> Strips our leaden-weighted woes
> Of their well-forged armor
> And with ruthless, Puckish foot
> Kicks over the cup of dignified Care
> And holds the mirror of Ridicule
> Before wry-faced misfortune. . .[44]

These comments add poignancy to a recollection from a member of Arvey's circle in the early 1930s. Fifteen years later, following World War II, its writer returned to Los Angeles, where he renewed his friendship with some dancers from the old Norma Gould studio, where Arvey had often played and where she had presented her New Music Symposium in 1935. He writes,

> I asked [people] like Waldeen Falkenstein or Teru [Izumida; both dancers for whom Arvey had once played] about Verna, and was told "Oh, she's absolutely changed since her marriage: all that laughter and sparkle has totally disappeared. D'ya remember how—at times—she could be almost winsome? That's all gone." Lester [Horton] even said "if you can believe it, she's even pushy and sort of tiresome now."[45]

How does one account for this transformation? Several events must be considered, though none really explains it. The resolution of the triangle with Forsythe and Still may have been traumatic for Arvey, as it was clearly devastating for Forsythe. She had resisted Forsythe's formulation of a triangle to begin with, writing to him, "There is one Billy and one Harold. They each have their particular niche. I have never been able to confine myself to one particular friend. . . . That should not alter a friendship as old as ours has been. Why can't we all three be together, instead of two . . . or two? I am always your friend whether you like it or not." She also may have precipitated the crisis through what seems her heartfelt advocacy of Forsythe's writing. She had introduced herself by mail to Carl Van Vechten, a major patron of the Harlem Renaissance, and represented Forsythe to him with an eloquence notably missing from much of her writing about Still. The letters from Forsythe to Van Vechten, first informative and assertive, then crushed, along with Arvey's rather stiff reply to Van Vechten's obviously worried query ("I think you have done Harold a far greater service by doing exactly what you did. . . . [A] little personal triumph is relatively unimportant when it comes to making finer human beings of people!"),[46] are quoted in the chapter on Forsythe above. The undated "Scribbling" that identifies him as a "drunkard" who "lied" about her probably dates from 1935, at about the same time. She had known of Forsythe's deafness earlier, though she seemed unaware of its progressive nature, and she believed he had tuberculosis. What looks like his accelerating physical deterioration at this time, combined with her helplessness and perhaps even guilt about it, must have been painful.

Both Arvey and Forsythe had worked with Still; now Forsythe's working relationship with Still was broken off and Arvey's began to replace it. Presently Forsythe's poem for the score of *Dismal Swamp,* just in preparation in 1935 for the New Music Edition, was removed in favor of another, inferior one by Arvey. (See the appendix to this chapter for both texts.) The ballet *Central Avenue,* for which Forsythe had provided the scenario, was eventually listed as withdrawn, replaced by the similar *Lenox Avenue,* to a scenario by Arvey. (Here the reasons for the switch are not so clear.)[47] Of the music from this relatively short period, only the score to *Blue Steel* continued to circulate to conductors. Arvey continued to write about it enthusiastically in her 1938 monograph. It was withdrawn only when *Troubled Island* was completed several years later, probably to give the new score a clearer field.

Having drawn closer to Still, Arvey now had to face public opprobrium over the interracial relationship. Still's 1938 suit for divorce was front-page news in the Negro press. The harassment Arvey sustained from a handful of African American women when her relationship with Still became known was intimidating and unexpected:

> Dear Langston,
>
> . . . We have had a barrage of the dirtiest, lousiest, most malicious anonymous letters you can imagine. They even sent them to newspapers, in an effort to turn people against Billy on my account.[48]

In response, the couple kept their address as secret as they could and maintained an unlisted telephone number; Arvey even hired a private detective on one occasion.

The change in their lifestyle after their marriage may have been much more difficult for Arvey than is suggested by a fragmentary "autobiography" of Still, which she undertook to write in his voice rather than her own: "We began to live a quiet life. Now that I had a real home I wanted to stay in it and enjoy it as much as possible. . . . Our staid life would scarcely appeal to lovers of thrills, but for us it is the only real romance."[49] If Still worked ceaselessly at composition, Arvey, too, applied herself diligently. She continued to write on dance, in addition to undertaking many articles on Still and helping him with his correspondence. In preparation for writing, she amassed numerous scrapbooks on race, anticommunism, and other topics.[50] She copied out extended passages from books on topics of interest, such as on Dvořák's sojourn in America.

In fact, Arvey seems to have tried hard to surrender her identity to Still's, willingly adjusting her views to his, being consumed by the slights he and his work experienced, and accepting the subordinate role that Still's working method required of his librettists. She may well have been disappointed that their marriage and their working relationship did not bring about the major change in race relations that she desired and Still

accepted as a basic purpose in his life. Her account of the 1935 symposium's outcome in the Still "autobiography" quoted above eerily projects how fully she would eventually abandon her own persona: "My
wife says that if any more composers' symposiums are given, someone
else will have to give them. She spent the following day in bed." [51]
Forsythe's question—"can you do it Without Bitterness?"—was very
much to the point. Arvey's disappointment at not getting to study at
USC left a residuum of anger; indeed, her bitterness at the ability of
some of their friends to travel to New York for the 1949 production
of *Troubled Island* when she could not is apparent in her letters to Still
before the production.

Whatever the reasons, the result was that Arvey and Still reinforced
each other's developing anxieties, helping each other as they lost their
individual perspectives sufficiently to blame their troubles increasingly
on a grand communist plot (discussed in "'Harlem Renaissance Man'
Revisited" below). This began to be evident in the years immediately following World War II. After 1949, the process was carried to an extreme.
It would seem that Arvey had conscientiously reflected Still's ideas and
his language in writing for and about him in the early years of their relationship. Her conscientiousness continued, but the language became
more and more her own. In the process, it became more forced and convoluted. The conclusion of her very late (1969, post–Black Arts movement) discussion of the "I Got Rhythm" controversy is carefully coded
to invoke distinctions about class and class-based genre, chosen with a
certain implicit snobbery:

> As composers, the difference between Gershwin and Still is obvious. Gersh-
> win approached Negro music as an outsider, and his own concepts helped to
> make it a Gershwin-Negro fusion, lusty and stereotyped racially, more pop-
> ular in flavor. Still's approach to Negro music was from within, refining and
> developing it with the craftsmanship and inspiration of a trained composer. [57]

Her avoidance of opposites for "Gershwin-Negro fusion," "lusty," and
"stereotyped racially" that might apply to Still is surprising, given the
opening of the paragraph. She introduces the racial issue with these
phrases and then fails to follow through on the terms she herself proposes. The suggestion instead that something "popular in flavor" does
not admit of "craftsmanship and inspiration" or cannot come from a
"trained composer" goes against the grain for many readers and writers
who cherish (as an ideal, anyway) a more egalitarian approach to aesthetic evaluations; in fact, it rejects the craftsmanship Still brought to his

commercial work. The use of "from within" in opposition to "outsider" is an attempt to evade a simple inside-outside contrast in favor of the suggestion of something more uplifting on Still's part. The result is an argument that, through its failure to follow through, does Still no good. The paragraph adds up to a late and not well thought out attempt to defend Still. In any case, Still allowed Arvey to take the lead only in one matter, the family's political posturing about anticommunism. It was no easy thing to stay balanced on their own personal troubled island under the pressures she attempted to carry for them both.

The issue of the quality of the librettos she provided for Still should also be addressed, however briefly. The later ones are indeed disappointingly similar, tending to dwell on the common themes of loyalty and retribution despite their varying locales. *Costaso,* Still's fifth opera (composed 1949–early 1950), engages with themes of loyalty and friendship, major issues in the Stills' lives as they worked on it. Arvey's text repeatedly extols these values, along with domestic serenity over an extended period. For example, Carmela, in her first-act aria about Costaso, does not sing of her passion for him; instead, she sings of their common peacefulness and serenity, for which they have abandoned passion and high ambition, perhaps as Still had done by going to Los Angeles:

> Far off riches beckon, false in their promised yield, / while here fortune lingers steadfast and secure. . . . / When life moves on serenely, when friendship's glow surrounds us, time itself becomes timeless. / The moments pile on moments, the hours grow into days, lengthen into years, to eternity. . . . / Our golden moments bring us joy forever!

When given the order to leave home and search for the city of gold, Costaso sings:

> Love bids me stay at home / where peace and devotion occupy our thoughts, / where comfort is our watchword.

In the desert, as they despair of rescue, Costaso's friend Manuel voices the value of friendship and loyalty in the opera's most forthright declaration of love:

> Your friendship more than repays me. / On the highway, in the town, / people pass and glance in friendly fashion. . . . / Where devotion? Where everlasting love?. . . / When at least the spark is found, when among strangers a friend appears, / then I return his love full measure. . . . / One friend, and I search no more.

Plotting by individuals is the order of the day.[53] We see Armona plot almost from the beginning to send Costaso to his death in order to win Carmela to himself. We see Carmela confront Armona in Act II Scene 1 with unheroine-like strength and tenacity in her husband's behalf. Her counterplot emerges only in the final scene, a moment or two before Armona is undone by an emissary from the distant capital. The last-minute developments that bring about Armona's fall and Carmela's triumph may be autobiographical for both Still, who had come to believe that his triumphant production of *Troubled Island* had been made to vanish with comparable unexpected suddenness, and Arvey, whose heroine managed at the last moment to subvert the passive-love object role expected of her as a matter of operatic tradition.

Thus Arvey's libretto and the jointly devised plot of *Costaso* reflect a view of the world in which heroes are isolated and manipulated by the plotting of either "bad guys" in positions of authority or "good guys" in the form of wives and other loyal but subordinate friends dedicated to the proposition that "Costaso always wins." Arvey's language is often neither graceful nor telling.

Yet Arvey's presence and willingness to collaborate cannot be dismissed as purely negative. She proved a reliable supplier of texts, and Still was a full participant in the devising of the plots he set. In New York, Still had found it difficult to find librettos and librettists with whom he could work. Still's choice of librettists was typically governed by their accessibility as much as or more than by their literary distinction. Grace Bundy, his first wife, had supplied song lyrics as early as 1916; later she wrote letters in his behalf, just as Arvey did later on. In the late 1920s Still began work on an opera ("Rashana") that was based on the plot of an unpublished novel by Bundy. It was to be versified by Countee Cullen, but Cullen was distracted by his personal life and never pursued the project. In Los Angeles, Forsythe was at hand (displacing Bundy, as Arvey was to displace him) to work on *Blue Steel*. When Langston Hughes agreed to provide the libretto to *Troubled Island*, Still wrote to him, "Please remember that it is absolutely necessary for us to keep in touch if we are to collaborate."[54] Arvey's collaboration on librettos did not begin until Still himself grew impatient with Hughes's inattention. As late as 1939, he asked Arna Bontemps for a libretto; he collaborated soon afterward with Katherine Garrison Chapin on *And They Lynched Him on a Tree*.[55] The possibility that Arvey's convenient accessibility as a librettist discouraged him from seeking out and setting a richer variety of opera texts must be balanced against his early difficulty in finding satisfactory texts to set at all.

There is evidence, published and unpublished, about how the Stills' collaborations worked. For example, Still wrote to the *New York Times* critic Howard Taubman some months after the New York production of *Troubled Island* concerning the new opera (*Costaso*) he was working on in collaboration with Arvey.

> The libretto is by my wife—Verna Arvey, and we are working in a way which seems to us satisfactory, though not usual. The plot we developed together, then she wrote out the libretto, each recitative indicated exactly, but each aria indicated only by the opening lines. I then set the opening lines of the arias and went on from there, developing each aria musically. Afterward, she put the remaining words to the music. This method has given me more leeway than I would have if I had a set libretto from which no deviation is possible. At present I am completing Act II of the opera as far as the music is concerned, but the entire libretto is finished.[56]

Like most of Still's letters after their marriage, this one was typed on Arvey's typewriter, most likely by her, and signed by Still. The question arises, who wrote it? In my opinion, after receiving the inquiry from Taubman, they discussed what topics to address, Arvey wrote out a draft reply, and Still signed it, with or without changes. This letter survives in a carbon of its finished form, so any changes made on the original in longhand are not present. Since it was clearly intended for publication, Arvey was performing a useful public relations function, giving Still this opportunity for publicity while sparing him the necessity of writing it himself.

There is draft evidence about one earlier collaboration, containing material that involved the film industry and other composers, from several years earlier. Still responded in 1940 to a symposium-by-mailed-questionnaire on film music; his answers are quoted at length in "Finding His Voice," above. A draft of his replies shows that Arvey typed out the questions, leaving space for his answers. She appears to have written down his comments as he spoke them, preserving language that is reminiscent of Still's writing style from his earlier, New York period.[57]

The anticommunist writings present a more difficult problem, since the Stills' shared position on this topic played a part in their later isolation. Authorship of the 1951 speech read by Still in which he named a rather long list of persons he believed, without real evidence, to be communists (quoted in "'Harlem Renaissance Man' Revisited," below) was claimed by Arvey in her correspondence with the editor of the *American*

Mercury. One begins by assuming that she is the author of other anti-communist talks given by Still, but that is not the case. In May 1949, Still spoke at Mount St. Mary's College in Los Angeles on the general topic of problems faced by the composer of "serious" music. He divided the problems into external ones, such as taking the critics seriously, and internal ones, such as deciding on a style and finding inspiration. He drafted the speech himself (see fig. 11), then reordered the paragraphs for Arvey to type. His paragraph on the communist threat is quoted in full here. Where Arvey made changes in her typescript, Still's words are bracketed. Her substitutions appear in boldface.

> I turn now to one tremendous problem that confronts only those composers in our country who are loyal Americans. It is a problem created by the opposition of Communists to all who do not subscribe to their beliefs; a unique problem in that individuals responsible for it cover up so effectively their affiliation with the [party] **Soviet controlled group** that people who know of it hesitate to make any accusation on account of the difficulty of offering substantial proof of the guilt of these people. Apparently [they] **these Reds** do not realize that music and politics have nothing in common. Their code appears to be one that makes art subservient to the Soviet government; a code that says, "All who disagree with us must be destroyed." Through underhanded manoeuvering they have placed their emissaries in [important] **key** positions where they very effectively [keep the] **prevent** loyal American composers from being heard whenever and wherever possible. From a person [employed in the Victor Record Co.,] **in the employ of one of our most prominent recording companies;** a person in a position to know **what goes on,** I learned that a small group of Communists dictate what music shall **and shall not** be recorded **by that company.** [crossed out material] I shudder to think of what could happen if these people had greater power. One thing is certain[.]; Greater power they will surely have unless something is done to curb them. Incidentally, I suggest, if you have not already seen it, that you look over the group of Communists whose photos appear in the April 4th issue of LIFE. In it you will find **listed** three men very prominent in American music.—I'm quite [underline removed] certain Life made no mistake in these three instances.

Her editing is light, occasionally intensifying Still's language, and in one case, the reference to the Victor Record Co., serving to weaken it.

How, then, did Arvey influence Still's career? She brought common interests, useful skills, and total dedication; most of her actions in his behalf were based on her best judgment about his interests and in fact often amounted to simply carrying out his wishes. Several factors need to be considered in reevaluating her judgment now. The role of race clearly

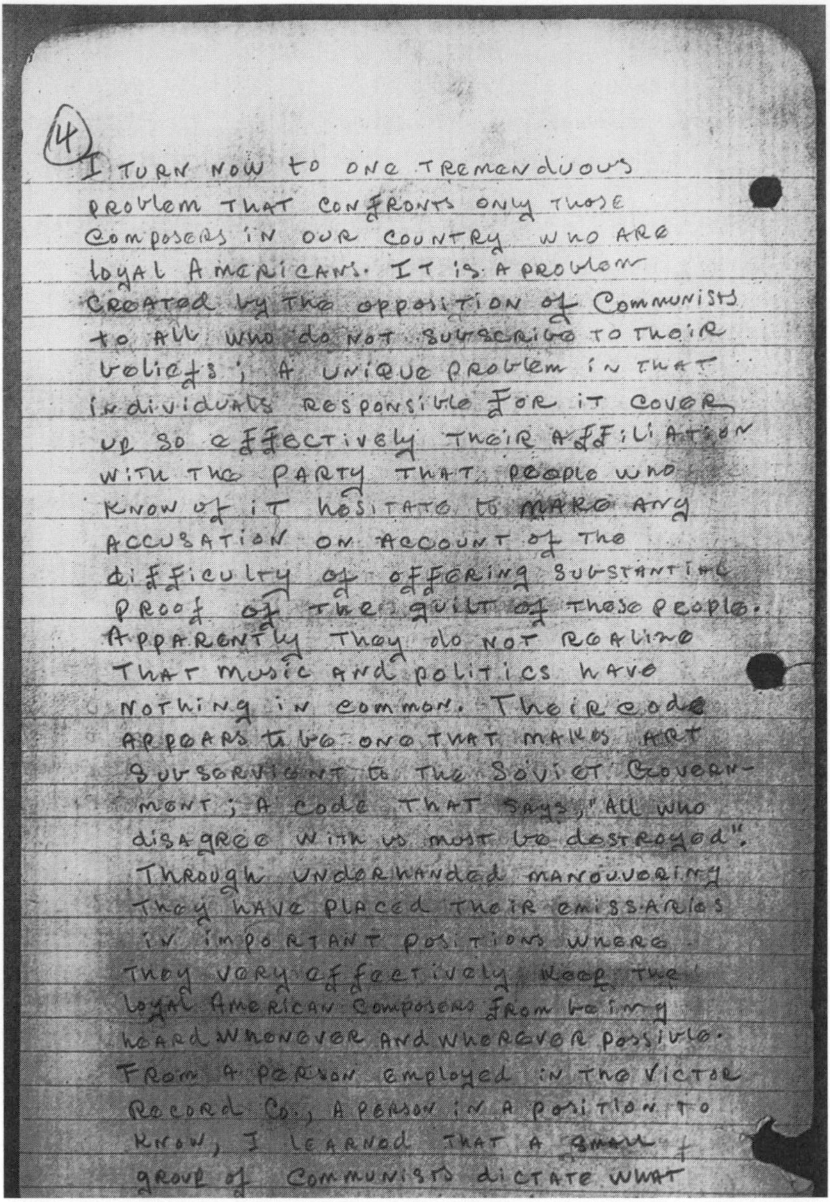

(4) I TURN NOW to ONE TREMENDUOUS
PROBLEM THAT CONFRONTS ONLY THOSE
COMPOSERS IN OUR COUNTRY WHO ARE
LOYAL AMERICANS. IT IS A PROBLEM
CREATED by THE OPPOSITION OF COMMUNISTS
to ALL WHO do NOT SUBSCRIBE TO THEIR
BELIEFS; A UNIQUE PROBLEM IN THAT
INDIVIDUALS RESPONSIBLE FOR IT COVER
UP SO EFFECTIVELY THEIR AFFILIATION
WITH THE PARTY THAT PEOPLE WHO
KNOW OF IT HESITATE to MAKE ANY
ACCUSATION ON ACCOUNT OF THE
DIFFICULTY OF OFFERING SUBSTANTIAL
PROOF OF THE GUILT OF THESE PEOPLE.
APPARENTLY THEY do NOT REALIZE
THAT MUSIC AND POLITICS HAVE
NOTHING IN COMMON. THEIR CODE
APPEARS to be ONE THAT MAKES ART
SUBSERVIENT to THE SOVIET GOVERN-
MENT; A CODE THAT SAYS, "ALL WHO
DISAGREE WITH US MUST be DESTROYED".
THROUGH UNDERHANDED MANOUVERING
THEY HAVE PLACED THEIR EMISSARIES
IN IMPORTANT POSITIONS WHERE
THEY VERY EFFECTIVELY KEEP THE
LOYAL AMERICAN COMPOSERS FROM being
HEARD WHENEVER AND WHEREVER POSSIBLE.
FROM A PERSON EMPLOYED IN THE VICTOR
RECORD Co., A PERSON IN A POSITION TO
KNOW, I LEARNED THAT A SMALL
GROUP OF COMMUNISTS DICTATE WHAT

Figure 11. Page from draft of Still's speech for Mount St. Mary's College,
1949. Courtesy of William Grant Still Music.

Figure 12. Still and Arvey at work. Courtesy of William Grant Still Music.

affects our perception of her position. From the days of Still's earliest
successes as Varèse's protégé in New York's modernist circles, it seems
that virtually everyone who knew him or knew of him or his work had
an agenda for him that turned on racial difference. So did Still himself; so did the critics (see the introduction and "'Harlem Renaissance
Man' Revisited"); so did both Forsythe and Arvey; and so do we. It is
easy but not very enlightening to blame her for those decisions by Still
that seem to go against the grain in one way or another. Most of these
were set forth by Still in typescripts that preceded his arrival in Los
Angeles. Class distinctions of various kinds are also an underlying issue.
The concert music and operas Still composed, although intended to
have broad listener appeal, were intended for performing organizations
and venues (mainly symphony orchestras and opera houses) that drew
middle-class, largely white audiences. Moreover, the quiet lifestyle
chosen by Still and protected by Arvey served to reinforce the "peculiar
isolation from [his] race" that Forsythe had noted in 1930, years before
Arvey and Still married.

Gender issues likewise play a role in our evaluation of this complex relationship. The formulation of aesthetic distinctions by the modernists that served eventually to marginalize Still's work bears an uncanny resemblance to the process by which women, too, were marginalized; misogyny was a significant aspect of the aesthetic approach of the male American modernists of the 1920s.[58] If Arvey can be blamed for Still's aesthetic decisions, then the modernists' hostility toward Still can be explained away on quasi-"objective" grounds unrelated, on the surface, to these tricky issues of race and class. From another direction, theorists of black culture, specifically including writers on the blues, have tended to formulate their ideas in masculinist terms, making it easy to avoid the gender-related questions that are important to understanding Arvey's role in Still's life and career.[59] Both of these approaches may help explain Arvey's position as a lightning rod for attacks really aimed at Still, attacks that obscure both Still's thought and Arvey's. That these have not yet been addressed is illustrated by the treatment of her *In One Lifetime* by its editors as a book on Still rather than one on Still and Arvey, resulting in both the deletion of material that describes her development and the mishandling of other materials. The recent bio-bibliography of Still includes a listing of "Writings by William Grant Still and Verna Arvey." Only thirty-four of the 168 articles she published after leaving school are included; while many of these do not relate to Still, there is no indication in the headnote that the list is a selective one.[60]

One might think fruitfully about Arvey in terms suggested by Bonnie G. Smith's article, "Historiography, Objectivity, and the Case of the Abusive Widow," in which a "consistent pattern of diatribes" is shown, aimed at a series of widows of literary figures who either "managed a dead husband's reputation, edited his work, or claimed an independent intellectual status for herself." Smith discusses in detail numerous attacks by scholars on the reputation of Athénais Mialeret-Michelet, the widow of the French historian Jules Michelet. She concludes that while Mialeret-Michelet was inferior to her spouse as an author and scholar, the attacks on her have been so extreme as to suggest some other underlying issue, one she finds to be misogyny. "Wrapped in the mantle of science and impartiality, the saga of Michelet mutilated by his widow and rescued by heroic researchers is a melodrama whose psychological dimensions we should begin attending to, if only to understand the world of history better."[61] In Arvey's case, it would seem desirable to avoid complicity in the male modernist composers' virtually automatic anti-woman rhetoric, a reaction against the prevailing characterization of music as an effeminate occupation in the world of middle-class whites.[62] Arvey, after all, had established a local reputation as a performer, writer, and advocate of contemporary music; she had been invited to teach in New York City as a result of her presentations of unfamiliar music. These things she either gave up or placed at Still's disposal.

If many of the things for which Arvey is held accountable really reflect Still's choices that may have been contradictory to the expectations of his friends and supporters, then she has been unfairly blamed for carrying out his wishes. Arvey often stated that she regarded their professional relationship as a partnership, a position that may have helped her become a target. It is clear from the record that Still, a major creative force, was in fact dominant. If for no other reason than her constant presence from 1934 on, it is important to consider what she brought to the relationship, and how the relationship changed them both.

As in the case of the "abusive widow," Arvey was indeed a talent far inferior to Still. If she became, especially after 1949, his political voice, she also represented his artistic and political wishes faithfully in the years that preceded the production of *Troubled Island,* that is, from 1934. Her activity as a gatekeeper for him, protecting his composition time, was something he clearly welcomed. But the isolation that eventually resulted may have created a more destructive situation than necessary, seen best in their mutual difficulty with the Black Arts movement and other political developments of the 1960s. Even before that, Arvey was the writer of his intemperate and uncharacteristic anticommunist speech and must bear that responsibility, while Still was responsible for delegating his political agency to her and for reading her words in public. Yet Still's aesthetic judgments about his music were always his own, including those on which the latter part of his career is based. I am convinced that Still's concern over the representation of Africa and African Americans in his music, and therefore his decisions about what to compose and how, antedated his relationship with Arvey, and that he explicitly retained aesthetic control over his artistic decisions. Recognizing that his artistic judgment was set, it was Arvey who accepted it as absolute and gave up her own personality in service to Still and to his work. Very likely she was the one who attempted to take on the burden of racial resentment, thus freeing Still to continue creating but assuming for herself an unbearable emotional burden. The relentless poverty that was their lot after World War II must have contributed to her alienation as well. This, along with her unconscious resentment at having submerged her identity so fully in his, could well explain the anger of her later writing. If Still's position as an African American brought him unusual challenges and set him a path demanding extraordinary resourcefulness, and if he chose solutions that raise their own questions, we are better served by addressing these issues directly rather than by blaming Arvey.

To conclude, it is clear that Arvey began with an artistic persona of her own, however fragile it turned out to be. Early on, one can see emerging a mix of talent, energy, chutzpah, and self-doubt. Her broad interests represented something of a Los Angeles version of the "new," less fiercely grounded in rebellion against the nineteenth-century musical canon than we have come to expect elsewhere, more receptive to the work of "others," including Still, Forsythe, and herself. Later on there appears the weakness that resulted from submerging herself in the work first of Forsythe, then of Still; the suspicion that developed from her own distance and the exclusion and subordination of her own creative energy; the defensiveness that grew from the ugly incidents that went along with her racially mixed marriage; the narrowness of view that allowed her to perceive the indifference or opposition that was Still's lot as a pioneer as a communist plot. To return to the initial query about what Arvey brought to her relationship with Still, it would seem that her early eclecticism was more compatible with Still's ideas and his music than was the "new" in New York. She brought competence in handling his affairs, sympathy with his political views, an interest in dance and theater, energy and enthusiasm and willingness to subordinate herself to his needs. If anything, she served him too well. Whether she deflected Still from his purpose or facilitated his chosen path seems to be a judgment that depends on the observer's interpretation and perhaps on what part of Still's career is being considered, at least for now.

APPENDIX
DISMAL SWAMP [63]

[Forsythe's text, suppressed]

> My heart pierces the thick pulpy wall of your body
> To be caught in the delicately spun web of your spirit,

And drawn deeply into a core beyond the world, where
Resonantly a strong voice sounds for me your final Truth.

[Arvey's alternate text, as published:]

Oh, swamp! your gloomy surface strikes me cold
Your sombre stumps no joy awake
Yet beyond your rotting, odorous mould
Strange charm greets those who penetrate.

No longer dismal, swamp!
Wild ferns, green moss, small twigs a-spin
Your beauty acrid; verdure damp
What joy for those who gaze within! [64]

THE BLACK MAN DANCES

[Forsythe's texts for each of the four movements; this entire piece was
not published or performed.]

In the night the young man's flute is a shadow
Trailing from the spirit of his lost love.
Deep in the jungle; gloomed darkly in his song,
Slowly dances the heart of the lonely lover.

Sharp red lights crackle in the [jungle],
Dancing to the pounding of feet.
The poignant slowness of a hidden sorrow
Slows, once, the clear brightness of rhythm.

Their feet are leaves from an autumn tree,
They float, O Jazz River, on your bosom,
The piano swells thru smoke and gin,
The cabaret walls stand like a levee.

"Strut it, sistuhs an' brothuhs, Rent man on de way!"
Shout it voices, shoulders, hips . . .
Blacks and browns, clap hands and shout:
"Shout it sistuhs an' brothuhs, Rent man on de way!"

NOTES

1. The program she reviewed was a Saturday Morning Musicale given by
Adolf Tandler's Little Symphony on January 9, 1926, of music by Bach, Sibelius,
and Cowell. Two months earlier, on October 22, 1925, Tandler and his orchestra had participated in the first concert of Henry Cowell's New Music Society,
which was presented in Los Angeles. Rita Mead, *Henry Cowell's New Music*

1925–1936: The Society, the Music Editions, and the Recordings (Ann Arbor: UMI Research Press, 1981), chap. 3, "The New Music Society," 31–49. That program, which both Arvey and Forsythe probably attended, consisted of Dane Rudhyar, "Surge of Fire"; Varèse, "Octandre"; Ruggles, "Angels"; and Schoenberg, "Sechs kleine Klavierstücke."

2. Los Angeles before the famous émigrés from Hitler had its own style of modernism, described for music in Catherine Parsons Smith and C. S. Richardson, *Mary Carr Moore, American Composer* (Ann Arbor: University of Michigan Press, 1978). See especially chap. 12, "The First Los Angeles School," and chapters 17–19, "The Federal Music Project," "The Ultra-Moderns," and "Musical Americanism." For a more recent approach that involves art and architecture, see Paul J. Karlstrom, ed., *On the Edge of America: California Modernist Art 1900–1950* (Berkeley and Los Angeles: University of California Press, 1996).

3. Jon Michael Spencer, "An Introduction to William Grant Still," in Spencer, *Reader,* 1–60. In "William Grant Still: Eclectic Religionist," *Theomusicology: A Special Issue of Black Sacred Music: A Journal of Theomusicology* 3, no. 1 (Spring 1994): 135–156, Spencer considers Arvey and Still's interest in spiritualism. Spencer was unaware of Forsythe's presence when he wrote these essays, and so did not speculate on Forsythe's connection with Still or Arvey.

4. Arvey, *IOL.* Little of the vital young adult is suggested in this infelicitous book. In the editing of the book, the few clues that might have illuminated her character and her pre-Still career were removed, along with considerable repetition. In an interview with Lance Bowling, April 3, 1987, Arvey described how her book had been edited. Most striking, she had prepared a long list of the prominent figures in music, film, and theater she had interviewed, going back to her high school years. In the published book, the list becomes a disproportionately long appendix entitled "Who's Who in the Life of William Grant Still," with new annotations that ignore both Still and Arvey. Arvey told Bowling: "That section at the end, you know, where I told about some of the people that I'd interviewed, . . . when the man came to write his notes, the explanatory notes, he said that all these people were known to William Grant Still. Well, they weren't, because I wrote those interviews before he came out here. . . . We didn't even see the galley proofs for that, you know."

For one critical reaction, see D. Antoinette Handy's negative review in *AM* 5, no. 4 (1987): 456–458.

5. Interviews with Carlton Moss, the author of the short story on which *Blue Steel* is based, and Harry Hay, an early associate of Forsythe and Arvey.

6. Donald Dorr, "Chosen Image: The Afro-American Vision in the Operas of William Grant Still," *Opera Quarterly* 4, no. 2 (Summer 1986): 1–23.

7. See below, Harold Bruce Forsythe, "William Grant Still: A Study in Contradictions," n. 16.

8. Verna Arvey, "Time for the Old Ox," typescript, p. 88, Still-Arvey Papers, an early version of her memoir. This and several other quotations below were cut from *In One Lifetime.* (See n. 4.)

9. "Commencement memories," Arvey, Scrapbook #49, Still-Arvey Papers. In 1926 the campus of the University of California–Southern Branch was still on Vermont Avenue, although construction on the present Westwood campus

was beginning. Students who wanted to study music theory and history or enroll for applied lessons studied across the street at the California Christian College (later Chapman College). The University of Southern California, a private institution, would have been beyond Arvey's financial reach.

10. Later scrapbooks, now at WGSM, reflect her increasing interest in race and politics.

11. Arvey's letter was addressed to a Chicago theater manager/film distributor. For information on Jacob Arvey, see Milton L. Rakove, *Don't Make No Waves, Don't Back No Losers: An Insider's Analysis of the Daley Machine* (Bloomington: Indiana University Press, 1975), 112–113, 144–145. Alex Gottfried, *Boss Cermak of Chicago* (Seattle: University of Washington Press, 1962), describes Jacob Arvey's 1923 role in the shady financial dealings of Chicago machine politics.

12. "Present Day Musical Films and How They Are Possible," *Etude* (January 1931): 16–18, 61, 72.

13. These were, respectively, Victor Baravalle, Martin Broones, Arthur Kay, and Heinz Roemheld. Her article was featured in a two-page spread with photos of the individuals interviewed.

14. See column by Arthur Corey, *American Dancer,* November 1933.

15. Ruth Eleanor Howard, "Dancing in Southern California: Terpsichorean Los Angeles Takes Second Place Only to New York," in Bruno David Ussher, ed., *Who's Who in Music and Dance in Southern California* (Hollywood: Bureau of Musical Research, 1933), 52–53. Among those with whom Arvey was associated are Ernest Belcher, Melissa Blake, Rosa Buruel, Waldeen Falkenstein, Eleanore Flaig, Norma Gould, Michio Ito, Teru Izumida, Dorothy Lyndall, Manual Perez, Charles Teske, Bertha Wardell, and Charles Zemach. Belcher, Falkenstein, Flaig, Gould, Lyndall, Perez, Teske, Wagner, and Zemach are listed in Ussher. For more on dance in Los Angeles between the wars, see Naima Prevots, *Dancing in the Sun: Hollywood Choreographers, 1915–1937* (Ann Arbor: UMI Research Press, 1987).

16. Verna Arvey, "Trio: Music for Dancers," *American Dancer,* January 1933.

17. Verna Arvey, *Choreographic Music: Music for the Dance* (New York: E. P. Dutton, 1941), 433, end of chap. 29, the end of the text.

18. Bowling-Arvey Interview, 1987, p. 4. Arvey's younger sister, Dolly, remembered little music in the household, however.

19. Ussher, *Who's Who in Music and Dance,* 188. The entry in full: "Eachus, Ann J. Pianiste, Teacher; b. Duarte, Calif.; studied exclusively w. Thilo Becker; asst. teacher w. Thilo Becker many yrs; teacher of Marguerite Bitter, Margaretha Lohman, Bernice Morrison. Add.: 310 S. Hoover St., Los Angeles." Thilo Becker, a German-trained pianist of Australian origin, was the premier piano teacher in southern California from the turn of the century; his students included Paloma Schramm and Olga Steeb. There is no direct evidence as to when Arvey stopped studying. In 1932 she gave a recital at Eachus's studio.

20. *American Dancer,* June 1932. Review of an evening of dance by the Flaig group, signed "O.S.F." Arvey Scrapbook.

21. August 30, 1933. "Listening In with Ben Gross." The clipping is in

Arvey's scrapbook. In response to Arvey's inquiry, Gershwin wrote that the tempos were too slow.

22. Undated letter, Still to Arvey, Still-Arvey Papers. The return address is 408 Manhattan Avenue, New York City.

23. "Time for the Old Ox," 91. She may have been referring to Forsythe.

24. Forsythe to Arvey, March 15, 1934, Forsythe Papers. This is from one of two letters bearing the same date.

25. See my article "Athena at the Manuscript Club: Reflections on John Cage and Mary Carr Moore," *Musical Quarterly* 79, no. 2 (1995): 351–367. Hay is now an important informant for me and for John Cage's biographer, Frans Van Rossum.

26. She had expected to give a recital with Benjamin Zemach, a dancer with whom she had worked in Los Angeles. Zemach backed out at the last minute, but Arvey went through with the concert anyway. According to her typewritten memoir, the backing and filling that went on before the concert—she rejected the theater booked for her initially by the Mexican government because the stage was too small to accommodate the anticipated dancer—put off her sponsors; neither the composers associated with the Conservatory nor the appropriate government officials actually attended the performance. "The govt officials were conspicuous by their absence, for Chavez, out of pique or something else, had called a 'junta' at which they all had to be present elsewhere." Typescript from notebook "Verna Arvey's scribblings from her notebook of subjects for future writings," courtesy WGSM.

27. The program, as given in Los Angeles, November 4, 1934, The Dance Theater, Norma Gould Studios, 118 North Larchmont:

Giga from Sonata in D	Galuppi
Minuet in D	Bach
Danza Indigena Mexicana No. 2	Rolon
The Dances of King David	Castelnuovo-Tedesco
(Hebraic Rhapsody on Traditional Themes)	

a. Violento ed impetuoso	e. Rude e ben ritmato
b. Ieratico	f. Malinconico e supplichevole
c. Rapido e selvaggiog.	g. Allegro Guerriero
d. Lento e sognante	

Intermission	
Norwegian Dance	Neupert
Trois Ecossaises	Chopin
Minuet (from Sonatine)	Ravel
Rigaudon	Ravel
Wiener-Tänze No. 2	Friedman-Gaertner
Two Spanish Epigrams	Arvey
Waltz	
Cockfight	
Polka	Smetana
Two Dances from La Guiablesse	Still
Brazilian Dance (Corcovado)	Milhaud
St. Louis Blues	Handy-Bloom-Lawrence

28. *Los Angeles Evening Herald and Express,* October 23, 1934.

29. *Rob Wagner's Script* (Beverly Hills, Calif.), November 10, 1934. A letter, this one from Forsythe, sheds some light too:

I cannot forego the pleasure of telling you briefly how much I enjoyed your recital. But strangely, Verna, I still think that you played that night at Eachus' better than ever before or since. You were possessed that night. Last evening I'll be darned if once or twice you didn't actually act as if you were indifferent to audience and music! . . . I just couldn't . . . forbear to mention Ravel and the minuet. This is exquisite music, and it was exquisitely performed. By far the high water mark of the program. . . . It was a beautiful moment, for once more your potential ability was made known to me. . . . Of course you played other things well too. . . . I thought the 2nd Guiablesse dance delicately done, and that amusing Brazilian Dance! and the opening Galuppi . . . intelligent, reserved, innately well bred.

. . . [Y]ears from now I'll be expounding the art of Verna Arvey and bragging that on page 344 of Frailest Leaves is a swell description of her approach to music. HBF

30. Letter, Cowell to Dear Miss Arvey, February 9, 1935, Still-Arvey Papers. The papers he listed whose critics were present included the *Musical Courier, Musical America,* and *Musical Leader* as well as *Trend, Nation, New Republic, Daily Worker,* and *New Masses.*

31. Postcard, Cowell to Arvey, Still-Arvey Papers. Unfortunately, there is no record of this event in the archives of the New School. I am grateful to Margaret Rose, Archivist/librarian, for searching the records in my behalf.

32. Hedi Korngold Katz, b. ca. 1890, Budapest, d. December 7, 1960. Katz, a violinist, graduated from the Royal Academy of Music, Vienna, and studied in London and Berlin. According to her obituary notice (*New York Times,* December 8, 1960), she was first violinist of the Symphony Orchestra of The Hague from 1919 to 1923, when she came to the United States. She founded the music school of the Henry Street Settlement in New York in 1927 and was director for eight years; later she helped found two other music schools in New York City.

33. Letter, Mrs. Hedi Katz, director, The Music School of the Henry Street Settlement, NYC, to Miss Verna Arvey, Los Angeles, December 10, 1934, Still-Arvey Papers.

34. Letter, Artie Mason Carter to Verna Arvey, August 12, 1935, Still-Arvey Papers.

35. Letter, August 16, 1935, letterhead "Charles E. Pemberton, Mus.M., University of Southern California / Private Studio," to "My dear Miss Arvey," Still-Arvey Papers.

36. Further information from pp. 248–249, incomplete typed memoir in Still-Arvey Papers. Rogers later performed *The Book of the Hanging Gardens* at an Evenings on the Roof concert.

37. High school commencement brochure, Still-Arvey Papers.

38. See quotations in "An Unknown 'New Negro,'" above.

39. An earlier version exists in the Forsythe Papers.

40. Please see "'Dean of Afro-American Composers' or 'Harlem Renaissance Man,'" "An Unknown 'New Negro,'" and Forsythe's "A Study in Contradictions," elsewhere in this volume.

41. Letter, Forsythe to Arvey, March 15, 1934, one of two bearing this date, Forsythe Papers.

42. This and other quotations from Arvey's letters to Forsythe appear in several pages of such quotations at WGSM. She must have excerpted them later from carbons she kept of her letters to him. None of her letters to Forsythe survive.

43. The example she chose to illustrate one of these "nuggets" was her experience of interviewing Francis Joseph Hickson, director of an otherwise unidentified experimental little theater. Hickson gave her a pattern for the development of a drama; she reports, "Years later, when I began to write libretti for my husband's operas, these simple precepts helped in the formation of our ideas."

> Act i: The characters and situation are presented.
>
> Act ii: The conflict develops and is left unresolved at the end of the act.
>
> Act iii: The characters unravel their difficulties and arrive at a satisfying conclusion.

44. Eleanora Flaig, quoted in "Time for the Old Ox," 94, Still-Arvey Papers.

45. Letter, Harry Hay to the author, March 19, 1994. Hay returned to Los Angeles ca. 1950. Falkenstein and Izumida were dancers whose recitals Arvey had accompanied on several occasions.

46. Carl Van Vechten letters, JWJ. There are no pre-1940 letters from Van Vechten to Arvey or Still in the Still-Arvey Papers.

47. See "Finding His Voice," above.

48. Letter, Arvey to Langston Hughes, n.d., Langston Hughes papers, JWJ. The letter is written on Arvey's own letterhead, and includes a copy of a program dated November 21, 1937. It may have been written after Still filed for divorce in May 1938, however; the filing received front-page treatment in the *Pittsburgh Courier*.

49. Typescript, undated autobiography of Still, p. 212, Still-Arvey Papers. Pages 11–151 are missing.

50. Several boxes containing dozens of scrapbooks on these two topics alone are at WGSM.

51. MS autobiography, Still-Arvey Papers.

52. Verna Arvey, "Memo for Musicologists," reprinted in *Fusion 2*, 21–25. To judge from the citation in the *Bio-Bibliography* (A30), which quotes a sentence reproduced in the quotation here, it is probably an expansion of Arvey's "Afro-American Music Memo," *Music Journal* 27 (November 1969): 36, 68. Arvey goes on to discuss Dvořák's use of "national American melodies" in the symphony *From the New World,* in her view strongly influenced by the singing of "Plantation songs and Hoe-downs" by Harry T. Burleigh.

53. Although the original story seems to have called for an appearance by the Virgin, who shows the two men the way to safety, she does not appear in the opera.

54. Postcard, Still to Langston Hughes, December 16, 1935, JWJ.

55. Still to Bontemps, 1939, Still-Arvey Papers. For details of the Chapin collaboration, see Wayne D. Shirley, "William Grant Still's Choral Ballad *And They Lynched Him on a Tree,*" AM 12 (Winter 1994): 425–461.

56. Carbon copy, letter, September 20, 1949, WGS to Howard Taubman, Still-Arvey Papers.

57. "Music in Films, a Symposium of Composers," *Films* 1, no. 4 (Winter 1940): 5–18.

58. Catherine Parsons Smith, "'A Distinguishing Virility': On Feminism and Modernism in American Concert Music," in Susan Cook and Judith Tsou, eds., *Cecilia Reclaimed: Essays on Gender and Music* (Urbana: University of Illinois Press, 1994). Literary critics have documented this even more fully. See, for example, Sandra M. Gilbert and Susan Gubar, *No Man's Land: The Place of the Woman Writer in the Twentieth Century,* vol. 1, *The War of the Words* (New Haven: Yale University Press, 1987).

59. See, for example, Imamu Amiri Baraka, *Blues People: Negro Music in White America* (New York: William Morrow, 1963); Albert Murray, *The Hero and the Blues* (1973; New York: Vintage Books, 1995); Paul Oliver, *Blues Fell this Morning,* 2d ed. (Cambridge: Cambridge University Press, 1990).

60. *Bio-Bibliography.* The number 168 is Judith Anne Still's count of her mother's work.

61. Bonnie G. Smith, "Historiography, Objectivity, and the Case of the Abusive Widow," in Ann-Louise Shapiro, ed., *Feminists Revision History* (New Brunswick, N.J.: Rutgers University Press, 1994), 24–46.

62. See Smith, "'A Distinguishing Virility.'"

63. Published by New Music Edition.

64. Forsythe's poem is attached to the draft score of *Dismal Swamp* in the Still-Arvey Papers; Arvey's appears in the published score (1937).

"Harlem Renaissance Man" Revisited

The Politics of Race and Class in Still's Late Career

Still reached his artistic maturity as a versatile and innovative commercial musician and composer of concert music in Harlem in the 1920s. He sought to break down race-based limitations on the mixing of African American and European techniques, forms, and styles through the use of blues-based harmonic progressions, melodic turns, forms, and sometimes rhythms in his symphonic music as well as to blur class-based boundaries between the "popular" and the "serious." Unlike his white modernist colleagues, Still had nothing to gain and everything to lose by using the exclusionary, modernist creative languages such as serialism or atonality. His personal interest lay with integration into the larger society and the larger musical language—in becoming, as he said, "another American voice" whose work confounded both race- and class-based distinctions. His 1934 move to Los Angeles now appears to be an act of self-exile, one that allowed him to work out his own highly individual creative position—a position that continues to problematize his contribution to American music for both white and black observers. By leaving New York City, he distanced himself psychologically as well as geographically from the interconnected aesthetics and politics of white modernist composers and black intellectuals of the Harlem Renaissance. He repudiated essentialist racial distinctions but embraced and even exploited cultural difference in his art. In pursuing his own creative imperative, he was forced throughout his career to untangle and then reweave in his music (as in his life) many strands of American culture, strands involving race and musical genre, class differences and political loyalties, gender and geography.

Over a period of a quarter century, his audience grew steadily. Yet his music often drew ambivalent critical responses that were permeated with stereotypically race-based expectations. The 1949 production of *Troubled Island* by the New York City Opera, a case in point, formed the apogee of Still's rise as a composer. But after that production, he came to believe that he was the target of a communist conspiracy. Here I want to discuss Still's outspoken anticommunism. Far from being a frivolous stance easily dismissed as personal paranoia, I propose that Still's anticommunism and his acceptance of what I will call the "plot theory" are closely connected to the race-based critical expectations often assigned to his music across his career. I make no attempt to explain or justify Still's public denunciations of other individuals; rather, I limit myself to an attempt to understand the political position that lay behind his unfortunate public statements.

Before addressing the questions about how it was that Still came to subscribe to a communist-inspired conspiracy theory and participate in the anticommunist movement, it is necessary to say a few things about Still's politics, his relationship to communism, and the anticommunist movement itself. Controversy over communism and the Communist party was lively and pervasive in the 1920s, 1930s, and 1940s. Despite the monumental indifference to matters political ascribed to him by his friends, Still could hardly have avoided contact with creative artists who were both politically involved and interested in communism in his New York years.[1] Carlton Moss describes dining with Still at the Harlem YMCA, "the only decent place to eat in Harlem" and a major gathering place where political discussions must have swirled around him; he could scarcely have shut them all out.[2] In the late 1920s and 1930s, Still worked with at least two writers who were close to the party. One of them was Moss, who supplied the short story on which Still's first opera, *Blue Steel,* is based; the other was Langston Hughes, author of the libretto for *Troubled Island.* Still welcomed the opportunity to compose these operas, both on black subjects. He collaborated amicably enough with Hughes on the project until Hughes left for the Spanish Civil War. He was even interested enough to put his name on two Popular Front-style letters supporting the Spanish Civil War, a liberal cause that was co-opted by the Soviets.[3] Given the disruption of Harlem society in the course of the Great Depression of the 1930s, it is possible that he shared at least a passing interest in communism with a good many Americans, including many modernist composers. In *A History of Musical Americanism*, Barbara Zuck gives a long-accepted explanation for this passing interest: "The Communist Party had an important sociopolitical function at this time in its organized agitation against groups fostering discrimination and racial hatred. Thus, political leftism in the 1930s simply became a common framework in which the American intelligentsia expressed their idealism and humanitarianism."[4] Still's anticommunism flies in the face of this long-accepted explanation.

From the first public performances of his works in new music concerts in the 1920s, critics sought to pinpoint musical indications of Still's racial identity. They frequently evaluated his work in terms of their success at finding what they understood to be such features. In early 1925, for example, the *New York Times* critic Olin Downes (not himself a modernist) scolded Still for experimenting with modernist effects in *From the Land of Dreams*, thus by implication abandoning Downes's expectations: "Is Mr. Still unaware that the cheapest melody in the revues he has orchestrated has more reality and inspiration in it than the curious noises he has manufactured?"[5] (Still followed *From the Land of Dreams* a year later with *Levee Land*, a self-styled "stunt" that brought the blues singer Florence Mills to the concert stage, creating a sensation in which his point remained unremarked.) Downes's expectations of "exotic folksong and popular rhythms" in his review of the 1949 production of *Troubled Island* is a much later expression of the same practice.[6] It would seem that the challenge of composing concert music that was "recognizably Negroid" and at the same time avoided popular and commercial stereotypes was one reason Still turned away from his short-lived "modernist" phase of the early 1920s to focus on making his already-present "racial" expression more obvious. Still's self-characterized "racial" period lasted until 1932, but he continued to write pieces with "racial" features long after that date.[7]

The first performances of the major works from Still's racial period, the *Afro-American Symphony* and the ballet *Sahdji*, took place in 1930 and 1931. These performances, which were given in Rochester, were covered by critics whose comments also reflected race-based expectations. For example, Emanuel Balaban's report to *Modern Music* (the "little magazine" of the musical modernists) on the premiere of the *Afro-American Symphony* rejected the idea that Still had composed an "acceptable" symphony, insisting instead that it was merely a "suite" and stressing the work's simplicity, sincerity, and use of "racial color," qualities safely attributable to an African American composer.

> William Grant Still's *Afro-American Symphony* would be more acceptable had he called it a suite. It is not cyclical nor symphonic in the accepted sense. Rather does it make use of dance forms. . . . The work is quite simple harmonically; in instrumental color typical of Still at his best. He derives extraordinary color with the scantiest of means, color that is essentially racial. Sincerity and naivete are among the most important elements in his work.[8]

Balaban's report was merely wrong and stereotype-laden. It did not contain the vituperation the same symphony attracted a few years later, when it was performed in New York City.

New York-based modernists wrote about the *Afro-American Symphony* in late 1935, after it was presented by the New York Philharmonic. Marc Blitzstein reviewed the 1935 performance for *Modern Music*. He attacked the symphony on ideological grounds, criticizing Still's "servility, . . . [his] willingness to debauch a true folk-lore for high-class concert-hall consumption," thus turning the *Afro-American Symphony* into something "vulgar."[9] The delay of four years between the Rochester premiere and the New York performance may have affected Blitzstein's reaction, as will be seen below in the discussion of the Composers' Collective. Soon after Blitzstein's diatribe, Aaron Copland wrote disdainfully of Still's music in general:

> William Grant Still began about twelve years ago as the composer of a somewhat esoteric music for voice and a few instruments. Since that time he has completely changed his musical speech, which has become almost popular in tone. He has a certain natural musicality and charm, but there is a marked leaning toward the sweetly saccharine that one should like to see eliminated.

And of a piece that Still had striven to make "modern":

> There is the "naive" kind [of American music] such as William Grant Still's . . . often based on the slushier side of jazz and mak[ing] a frank bid for popular appeal. . . . [O]ne can't help wishing that their musical content were more distinguished.[10]

These remarks by Copland long irked Still, for their effect was to dismiss Still's efforts at crossing race- and class-related barriers of genre as merely profit oriented and sentimental.[11]

In between the symphony's 1931 premiere and its first New York performance (1935), the Composers' Collective, affiliated with the Workers' Music League, an arm of the American Communist party, was formed by some of the New York modernists.[12] The collective's composers, including Blitzstein (the group's secretary), attempted to compose music that would appeal to the masses. (Still, who had used folk materials for years in his concert music, must have seen this as an attempt to reinvent his example, one that was not acknowledged by the composers of the collective.)[13] After the Composers' Collective's efforts to write new songs for workers to sing had ended in failure and the collective itself had dispersed in the late 1930s, folk song was adopted by the American Communist party as a means to promote its revolutionary ideas. A part of its Popular Front approach, the party's position coincided with wide interest in folk music and New Deal support for the arts.[14] Blitzstein's scathing attack may have been less a personal matter than an exercise in the application of party policy, uncritically borrowed from the Soviet approach to the folk musics of its various republics and not thought through in terms that fitted the racism of American society.[15] At about the same time, for example, Marian Anderson was attacked in the pages of *New Masses* for her recordings of spirituals that were "lacking the requisite rhythmic fire," "far too polite for comfort," and "castrated replicas of the original."[16] For Still, Blitzstein's and Copland's critical attacks in the pages of *Modern Music* constituted more attempts to circumscribe his creative voice and tell him how he ought to compose. They represented a pernicious old stereotype dressed in new, left-wing clothes. As a prominent African American, Still was seen by the party as an attractive potential recruit. His experience with the members of the Composers' Collective, however, may well have reinforced him in his decision to reject any overtures he may have received from the party.

In the early 1940s, many creative artists who had been drawn to communism as an expression of their "idealism and humanitarianism," in Zuck's words, became disillusioned and either left the party or ceased to cooperate with it. While some African Americans remained loyal to the party publicly, others became seriously disenchanted. The prominent Harlem Renaissance writer Claude McKay had articulated his objections in 1937. I quote them here as a likely statement of Still's position as well:

(1) I reject absolutely the idea of government by dictatorship, which is the pillar of political Communism.

(2) I am intellectually against the Jesuitical tactics of the Communists: (a) their professed conversion to the principles of Democracy . . . ; (b) their skulking behind the smoke screen of People's Front and Collective Security . . . ; (c) their criminal slandering and persecution of their opponents.[17]

Particularly relevant for Still, a steadfast integrationist, was McKay's view that, Popular Front and party claims to the contrary, the party really advocated black separatism: "Negro Nationalism in the United States . . . is the brain child of the American Communists and the real Negro nationalists are the Communists. They have advocated the creation of a separate Negro state within the American nation."[18] Along with his own experiences in the world of concert music, the position stated by McKay was at the heart of Still's anticommunism and of his plot theory as well.

The comments by Blitzstein and Copland marked a general change in the critical reception of Still's work at least from 1936, the end of the period when his music, though it often drew stereotyped critical responses, regularly attracted critical admiration as well. In the mid-1930s it was the modernists who rejected this music; by the mid-1940s the attitude had become more general. By 1946 Olin Downes had arrived at a formula for discussing Still's music that conflated the class-based genre barrier with the frankly racial one:

The composer's expression is diluted in a way that deprives it of racial essence. . . . Years ago we heard music by Mr. Still, of a exoticism and imagination that recompensed considerably for the immaturity of its workmanship. . . . [Now, Still] appears to have smoothed out as a composer— conventionalized. This is unfortunate. It is to be hoped that in later scores Mr. Still will return to what hide-bound academicians might call the original error of his ways.[19]

Troubled Island was premiered in 1949, eight years after its completion and eight years after the campaign for a production began. Following a rejection from the Metropolitan Opera, the campaign paused during the early years of World War II and then centered on the infant New York City Center for Music and Drama, which organized its own opera company not long after the war ended. It became a liberal cause célèbre in

which librettist Langston Hughes's high visibility on the left played a
role, as did Eleanor Roosevelt and New York's Mayor Fiorello La
Guardia. In 1944 Still wrote about the opera to Leopold Stokowski,
who had conducted several of Still's orchestral scores and was in his first
year as conductor of the New York City Symphony, a one-year-old arm
of the City Center for Music and Drama. Stokowski was enthusiastic,
leading Still to expect a concert performance in the 1944–1945 season,
to be followed by a fully staged production the following year.[20] That
plan ended because Stokowski's association with the symphony lasted
only one season; he left without conducting an opera. Nevertheless,
the company continued to indicate an interest in producing the opera.
Newbold Morris, board chairman of the City Center of Music and
Drama, Inc., wrote to contributors to a "Troubled Island Fund" on
July 8, 1946:

> I am writing to advise you that since Leopold Stokowski has left the City
> Center, we have recommended that this great opera by William Grant Still be
> included in the regular repertory of the New York City Opera Company dur-
> ing the 1946–1947 season. Mr. Halász, director of the Opera Company,
> feels that this production should be presented because we have not yet given
> to the public the work of an American composer.

This was not the first plan for producing the opera, as the next paragraph suggests:

> It is felt that this method of presentation would be a distinct advantage over
> our original idea of producing the opera all by itself. It will give an opportu-
> nity to music critics and music lovers to hear this work and then, of course,
> if the response is what we hope it will be and impressive financial interests
> are attracted to it, it might be possible to send it on tour throughout the
> country.[21]

More delays and a further lowering of expectations ensued.[22] There was
plenty of time for both composer (Still) and librettist (Hughes) to get
discouraged and grow suspicious at the convoluted and seemingly endless process. Toward the end of this difficult period, Stokowski's own
negative experience with the City Center may have encouraged Still's
suspicions: "My experience with them was far from good. Confiden-
tially, I would be careful with them if I were you."[23] Through the years
of waiting, Still clung stubbornly to his faith that the intrinsic quality of
his work would eventually overcome the obstacles. The hoped-for result
would not only be a production of *Troubled Island* but also a fundamental breakthrough in race relations in America—an aspiration he

had once attached to the *Afro-American Symphony*. When he was finally sure that the opera would be produced, he wrote, "I pray that the opera will be done successfully. Fears arise. I've waited thirty-seven years for it. All is in God's hands."[24]

The opening night audience gave *Troubled Island* a prolonged ovation; Still took twenty bows. This memorable outpouring was offset by the critics' lukewarm reception. In particular, Olin Downes's review in the *New York Times* began by addressing Still's crossing of genres, starting with the opera's "cliches of Broadway and Hollywood" and complaining that "very little is new." Toward the end of the evening, in the market scene that opens the last act, Downes found a hint of the racial stereotype he had expected, a clear representation of "exotic folksong and popular rhythms." (Perhaps not coincidentally, the scene includes extraneous sexual byplay, which, also not coincidentally, Still removed in a later, unperformed revision described below.) Only in the small print did he grant Still's gift as a composer of opera who had created "a structure of considerable breadth and melodic curve." Other reviews in the white press followed Downes's model. Two additional performances, scheduled before the season began, did not change the critics' minds.[25] Returning to Los Angeles after the intoxicating experience of the premiere, Still anticipated Voice of America broadcasts of the dress rehearsal, which had been recorded for that purpose.[26] He also set about revisions in preparation for another production, for several possibilities had been mentioned.

Troubled Island is about the Haitian revolutionary Jean-Jacques Dessalines, who was murdered in 1806. In Act I, as the revolution is about to begin, Dessalines is treated as the hero-to-be. In Acts II and III, he is portrayed as the emperor of Haiti, debauched, illiterate, and unable to govern. Finally in Act IV he is murdered by his erstwhile followers; his first wife, abandoned in the years of debauchery, returns to sing a final aria over his body.

So convinced was Still that there would be further productions that he set about a revision that would give the denouement more weight, bringing the tragedy of the hero's high early aspirations and his subsequent destruction into more telling perspective. In the market scene that precedes the assassination, Still removed the lighthearted give-and-take

Example 7. Excerpt from the revised version of *Troubled Island,* Act IV, final scene, words added after the 1949 premiere performance at the New York City Opera. Underlying chords in the strings in an eighth note–dotted quarter pattern from measure 273 on are omitted from the piano-vocal score. Copyright 1976 by Southern Music Pub. Co., Inc. Reprinted by permission.

Example 7. (*continued*)

that had attracted Olin Downes's approval as suitably "exotic," deleting an exchange between a female fruit vendor and a fisherman of the chorus and substituting repetitions of text already sung for the excised words. The deleted text, sung by the fruit vendor and echoed by the chorus, includes this couplet:

Out of my way and let me pass!
All men's tongues are full of sass!

In the revised closing scene, Azelia (the abandoned first wife), comes upon Dessalines as he lies fatally wounded (but not, in this version, dead) from the assassins' attack. This is part of the text (supplied by Verna Arvey) that Still interpolated to follow Azelia's discovery of Dessalines:

> *[She kneels at Dessalines' side. Suddenly her face is frozen with the horror and pain of recognition. Dessalines stirs.]*
>
> AZELIA: Jean Jacques!
> DESSALINES: Azelia! They've all gone?
> AZELIA: They were never with you.
> DESSALINES: Only you remain.
> AZELIA: Yes, Jean Jacques.
> DESSALINES: And you forgive me?
> AZELIA: I love you.
>
> *[Dessalines dies.]*[27]

The text was added to a passage that was purely instrumental in the production.

Presently it became clear that none of Still's expectations for further performances and productions would be realized and that his opening night triumph had led to nothing. As his disappointment grew, he came to believe that the cause of these nonoutcomes lay with the unfair reviews by the New York critics, especially Downes, whom he had once counted as a supporter. The revised ending of *Troubled Island*, devised to enhance the power of the closing scene with a minimum of change, reflects his feelings. "They were never with you," one of the lines supplied by Arvey in this revised ending, takes on added meaning in the real-life context of fear and suspicion that had begun in the campaign to achieve a production.[28]

After the *Troubled Island* production, Still became increasingly withdrawn. A sense of preoccupation and distance from his fellows had been a characteristic of his demeanor even in 1930; in his later years, it was carried to an unhappy extreme. He believed, as does his daughter, Judith Anne Still, to this day, that a communist-inspired conspiracy produced the destructive reviews and robbed him of the recognition that was his due. She recalls from her childhood (age seven):

> My father returned from the New York production wrenched by disappointment. I remember how he looked in his long, charcoal grey overcoat and brown, wide-brimmed hat, wearily taking his suitcases out of our '36 Ford after we had brought him home from the airport. . . . He took out the little notebook in which he always jotted down notes when he did not have my

mother there to remember things for him, and he glanced through it. "Well, Verna," he said, "I just don't know. I just don't know what to say."[29]

She describes her father reading from the little notebook, telling of a pre-performance visit to his hotel room by the *Times* drama critic Howard Taubman. Taubman, she reports, warned Still that the white critics had decided "the colored boy has gone far enough" and that the production would be panned. An inquiry by a New York singer friend drew the reply, "You know we're only going to let just so many Negroes through."[30] She believes the notebook may survive, though it remains unlocated.[31] Judith Anne Still's often-repeated personal testimony, which should not be dismissed out of hand, and that of her parents remain the strongest evidence for a specific plot to deny Still an unqualified operatic success.

One may track the development of the plot theory in Still's diary in the months following the production. On first hearing the recording made by the State Department for foreign broadcast, he reacted nega-tively to what he had heard on musical, not political, grounds, perhaps reflecting a postproduction letdown: "June 14 . . . Got dubs of records. Disappointed. Halász did a very poor job as director. Winter's ama-teurish. Some others not satisfactory."[32] Later, after the Voice of Amer-ica recording had been broadcast in Paris and Brussels, the State Depart-ment recalled the recording and advised Still that it was "mauvais."[33] Stokowski's comment, "I am afraid there has been some intrigue going on against your *Troubled Island*," refers to this incident.[34] The plot theory appears full-blown in Still's diary in October 1949, some five months after the production: "Disquieting news re the persecution we are receiving from the Communists. Unfortunately we cannot tell people of this because they would not believe us. Only God can help us. I be-lieve He will."[35] Lumping the New York critics (especially Downes) with the modernists, Still wrote that he was "downcast over attitude of the so called 'musical intellectuals' toward my music."[36] By the follow-ing February, he concluded sadly, "I marvel on listening to the records of [*Troubled Island*] at the critics' reaction. But they were biased for sev-eral reasons. I hate to be forced to admit that racial prejudice entered into it."[37]

Still summed up his view about the coterie that opposed him in a let-ter to Howard Hanson that discussed the State Department's with-drawal of the recording from radio stations in Europe in August 1950: "Although I have recognized the fact that you, and I, and other Ameri-can composers have had strong opposition for years, this is the first *legal* evidence I have had, outside of a number of disparaging clippings written by members of the clicque [*sic*]." [38]

Still had started to speak out against communist exploitation of racial issues and recruitment of African Americans for the communist cause after the canceled production of 1946. To begin with, he published "Politics in Music" in a small southern California music periodical. After a slap at the "cerebral pseudo-music" of unnamed modernists who had, through intrigue, "done American music . . . a grave disservice," he distanced himself from the "many who subordinate their art to [communist] political propaganda," and named Paul Robeson and Earl Robinson as examples of the "many." He wrote of his own refusal to allow himself or his name "to be used indiscriminately by political leftwingers" and concluded, "I believe that most of us in the arts are liberal, but not Leftists. I believe that the American tradition itself is liberal. . . . Some Americans have chosen to make their liberality the servant of a foreign political ideology. . . . [S]uch a choice is not mine." In support of his argument, he made the point that his outspoken protest pieces from the early 1940s had been commissioned and performed under the current social and political order, without the need for a violent revolution to enable him to speak. He asserted that, contrary to party claims, he had artistic freedom under the current system: "I thought back to two of my own compositions which were strongest in protest against existing conditions (*And They Lynched Him on a Tree* and *Plain Chant for America*) and remembered that both of them were initiated by a member of what is called our capitalistic class, the poet Katherine Garrison Chapin." [39]

Three years later, he continued this theme in "Fifty Years of Progress in Music," a more widely distributed essay citing several African Americans (Harry T. Burleigh, Roland Hayes, Marian Anderson) who either had reversed or were helping to reverse the stereotype that "Negroes were talented only in folk or theatrical music." He wrote of the effort that white symphony conductors had to make to hire African American musicians in the face of rigidly segregated musicians' unions; of the one black impresario in the United States (M. H. Fleming of Salt Lake City); of the tremendous success and worldwide influence of jazz as opposed to the ban against black singers at the Metropolitan Opera and the continuing difficulty that African American composers of concert music had gaining recognition. Turning to his recent experiences with *Troubled*

Island, he described the even higher barriers faced by black composers when they undertook to get an opera produced. For the first time, he publicly attacked two white modernist composers as enforcers of a communist-inspired, aesthetically doctrinaire strategy with racist as well as political implications:

> It is a fact that there is in New York a powerful clique of white composers who exclude all others, white as well as colored. . . . It is interesting to know that Aaron Copland and Leonard Bernstein, the leaders of the clique, were also publicized in *Life* magazine's April 4, 1949, issue, in an expose of "Dupes and Fellow Travelers." The connection is all too obvious!
>
> Having refused to follow Leftist doctrines, certain colored and white composers have been opposed by this clique for many years. Among other things, the door to adequate recordings of our music—always a sore spot—has been closed to us. Thus the New York clique had made a totally unnecessary obstacle for many of us—an obstacle that has wider implications than the merely racial or personal.[40]

In 1951, Still was reported by the *Hollywood Citizen-News* as having asked to testify before the House Un-American Activities Committee.[41] The following year, he wrote at length to the *Arkansas Gazette,* not to name names this time, but to set forth his earnest conviction that the Communist party had no program to improve race relations in the United States and to cite evidence that the party had actually proposed (some years earlier) further segregation of the races as a solution.[42]

In May 1953, he read a potentially incendiary speech to the San Jose, California, Chamber of Commerce. This time he neither argued the communist position on race relations nor settled for naming a couple of people who had sold out to a foreign power or were part of a politically motivated music conspiracy. The typescript of his remarks is entitled "Communism in Music." Some excerpts:

> Although America has not been taken over by the Soviets in fact, it is true that Moscow has had a subtle but effective hand in our arts for many years. . . . [I]n no instance am I accusing any American citizen of being a Communist, because I am not in a position to say who carries a Party card and who does not. . . . I am able to mention a series of coincidences, backed up by printed documentation, and ask the reader to draw his own conclusions.

Still's list of those who furthered Moscow's "subtle but effective hand" is long, varied, and deserving of skepticism. Roy Harris is named for dedicating his *Fifth Symphony* to the Soviet Union; Aaron Copland, for allegedly being a member of twenty-eight communist-front groups. Also named are Leonard Bernstein, Serge Koussevitzky, Olin Downes, Marc

Blitzstein, Newbold Morris (board chairman of the New York City Opera), and Kurt Weill. For good luck, perhaps, he named some others "whose names appear on such lists [of un-Americans] regularly": Larry Adler, Dean Dixon, Morton Gould, Earl Robinson, Margaret Webster, Garson Kanin. Even his old friend Henry Cowell, whom both Still and Arvey had stuck by all through the San Quentin years, is mentioned.[43] In addition, Douglas Moore, Oscar Hammerstein II, Ira Gershwin, and Hanns Eisler are named, along with the sponsors of a concert of Eisler's music: Copland, Bernstein, David Diamond, Harris, Walter Piston, Roger Sessions, and Randall Thompson. On the other side, he gave a much shorter list of composers whose work had been intentionally shut out: Charles Wakefield Cadman, Deems Taylor, and Paul Creston were named as loyal white American composers. In addition, Still reported, "On one occasion, I was made so uncomfortable in a studio job that I resigned, only to have my place taken by a known Communist." At the same time, he emphasized that his primary concern was race-based:

> Here, a word must be said concerning the part played in all this by the racial angle. When the communists decided to take over America, they also decided that American Negroes would be their shock troops and lead a revolution for them. American Negroes have thus been under great pressure but, speaking in general terms, they have not as a whole fallen in with this plan. However, the pressure on them still continues, and any Negro leader who dares to think for himself is a target of special attention. So, both musically and racially, my work has been opposed.[44]

In reading the speech, Still omitted these sentences by Arvey: "In the final analysis, Party membership may be only a technicality. The big question is: to what extent have certain musicians used their talents and their positions to further the aims of Soviet Russia?" Though Still did not identify his informant, he added his story about Howard Taubman's preperformance visit and warning. He also remarked on Newbold Morris's role in the firing of László Halász, the music director who had chosen to produce *Troubled Island,* and (erroneously) the subsequent decision to produce a work by Kurt Weill, whom he added to his list of communists.[45] Neither Still nor Arvey changed their minds in later years; this speech, however, marks the end of Still's career as a public speaker on the issue of anticommunism.

One returns to the following overriding questions. Why did Still come to a conspiracy theory to explain the critical reception of his music (especially *Troubled Island*) and the lack of recordings of his music? After all, many an opera by an American composer has sunk into the unmarked depths after a few performances, certainly some that may not have deserved that fate.[46] Why the anticommunist position that laid the "failure" of *Troubled Island* on this doorstep and so soured both Still and Arvey toward much of the concert music establishment, especially considering that Still's concern with the racial issue is evident throughout? My purpose here is to understand how Still came to the conspiracy theory and to anticommunism, both of which are difficult to accept.

Other incidents, in conjunction with political developments, probably reinforced Still's perception of a pattern of communist-inspired racial persecution that he began to dwell on as the *Troubled Island* production developed. Noisy competition among political factions suffused the Hollywood film colony in the 1930s and 1940s. The rise to power of the leftist Screenwriters' Guild by 1940 was countered by the 1944 formation of the Motion Picture Alliance for the Preservation of American Ideals, organized by film producers to "combat what we regard as a growing menace within our own industry of Communists and to some degree Fascists."[47] After years of shrill political debate (fanned in part by the intransigently antiunion *Los Angeles Times*), the 1947 hearings on alleged communist influences in the Hollywood film colony may have predisposed Still toward his anticommunist position. It may have led him to wonder whether his treatment at the hands of Twentieth-Century Fox over *Stormy Weather* had been politically motivated. (In 1943, Still resigned from a lucrative studio contract, partly because he disapproved of the image of African Americans projected in *Stormy Weather*, the film he had been signed to work on and the "studio job" mentioned in the 1953 San Jose speech.)[48]

Circumstances surrounding the premiere of Still's choral ballad *And They Lynched Him on a Tree* in New York City in June 1940 may also have fostered Still's developing sense of distrust, even though (or even because) its positive critical reception showed no obvious sign of the pattern I have described in connection with the *Afro-American Symphony* and *Troubled Island*. Still learned a few days before the premiere that another new work calling for roughly similar performing forces, Roy Harris's *Challenge 1940*, would be performed at the same concert. Many years later, Arvey wondered aloud how Harris, once a member of the Composers' Collective, had managed to push his way onto this program and deflect some of the glory away from Still. The presence of Paul Robeson and of Earl Robinson's music, which Still knew about in advance, added to the surprise presence of Harris's music, may also have left Still feeling used by these leftist composers.[49] Still had been aware earlier of conductor Artur Rodzinski's concerns about programming so timely and controversial a text as Still's piece employed. He probably never knew, however, that Rodzinski had commissioned Harris for another new work that would focus on a more traditionally patriotic and therefore "safer" topic. Because he did not go East for the concert and it was not broadcast in Los Angeles, he was unaware of how negligible Harris's contribution actually was.

With *And They Lynched Him on a Tree,* premiered in New York City in 1940, not only Still's highest aspirations for his music but also his single strongest public expression in music about racial oppression had been, as both Arvey and Still viewed it later, co-opted at its premiere by the left. Still's absence from the performance may have bolstered a sense of helplessness in the shaping of distant events. He may even have attributed the warm critical reception his own work received to the presence of music by Robinson and Harris, both of them far to his left, on the program. The feeling of co-optation became increasingly uncomfortable, at least in hindsight, for a man who was convinced that the Communist party was cynically exploiting racial violence in the United States with no program or expectation of improving the situation.

Another incident that may have influenced Still's thinking about communism cannot be dated. Judith Anne Still reports an occasion when her father was invited to a meeting in an "elegant apartment" where he was promised support as a composer and urged to become a party member as some other prominent African American artists had done. Langston Hughes was in Los Angeles in 1939 to work with Still on *Troubled Island.* Judith Anne Still suggests that Hughes arranged such a meeting at that time. Whenever it happened, the result seemed to be to create suspicion rather than interest on Still's part. The coolness that developed between Still and Hughes, which became public shortly before the opera's 1949 premiere, resulted in part from Hughes's departure for the Spanish Civil War before the *Troubled Island* libretto was completed to Still's satisfaction, but it may well have fed off their increasing political differences as well.

The situation with the New York City Opera beyond Still's previously described negotiations may also have encouraged the plot theory. Newbold Morris, the official who was the liaison between the City of New York and the opera company, was heavily involved in politics and often a center of public controversy because of his position with the city.

Among the board members and those on the "Troubled Island [fund-raising] Committee" was Claire M. Reis, longtime administrator of the League of Composers. Though the league had commissioned Still and given him early performance opportunities, it was also the sponsor of the journal that had led the critical attack on his work, *Modern Music*. Reis, who functioned as secretary of the opera board and had been one of the original donors, appears to have favored board involvement in artistic decisions, something that appears in Martin Sokol's account of Halász's firing in 1951.[50] Divisions and politicking on the board were, apparently, well reported in the press, a situation that may have encouraged Still's dissatisfaction.

Around 1950, Still's income began to diminish. His fellowships (a Guggenheim, twice renewed, followed by a Rosenwald, renewed once) had long since run out. Commissions for new works and opportunities for commercial work likewise dwindled. He ascribed the problem to the conspiracy: "Funny that people think we have money when on the one hand I am denied employment in the movie studios as a composer, and on the other the intellectual & Communist musical people (who are in control) keep us from getting recordings and performances. They would have me starve."[51]

None of the concerns I have mentioned—the stereotyping of his concert music throughout his career, the critical treatment of the *Afro-American Symphony*, the performance circumstances of *And They Lynched Him on a Tree*, the controversy over the music for *Stormy Weather*, the politicization of the New York City Opera, disappointment over the curtailed European broadcasts of *Troubled Island* as well as its critical reception in New York, even the loss of paying work—seems to be serious enough to warrant Still's increasing suspicion and his conversion to the communist plot theory in itself, let alone his public espousal of these positions. Yet, taken together, and given the atmosphere of mystification and manipulation that surrounded the activity of the party,[52] one can see why someone in Still's position might well have discerned a pattern of obstructionism. Certainly one can recognize the desperation and the suggestion of paranoia in Still's journal entries quoted above over the months following the production.

One may infer that Still's anticommunism was the end product of a line of reasoning that his experience as a composer of concert music led him to ascribe to his critics: he was an African American, and African Americans were by stereotyped assumption considered not capable of composing in elite "higher forms." Hence the evaluations by white critics and composers that he was not really composing in the "higher forms" at all but must be writing commercial music. If that was the line of reasoning that led him to attack stereotyped, race-based expectations of his music, the reasoning he apparently applied in arriving at his anti-communist position formed a parallel, equally weak syllogism: Still composed (for whatever reason) conservative, less dissonant music and was himself politically conservative. The composers of the "New York clique" wrote more dissonant music, and many of its members or associates had flirted with communism, perhaps even joined the party, and had certainly espoused more liberal politics than he. Therefore dissonant music was part of a communist plot to undermine American music, and critical attacks on his music were a part of this plot. One of the ugly aspects of the anticommunist movement around 1950 was that "communist" was sometimes understood as a code word for "Jewish" and/or "homosexual." The homophobic and anti-Semitic implications here problematize the Stills' position even further. Still's African American identity made him a very visible composer of concert music who had long been a target for recruitment by the party. However alienated he had become from Copland, Blitzstein, and Harris et al., he had once been a New York modernist himself. He had once been grateful to Downes for addressing his work at all; now he was frustrated that Downes and other critics would not outgrow their racially stereotyped views of his music. His connections with Hollywood might have served to make him even more of a target of the anticommunist witch hunt. In addition, Arvey's heritage was Jewish. Her uncle, Jacob Arvey, occupied a prominent position in the Democratic machine that controlled Chicago politics; Uncle Jake's record of opposition to communist-controlled unions might not have protected either him or his relatives from what was, among other things, a partisan political movement.[53] Still may thus have acted in part out of concern and support for Arvey. He granted the role of generic racism in what he had come to see as the *Troubled Island* debacle only in a moment of despair, months after the fact; it must have been less painful for him to perceive the "failure" of that production as contrived by a specific coterie than to see himself as a helpless victim of institutionalized racism. Under these circumstances, the flawed reasoning evident here may have had much less to do with Still's actions (and Arvey's) than with the fact that Still was culturally positioned in a way that left the path he chose as the one least objectionable. Perhaps the final irony of his entire involvement with anticommunism was that the McCarthyite movement rent American society in an excruciating way, one whose scars remain visible; yet, except as a more or less theoretical civil liberties issue, it did nothing whatever to address the issue of racism. All it did, on either side, was to distract attention. Still's anticommunism—by far his most controversial public position—was thus irrelevant to his principal cause, which was to end racism.

If I have indeed tracked some of the reasons for Still's early perception that the radical left had no sympathy for his artistic aspirations and no agenda to improve race relations in America, and if the critical attacks on his music in the 1930s and later were partially motivated by doctrinaire political considerations, as now seems entirely possible, it may be necessary to rethink the charge of "paranoia." It must be remembered here that, despite the apparent opposition suggested by the term "anticommunism," the issue was never a simple question of "communists" versus "anticommunists." The crude polarized language that marked this movement fostered confusion at the time and continues to complicate discussions. The outspoken "anticommunists" were a relatively small group who shared right-wing, nativist views. They labeled many more liberal Republicans and Democrats, most of whom had long opposed the Communist Party, as "communists" or "communist sympathizers." It is now clear that many careers were destroyed by the extreme anticommunism of the McCarthy era. It is also clear that the party attempted to destroy the careers of prominent writers and artists who left it (e.g., Ralph Ellison and Richard Wright). We also know that critical judgments of artistic production have often been based on nonobjective criteria and that racism was pervasive among both liberals and conservatives. One could claim that Still was as much a victim of those battles as a participant. Such a claim has the advantage of insisting on the complicated contextual web in which Still took his position but denies Still's agency as an individual capable of making his own decisions. Whatever the whole story may be, individual paranoia is not a satisfactory explanation.

Whether there was a conspiracy or not seems less important at this point than that Still firmly believed that there was one and that he acted on that belief. Like his long-standing conservative politics and his often-stated belief in God, anticommunism became a way to confront and separate himself from the white liberal establishment that had both supported and thwarted him for so long. Forsythe's insight (perhaps gleaned from his conversations with Still) presents an aspect of the modernism that Still came to oppose at such cost and is relevant here despite

its incompleteness: "The intellectualism of modern music is more psychopathic than has been generally understood." [54]

Yet racism remained Still's principal issue. In the early 1940s, Arvey
had written,

> Very few people regard racial matters as a vital topic in this war. How wrong
> they are will only be seen after the war is over, and perhaps even before it
> ends. We who are close to the heart of the matter know that is one of the chief
> reasons for the war and, after it's all over, this will be seen as a major objec-
> tive. It's one of the necessary topics. [55]

Jon Michael Spencer has recently documented Still's continuing statements against racism, showing them to form a long-standing and consistent pattern. [56] Nevertheless, in the late 1950s and 1960s Still's public
position as a McCarthyite remained unchanged.

The complexity of the situation in which the racial issue and Still's creative efforts were repeatedly submerged in other, irrelevant issues provides a background for the arguments about racial separation and integration that arose afresh in the 1960s. Not least among the ironies of
Still's anticommunism is that in the twilight of his career he wound up
in bitter opposition to the Black Power and Black Arts movements. Still
had long been committed to racial integration, and he did not change
his position; yet his difficulties in keeping the focus on the racial issue almost seem a textbook argument in favor of separatism, a doctrine he
had addressed in another context decades earlier, in the course of his racial period. Yet a great part of Still's musical utterance had addressed the
development of an authentic African American voice for concert music
where there had been almost no such voice. It appears that he had hashed
out the issue, probably not for the first time, with his Los Angeles friend
Forsythe, who in 1930 was the first to write at length about Still's work.
Forsythe ascribed the "dark-heart" to Still and celebrated Still's compositional achievements with the insights and the resolve born of his own
struggle to produce literature and music that might reflect his own identity as an African American. [57] The upshot was that Still rejected the
principle of black separatism along with Forsythe's rhetoric, but not,
where his music was concerned, the practice of self-conscious racial expression. His resistance to the prescriptions of the Black Arts movement
of the 1960s simply repeated the position he had reached in his discussions a generation earlier with Forsythe and elsewhere. Since then, the

practice of ignoring middle-class African American cultural contributions has militated against knowledge, let alone acceptance, of Still's life and work by a wide American or African American audience.[58] In what seems the greatest irony of all for the composer of *Africa* and the *Afro-American Symphony,* the Black Arts movement saw Still's great "classical" aesthetic experiment as irrelevant, if they knew about it at all.[59]

Still's use of African American materials embodied a different approach from that of white composers, carrying the potential for subverting or even upsetting the racial status quo. Who might present "black" musical ideas as concert music and in what format and to what audience were clearly at issue as Still (and other African Americans) entered the arenas of concert music and opera. Still addressed this issue directly in his work.[60] The critical reception of Still's music as too commercial, even too polished (however ironic in view of his early struggles to master his art), suggests that his long-term efforts were indeed successful at raising questions about the artificial barriers of genre that mirrored racial distinctions, that he was occupying new ground, opening an unfamiliar and not entirely welcome territory. The critical misunderstanding he attracted suggests that his challenge to a wide array of cultural stereotypes met with resistance, however poorly articulated, from both races.

It is worth remembering here that Still participated in not one but several transformations of the blues, including not only the "uplifting" transformation found in the *Afro-American Symphony* but also W. C. Handy's earlier metamorphosis of blues from a folk practice to the commercially viable (and sexually suggestive) "classic" blues of the 1920s and even Paul Whiteman's "sweet" synthesis of blues and jazz for large orchestra. Still's racial doubleness figures in each of these changes. Hindsight locates Still in the role of the mythical West African trickster, a figure he may not even have known about, as his career evolved.[61] The self-consciousness with which he went about his compositional practices, his contrasting and complementary double personae as modernist and Harlem Renaissance man as well as the multiplicity of adaptations of African American cultural practice he experienced in the crucibles of Harlem and Broadway, make this a valuable insight. His response to the reception of *From the Land of Dreams* in 1925 had been to offer *Levee Land,* featuring a blues singer performing the blues to a "modern" accompaniment, to the same audience the next year. As we have seen, the *Afro-American Symphony* contained its own response to white commercial borrowings from African American folk music. His firing from Columbia Pictures in 1936 for inserting "The Music Goes Round and

Round" into a rehearsal of a quiet passage for the film *Lost Horizon* was surely a tricksterish gesture as well. It is possible, too, that the social change of the 1960s involved at last one too many adaptations for a single human being to negotiate. How does one accommodate to a cultural change that appears ready to bury one's entire creative output? (Close analysis by other scholars may show that, in his music, he did negotiate it.)

Still's anticommunist position hints at how complicated his chosen path was. His identification as an African American who confounded a range of sometimes conflicting popular stereotypes—raised in an urban Southern environment in a tight-knit family with aspirations to uplift the race; active and successful in the separate, culturally opposed worlds of commercial and concert music; more the modernist and Harlem Renaissance man than he would have cared to admit, self-exile notwithstanding—assured that his aesthetic synthesis would be a unique and valuable contribution to American culture. The uniqueness of Still's creative path meant that even when audiences received his music warmly, as they often did, his formal and technical achievement would go largely unrecognized. There was little room for this experiment, for the inflections of class distinction and racial expressivism that were essential features of Still's art, in the fierce and reactionary political and social binarisms of the 1950s. In this light, Verna Arvey's aphorism, "they were never with you," takes on a far richer meaning. When it comes right down to it, they—whoever "they" might have been, then or now—were probably never entirely against him, either. They just didn't, and don't, know quite what to make of him. By now, we may be ready to rethink the person and rehear the music.

NOTES

1. Both Carlton Moss, in the interview of February 21, 1993, cited in "Finding His Voice," and Harold Bruce Forsythe, in "William Grant Still: A Study in Contradictions," describe Still's preoccupation with music to the exclusion of other things going on around him.

2. Interview with Carlton Moss.

3. Scrapbook #10, Still-Arvey Papers. Both letters are undated and mimeographed, ca. 1939. The Communist party's use of loosely affiliated organizations with tangentially related interests led to a great deal of confusion about its

influence, then and later. (See Claude McKay's comments about this practice below.) The Musicians' Committee to Aid Spanish Democracy, for example, includes on its letterhead the names of Pablo Casals, Charles Wakefield Cadman, John Alden Carpenter, Aaron Copland, Olin Downes, Howard Hanson, Hall Johnson, Daniel Gregory Mason, Paul Robeson, Still, and Edgard Varèse. Among these names selected from the long list, Cadman, Carpenter, Hanson, and Mason may be considered as especially far to the right of the Communist party in their politics.

The second is from the Negro Peoples' Committee . . . to Aid Spanish Democracy; among the names on its letterhead are Countee Cullen, Langston Hughes, Still, Richard Wright, and Adam Clayton Powell. The same caveat applies to them.

4. Barbara Zuck, *A History of Musical Americanism* (Ann Arbor: UMI Research Press, 1980), 107. The comment about the party's "important sociopolitical function" is drawn from Paul Bowles, *Without Stopping* (New York: G. P. Putnam's Sons, 1972), 80.

5. Olin Downes, "Music," *New York Times,* February 9, 1925, 15. As stated in the introduction, Downes and other listeners missed the blues allusions in the work.

6. Olin Downes, "Halász Presents New Still Opera," *New York Times,* April 1, 1949, 15:1.

7. Murchison outlines Still's style periods as "modern" (1923–1925), "racial" (1925–1932), and "universal" (1932-), based on Still's own writing about his music.

8. Emanual Balaban, "Progress at Rochester," *MM* 4, no. 4 (May–June 1932): 182–184. The ballet *Sahdji* was premiered on May 22, 1931; the *Afro-American Symphony* on October 29, 1931. *Africa,* another large work from this period, was premiered in 1930 but was revised several times after that. Its complicated history is documented in the *Bio-Bibliography*. See the foreword for a recent revival.

9. Marc Blitzstein, "New York Medley, Winter, 1935," *MM* 13, no. 2 (January–February 1936): 34–40.

10. Aaron Copland, "Our Younger Generation—Ten Years Later," *MM* 13, no. 4 (May–June 1936): 3–11; Copland, "Scores and Records" (arranger Otto Cesana is named along with Still), *MM* 15, no. 1 (November–December 1937): 45–48. In the latter review, Copland was discussing Still's *Dismal Swamp,* a League of Composers commission. For more on the early history of the League of Composers, see David Metzer, "The League of Composers: The Initial Years," *AM* 15, no. 1 (Spring 1997): 45–69.

11. Some fifteen years later, in making notes for the 1953 anticommunist speech discussed at length below, Arvey included this item: "Copland slushy jazz; his own jazz; and the Communist party line regarding jazz." "Extra notes for *Communism in Music* article, and for the book," Still-Arvey Papers. It appears that in preparing the essay, she made notes of things she had heard Still discuss. This particular note was not developed in the speech. However, Copland's comment rankled enough so that, in 1941, Arvey wrote to Claire Reis,

who directed the League of Composers, suggesting that *Modern Music* favored Copland unfairly over all other composers. (Reis, of course, rejected Arvey's complaint.)

The class-related "commercial" stereotype had already been assigned to white composers of successful commercial music who ventured to compose in larger forms (George Gershwin is the most obvious example).

12. For more on the Composers' Collective, see Zuck, *A History of Musical Americanism,* and Carol J. Oja, "Composer with a Conscience: Elie Siegmeister in Profile," *AM* 6, no. 2 (Summer 1988): 158–180. Not all the collective's members were members of the Communist party, though some were.

Soon after Still left New York, for example, one estimate had it that "75% of black cultural figures" were party members or "maintained regular meaningful contact with the Party." Mark Naison, "Communism and Harlem Intellectuals in the Popular Front: Anti-Fascism and the Politics of Black Culture," *Journal of Ethnic Studies* 9, no. 1 (1981): 1–25. Naison is here quoting from a 1977 interview with Howard Johnson, a party organizer in Harlem in the 1930s. Since anyone might come in contact with a member of an organization that had a loose connection with the party through a few of its members, the estimate is meaningless.

13. Blitzstein's first social protest theater work dates from 1935; and Copland began working on *El Salon Mexico,* a self-consciously "popular" work, in 1933.

For more on performances of Still's concert music in the 1920s and their folk/blues connections, see Carol J. Oja, "'New Music' and the 'New Negro': The Background of William Grant Still's *Afro-American Symphony,*" *BMRJ* 12, no. 2 (Fall 1992): 145–169; and "The *Afro-American Symphony* and Its Scherzo," above.

14. Robbie Lieberman, *"My Song Is My Weapon": People's Songs, American Communism, and the Politics of Culture, 1930–1950* (Urbana: University of Illinois Press, 1989), 31.

15. The Composers' Collective seems to have echoed, or perhaps influenced, a party position taken in the early 1930s, "when its critics demanded a Black music free from 'commercial influences.'" The party, as part of its Popular Front phase from 1935, changed its policy in order "to speak of the Black arts (with the exception of vaudeville and musical comedy with sexually explicit themes) as politically "'progressive' in and of themselves," thus accepting "commercialism" in order to attract black musicians. See Naison, "Communism and Harlem Intellectuals in the Popular Front."

16. Henry Johnson, music column in *New Masses* 19 (April 14, 1936): 29–30, reviewing a Victor recording of spirituals sung by Anderson.

17. Claude McKay, "Negro Author Sees Disaster If the Communist Party Gains Control of Negro Workers," *New Leader* (September 10, 1928): 3, as quoted in Wayne F. Cooper, ed., *The Passion of Claude McKay: Selected Poetry and Prose, 1912–1948* (New York: Schocken Books, 1973), 228–229, under the title "Communism and the Negro." Ralph Ellison's *Invisible Man* (1952) owed at least some of its success and perhaps its National Book Award not only

to the excellence of its writing but also to its subject, the recruitment and subsequent betrayal by the party of an African American political activist.

18. Claude McKay, "Claude McKay versus Powell," (New York) *Amsterdam News,* November 6, 1937, 4, as quoted in *The Passion of Claude McKay,* 250–252, as "On Adam Clayton Powell, Jr.: A Response."

19. Olin Downes, *New York Times,* April 5, 1946, 19, writing of the *Poem for Orchestra* on a program featuring "Music of Negroes" that included Still's work, "Spirituals for String Choir and Orchestra" by Morton Gould "freely in Negro style," and Marian Anderson singing Mahler and Donizetti. On the same page is a report of a speech by Gov. Harold Stassen of Minnesota (later a candidate for president) entitled "Stassen Assails Bigotry in Nation."

20. Letter, Leopold Stokowski to Still, May 1, 1944, Still-Arvey Papers.

21. Letter, Newbold Morris to Mr. and Mrs. Louis Kaufman, July 8, 1946, courtesy of Annette Kaufman. The mimeographed letter, which asked the Kaufmans to look for other contributors to the City Center Troubled Island Fund, concluded, "We would like any suggestions you may have as to ways and means of raising the $20,000 necessary for the production of this opera, so that we may be certain to have the money we need to include this production in the 1946–1947 City Center Opera Season. Let us remember that if this opera proves to be as successful as we hope it will be, it will continue to be included in the regular operatic performances by the New York City Opera Company." Stokowski wrote to Still with the idea of performing an orchestral suite from *Troubled Island,* then a staged version of the opera, then a full production. Letter, Stokowski to Still, May 17, 1944, Still-Arvey Papers.

For a published account of the formation of the New York City Opera, see Martin L. Sokol, *The New York City Opera* (New York: Macmillan, 1981). Sokol focuses on László Halász's contributions to the company and on the events leading to his firing in late 1951; his bias is toward defending Halász. Since Stokowski was associated with the New York City Symphony and not the opera company, his name does not appear until much later in the chronicle. Moreover, Sokol's annals do not include the Voice of America recording of *Troubled Island,* which was the first such recording of a company production. (Tapes transcribed from this recording are available through WGSM.)

A typescript account of the New York City Center's early years, missing its first 118 pages but giving a somewhat more balanced version, is in the Heddy Baum Collection, Music Division, New York Public Library, Lincoln Center.

22. Tammy Lynn Kernodle, "Still's *Troubled Island,* a Troubled Opera: Its Creation, Performance, and Reception" (M.A. thesis, Ohio State University, 1993), details the struggles of Still and Hughes to get the opera produced, including the rejection of the work by the Metropolitan Opera and the correspondence from 1944 with conductors Leopold Stokowski, Pierre Monteux, and Laszlo Halász as well as city official Newbold Morris and others (see esp. 25–37). Kernodle concludes that the public record does not demonstrate a plot against Still. Verna Arvey's account appears in *IOL,* 141–145. In addition to these sources and others in note 24 below, Arvey's letters to Louis and Annette Kaufman (unknown to Kernodle) recount the story as it developed.

23. Letter, Stokowski to Still, May 19, 1948. The letter specifically addressed Still's question as to whether the contribution Stokowski had made to the opera's production fund had been returned as promised. Still-Arvey Papers.

24. Still, Diary, January 28, 1949, Still-Arvey Papers.

25. Olin Downes, *New York Times,* April 1, 1949, 15:1. In his introduction to "The Life of William Grant Still" (Ph.D. dissertation, Harvard University, 1987), Benjamin Griffith Edwards writes that the opera received "only" three performances because of its poor reviews. Edwards does not take into account that only three performances were scheduled to begin with. Arvey, *IOL,* 143, reports that the opera was "scrapped" after three performances, also leading to the impression that the production was closed before initially planned. In fairness, it must be added that, at this early point in its history, the New York City Opera company was able to schedule extra performances on two or three occasions in response to audience demand.

26. Letter, Still to Leopold Stokowski, September 9, 1950, Still-Arvey Papers, refers to the second performance as the one that was recorded. In all other sources, the recording was said to have been made at the dress rehearsal.

27. The altered and added texts appear in both the piano-vocal score and the full score but not in the typed libretto at WGSM. The action is not described in the argument that appears at the beginning of both scores.

28. Arvey's text for *Costaso,* the opera Still composed in the year of *Troubled Island*'s production, described briefly in "*they,* Verna and Billy," above, reflects the beleaguered quality suggested by this line throughout.

29. Judith Anne Still, "In My Father's House . . . ," *BPiM* 3 (May 1975): 199–206.

30. This statement also appears in Still, "Fifty Years of Progress in Music," *Pittsburgh Courier,* November 11, 1950, 15. Reprinted in Spencer, *Reader,* 177–188. In a private communication dated February 27, 1996, Taubman's son, William C. Taubman, advised me that he does not remember his father mentioning either Still or his opera.

31. Telephone conversation with Judith Anne Still, December 15, 1994. This statement is a regular part of her slide lecture on her father.

32. Still, Diary, June 14, 1949. "Winter" is the baritone Lawrence Winters, who sang the role of Dessalines on the recording and in the production. Still-Arvey Papers.

33. Letter, Still to Leopold Stokowski, September 9, 1950, Still-Arvey Papers.

34. Letter, Leopold Stokowski to Still, September 18, 1950, Still-Arvey Papers. Stokowski's letter continues, "Is there something I can do in Bruxelles to assist you regarding this?" Still replied (September 25, 1950) by thanking Stokowski for his offer and rejecting it: "I feel that the intrigue is going on here in America, and that it is only a continuation of the intrigue that went on before."

35. Still, Diary, October 4, 1949, Still-Arvey Papers.

36. Still was arguably a modernist himself (see Murchison's chapter, above). In terms of his rigorous approach to composition, he was an intellectual as well, one with strong neoclassical leanings. In his music Still aimed for both formal sophistication and emotional expressiveness: "I am unable to understand how

one can rely solely on feeling when composing. . . . [A] fragment of a musical composition may be conceived through inspiration or feeling, but its development lies altogether within the realm of intellect." William Grant Still, "An Afro-American Composer's Viewpoint," in Henry Cowell, ed., *American Composers on American Music* (Stanford: Stanford University Press, 1932), 182–183, and reprinted in Spencer, *Reader,* 232, and *Fusion 2,* 52.

Moreover, in a talk on orchestration delivered at Eastman in 1932 which seems to focus on his then-current work for the "Deep River Hour" radio show, Still spoke repeatedly of the need for "clarity, balance, and a tasteful variety of tone color" to achieve successful, effective orchestration. The statement suggests the high neoclassicism of many modernists. William Grant Still, "On Orchestration," *Fusion 2,* 35–39. (The essay is the text of the Eastman lecture.) In spite of his neoclassical approach, Still deplored the modernist notion of music as strictly objective as well as the charge of "slushiness" directed at his own work.

37. Still, Diary, October 24, 1949, and February 21, 1950, Still-Arvey Papers.

38. Letter, Still to Howard Hanson, September 20, 1950, Still-Arvey Papers. The letter continues with a reference to a report of an interview with Leonard Bernstein. The report refers to Still's "music, and the music of certain other Americans, whereupon Bernstein replied, 'We don't admit those composers.'" The State Department had suggested the substitution of two short operas, "The Telephone" and "The Medium," by Gian-Carlo Menotti.

39. William Grant Still, "Politics in Music," *Opera, Concert and Symphony,* August 1947, reprinted in Spencer, *Reader,* 144–149.

40. Still, "Fifty Years of Progress in Music." Leonard Bernstein never conducted Still's music, then or later.

41. These articles are listed in the *Bio-Bibliography.* The item numbers and annotations are given here: B196, "Editorials." (Hollywood) *Citizen-News,* September 25, 1951. "Report that Still 'asked Rep. Donald L. Jackson to let him testify before the Congressional Committee on Un-American Activities. . . . Communists, said the Negro composer, do not speak for the Negro race.'" B242, "'I Pity Negro Communists.' *Los Angeles Tidings,* June 13, 1952. Lengthy article on Still's views pertaining to communists and their attempts to use members of his own race for the communist cause."

42. "Negro Composer Warns His Race About Reds' Lies," *Arkansas Gazette,* April 7, 1952. Still-Arvey Papers.

43. Both Still and Arvey visited and corresponded with Cowell while he was in San Quentin. See also Michael Hicks, "The Imprisonment of Henry Cowell," *Journal of the American Musicological Society* 44, no. 1 (1991): 92–119; and letters in Still-Arvey Papers.

44. William Grant Still, "Communism in Music," speech read to San Jose Chamber of Commerce, May 22, 1953. A tape at WGSM shows that Still deviated slightly from the prepared text, which was revised further and published under his name as "Music: Cog in the Machinery for World Domination" in the *American Mercury,* August 1954. On August 29, 1953, Arvey wrote to Joseph C. Keeley, editor, *American Legion Magazine,* offering him a revised version of the same speech. In a cover letter, she wrote, "You will note that although I

wrote the article . . . my husband's name is on it for the reason that it was he who delivered it in its original form as a speech. . . . [A]s the views expressed are shared by both of us, I didn't think it mattered whose name appeared as author."

Arvey drew much of her material from *Red Channels: The Report of Communist Influence in Radio and Television* (New York: American Business Consultants, 1950), a privately published collection of citations from witnesses sympathetic to the House Un-American Activities Committee. The citations associate prominent entertainers with communism on very flimsy grounds. Langston Hughes has a long list of citations in this report; those for Downes and Copland are likewise quite long. Harris, who was not similarly prominent, is not mentioned.

In an oral history given for the Library of Congress in 1996, David Raksin identifies himself as having been assigned to take Still's place on *Stormy Weather* after Still left the film in 1943. His statement exemplifies the confusion that continues to surround the innumerable charges and countercharges characteristic of the anticommunist movement. Still had resigned from *Stormy Weather,* giving as his reason that he disapproved of the image of African Americans projected in that film. This was the "studio job" mentioned in his San Jose speech. Raksin reports in error that Still was fired. Benny Carter was hired after Still departed; Emil Newman is listed as Music Director on the film credits. Others may have been involved as well. Thus, as with most of the persons named in the speech, the charge against Raksin, Carter, Newman, or whoever, was and remains an unconfirmed allegation.

45. Sokol does not report the production of a Weill opera by the New York City Opera until five years later (*Lost in the Stars,* 1958). However, Marc Blitzstein's *Regina* was produced in 1953, about a month before Still gave this speech. Halász too was fired in 1953.

46. Some examples: Mary Carr Moore's *Narcissa* (1912); Horatio Parker's *Fairyland* (1915); Charles Wakefield Cadman's *Shanewis* (1918); Howard Hanson's *Merry Mount* (1934); Aaron Copland's *The Tender Land* (1954). While some of these have had revivals, none has entered the operatic canon.

47. The introductory essay to Bernard F. Dick, *Radical Innocence: A Critical Study of the Hollywood Ten* (Lexington: University Press of Kentucky, 1989), summarizes the events that led up to the prosecution of the Hollywood Ten for refusing to cooperate with the investigations of leftist activities and cites a few of the apparent contradictions in the selection and treatment of witnesses. For a more detailed account, see Larry Ceplair and Steven Englund, *The Inquisition in Hollywood: Politics in the Film Community* (Garden City, N.Y.: Anchor Press/Doubleday, 1980).

48. See "Finding His Voice," above.

49. Smith, interview with Arvey, Los Angeles, 1981; Arvey, *IOL,* 116. Arvey incorrectly reports that the performing forces (orchestra, white chorus and Negro chorus) were identical. Wayne D. Shirley, "William Grant Still's Choral Ballad *And They Lynched Him on a Tree,*" *AM* 12 (Winter 1994): 426–461, documents the genesis of this work in some detail. I am grateful to him for pointing out that Harris did not, as Arvey reports, specify two choruses. He did, however, suggest that, since both choruses were already on stage, they should both

sing his piece. The two works also called for different solo voices, a point not mentioned by Arvey.

Earl Robinson, like Blitzstein, was a member of the Composers' Collective. The *Ballad for Americans* "made use of both folk and art music traditions while synthesizing the patriotic, egalitarian, democratic strains of Popular Front culture." Lieberman, *"My Song Is My Weapon,"* 40. By 1949, Arvey was writing to Still, in New York for the premiere of *Troubled Island*, warning him of a *Times* staff member she thought might be a "Commie."

50. Sokol, *The New York City Opera*, 82–86. Reis's minutes for the meeting at which the board decided to fire Halász are reproduced in full in Sokol's book. See n. 11 above for Arvey's earlier correspondence with Reis.

51. Still, Diary, October 24, 1949, Still-Arvey Papers.

52. Lieberman, *"My Song Is My Weapon."* Lieberman points out that former communists who wrote about their experiences in the party often put its failure down to "manipulation, corruption, and betrayal" (xxi), much in keeping with the atmosphere of deception cultivated by the party itself. In a curious way, the Stills' plot theory mirrors this atmosphere of deception.

53. For information on Jacob Arvey, see Milton L. Rakove, *Don't Make No Waves, Don't Back No Losers: An Insider's Analysis of the Daley Machine* (Bloomington: Indiana University Press, 1975), 112–113, 144–145.

54. "Frailest Leaves," 445, Forsythe Papers.

55. Letter, Verna Arvey to Carl Van Vechten, March 24, 1943, Van Vechten Papers, JWJ.

56. Jon Michael Spencer, "The Terrible Handicap of Working as a Negro Composer," in *The New Negroes and Their Music: The Success of the Harlem Renaissance* (Knoxville: University of Tennessee Press, 1997), chap. 3, 72–106.

57. See Forsythe, "William Grant Still: A Study in Contradictions," below.

58. The black middle class is described as "surely one of the most disparaged social groups in all of modern history" by Andrew Ross in *No Respect: Intellectuals and Popular Culture* (New York: Routledge, 1989), 76; quoted in Ingrid Monson, "The Problem with White Hipness: Race, Gender, and Cultural Conceptions in Jazz Historical Discourse," *Journal of the American Musicological Society* 48, no. 3 (Fall 1995): 396–422. The trashing of this class goes back as far as E. Franklin Frazier's *Black Bourgeoisie* (New York: Free Press, 1957).

59. For example, Kevin K. Gaines, *Uplifting the Race: Black Leadership, Politics, and Culture in the Twentieth Century* (Chapel Hill: University of North Carolina Press, 1996), 76, argues that "uplift" meant in practice the adaptation of elite white social practices that widened class distinctions within the African American community and engendered class-based hostility within the race. Gaines does not appear to be familiar with Still's work. In *The New Negroes and Their Music,* Spencer argues in Still's behalf: "There is no evidence in his remarks that his intent to 'elevate' this music was indicative of a clandestine contempt for it or for the common folk who created it. To the contrary, Still viewed himself as fulfilling the wishes of his forebears who wished for the advancement of their children and the race as a whole" (84).

60. Lawrence Kramer, "Powers of Blackness: Africanist Discourse in Modern Concert Music," *BMRJ* 16, no. 1 (Spring 1996): 53–70, argues that white

American and European composers of the modernist period employed African-ist (including African American) musical usages in ways that enclose and subor-dinate them, thus reflecting the dominant social structure. By subordinating the "black" usages without disturbing primary European-based formal structures, Kramer proposes, a definition of American whiteness as superior to African or American blackness was reinforced.

61. See "The *Afro-American Symphony* and Its Scherzo," above.

SOURCES

Personal Notes

William Grant Still

Born Woodville, Miss., May 11, 1895.

My father was musically inclined, and did some composing. I have no record of any of his work along that line. His instrument was the cornet, and he was a band leader.

My mother leaned toward things of a literary nature. She taught literature in the high school in Little Rock, Ark. She was quite active in N.A.A.C.P. work in Little Rock. As a matter of fact, she was interested in and took an active part in everything of a cultural nature (I have not expressed myself well here. I mean to say in everything that she could take a part in.) She was an excellent public speaker also.

The love affair of my mother and father started in an Alabama school where both were teaching. This was Mr. Council's school. "Normal," they called it.[1]

My father died when I was three months old. My mother related some unusual occurrences connected with his death. (You need not include these for I am merely telling you of them.) One was that an owl

---

This narrative was written by Still in response to Harold Bruce Forsythe's 1933 letter requesting materials for the proposed biography. The typescript is in the Forsythe Papers. Changes are indicated by brackets or notes. The paragraph separations are occasionally conjectural, as Still, who did not believe in wasting space, indicated them only by a return, with no extra space or indentation. The titles of shows and music are italicized by the editor.

persisted in perching on the roof of the house despite all efforts to drive him away. If I remember correctly the bird remained there for a number of days, and would not leave until my father had died. It would not seem strange were it not for the old superstition concerning owls and death.——My mother also told me of the beautiful vision my father had when he was expiring. I think his ailment was typhus. Just before he passed out he rose in the bed and told those present of an angelic being that he saw approaching him. He described this beautiful entity to them, telling them that it was coming for him and then died.

My mother moved then to Little Rock, Ark. where I spent the earlier part of my life—to be exact—until I was sixteen years of age. I was taken many places of course during the sixteen years.

My mother had high aims for me, and she started working toward them, i.e. molding my method of thought at a very early age. I had to read the books she chose—and I'm grateful to her now for it. She constantly impressed me with the thought that I should achieve something worth while in life. She sought to aid me reach the state of mind that leave one unhappy when he has failed to put forth his best effort.[2] She wanted me to be a man and, for that reason, dealt with me in a manner that would have seemed strange to some mothers who are inclined to coddle their children. But my mother knew what I needed, and I am thankful for it. She sought at all times to give me every advantage that she possibly could. (I rarely missed passing through a day without a licking. But I needed them. Had my mother not employed that means of teaching me to control myself I don't know what the results would have been. Certainly with such a stubborn will as mine things would have gone wrong somewhere.)

I spent much of time in childhood around my maternal grandmother. I have much to thank her for. She was one of the old fashioned devout Christians. She had been a slave, although she was one of the fortunate ones who did not have to work in the fields. She had seen slaves being herded along the country roads of Georgia on the way to the slave mart. She knew and sang the old songs that voiced the slaves' belief that God would not forget them. Because of her influence I have been enabled to realize the value of things spiritual, and to love them. In me the fleshly tendencies are strong. Were it not for the training I received through contact with my grandmother I could not restrain them. God was good to me to give me such a grandmother. She loved me, Harold.[3] Each day when I would come home from school she would have something special prepared for me. Pies, cookies, candy or something good that she had made. Later on her memory became affected. She seemed at times to forget everyone. But she never forgot me. In my memory she and my mother still live. It is they who are largely responsible for what I have been able to accomplish. Would that more of our women of color had high ideals, and sought to instill in their children the thought that they must not be content to stop halfway but to keep right on until they are prepared to cope with any man. (I do not mean to say that I am thus prepared, but I do say that I would probably have followed the line of least resistance if the thought of making good had not [been] drilled into me.)

Later, when I was about nine or ten years of age, my mother married again. Mr. Shepperson, her second husband, was a splendid stepfather. In truth, a father could not have been more considerate. He and I spent many pleasant and profitable moments together. He too liked music. [I] learned at an early age to appreciate the better sort of music through the records he would buy. (It's funny how bad those things sound now, but they seemed fine in those days. Until the year just past I kept the old Victor machine on which I used to play operatic records for hours at a time.)

I attended grammar and high school in Little Rock. Was valedictorian of my class in high school. I had to be because my mother made up her mind that I must be, and she made me study. She would never work out any problems that presented themselves for me but would force me to work them out for myself. I[t] was she who had me begin taking violin lessons after I had entered high school. Just as soon as I learned to read music I began making efforts to compose. After having completed high school I was sent to Wilberforce. There I was thrown in contact with some fellows who were lovers of music. These contacts were helpful.

Upon returning home after my first year at college I begged my mother to send me to Oberlin. But she had mapped out a career for me. I was to finish Wilberforce and then to go to Oxford. That did not interest me. I wanted to study music. And so I wasted time in college just barely making my grades; always in trouble for playing pranks; spending most of my time studying music, attempting to write and playing the violin. Finally in my senior year, just about six weeks before I would have graduated I got mixed up in another prank. This was of a more serious nature—to be exact it appeared serious to others although nothing was [done] by any concerned that was at all wrong. i.e. morally. After this affair I left college and went to Columbus, Ohio to make my own way. Managed to get a job. Made six dollars per week. Finally got a job with an orchestra. Did very well while the job lasted. After that I had to go a little easy on the eating so that there would be enough to eat a little each day. Nevertheless, in the fall of that year (1915) I got married.[4]— (entered college in 1911 at the age of sixteen years; made my exit in 1915 and got married)—I will say no more of the marriage other than to mention that my mother was sorely grieved because of it, and to mention the four kiddies of mine. Gee, but I love those kids, Harold. I never fully know how greatly I was wrapped up in them until I was separated from them.

After a brief period I received a small amount of money that my father left me. With a portion of this I began studying at Oberlin. They were very kind to me there. Gave me work in the school assisting the janitor. This helped pay room rent. Dr. and Mrs. Stevens, colored people who kept and boarded some of the colored girls attending the school allowed me to wait table at their place. This provided food. I also played in the moving picture house there on some nights. This brought in a little more. Of course the money I received was little. I often was unable to keep quite as neat as I would have liked to be. It's not easy to stretch a few worn articles of clothing (I had to buy my suits in a second hand store during this period i.e. whenever I was fortunate enough to be able to get a suit). While in Oberlin Prof. Lehman, who taught me theory, seemed impressed with my work in the class. He asked me one day why I did not study composition. I told him that I did not have the money. He then brought the matter to the attention of the theory committee. As a result Dr. Geo. Andrews was asked and consented to teach me composition free of charge.

During the war I came to New York and enlisted in the navy. Was discharged shortly after the armistice.

Worked then in a shipyard over in New Jersey. Working in winter. Had often to go in the double bottoms and bail out water. This did not agree with me.

Went to Kentucky, where my wife and children were, later the same winter. You need not mention the following. Received a wire supposedly sent by my wife's father stating that she was dead. Left hurriedly only to find her alive and perfectly well when I arrived in Kentucky. Remained there a short while, and then went to Columbus hoping to get work.

No work in Columbus. Remained there looking and hoping. Was down to my last dollar. Really I had just one dollar left. That same night some musicians who lived in the same hotel where I stopped knocked on my door and told me that I could go to work with them the following night. The violinist who had been playing with them had gotten drunk and thrown them down on the job.

Worked in Columbus for quite a while. Finally had some money ahead and returned to Oberlin. Stayed there for a period. The end of the session. Had written Handy about work in New York.[5] He had been here about a couple of years then. He agreed to give me a job. (I had worked with him a few years before in Memphis. One summer only.) My wife went back to Kentucky and I came back here.

Worked about two years with Handy. Reverses forced him to dispense with some of his employees. I was one.

Played around town with Deacon Johnson[6] then for a while. Never stopped studying and attempting to write.

Then *Shuffle Along* came into being [opened May 23, 1921].[7] Some of the fellows had heard me play oboe. They wanted an oboist in the orchestra. I was elected. During those days Wm. Service Bell[8] and I were close friends. He and Revella Hughes sang some of my songs in recital in Harlem. Remained with *Shuffle Along* for more than a year. Finally left the show when it closed in Boston. I returned to New York to be Recording Mgr. of the Black Swan Phonograph Co. While in Boston with the show I studied with Mr. Chadwick,[9] who would not accept any money for his services.

My family had come to New York before *Shuffle Along* closed in New York.

While connected with Black Swan I happened to be talking to a stenographer one day. Glancing down at what he was writing I discovered that he was replying to a letter announcing that Edgard Varèse[10] was offering a scholarship. (His reply was to the effect that the party for whom he was writing knew of no one to suggest for the scholarship.) I got busy, got the information, and wrote Varèse. In the end I received it. The period of study with Mr. Varèse helped me wonderfully. It taught me to be independent; to break away from the barriers that had repressed—(you fill this in, I can't think now). Any way I began finding myself. I came to the point where I could—(what shall I say? NOTHING.) Well, I liked Varèse, and I still like him. I think he is an exceptional man. He was my friend in the true sense of the word. He stood firmly for me. I shall always be indebted to him.

Black Swan went along for a while, and then went on the rocks. I was again out of a job. Stayed out too for quite a few months. (Orchestrated *Runnin' Wild* [opened September 29, 1923] while with Black Swan.)

Then Luckyeth Roberts came along with a colored show. I orchestrated it. The show lasted about four weeks. I was again out of a job, and had not been paid all that was due me for orchestrating the show. However that was not Roberts' fault.[11]

Hung on by the hardest over a period of some months and then got a job with *Dixie To Broadway* [opened September 29, 1924; ran for eight weeks]. Stayed with that show for quite a while. The show closed.

Worked at the Plantation then.[12] Directed the show. It was during this time when Florence [Mills] sang *Levee Land* [January 24, 1926].

Leroy Smith offered me a job. The remuneration was greater by far than what I was receiving. So I accepted. Remained with him for about six months. Left him to orchestrate an edition of *Earl Carroll's Vanities*[13] [. . . *of 1926;* opened August 24, 1926]. This came through Don Voorhees who was Carroll's musical director.[14] Don had work on the radio and needed arrangements. That caused me to stop playing and to devote myself to writing, i.e. orchestrating principally. Composing whenever I had time. You [Forsythe] came to New York during that period [September 1927].

Remained with Don for about two and one half years. Orchestrated *Rain or Shine* [opened 2/9/1928. One critical comment: "Stung by the jazzy lash of Dan [sic] Voorhees and his squealing band, the music sweeps like a breaking wave."],[15] other Carroll shows [*Vanities of 1928,* opened August 6, 1928], and an edition of *Americana* [opened October 30, 1928] that failed. Received a Harmon second award in music [1928]. Clarence White was given the first.

Somewhere along there I trained a special orchestra that I conducted later in a program of Negro music before the Crown Prince of Sweden.

And then the chance came along to go with Whiteman. Not long after that I saw you. The job ended. [Still returned to New York in June 1930.]

I was out of work for about fourteen months. Things often looked critical. But God is good. I am thankful that He brought me through. The job with Willard Robison's Deep River Orchestra [ca. August 1931] came up. At first I merely orchestrated. The program went to WOR. After a short while I was chosen to conduct the orchestra. A group of splendid white musicians. I have never been accorded greater courtesy nor have I ever received greater cooperation than from those fellows. The program succeeded. Was spoken of highly, especially by musicians. The contract expired the early part of this month [December 1932].

The program has gone to WJZ. Unfortunately the folks at NBC are not broadminded.[16] They don't want a Negro conductor. So I am now [1933] serving merely as an arranger. But it's OK. Everything will work out.

Scored the Prelude and Entr'Acte of Clarence White's opera for him.[17] Delivered a lecture on Orchestration at the Eastman School last year [in conjunction with the second performance of the *Afro-American Symphony,* 1932].

MISCELLANEOUS

Don't forget to say a lot about Dr. [Howard] Hanson.[18] There is not a finer man in the world than Dr. Hanson. A splendid musician; big hearted; broad minded, and all the other good things thrown in. Even then he is not done justice. He has made it possible for me to hear my efforts. He has encouraged me. He has aided me materially. He has been a FRIEND.

Please mention these:—

Georges Barrère:—For performing some of my efforts.

Quinto Maganini: For placing the second Mov. of *Africa* on his program.

Olin Downes: For his interest and encouraging remarks.

John Tasker Howard: For mentioning me in *Our American Music* [New York: Thomas Y. Crowell, 1931].

Paul Whiteman: For giving me a good job and paying me well. For including the last movement of *Africa* on his program.

Frank Patterson: For his interest and some nice things he has done in my behalf.

Varèse——(You know)

Lehman and Dr. Andrews and Geo. Chadwick—(You know)

ALSO:

Irving Schwerké: Through his efforts *Africa* was performed during the Festival of American Music in Germany; *Africa* was accepted for performance by the Pasdeloup orchestra in Paris; the symphony has been brought to the attention of Weingartner.

I am a firm believer in God, and I certainly have every reason to be so. I am thankful that He has suffered me to go through a troublous period.

It was what I needed. Spiritual development is necessary to one who would compose. Through suffering the ego is overcome; one learns the lesson of humility; when one is humble he can hear the voice of God, and he can learn the lessons that will profit him most.

I have now but one great desire. That is to serve humanity. It matters not if I fail to amass money or to win great esteem. But it does matter if I fail to help others.

You'll have to ask me the rest. My old brain refuses to work any more right now.

[Billy]

COMPOSITIONS

FROM THE LAND OF DREAMS (FOR CHAMBER ORCHESTRA AND THREE FEMALE VOICES TREATED INSTRUMENTALLY)

In three movements—Lento; Allegretto; Allegro Moderato. Completed in 1924.

Performed at a concert of the International Composers' Guild in New York, Feb. 8, 1925.

Conducted by Vladimir Shavitch, who was at that time conductor of the Syracuse Symphony Orchestra.

The first of my efforts to be performed in New York. I was so nervous when it was being played that I scarcely heard it.

Press Comments:—

William Grant Still tried the instrumental use of human voices in an incoherent fantasy, *From the Land of Dreams,* and succeeded in making them sound once or twice like Wagner's Rhine Maidens.

One hoped for better things from Still. . . . Is Mr. Still unaware that the cheapest melody in the revues he has orchestrated has more reality and inspiration than the curious noises he has manufactured? . . . This is music unprofitable to compose or listen to.— Olin Downes

From the Land of Dreams, the work for small harmonic orchestra and voices instrumentally treated by WGS, well known for his orchestration of many Negro revues, adds another member to the company of American musical embryonics. Still has learned much from Edgard Varèse, his instructor, although he has not yet quite learned to speak out freely. . . . But Mr. Still has a very sensuous approach to music. His employment of his instruments is at once rich and nude and decided. The upper ranges of his high soprano have an original penetrating colour. And the use of jazz motives in the last section of his work is more genuinely musical than any to which they have been put, by Milhaud, Gershwin, or any one else.—Paul Rosenfeld.

My Personal Opinion: It is not Still but Varèse who speaks in *From the Land of Dreams*. The realization of this fact enabled me to see that it was necessary for me to find an idiom that would be modern but not so much so that it would fail to be recognized at once as Negroid.

LEVEE LAND (FOR SOPRANO SOLOIST AND CHAMBER ORCHESTRA)

In four parts—"Levee Song"; "Hey-Hey"; "Croon"; "The Back-slider."

Completed in 1925.

Performed at a concert of the International Composers' Guild in New York, Jan. 24, 1926.

Sung by Florence Mills.

Conducted by Eugene Goossens.

A very large audience many of whom, in my opinion, came merely to witness Florence Mills in the role of a concert artist.

Press Comments:—

One simply could not help defying the streptococci germs and braving the chill winds of night to see what Miss Mills would do with her numbers and her audience.

Miss Mills sang a group of songs by William Grant Still entitled, *Levee Land*. Curious and elemental were these songs by this brilliant young Negro composer, plaintive in part, blue, crooning and sparkling with humor, and Miss Mills gave them a perfect interpretation. . . . Now, it's true though possibly a bit rash to come right out and say that Florence Mills packed the house.—*New York World*

The interest of the performance, the real interest and value such as it was, came from the performer. . . . She would have made a flatter piece of music amusing by her diction. . . . The "Levee Song" is the best. The last, "The Backslider," is effective when it has Miss Mills to do it. Both of them seem artificial, neither real jazz, nor real modernism, with forced and sentimental affectation.— Olin Downes

William Grant Still is a Negro musician with a first rate education. . . . Last year he had a piece performed at an I.C.G. concert which was nothing more or less than a slavish imitation of the noises which Edgard Varèse calls compositions. This year he had safely escaped from that baleful influence and gave the public four foolish jazz jokes—sung by Florence Mills in a true and proper Broadway manner—and greatly enjoyed by the public. These works are so good, healthy, sane—such good musical fooling—that they place this Negro composer on a high plane in the super-jazz field just now in vogue.— *Musical Courier*

William Grant Still has attempted in *Levee Land* to combine jazz with sophisticated harmony, and the result of the union is not happy.—*Musical America*

My Opinion: *Levee Land* was a step nearer the idiom I was seeking, yet it was still too extreme.[19]

Levee Land was also performed in Germany. Sung by Juan Harrison over the radio, Frankfurt-on-the-Main.

FROM THE JOURNAL OF A WANDERER (SYMPHONIC SUITE)

Completed 1925.

Performed by the North Shore Festival Orchestra [Chicago] under the direction of Frederick Stock, 1926.

Performed by the Rochester Symphony under Dr. Howard Hanson, 1928.

Press Comments (North Shore Orchestra):—

From the Journal of a Wanderer, five short pieces of futile instrumental vagaries without much rime or reason.—Maurice Rosenfield

Press Comments (Rochester):—

Mr. Still's *Darker America* interested this writer when it was played here. . . . His suite yesterday was more versatilely written; more spectacularly conceived; in it was instrumental and harmonic invention of originality and at times of appeal.—Stewart R. Sabin

DARKER AMERICA (SYMPHONIC POEM)

Completed 1924.

Performed first at a concert of the International Composers Guild, New York, 1926, with Eugene Goossens conducting.

Press Comments (I.C.G. performance):—

With respect to the works of Messrs. McPhee, Goossens and Still there is hardly a choice between saying a great deal or nothing at all.—*New York Telegram*

The best music last night was that of *Darker America*. . . . It communicates an atmosphere. What is lacking is actual development and organic growth of the ideas. This music, however, has direction and feeling in it, qualities usually lacking in contemporaneous music.—Olin Downes

The actual high spot was a new work by that greatly gifted Negro composer, William Grant Still. . . . This composer is still slightly under the influence of his teacher, Edgard Varèse. Some day he will escape entirely from this influence and when that day comes he will blossom forth as one of America's really great composers. He already has a splendid technic and is obviously full of ideas. Just at present his ideas are clouded by modernistic harmonies (i.e. dissonances) which spoil them. However, there is no doubting the man's power, and his music on this particular occasion was like a bright spot amid a lot of muddy grime.—*Musical Courier*

Mr. Still has progressed notably in his mastery of expression since his *Levee Land* . . . . In *Darker America* he has essayed to voice some phases of the spiritual life of his race. . . . The harmonic influence of Varèse is apparent in the treatment of Negro themes, and the work is weak in development. But the earnestness of the writing, the driving energy of the rhythmic movement and the ingenious scoring are worthy of praise. The music has a powerful emotional urge and convincing sincerity.—*Musical America*

Press Comments (Rochester):—

A large audience and a jury of six musicians and music critics attended a concert tonight in Kilbourn Hall, at which four manuscript orchestral works by American composers were played. Audience and jury, voting jointly, designated two of the four works for early publication. . . . The composers whose works were selected for this purpose tonight were Douglass Moore, [whose] *Pageant of P. T. Barnum* received the unanimous vote of the jury and a majority vote of the audience, and William Grant Still, whose *Darker America* was given second place by the jury.—*New York Times*

Program Notes: *Darker America* is representative of the American Negro, and suggests triumph over sorrows through fervent prayer.

My Opinion: *Darker America* has quite a few faults, viz. lack of consistency in form; too much material for such a short composition; faulty harmonization in places.

FROM THE BLACK BELT (SUITE OF MINIATURES FOR CHAMBER ORCHESTRA)

This is a group of short, humorous pieces.
Performances:

Barrère Little Symphony, 1927, New York

Barrère Little Symphony 1932, New York

Press Comments:—

Mr. Still's opening "Dance" closed at about the sixth measure. The ensuing music proved tuneful and showed skill in the use of instrumental sonorities. . . . The last section, "Des Keep on Shovin'," was another fragment, closing a likeable piece.—*Herald Tribune*

My Opinion: This group was conceived with view to amusing the audience. It has done that, for the audience did laugh each time it was performed in New York. Mr. Barrère told me that the same thing occurred when he performed it in Washington.

"THE BREATH OF A ROSE" (SETTING OF LANGSTON HUGHES' POEM) / "WINTER'S APPROACH" (SETTING OF PAUL LAURENCE DUNBAR'S POEM)

These two songs are not important. I mention them because they were completed in 1927, and heard for the first time in public. These are the songs published by [G.] Schirmer.

"The Breath of a Rose" was written for a proposed stage production that never got beyond the period of planning.

"Winter's Approach" was written for Madam Marya Freund, a European singer.

LOG CABIN BALLADS (SUITE FOR CHAMBER ORCHESTRA)

Completed 1927

Performed by Barrère Little Symphony, 1928, in New York

The press comments were favorable. I will not include them for this is not an important work. The three pieces composing the suite are, "Long To'ds Night," "Beneaf De Willers," and "Miss Malindy." Florence Mills was particularly fond of "Miss Malindy," and wanted me to have lyrics set to the tune so she could sing it.

PURITAN EPIC (SYMPHONIC POEM)

Completed 1928.

This has never been performed, and will probably never be heard because I don't like it. I had intended calling it, "From the Heart Of A Believer." But I decided to change the title after the Victor Contest was announced and to enter the piece in the contest.[20]

AFRICA (POEM FOR ORCHESTRA IN THREE MOVEMENTS)

i-Land of Peace. ii-Land of Romance. iii-Land of Superstition.

Completed 1930.

Performances:

1930—special arrangement—Barrère Little Symphony in New York.

1930—Rochester Symphony under Dr. Hanson

1931—Festival of American Music—Bad Homburg, Germany under Dr. Holger.

Third movement to be played by Paul Whiteman's group in Carnegie Hall, Jan. 25, 1933.

Second movement to be played by the New York Sinfonietta in Town Hall, March 1933.

The entire work to be performed by the Pasdeloup Orchestra in Paris this season, under Rhené Baton.

Press Comments (Rochester):—

Mr. Still's Africa was heard by the writer with genuine pleasure. . . . The finale hints at something that one believes comes individually in conception to a composer.—Stewart R. Sabin

Judging by the applause the greatest approval of the audience went to the *Africa Suite*. . . . The music of the suite is impressionistic, strongly marked in rhythm, with passages that are richly harmonious alternating with others of barbaric discord.—Amy H. Croughton

To my mind the highlight of the evening came in the superb playing of W.G.S.'s third movement entitled "Land of Superstition" of his suite *Africa*.—Samuel Shulsky

I have many clippings from German papers concerning the Bad Homburg performance. I can't read them, and I have forgotten what the German fellow who read them to me said. But Irving Schwerké wrote me that *Africa* was the sensation of the festival. I did not believe him, thinking that he merely wanted to make me feel good. But this year I met Marvin Wessel, a young composer who has been living in Vienna. He knows Schwerké (and does not like him so well . . . that's confidential mark you . . .). He told me that Schwerké told him the same thing.

Now, let me tell you a few things about *Africa*. I have never worked on any composition as long as I have worked on *Africa*. This period of work has extended over five years. The entire structure of *Africa* has changed in that time. Harmonizations, developments and instrumental colours have been altered. And now I am making the final score. When that is done *Africa* will at last be completed. If one should hear this last version, and then hear the first he would not recognize the latter. [See Arvey monograph for additional revision.] I believe Africa will endure. Here is the explanation of (I mean program notes). . . . (Gee!)

An American Negro has formed a concept of the land of his ancestors based largely on its folklore, and influenced by his contact with American civilization. He beholds in his mind's eye not the Africa of reality but an Africa mirrored in fancy, and radiantly ideal.

I   —He views it first as a land of peace; peace that is partly pastoral in nature and partly spiritual.

II —It is to him also a land of fanciful and mysterious romance; romance tinged with ineffable sorrow.

III —Contact with American civilization has not enabled him to completely overcome his inherent superstitious nature. It is that heritage of his forebears binding him irrevocably to the past, and making it possible for him to form the most accurate (or definite?) concept of Africa.

SAHDJI (FOR CORPS DE BALLET, CHORUS AND BASS SOLOIST; TEXT BY RICHARD BRUCE AND ALAIN LOCKE)

Produced at the Eastman Theatre, Rochester, N.Y., May 1931. Choreography by Thelma Biracree. Chorus trained by Herman Genhart. Scenery by Clarence Hall. Costumes by Mrs. Alice Couch. Conducted by Dr. Hanson. (The work is also dedicated to Dr. [Howard] Hanson. Don't forget this.)

The story is of Sahdji, favorite wife of Konombju, chieftain of the tribe, who betrays the chief through infatuation for his nephew and heir, Mrabo. Konombju is killed while on a hunting expedition. Mrabo, intimidated by the attitude of the Medicine Man and Counselors, repudiates Sahdji who then stabs herself with a sacrificial dagger.—(Very poorly told. If you can get the book of Negro Plays by Locke you will find the story of Sahdji in it.)[21]

The story of Sahdji is told in pantomime by the dancers. The chorus, in addition to being used in the customary manner, is used in a sort of percussive way. The form approximates that of the old Greek dramatic model. The Chanter (bass soloist) recites (or chants) African proverbs which are both in comment on and explanation of the action.

Press Comments:—

The choral ballet is a vividly impressive work. Mr. Still . . . has written a musical score that appeals as one of the most direct and lucid in dramatic suggestion of recent compositions of its sort. . . . Mr. Still gives evidence of an excellent sense of dramatic appeal in stage music, and he wastes no time or measures on music that does not count in the drama.—Stewart R. Sabin

Mr. Still's score is a most interesting one, dramatically effective and having distinct racial qualities.—Amy S. Croughton

In *Sahdji* Mr. Still, whose symphonic works have aroused favorable comment here, again offers music of a direct nature. His composition seemed to fit in perfectly with the character of the people portrayed on the stage and thus much was gained for the work's unity.—Samuel Shulsky

Mr. Still is a composer of marked talent. . . . The ballet *Sahdji* is fully as racial in content as the former work, and it appears clearer and not less rich in style. It is not so effective on the stage, or was not so effective on the stage tonight, as it is when the music is examined or heard by itself. The reason for this lay partly in the problem of presentation. It also lay in Mr. Still's rapidly growing but not complete mastery, as yet, of his medium and his necessary state as a composer for the theatre. But this is real music, music of a composer of exotic talent and temperament, who has a keen sense of beauty, sensuousness which is controlled by taste, and incipient aptitude for the theatre.—Olin Downes, *New York Times*

Before attempting to answer these queries, it must be admitted at the outset that too few Negro composers have composed music which is worthy of presentation in concert-halls. But one of these, a William Grant Still (*), for example, with a ballet entitled *Sahdji,* represented his race at the concerts of the recent May Festival of American Music at Rochester, N.Y. . . . Yet Still's score, which the critic Olin Downes reported as showing "unmistakable talent, etc.," probably is no more a token of the spirit which any group of our authorities would agree upon as being essentially American than the music of Koscak Yamada.—An excerpt from "The Negro in American Music" by Carl E. Gehring in *Procession,* Feb. 1932

My Opinion: I was pleased with the outcome of *Sahdji* although there were some spots in the orchestration that were not quite right. I plan to rescore the work, and probably change the last dance, i.e. to write a new dance.

Sergei Radamsky took a score of Sahdji to Russia with him last year. Shortly afterwards an article appeared in the *New York Times* stating that the work would be performed in Russia. I have never learned whether or not it was done.

It was quite interesting to have a white man from Mississippi in replying to an article bemoaning the dearth of ballet music by American composers mention *Sahdji.*

Neither Locke nor Bruce attended the performance. However, I can truthfully say that I bear neither of them any ill will. They would surely have come if they had been able.

Sahdji was started in June 1930 and completed by August.[22] The composition of this work was comparatively easy.

AFRO-AMERICAN SYMPHONY—MODERATO ASSAI; ADAGIO; ANIMATO; LENTO CON RESOLUZIONE

Completed 1931.

First Performance—Rochester Symphony, Oct. 28, 1931.

The entire work is based on a simple little blues theme. This theme plays an important part in each movement except the scherzo, where it appears merely as an accompanying figure. The four movements present successively the pathetic, sorrowful, humorous and sincere (or noble) sides of the American Negro.

Press Comments (1st performance):—

This headline appeared in the Rochester Evening Journal, "NEW SYMPHONIC WORK ACCLAIMED AT FIRST PLAYING IN AMERICAN COMPOSER'S CONCERT." Following are excerpts from the article under the above headline.

> Interest in the program, however, centered chiefly in Arthur Farwell's "Gods of the Mountain" Suite and William Grant Still's "Afro-American Symphony." Both rank among the best constructed and most provocative compositions heard in the history of these concerts. Mr. Still's symphony was especially intriguing. . . . Throughout the symphony has life and sparkle when needed and a deep haunting beauty that aids in conveying a picture of the mercurial temperament of the Negro. The symphony sometimes shuffles its feet, at other times dances. It laughs unrestrainedly, it mourns dolefully and sways often in the barbaric rhythm of its subject. And always it sings. . . . Finally, Mr. Still has succeeded in being original without any self conscious effort.—David Kessler

> Mr. Still's symphony is by far the most direct in appeal to a general audience of any of his music heard here. . . . Mr. Still has done his work well in this new composition, but to some extent he has replaced that arresting vigor one has admired by deft sophistication.—Stewart R. Sabin

> Mr. Still's *Afro-American Symphony* is built up from a "Blues" theme which he develops into a composition of poignant beauty through which one feels intense . . . emotion held within bounds by a fine intelligence. There is not a cheap or banal passage in the entire composition, and none which impresses one as having been set down merely for the sake of keeping the instruments busy or covering a set amount of manuscript paper. To give one such composer as Mr. Still an opportunity to have his compositions heard and to hear

them himself would justify the entire American Composers' Movement.—
Amy H. Croughton

2nd performance—Rochester Symphony—Mar. 3, 1932
Press Comments (2nd performance):—

It is honest, sincere music . . . etc. . . . Mr. Still and his music were given an
ovation by the audience.—Amy H. Croughton

[See also critical comments in the introduction, above.]

(Let me explain here that I was present at this concert. I missed the
first because Dr. Hanson's secretary failed to notify me in time. As is
characteristic of Dr. Hanson, when he discovered that it would be too
late for me to get there in time by train he wired me to come by airplane
at the expense of the school. But the day was so bad that the companies
operating planes would not take passengers. . . . When *Sahdji* was produced I was broke, and did not have the money to get to Rochester.
Dr. Hanson sent me $100.00 to make the trip. Do you see now why I
admire him so much when, in addition to encouraging as me does, he
offers me material aid of that sort?)
    Let's get back to the subject.

He has written a symphonic piece that will be heard with pleasure by audiences at large.—Stewart R. Sabin

The *Afro-American Symphony* seemed a much more important work on second hearing than it did the first time it was played in this series.—David
Kessler

Press Comments (3rd performance):—
Some explanation is necessary here. After this second performance
the Scherzo of the symphony was broadcast in a special broadcast to
Germany. Now to get to the third performance. In December Dr. Hanson sailed to Germany to conduct the Berlin Philharmonic in a special
concert of American music. The Scherzo of the symphony was included
on the program. The following is an excerpt from an article that ap-

peared in the *New York Times* concerning the concert: "The audience demanded a repetition of Still's scherzo."

My Opinion: This symphony approaches but does not attain to the profound symphonic work I hope to write; a work presenting a great truth that will be of value to mankind in general. I have good reasons to expect its performance in Switzerland soon, and probably in England.[23]

NOTES

1. Organized in 1875 by a former slave as Huntsville Normal School, it was known from 1878 to 1919 as State Normal and Industrial School. It became a land grant college in 1891. Its current name is Alabama Agricultural and Mechanical University, Huntsville, Alabama.

2. Still "leave one," a typographical error.

3. Still "loned," a typographical error.

4. Still left Wilberforce University in 1915 and married Grace Bundy on October 4 of the same year; "1916" is an error.

5. W. C. Handy, 1873–1958, composer and music publisher, "Father of the Blues." For his relationship with Still, see "In Retrospect: Letters from W. C. Handy to William Grant Still," *BPiM* 7 (1979): 199–234; 8 (1980): 65–119.

6. Associated with the Clef Club, an organization of male African American musicians in New York.

7. Opening dates in brackets are taken from Gerald M. Bordman, *American Musical Theatre: A Chronicle,* 2d ed. (New York: Oxford University Press, 1992), unless otherwise noted.

8. William Service Bell was a baritone. Still's song *Good Night,* composed in 1917 while Still was at Oberlin College, is dedicated to Bell. Bell sang it at a concert on October 21, 1921, at the Newark (N.J.) YWCA; his accompanist was Tourgee DeBose. *Bio-Bibliography,* W58.

9. George Whitefield Chadwick (1854–1931), composer and longtime director of the New England Conservatory.

10. Edgard Varèse (1883–1965), avant-garde composer.

11. Luckey [Luckeyth, Luckyeth] Roberts (1887–1968), jazz pianist and band leader, composed fourteen musical comedies; the identity of the one orchestrated by Still is uncertain, though the opening date of *Charlee,* November 23, 1923, seems about right. A second Roberts show at about the same time is mentioned by Bordman, but its opening date is not given.

12. The Plantation was a nightclub in Harlem. Will Vodery was the music director of record.

13. For a biography of Carroll (1893–1947), see Ken Murray, *The Body Merchant: The Story of Earl Carroll* (Pasadena, Calif.: Ward Ritchie Press, 1976).

14. Donald Voorhees (1903–1989) conducted five editions of *Earl Carroll's Vanities,* starting at age twenty, and many other shows. He is best known as the conductor of the "Bell Telephone Hour" for twenty-nine years, the last nine of them on television, from 1940.

15. J. Brooks Atkinson in the *New York Times,* February 27, 1928, 26:3, reproduced in the *New York Times Directory of the Theater* (New York: Arno Press in cooperation with the Quadrangle/New York Times Book Company, 1973).

16. The first performance on WJZ is listed in the *New York Times* (January 1, 1933) as taking place on Tuesday, January 3, 1933, 9:30–10:00 P.M. Frank Black was the musical director at WJZ; it is not known who made the decision to bar Still as a conductor.

17. *Ouanga,* 1932.

18. Howard Hanson (1896–1981), composer, directed the Eastman School of Music from 1924 to 1964, organized annual festivals of American music, and conducted many of Still's works from the 1920s on.

19. Marya Freund (b. Poland 1876, d. Paris 1966), known for singing the music of many twentieth-century composers.

20. "Puritan Epic" is crossed off the title page of the score at WGSM and "From the Heart of a Believer" is substituted. Perhaps Still began with the latter title, changed it for the competition, then changed it back again.

21. Alain Locke and M. Gregory, eds., *Plays of Negro Life: A Sourcebook of Native American Drama* (New York: Harper and Row, 1927).

22. Another slip by Still. Still's diary shows 1930 as the year of composition, not 1931. The work was premiered on May 22, 1931.

23. There is no evidence that these performances took place.

William Grant Still
and Irving Schwerké

*Documents from a
Long-Distance Friendship*

Edited by Wayne D. Shirley

"He does not dedicate music lightly," said Verna Arvey of William Grant Still.[1] And indeed Still's works are dedicated to major cultural figures who were helpful to him—Edgard Varèse, Howard Hanson, Georges Barrère, Henry Allen Moe of the Guggenheim Foundation, Leopold Stokowski. Still's *Afro-American Symphony* is dedicated "to my friend, Irving Schwerké."[2] Who is Irving Schwerké, who bears the most prestigious of Still's dedications?

Looking in *Amerigrove,* we find that Irving Schwerké (1893–1975), "pianist, teacher, and writer on music," was music and drama critic for "the Paris *Tribune*" (i.e., the Paris edition of the Chicago *Tribune*) from 1921 to 1934. He was Paris correspondent for the New York periodical *Musical Digest* for the years 1922–1929 and for the *Musical Courier* for the years 1932–1941. He returned to the United States in 1941 (fleeing from the Nazi occupation of France, we correctly guess) and settled in his hometown of Appleton, Wisconsin, "to teach and write."[3]

We find out more about Schwerké from his papers, which he bequeathed to the Music Division of the Library of Congress. In them we see the latter years of Schwerké's life, spent as a well-loved piano teacher; we also see him as a collector of autographs (film as well as music and stage), photographer, and champion of American music. The Schwerké Collection contains significant correspondence with many composers, American and European; yet it is the letters of William Grant Still, running from 1930 to 1964, that are the unquestioned glory of the collection. Two further items, given by Schwerké to the Library of Congress in 1966, add to its importance: the holograph manuscripts of the original versions of Still's *Africa* and *Afro-American Symphony*.

One fact neither the *Amerigrove* article nor the Schwerké Collection tells us: Still and Schwerké never met.[4] Their friendship developed entirely through correspondence, a correspondence that is now preserved in the Irving Schwerké Collection in the Library of Congress and the William Grant Still–Verna Arvey Collection in the Department of Special Collections of the Fulbright Library at the University of Arkansas in Fayetteville. For the early years we have few of Schwerké's letters—the young Still, unlike Schwerké, was not a systematic organizer of his correspondence, and he may have left much of his correspondence behind when he moved to California in 1934. From 1937 on we have both sides of the correspondence.[5]

The correspondence as we now possess it begins in 1930. The opening letters invoke two figures important in Still's life during the 1920s but are otherwise unremarkable:[6]

[July 17, 1930?][7]

108–15 172nd St.,
Jamaica, N.Y., U.S.A.

Dear Mr. Schwerke:—

Kindly allow Mr. Varese, c/o Morgan & Co., 14 Place Vendome, Paris, to see the sketch by Bruce Forsythe before you return it to me.

Sincerely,[8]

William Grant Still

(Forsythe's "sketch," we can infer from Schwerké's later interest in *Darker America,* is probably a draft of "A Study in Contradictions," which appears below in this volume.[9] Varèse lived in Paris from fall 1928 to summer 1933.)

18, rue Juliette Lamber
Paris, Oct. 9, 1930

Dear Mr. Still,

Yours of July 17th has followed me all over Europe—I have at last received it and hasten to thank you for your kindness. The Forsyth study has helped me much, and I am now writing our friend Varese, to give it to him—I should have done so before, had I known your wishes in the matter. I hope you will send me another example of your MS, similar to the one you sent me some time ago, as I shall want to decorate my article with two facsimile[10]—if I have them! And for my personal vanity, please don't forget to

Figure 13. Irving Schwerké with singer Sophie Tucker, for whom Still made arrangements. From the collections of the Music Division, Library of Congress. Courtesy of Library of Congress.

send me some time, your photo with dedicace and also one of your compositions with inscription. If I had something for piano or voice, I could easily place it on programmes here. With good wishes and again my thanks, believe me,

Faithfully yours,

Irving Schwerké

P.S. Re Osgood's "So This is Jazz," I tried to obtain a copy of this book for review in the Chicago Tribune, but no luck. I *too* hope to have the pleasure to meet you sometime.

Still replied on October 29:

Dear Mr. Schwerke:

Your letter was indeed welcome. Hence the prompt though brief response.
   Let me pause here to thank you for sending Forsythe's account to Mr. Varese.
   Here are copies of two songs, a snapshot and an example of my poor manuscript.[11] Am more than glad to send them.
   Please pardon the appearance of the songs. I want to get them off today. They are the only copies I have here and the inclement weather makes it inconvenient to get to New York.
   As soon as I can get the nerve I will have some photographs made and send them to you.
   Please drop me a line when you find time. Shall look forward to it.

Yours sincerely,

William Grant Still

A pleasant and enjoyable correspondence, but not a remarkable one. Still's next letter is very different in tone: Schwerké is suddenly Still's confidant, the "sympathetic ear" to whom he can tell his troubles. (Had Schwerké, in a letter to Still, assured the young composer that the writer had "a sympathetic ear" for his troubles? Still's use of the phrase suggests that he is responding to a statement by Schwerké.) This remarkable letter is worth quoting in extenso:

Jan. 9, 1931

Mr. Irving Schwerke,
18 rue Juliette Lamber,
Paris, France.

My dear Mr. Schwerke:

Greetings and sincere wishes for your happiness and prosperity during this year to which we have so recently been introduced.

The first of this week saw the completion of my latest effort. Its title, Afro-American Symphony, is self explanatory. I believe that the use of a theme in Blues idiom in a work of this sort for the purpose of welding it together is absolutely unique. And its rhythmic interest should prove to be equally as great as its melodic interest. But I must not bore you with more details.

The reaction has set in. This, as well as present conditions, has served to bring on a spell of depression. A sympathetic ear is indeed the most effective relief for such an ailment. Please do not think hard of me for becoming confidential. Strange to say, considering that we have had no personal contact, I have felt from the first that in you I have a friend.

It is unfortunate for a man of color who is ambitious to live in America. True (and I gladly admit it) there are many splendid people here; broad minded; unselfish; judging a man from the standpoint of his worth rather than his color. Such men as Dr. Howard Hanson, Frank Patterson and many others. Such a man as my friend Varese proved to be when he was here. But there is a preponderance of those who are exactly the opposite. And the views of the former must, of necessity, conform more or less to those of the latter.

I have never felt this so keenly as in the past few months. Friends who would lend me a helping hand, who would make it possible for me to make a living for my family[,] are unable to do anything because of those who are opposed to placing a colored man in any position of prominence. That is stating it mildly.

As for my people . . . well, there are many who have allowed themselves to become bitter over conditions. But, thank God, there are those who have sufficient wisdom to refrain from becoming bitter; who long for and labor to attain the day when the two racial groups may reach a state of perfect harmony or merge into a new group. With the latter I am in perfect accord.

Unless there is a change soon I will be forced to abandon my aspirations and look to other means of gaining a livlihood [sic] or to go where such conditions do not exist.

I shall look forward to hearing from you[,] for your letters are always welcome.

Forgive me if I have taken too great a liberty. I would not have done so had I not felt assured that you would understand with that sympathetic understanding born of friendship.

Yours sincerely,

William Grant Still

Schwerké was duly moved by Still's letter.

Paris, Feb. 6, 1931

Dear Mr. Still,

How friendly of you to write me that nice letter! It certainly was pleasant to receive it, and what you express therein, I assure you, is quite mutual. I am glad you feel we are friends, I believe we are. My letter has to be short, for I am not yet over a long siege of the flu, and have to watch my strength. Another time I'll write at length. This is, however, sufficient to bring you my good wishes and to say I am happy you feel the undersigned is a friend to whom you can talk as if to yourself!

Yours,

Irving Schwerké

Before he received this letter Still wrote apologizing for the letter that had so moved Schwerké:

Feb. 10, 1931

Dear Mr. Schwerke:

My present happiness exceeds by far the depression I experienced when I last wrote you.

Probably I told you of having written a work last summer for ballet, chorus and bass soloist. Sahdji is its title.[12]

Through the kindness of Dr. Howard Hanson, to whom it is dedicated, Sahdji will be produced in May.[. . .]

I am sorry now that I burdened you with my woes in that letter, and I wish that I could recall it. Won't you forgive me?

Please drop me a line.

Yours very sincerely,

William Grant Still

As Still was writing this letter, Schwerké was planning a three-day festival of American music to be held in Bad Homburg, Germany, that July. On February 16, 1931, he wrote Still asking him for a score of *Darker America*. It would be, said Schwerké, "the only composition by a Negro composer to be heard at the Festival." Still replied on February 27:

Dear Mr. Schwerke:

I know not how to begin thanking you for your great kindness to me. There is appreciation that causes one to be effusive in giving thanks, and there is that appreciation born in the heart of one's soul. The latter sort is not expressed with ease.[. . .]

I will send you score of DARKER AMERICA and score and parts of AFRICA. Please, if it be possible, program AFRICA instead of DARKER AMERICA.[. . .]

DARKER AMERICA, being an earlier work, has many faults. Lack of continuity, harmonization not altogether characteristic, insufficient development as well as other defects. AFRICA is a far more consistent work. It was performed this season by the Rochester Symphony.[. . .]In addition it will be easier for me to supply the parts [of AFRICA]. Finally the latter [i.e., AFRICA] is an unpublished work and it will not be necessary to pay a fee for performing it.

I plan, D.V.,[13] to go through the extra score of AFRICA I have here for the purpose of eliminating any errors it may contain, and I hope to mail both scores to you before the end of the coming week. I am writing today for the parts of AFRICA and will forward them as soon as they come.[. . .]

Bruce Forsythe's enthusiasm for *Darker America* was beginning to pose problems for Still, who felt he had moved beyond that work. Schwerké telegraphed Still to send the score of *Africa* only—a telegram that did not arrive in time to save Still from a fracas with the post office, which looked at the printed score of *Darker America* as a "book" and therefore unacceptable to French customs.[14] Still was still planning to send both scores when he wrote a letter giving instructions for the performance of *Africa:*[15]

If you decide in favor of "AFRICA" (and I sincerely hope you do) I suggest a cut from No. 17 to No. 20. On page two of the score you will find indicated a special pizzicato. F.N. Pizz. (Finger Nail pizzicato) is an invention of mine and has proved effective. It is produced by plucking the string as near as possible to the place where it is stopped. The plucking is to be done with the tip of the finger nail. Please call the conductor's attention to this, and to the Harmon and Fiber Mutes for Trumpets and Trombones. The Harmon Mute seems to contribute flexibility and is unusually good for delicate brass effects. It is rare now in this country to find trumpeters and trombonists who do not use this mute (with the exception of those in the symphony orchestras. They seem to be satisfied with the terrible [erased: metal] pear shaped mutes.) The Fiber Mutes produce a very pleasing tone and are, I believe[,] better for playing staccato passages. Where the three tom-toms are employed one player should be assigned to the 15 inch tom-tom and one player to the 12 inch and 10 inch tom-toms[. . .]from No. 3 on through the remainder of the composition only the normal pizzicato is to be employed.

In March Schwerké wrote Still suggesting that they drop the formal salutations "Dear Mr. Still" and "Dear Mr. Schwerke."[16] Still replied:

My dear Irving:

I am happy that we may dispense with formality. May our friendship ever grow, and may that day come when I may prove to you the deep regard I have for you.

From now on they are "Dear Still" and "Dear Irving"—and often "Dear Friend."

Friendship did not, alas, make the problems of international communication any easier: several letters of this period deal with the details of getting a work in a new style, in manuscript, with a set of revisions to be entered, ready for performance:

Paris, May 25, 1931

Dear Still:

It seems impossible to procure the Harmon and Fiber mutes for Trumpets and Trombones, in Europe. Will you have the proper number of these sent to

> Dr. Oskar Holger
> Ludwigstrasse 14
> Bad Homburg Germany,

upon receipt of this letter, if possible. The Bad Homburg people are anxious to do AFRICA as you wish, and have exhausted every means of getting these mutes[. . .]

June 3, 1931

Dear Irving:

After receiving your letter today I went to purchase the mutes, and to arrange for having them sent. But I discovered that the mutes cost almost fifty dollars, not including duty, etc. I then concluded that, under the circumstances, it will be best to employ ordinary mutes (i.e. the conical kind.)
    [. . .]When the Rochester Symphony performed AFRICA the trumpeters and trombonists used [conical] mutes and, though the color desired was not exactly obtained, it was approximated.[. . .]

Schwerké's reply to this letter notes also the receipt of a photograph of Still to be used in the program:

Paris, June 12, 1931

Mon cher Still:

I am happy and proud to have the photo, it certainly represents a "stunner!" Thanks for sending it. I shall tell the Bad Homburg people what you say re the mutes, and depend upon it they will do their best. The concert is 9:00 o'clock, evening of July 8th, and will be broadcast in America over New York Radio. Watch papers for further details. From nine to nine-fifteen I make a speech! Should like to send you a personal message at that time, but . . . I appreciate your kind words—you know how I feel towards Still and his music. I hope some day to know you personally.

Yours,

[signed] Irving

The Bad Homburg Festival of American Music duly came off on July 6 – 8, 1931.

Still wrote Schwerké on receiving the handsome and elaborate program book of the festival:

[July 29, 1931][17]

My dear Irving:

The programme book came today. Gee, but I am delighted with it! I am truly glad to have your picture and autograph. It may interest and amuse you to learn that the ladies who have seen your picture today have been favorably impressed. Others have remarked as to the kindliness of your expression. I am tempted to remove the picture and frame it.

Your sketch on American music is of great value. I agree with you as to the origin of American Music.[18] As I see it the music of the American Negro has resulted from the union of the religious songs you mentioned and the primitive songs of Africa.

I noted with great interest the foot-note on page 58 regarding "jazz".[19] Undoubtedly the word is of French origin for both it and the eccentric style of playing (as it was regarded in those days) to which it was applied were introduced in the Northern section of the United States by Creole musicians.

Although I am at best a poor judge, I know that you deserve great credit for the material contained in the programme book.

Please drop me a line when you have time.

Yours faithfully,

Still

On July 19 Schwerké wrote Still of the results of the Bad Homburg festival, and of his new plans for *Africa*. It is a long letter, but it deserves quoting at length.

Dear Grant:

Your AFRICA was the sensation of the Festival. It had a success and was comprehended, as I have never before seen. Throughout the length and breadth of Germany it has been written about in the most wonderful manner. Enclosed are a few articles—I wish I could send you the hundreds that have appeared. I wish you had been there—and as I listened to AFRICA I was not only grateful for its composer, but for the fact that he is my friend. No one but a man who has a great capacity for friendship could write like that. The work made such a stir, I see possibility of having it performed elsewhere in Europe, so instead of returning the score & parts to you, I have them with me in Paris, and unless you ask for them back right away, shall keep them here. I hope to place it with some important orchestras—if you wish I should—and naturally, this time, they will pay for the perform-

ing rights. If I hold out for $50.00, is that all right with you? I don't see
how, in the face of present conditions, we could ask for more and get it, if
that much. I think you have confidence in me in these matters? Other festivals will be under way:—have you, or will you have anything that could be
given as a first world performance? Let me know.[. . .]

Still answered in a letter dated by Schwerké as July 31, 1931:

Dear Irving:

There is so much I want to say that I scarcely know how or where to begin.
Your letter and the clippings came today. I feel exactly like a small child on
Christmas morning. I am happy to learn that AFRICA was received favorably, but the happiness aroused by your expression of commendation is far
greater.[. . .] Truly you are a friend, Irving. Indeed I will be glad for you to
keep the score and parts. Any arrangements you make for other performances will be agreeable to me. However, it would be neither friendly nor
fair for me to be the only one to profit. I insist that whatever sum is paid
for performing rights be divided equally between us.

The letter goes on—without even a paragraph break—to a topic of
greater importance:

I have a composition here that has not yet been performed. It is the "Afro-
American Symphony". In it I have sought to portray the American Negro
as he is. Dr. Damrosch has the score. I have been trying to get it back from
his secretary. As soon as she returns it I will send it to you.[. . .]

What Still did *not* tell Schwerké in this letter is that the score already
bore the dedication "Dedicated to my friend, Irving Schwerke." This
was to be a surprise for Schwerké. Like many surprises, this one was
plagued by unforeseen problems—Still forgot to put enough postage on
the package; Schwerké had to pay an extra fee and wrote Still what
seems to have been a somewhat peeved letter.[20] But when he examined
the score in detail and saw the dedication, Schwerké was much moved.
(Perhaps he sensed that he was now immortal.) Still answered Schwerké's
letter of thanks:

Sept. 5, 1931

My dear Irving,

I am more than glad to have your letter. I felt that you had not yet exam-
ined the score when I received the first letter you sent after having gotten it.
In truth, Irving, the dedication can only feebly express my regard for you.
May the ties of friendship that bind us ever grow stronger.

Faithfully,[21]

A further letter talks about Still's further plans and encloses a brief analysis of the symphony:

[October 5(?), 1931]

My dear Irving:

Your friend greets you, and hopes that you have returned from your vacation happier and in better physical condition than ever before. At last the parts of the symphony have been completed. I am sending them to you. They are, I believe, correct. More string parts will be needed. It will be undoubtedly best to have these made in Europe. By all means send me the bill. I will feel hurt if you fail to do so for it would be an imposition to expect you to bear this expense. Please don't fail me in this matter, Irving. You have undoubtedly received the score ere this. That was sent about ten days ago. The brief sketch enclosed will prove valuable for program notes. I hope that my next effort will be a stage work. Have applied for a Guggenheim Fellowship. If I receive it I intend to spend the period it affords in writing an African opera.[22] I have what I believe is a good libretto. Can tell better after a professional librettist has examined it. Shall look forward to a letter soon.

Your friend,

Still

[Enclosure]

The Afro-American Symphony is not a tone picture of the "New Negro." It portrays that class of American Negroes who still cling to the old standards and traditions; those sons of the soil who differ but little, if at all, from their forebears of ante-bellum days.

These are an humble people. Their wants are few and are generally child-like. Theirs are lives of utter simplicity. Therefore no complex or elaborate scheme of harmonization would prove befitting in a musical picture of them. 'Tis only the simpler harmonies, such as those employed, that can accurately portray them.

From the hearts of these people sprang Blues, plaintive songs reminiscent of African tribal chants. I do not hesitate to assert that Blues are more purely Negroid in character than very many spirituals. And I have employed as the basic theme of the symphony a melody in the Blues style. This theme appears in each movement as follows:

I. Principal theme.

II. Contrasting theme.

III. Combined with the principal theme of the Scherzo near the close of the movement.

IV(a). Contrasting theme.

IV(b). Vivace (6/8 time). Representing the Negro's good humor that can rarely be long suppressed by any serious or sorrowful mood.

Even before receiving the score of the *Afro-American Symphony* Schwerké had been busy promoting Still's music in other places than Bad Homburg. He had written Wilhelm Furtwängler in June or July 1931 about the score of *Africa*;[23] now he sent Furtwängler the score of the *Afro-American Symphony.* (In the event, Furtwängler's reply was courteous but gave no indication that he would be interested in performing the work.)[24]

While Schwerké waited for Furtwängler's reaction to the *Afro-American Symphony,* he sent the manuscript of *Africa* to Rhené-Baton, then conductor of the prestigious Concerts Pasdeloup in Paris. In May Rhené-Baton borrowed the manuscript scores of both *Africa* and the *Afro-American;* by fall he had decided to perform *Africa* at the Concerts Pasdeloup.[25]

Sometime early in 1932 Schwerké wrote to Still, describing his work for Still's music and relaying Rhené-Baton's enthusiasm for *Africa.* Schwerké seems to have written more than one letter on this subject. To the first of these[26] Still replied with a letter giving details of his current project:

My dear Irving:

How can I begin to tell you of my joy. AFRICA to be performed in Paris. . . . . well. . . . . . somehow it seems like a dream. Irving, I am so grateful to you. Yours is indeed true friendship.

I am working now on the score of La Guiablesse. The scenario is based on a legend of Martinique. In fact, it is the legend. As the story goes—the devilish spirit, La Guiablesse, comes down from the mountains into a village in the guise of a beautiful woman and lures Adou, the lover of Yzore, to follow her back up the mountain side. Just as he approaches her to embrace her she is transformed into a fiendish hag. He, shocked into unconsciousness[,] falls backward over the cliff. Ruth Page prepared the scenario. Dr. Hanson plans to produce it at the Eastman theatre next May.[27]

Must get back now to the music paper. Will write you again soon.

Faithfully,

Still

Still's other letter replying to the news of an impending Paris performance of *Africa,* a letter dated February 28, 1932, was to be fateful for their friendship:

My dear Irving:

There is so much I want to say. There is so much I should say.——I would say it if I but knew how to begin.

Your letters always bring me happiness, and the *last one*——!!! Well, I have not yet gotten back to earth.

How can I thank you enough? It can't be done. You have accomplished something not at all easy; something requiring the courage of a pioneer. And I am so grateful.

I will make inquiry concerning the mutes without delay, and inform you in the near future. I will also have some photographs made right away. If there is something else I may do be sure to let me know. And please thank M. Baton for me, and assure him that I am delighted over his opinion of AFRICA and his decision to perform it.

Yesterday I sent you a money order for two hundred and fifty francs. I have wanted for a long time to repay you for what you spent when the symphony was delivered[,] but had to wait until I got to work.[28] Things now (thank God) are going well. Now let us return to the money order. If possible I want to get three or four program books of the Bad Homburg Festival. Some friends have asked for them.

Won't it be great if Mr. Furtwangler decides to perform the symphony? I believe that God is with us, and that He will bless us unusually in this particular instance. Despite my great unworthiness He has shown me clearly that He hears my prayers by answering them. Moreover, He has even shown me that He has great blessings in store if I but obey in a certain work He has given me to do.[29] These assertions may sound strange to you, Irving, but they are absolutely true. Some miraculous things have been experienced by me in the past year.

I pray for you each day, and I shall continue doing so.

Write again when you can get to it. In the meantime I will look forward
to a letter.

Faithfully,

Still

Under the spell of this self-revealing letter Schwerké replied:

Paris, March 7, 1932

My dear Grant:

Those first two words in no way express it! No, what you say does not
sound strange to me. I, too, believe, and my faith and conviction are great,
but I pray constantly that they become greater. And I know that you and I
have been directed to each other to accomplish some purpose—we do not
know what it is, but one day we will. Tell me some of the miraculous things
that have happened to you this past year, so I can share the joy and wonder
of them with you.

The books have gone forward, and I'll be glad to have the photos. And
among the photos you send me, will there be one for your friend (my ambition, to be *the* friend) with an inscription you can write only to him? Unless
some catastrophe happens, Furtwangler and Rhene-Baton will play the
Symphony and AFRICA, and yesterday, in Brussels (I went to hear a new
work by Tansman), I prepared the way for Still with the wonderful orchestra there. I am praying to find some way to have some copies made of both
works—if I could, then I could get a number working at the same time. But
all that will come if we but remain true to the faith and the guidance we
know we have. I did not want you to send me that money, but since you
have, thanks. All good wishes, dear Grant, and let me hear from you often.

Faithfully and with love,

Irving

Still's letter is inarticulate gratitude; Schwerké's is something like court-
ship. Still replied in the time-honored way of those receiving unwanted
advances from a friend—answering the outward message warmly while
ignoring the subtext. Still's own subtext comes through in the obsessive
and embarrassed reassurances of friendship in this paragraphless letter:

My dear Irving:

Finally!! . . . The photographs and a letter that should have been written
long since.[30] I waited until I had the pictures made to write. How can I tell
you how grateful I am to you? What words can I use to describe the happiness you have brought me? Truly you are a friend, for your friendship is the
genuine sort that expresses itself in deeds of kindness.

(The door is closed—kindly but very firmly—on Schwerké's hopes of being "*the* friend.") Still continues:

> I pray for you daily, my dear friend, and I sincerely hope that God will bestow on you the greatest blessings that man can receive. God alone is able to reward such kindness as you have shown me. And I believe that He is going to reward you. I look forward to the day when I may see you and endeavor to tell you how dearly I prize your friendship. Please pardon such rambling expressions. Under such circumstances one cannot easily express himself coherently.

Still's letter then—without even a new paragraph—shifts to current news:

> Dr. Hanson evidently forgot to autograph the photo I sent him. I am sending him another. The Rochester Orchestra repeated the symphony last month. The critics agreed that it seemed more worth while on second hearing. The job[31] is going along well even though it is exacting. Am rewriting La Guiablesse. Will tell you more of it later. Have not forgotten the mutes. Probably it will be best for me to purchase them here and send them to you. The books[32] came. Thanks so much for sending them. Must get ready now to work. Remember that I hold nothing but good wishes for you, and write as soon as you can.
>
> Sincerely,
>
> Still

That July Still reported to Schwerké his reactions to his work on the "Deep River Hour":

> [July 1932][33]
>
> My dear Irving:
>
> [. . .] The days between this and my last letter have held for me nothing more than the usual routine. . . . . the broadcasts of one week leading immediately into preparation for those of the next week. But there is some fun in it[,] to say nothing of the valuable experience I am gaining. Truly, Irving, God has never suffered anything to occur in my life that has not been profitable.[. . .]
>
> Creative work is at a standstill for the present. This is a period of study and reflection. I believe it is a turning point leading me to a more thorough technical knowledge and a deeper spiritual understanding.[. . .]

In the event, it was not Rhené-Baton who conducted *Africa* at the Concerts Pasdeloup. Rhené-Baton, facing a revolt by the orchestra, resigned his conductorship late in October. He returned the score of

Africa to Schwerké on January 15, 1933; on that same day Schwerké made sure that it was received by Richard Lert, the young Austrian conductor who was to take over some of the conducting of the Concerts Pasdeloup orchestra. Lert agreed to program *Africa,* which was duly performed on February 4.[34] The photograph of Still in front of a framed poster for that program is one of the iconic photographs of Still.

Schwerké wrote to Still of these maneuvers and of the performance, cautiously grading his opening salutation:

Paris, February 10, 1933

My dear Composer:

What joy it was to have AFRICA performed in Paris! It was a prayer answered. I am sure you would like to hear the story. Rhené-Baton had taken the composition for performance with the Pasdeloup Orchestra; but he resigned and being without an orchestra, could do nothing. Then I met Lert, and the first thing he said, when we talked over his Paris programs, [was] "I wish I had a real novelty for Paris." I said "I have exactly the score you want!" So I rushed home, got the score, and Lert fell in love with it on the spot, and immediately announced it for performance. Since Paris, he has, I believe, also done it in Austria, and maybe Germany. At any rate, he is all for you and you have another staunch supporter in him. In Paris AFRICA had an overwhelming public success—I have heard thousands of concerts here, but seldom a first performance that so gripped a Parisian audience. Under separate cover, by registered mail, I am sending you a collection of papers, etc. on this performance,[35] so you can have a complete record for your scrap book of your introduction to the "capital of the world," and so you can see the publicity I did, etc.,—in case you ever come here and have to do things alone, you will thus have some idea of the local technic. Some of the criticisms are not good, but that need not trouble you in the least; you do not write for critics, but for the human heart, and the way your audience responded was proof of your success. In no case would or should I ever expect the French critics to do justice to an American work, for a number of reasons. Among them 1) they are down on all American musicians and composers, and cannot abide the thought that we have anything that is worthwhile; of course there are some exceptions, but I am speaking of French critics as a class. 2) most of them are composers themselves, and this in advance condemns any new composition that is successful artistically and with the public. In spite of this, however, your criticisms tend to the good side, and withal I am heartily happy over the whole venture.

I hope this finds you well and happy, and that you will go on composing more of your much-needed music. Best wishes and love from

Irving

[in ink]: Other articles will be sent as I find them—if there are more.

The reply to this letter is classic Still:

My dear Irving:

Again you have befriended me. I am so grateful. Could you but know what great happiness your kindness has brought me you would feel repaid. I scarcely know what to say concerning the reaction of the audience to AFRICA. Your reference to it made me think again of a vision I once had of AFRICA.

> In the dream I stood in the rear of a large concert hall where a symphony orchestra was rehearsing. My attention was centered on the orchestra until it was suddenly directed to one of the seats in the rear of the hall. On it I saw the score of AFRICA bound in a handsome red cover on which the title had been stamped in letters of gold.

I am sure this was a prophetic vision. The red cover was a symbol of happiness and the gold letters a symbol of success.

A person of a practical trend would surely scoff at such a conclusion. But I know God will direct, protect, and disclose to those who believe, events that lie in the future. Things of that sort have happened so often in my life. At times I have been shown symbols, the meanings of which were explained to me by an unseen entity. At others I have viewed coming events prior to their advent in the actual sequence (and with the same persons appearing in the dream who played a part in the events themselves) in which they occurred later. You can understand why I feel as I do about such things. They are facts, and important ones too. God will surely lead us steadily toward good ends if we but let Him.

Recently I have been led to make a new score of AFRICA. This is the final version. Errors of form, orchestration etc. that were present in former versions have been corrected.

I shall certainly be glad to receive the articles. Truly, Irving, you leave nothing undone. I thank you so much.

I am enclosing a note to Dr. Lertz [i.e., Richard Lert]. If I knew where to reach him I would not annoy you in this way. But circumstances force me to do so. I will be very grateful to you if you will forward this to him.

Affairs are progressing rather slowly here at the present. I believe the time is near when I will be called abroad to complete the work I must do on earth. So is it written.

LA GUIABLESSE is to be performed in May. I will let you know its outcome.

I pray that God will bless you, and will write you again in the near future.

Still[36]

After 1933 the correspondence lapses temporarily. Two letters of 1935 are useful for documenting Still's activities and for giving his initial reaction to a major American work that he is generally seen as standing in opposition to:

[1935]

1604 W. 35th. Place,
Los Angeles, Cal.

My dear Irving:

I can blame you not at all if you see fit to ignore this letter, for I have been exceedingly negligent.

The interim between this and my last letter to you has been literally crowded with activity. A Guggenheim Fellowship, that has just been renewed for six months, enabled me to compose the opera, BLUE STEEL, and two pieces for piano and orchestra, THE BLACK MAN DANCES, and KAINTUCK'. Truly, Irving, I had not realized the amount of work required to write an opera. For over one and one half years it demanded practically all of my attention and time.

I do hope you won't judge me too severely for having failed to write you. I want to hear from you very much, and promise that I will not again be guilty of my error of omission.

Sincerely,

Still

[October 1935][37]

My dear Irving:

Several good things have happened since I wrote you last. Pro Musica hears a two piano version of KAINTUCK', my poem for piano and orchestra, on Oct. 28. The Cincinnati Symphony will play the same piece this season. The New York Philharmonic is playing the AFRO-AMERICAN SYMPHONY this season. Since I sent you the score of this piece I have revised it, and it has been published. A new ballet, CENTRAL AVENUE, is almost ready. As a matter of fact, completing the extraction of the string parts is all that remains to be done. This is a humorous ballet. Although it bears the name of the main thoroughfare in the Negro District of Los Angeles' east side, it typifies the main streets in the Negro Districts of many American cities. Both Ruth Page and Zemach have asked for it.[. . .]

Your picture hangs on one of the walls of my living room. Many people see it, and ask me about you. In each instance a sales talk follows in which your virtues are enlarged upon.

The Chicago Opera Co. has done nothing about BLUE STEEL. In the interim I submitted it to the Metropolitan. Nothing happened. Unless something happens soon new plans will have to be laid out. It shall be produced.

PORGY met with success in New York, and I am glad. I felt all along that Gershwin would achieve splendid results.

Please drop me a line when you find time. Best wishes.

Sincerely,

Still

The correspondence resumes in 1937. Schwerké remains his cultured and amiable self; Still has shed the awkwardness of the young composer and writes with a new confidence in his stature. We do not have the opening letter of the correspondence—Still's letter ordering a copy of Schwerké's recently published book, *Views and Interviews*.[38] The first four extant letters run as follows:

March 1, 1937

Dear friend William:

Many thanks for yours of Feb. 5, 1937, and the check for a copy of VIEWS AND INTERVIEWS which has been mailed to you to-day (registered). I hope it reaches you in good condition—if not, let me know—and that you will find some virtue in it. Shall be mighty pleased to hear your candid opinion.

Will you please let me know if AFRICA and the AFRO-AMERICAN SYMPHONY have been published? I have had various opportunities of late to place them with certain conductors over here, but the copies which you sent me some time ago are now so used (I have had so many people study them!) that I do not think it safe to pass them on any more. The instrumental parts are, of course, still in good condition. The other day at The Hague, for instance, I told George Szell about you—he is up and coming and wants something fine from America; and if he found your works suitable to his feeling (for he does not undertake works that are contrary to his nature) he would do same in Scotland, Holland, Prague, etc. I am certain he would love your music, as anyone must who knows it. Also let me know if you are protected by the Society of Composers for any performing rights that might be due you. You might also send me notes about yourself to bring my file of you up to date. You see, I am always working for you whenever I have the chance—I love your music and esteem the author as friend. Has *my* symphony been done in America? The one dedicated to me? If so, I'd be thrilled to have the program.

Best of everything to you, and as ever,

Irving

1604 West 35th Place
Los Angeles, California

March 17, 1937

Dear Irving:

Your letter arrived safely, and the book today, in excellent condition. I spent some time cutting the pages, and looking over the contents, and

I assure you that I think it is splendid. I don't see how you manage to do so many things, and to do them all so well! I'm so happy that you autographed my copy—I shall prize that most of all.

No, Africa has not been published, although it has been in the hands of one for the past few years.[39] He is not at all energetic, and therefore, I am trying to push the Afro-American Symphony most of all, since that has been published by a most sympathetic, energetic, and intelligent man: George Fischer, at 119 West 40th Street New York. He has done a great deal to help this along, and I have written to tell him of your great interest in my music. Perhaps then, he will communicate with you—or would you rather communicate with him?

Don't you remember—this Afro-American Symphony is the one I dedicated to you? Before publishing it, it was necessary to revise it extensively, and in the resultant confusion, your name was left off the printed copy. However, I have always thought of it as being dedicated to you, and have agreed with the publisher that whenever a new edition is made, your name will appear on it as it should have done in the first place. I have also *revised Africa,* and for that reason, *the parts that you possess for each of these compositions are no longer any good.*[40] I think the new versions are much better than the old, and will be anxious to know what you think about them.

Yes, I am a member of ASCAP, and I am sending you the notes about me, as you asked.[41] Believe me, it is hard to tell you how very much your continued interest in my music means to me, I am grateful for everything you have done, and for everything you wish to do in my behalf. I would be most proud and happy if George Szell were to like my Afro-American Symphony well enough to do it.

It has been most successful since Stokowski and Hans Lange played it last year. Lange gave it a New York performance with the Philharmonic Orchestra, and Stokowski played the final movement on his tour across the United States. Then, when Lange played it twice in Chicago a few months ago, the ovation on each occasion was so tremendous that he had to repeat it a third time. Perhaps you read the account of that in the Musical Courier. Rene Devries was most enthusiastic, I thought. And did I tell you that I conducted the Philharmonic Orchestra here in the Hollywood Bowl in two of my compositions last summer? It was quite an occasion, as it was the first time in the history of the United States that such a thing had happened. It pleased me very much, I can assure you.

You asked me for some comments and a program of the symphony dedicated to you: one critic in New York said that the Scherzo of the Symphony crashes through the melancholy of the preceding movements with such verve and rhythmic gaiety that Carnegie Hall was electrified. In Chicago, Mr. Eugene Stinson said that "all lovers of music who are touched with the wonderful qualities of his race will rejoice to find in this work a simple, straightforward, unpretentious but extremely beautiful account of how the composer, from a decidedly superior viewpoint, beholds the world that is open to the Negro in the United States." I'm sorry the original clippings are pasted securely in my scrapbook, or I'd send them to you.

I wish you could find time to write and let me know what you are doing. I read you in the Musical Courier, of course, and I've especially enjoyed the little quips to Leonard Liebling for Variations—that you send from time to time.[42] They are very clever, and, on looking through the new book, I find that you have brightened it with many such pithy paragraphs: witty, but full of truth.

I'll be looking forward to hearing from you whenever you have a chance to write, and I surely thank you for the book and for the autograph! I value them highly. With best wishes always, I am

Sincerely,

Still

P.S. Did I tell you that Richard Lert is out here, and that I like him very much? Ernst Toch is here too. He is certainly a fine fellow.

April 10, 1937

William Grant Still
1604 West 35th Place
Los Angeles.

Dear Still,

Thanks for your good letter and all the nice things you say about my new book. I am happy you like it—and the autograph.

I shall look forward to seeing my name on the revised copy of the Afro-American Symphony. I am very happy to have this honor and thank you sincerely. In regard to the matter of the revised edition: shall I destroy the old orchestral parts which I have? I hope that you will not fail to send me score and parts of both the Symphony and Africa, as, if you still want that I should have these works played here in Europe, I must have entire new sets of the compositions. Please let me know as soon as possible so that I shall know what to do in regard to these matters.

I rejoice that everything goes so well with your work and am indeed happy to hear all the fine things said in your behalf. Write again soon, and believe me,

Yours sincerely,

Irving

May 5, 1937

Dear Irving:

I was surely glad to receive your letter—the more so since I have been spending the hours just before retiring in the pleasant pastime of reading your book. As I must have told you before, I'm enjoying it very much in-deed. It is instructive and interesting. Even the title is very well chosen. I heartily agree with what you expressed about modern music—that chapter is marked in my copy. I, too, feel that there are very few people today who are attempting to write sincere music, that is, music that stems from the Divine Source rather than from a limited human mind.[43] Not long ago, I gathered from one of Mr. Stokowski's letters that he also shares this view of modern music.[44]

I'm surprised that my publisher has not yet gotten in touch with you about the Afro-American Symphony, and I shall write soon to remind him of it. Yes, since the old orchestral parts of this symphony are now useless, I wish you would destroy them. I think you will agree with me that the new version is far better than the old.

Instead of sending you a new version of *Africa,* would you not prefer that I send you the score of a new tone poem? This one, "Dismal Swamp", lasts about fifteen minutes and should be off the press quite soon now. This afternoon I telephoned to inquire about it, and was told that in a very few days I may have a copy to give to you.

Last week, Langston Hughes (the poet) arrived in Los Angeles to collaborate with me on a new opera. We are both enthused over the subject, and by the musical possibilities inherent in the libretto that has been sketched. Langston plans to pass through Paris briefly in a few months, and I am going to ask him to see you meanwhile.[45] I think you will enjoy knowing each other. Have you read any of his books?

I have been unusually busy for the past few months. There is so much work to do, and the studio work has to be done so very rapidly that it keeps me rushing about. I'm trying, however, to complete a new Symphony.[46]

You know, I do appreciate more than I can tell you all that you are doing for me and my music, and all that you have done. I hope that you will have time to drop me a line occasionally to let me know of your own activities, for I missed your letters during those months when I did not hear from you, though I realized how busy you were.

Always with my very best wishes, I am

Sincerely,

Still

Schwerké's next letter to Still was to put a strain on their friendship. *Views and Interviews* had contained studies of four composers: Paul Dukas, Manuel de Falla, George Migot, and Serge Prokofieff. It had not, however, mentioned Still.[47] Schwerké had also, in 1931, published a monograph on Alexandre Tansman,[48] which had been the first detailed study of the composer (and which remains a useful book). Schwerké now proposed to do a "comprehensive" article on Still: perhaps (though this idea remained unarticulated) it might even become a book— *William Grant Still, compositeur américain.*

One fact Schwerké had not considered. His previous major writing on composers—the book on Tansman and the articles in *Views and Interviews*—had been to a significant extent the result of interviews carried on face-to-face.[49] Composer and writer could talk together; questions the composer thought of little importance could be quickly turned away ("You don't want to talk about my Third Quartet"). The book on Still, on the other hand, would involve intercontinental correspondence: anything Schwerké was to know, Still would have to send him. And a question becomes an assignment ("Dear Irving: You ask about my third string quartet. It's not a work I'm particularly proud of . . .").[50] Schwerké's letter proposing the book reads, in fact, distressingly like the letters sincere graduate students in search of a dissertation topic write to composers:

May 12, 1937

William Grant Still
Los Angeles

Dear Still,

I am preparing to write a comprehensive article about you and your work, for publication in Europe, and as I want this to be as complete and up to date as possible, I am writing to you to ask for the following information. If, when you have read over my request, you find that you do not have the time to prepare the data, please tell me quite frankly, and I shall understand.
    What I need is:—

1) detailed biographical notes; indications of personal traits of character, likes, dislikes, important influences in your life, important friendships, first (childhood) experiences in music, and so on. Any data that will help me to present Still the human being.

2) complete catalogue of your compositions, with titles, genre, date of composition; names of persons to whom the works are dedicated; dates of first world performance of each work, together with complete names of performers, name of hall, etc.

3) detailed description of each work (also, if possible, give inception of work) pointing out for what instruments it is written, any peculiarities in harmony, rhythm, melodic line, form; pointing out any qualities which make the work distinctly American in sentiment, meaning, and aesthetics.

4) as many press notices as you can send, about each work, be those notices pro or con.

5) until such time as the article shall go to press, keep me informed of unfinished works, giving detailed information as
above, so it will be complete down to the time of publication.

Do not try to be short in all this, but give me as much as possible. The
article must be such so that, when once published, it will never have to be
done again, and so that people can ever after refer to it again.
Other points on which you must think and send me information are:—

6) what is the effect in America of your work, what is the
peculiar uniqueness of your work;

7) what are the determining causes of this sensibility, what
are the relevant circumstances of your life which determined
it?

8) what is the sensibility which necessitated this expression?

9) by what means was this sensibility given expression; give a
technical examination of your style.

10) give close examination of some perfectly characteristic
passages in which your sensibility is completely expressed.

This, of course, means work, but unless we do it, nothing serious can be
achieved. After I have all this material from you, provided you can see your
way to sending it to me, I shall get to work and make a serious and complete study of you and your work, one which will be definite and able to
serve you and those interested in your art. Hoping to hear from you very
soon, and with all best wishes, I am

Sincerely yours,

Irving

A large-scale request! But Schwerké had done much for Still, and his
name was powerful. And for an American composer to have "a comprehensive article" published about him in Europe was rare. Still was
willing to cooperate, but there was a complication, which he explained
in his reply:

May 27, 1937

Your letter arrived yesterday, and your proposed article fills me with a deep
sense of gratitude, for I fully realize all that this will mean to me in my
work, and to my future. The more I read your own book, the more I ad-
mire your writing and your approach to your subjects, so you know that
I feel honored to have you wish to write such an article about me.
    Now, there is a rather strange situation in regard to this—one in which
I will rely upon your unfailing tact to set everything right.
    Do you recall reading articles by Verna Arvey in the Musical Courier?
I believe that she had one called Italian Piano Music, Contemporary and
Past—as well as one on South American and Cuban Music[51]—in maga-

zines in which articles by you also appeared, so perhaps you did see them. At any rate, for the past year Miss Arvey has been gathering material about me for a book she will write, and she has also lectured about me and played my music in various cities here. You can well imagine that I have given her all the available material about myself and my work. However, I have now asked her if she will answer your questions fully for me from the material I've already given her. She has promised to do this, also to add some details about the reactions of the public that I couldn't very well give as well as she—and then I will tell her a few facts which are especially for you, and will give her some clippings that may be of service.

She has done this for me because she admires your writing, but I think it would be nice if you were to acknowledge her help in some way when your article is finally printed. The manner of doing this would be up to you, and I know that you will devise some way to do this so that everyone will be happy over it. She would ask nothing except the public acknowledgement, which it seems right that she should have so that later, when her book comes out, it will not appear that she has copied her own data. On the other hand, you can manage to say such a thing so graciously and tactfully that it will not seem as though you had copied either, and then you have had enough experience with my music to write in much that neither one of us could possibly send you, for your sensitive reaction to music is one of your finest features.

What do you think about this? Of course, I am going to supervise whatever Miss Arvey sends, so you can be assured that there will be no inaccuracies.

Again, I thank you from the bottom of my heart for your good, helpful thoughts in my behalf and I hope to hear from you very soon.

Sincerely,

Still

Arvey's involvement with the project had both benefits and drawbacks. The major benefit was that she had already done the in-person interviewing necessary for such an article (who can sit down and write a letter giving "indications of personal traits of character, likes, dislikes, important influences, . . . important friendships, first [childhood] experiences in music, and so on"?) and had gathered much of the necessary data. The drawback was much greater: here was another work on Still already in progress, and one being written by someone in whom Still had already considerable personal interest. Still's asking Arvey to share her work with Schwerké shows Still's admiration for his old friend-by-correspondence—and possibly his consciousness that "a comprehensive article" on him in a major European journal would be a great help to his career.

Arvey wrote to Schwerké agreeing to cooperate:

[May? 1937]

Dear Mr. Schwerké:

Mr. Still has asked me to write and to send you this information about him.[52] He has given me some information which is especially for you, and then has asked me to add some of my own reactions gained through several years' association with his music. The clippings are, I think, duplicates of some that are pasted in his scrapbook.

He has also promised to write to you to inquire if you wish to acknowledge my help in some way—for that is indeed all I would ask. He has from time to time spoken of you with great affection and esteem, and I know that you must admire him in order to have done the wonderful things for him that you have done. Thus we surely must have a mutual admiration, and I feel as if that establishes a sort of bond between us. If this information does not satisfy you, or if I ever can be of service to you, do not hesitate to ask.

I know that Still has dedicated to you one of his most important works—and he does not dedicate music lightly. He has also shown me your new book, which I admire very much—and of course I've read most of your Paris dispatches in the Musical Courier, as well as the longer articles you write occasionally.[. . .]

With best wishes for your project and for all your endeavors, I am

Sincerely,

Verna Arvey

P.S. It is not worthwhile to mention "Central Avenue" which appears in some of the notices because it has been completely destroyed, and I think Mr. Still would rather not have it given even a passing notice. VA.[53]

Schwerké responded to Still and Arvey on June 12:

[. . .]

I[. . .]had a cordial letter from Miss Arvey, and now have yours of May 27, 1937. The reason why I have always gone directly to the composers about whom I write, is just to avoid such situations as has now seemingly arisen. I cannot as yet quite make up my mind what to do. You have no doubt noticed that in my articles I never lean on others— I collaborate with the composers, but do not lean upon my confreres. I quite understand and appreciate the situation, and I certainly do not want to be unjust to any one. . . . . But as I say, I have not yet really gone through the material, and cannot say definitely until I have done so. However, we won't worry and let us hope all will be right in the end. In the meantime, I appreciate the trouble Miss Arvey went to, and hope you will thank her for me.

With all good wishes I am,

Sincerely yours,

Irving

Schwerké and Arvey managed to maintain a semblance of friendship during this difficult time. Arvey even agreed to let Schwerké use her material without credit:

[June 1937?][54]

Dear Mr. Schwerke:

Mr. Still has just shown me your recent letter (you notice that I am writing this on his typewriter) and I want to assure you that you may use the material I've sent you without mentioning my name in connection with it if you wish. He feels that your article will be a splendid thing for him (and so do I) and I would not like to think that any action of mine had taken an opportunity from one who is so talented and who deserves all the help we can give.

Although some of the thoughts are my own, the greater part of the material stems directly from Mr. Still, as you will see when you read through it, so that you need have no fear as to its being authentic. He okayed it before I sent it to you. Moreover, knowing his reticence and modesty on matters concerning himself, I am sure that you have far more material in what I have sent than if he had written it out himself.

Please do use what you will need, and ask me for more information if you need it.

Sincerely,

Verna Arvey

Other correspondence of this busy year touched on other subjects. One of the more awkward was the omission of the dedication to Schwerké in the published edition of the *Afro-American Symphony*. Still had mentioned this in his letter of March 17. Schwerké alludes to it in his letter acknowledging the receipt of the score of the symphony:

Paris, May 21, 1937

Dear William,

Just a word in reply to yours of the 5th. By now you have no doubt received my letter saying that I received the scores from Fisher,[55] for which many, many thanks. The first person to whom I showed the symphony opined I must be a very untruthful person: I had told him the symphony was dedicated to me, and when he did not see my name on it, he called my bluff! Of course, I'll be happy to have the DISMAL SWAMP and to do all I can for it, as well as the others.

Should be happy to meet Langston Hughes and to do anything in my power to make his sojourn agreeable—this also applies to any other friends or acquaintances of yours who may be coming this way.

[. . .]

Still explained the circumstances again in his letter of June 8:

[. . .]

About the Afro-American Symphony: didn't I explain to you how it happened that the dedication was left off in the revision? It *is* dedicated to you, and to none other,—and the second printing, when it comes, will carry the printed acknowledgement. Those were my instructions to the publisher, and if the friend to whom you showed the Symphony still thinks you untruthful because the name doesn't appear, you have only to show him this letter and to tell him that it *was* on the original copy.

[. . .]

Despite Still's assurance, the dedication to Schwerké never appeared on any published edition of the *Afro-American Symphony;* a writer today, like Schwerké in 1937, can only follow Still's advice and "show [the doubters] this letter" to verify that Schwerké is the dedicatee.[56] This writer has, at least, one further resource: when I asked Verna Arvey late in her life whether Still might have withdrawn the dedication to Schwerké, she replied, "Certainly not! The work was dedicated to Schwerké and that dedication stands." It was as definite a statement as I heard that very definite lady make.

The year 1938 started with a final exchange of letters on the subject of Schwerké's proposed "comprehensive article."

Paris, February 25, 1938

Dear William,

I am working on a big study on my favorite STILL, but I do not progress very fast, for the principal reason, that I do not have much information about your compositions. I am enclosing a list of works on which I have only the merest fragments of hints, if anything at all, and hope that, sooner or later, you can let me have the material. Naturally, not having the scores and never having heard them performed, I can't say much about them, can I, hence must turn to you. I want this to be a "historical" study, one that people can turn to for information on any one of your works, and which will be authoritative from every point of view. Thanks in advance, and with best wishes and affectionate greetings,

Yours,

Irving

The enclosed list began with a request for an analysis of *Darker America*—Bruce Forsythe's article was still on Schwerké's mind—and went on to ask general questions about a number of works. Still's answer, which ran to two and a half pages of single-spaced typing, attempted to answer all of these questions.[57] It is here given complete, preceded by my attempt to reconstruct the now-lost enclosure with themes of *Darker America* that accompanied Still's letter.

[Reconstructed enclosure:]

Theme A

Theme B

Theme C

Theme D

Theme E

Theme F

A combination of themes A and C (more accurately, of themes A and F)[58]

First, you ask for an analysis of "Darker America". I am enclosing some themes, the lettering on which will correspond to the letters in the following description. "Darker America" was my first serious effort in a larger form and I now realize that it has many weaknesses. As its title suggests, it represents the American Negro. The introductory material is furnished by theme A on the separate sheet (presented at the outset by unison strings) and by theme C. At the 16th measure, theme B commences, given to English horn: this represents the sorrow of the American Negro. After 21 measures, theme C appears. Then follows a brief development built on themes A and C. After this, the episodic theme D appears, later leading back to a new treatment of theme B, interspersed with repetitions of theme D in various forms. After a brief development, theme E, which is a transformation of theme C, appears. This leads to theme F which is also a transformation of theme C. Following this comes a 3/4 section that I now wish I had omitted, for it seems forced. Then theme B, transformed, reappears, accompanied by theme D. This leads to a combination of themes A and C, with D appearing at intervals. This combination of themes A and C are shown at D.[59] That leads to the end. Now I know that I could have built a stronger composition with only two of these themes. As it is, it's fragmentary.

On the following points, my memory may be a little dim, but I'll try to cover everything you requested. "From the Land of Dreams" is dedicated to Edgar[d] Varese. It is for three voices and chamber orchestra and was first performed by the International Composers Guild Inc. in N.Y. on February 8, 1925, conducted by Vladimir Shavitz. I have now lost the score, so cannot analyse it further. "From the Journal of a Wanderer" is dedicated to Edgar[d] Varese and was first performed by the Chicago Symphony under Frederick Stock in 1926. It is an orchestral suite. "Levee Land" has no dedication. It was first performed in N.Y. in 1926 by the International Composers' Guild with Florence Mills as soloist and Eugene Goossens conducting. It is a humorous suite for soprano and chamber orchestra. "From the Black Belt" has no dedication. It is a suite for chamber orchestra composed of the following sections: Lil' Scamp, Honeysuckle, Dance, Blue, Brown Girl, Mah Bones Is Creakin', Clap Yo' Hands. "Log Cabin Ballads" has no dedication. It was first performed in 1928 by Georges Barrere and is 3 nostalgic pieces for chamber orchestra, entitled: Long To'ds Night, Beneaf de Willers, Miss Malindy.

"La Guiablesse" has no dedication. It is a ballet based on a Martinique legend, on which Ruth Page based her scenario. The legend speaks of the she-devil who assumes the guise of a beautiful woman in order to lure a susceptible village youth to his death. It was first performed at the Eastman Theatre in Rochester with Dr. Howard Hanson conducting in 1933.

I have destroyed "Puritan Epic." [60] "Sahdji" is an African ballet with a chorus and a chanter, a bass soloist who from time to time sings African proverbs to emphasize the meaning of the action. This chanter also sings a Prologue to the ballet, though this Prologue is a comparatively recent addition, added during the revision of the ballet. In this ballet Sahdji's dance before the chieftain, Sahdji's fire dance, and Sahdji's dance of death are the outstanding numbers. The first is the most exciting of them all. "Blue Steel" was composed in 1934–35, and is dedicated to the Founders of the Guggenheim Fellowships. It is an opera, the scene a mythical swamp, showing a man from a modern city who goes into a primitive Negro tribe and attempts to carry away with him the high priest's daughter—he does not love her, but he simply wishes another conquest. [61] In the end, he dies. The opera has never been performed in its entirety, but excerpts from it have been given.

"Kaintuck'" is dedicated to Verna Arvey, and is a tone poem for piano and orchestra depicting my emotions as I passed through a certain section of Kentucky on a misty summer day. It was first performed on two pianos at a Los Angeles Pro Musica concert in 1935 with Verna Arvey as soloist, [and] Robert V. Edwards at the second piano. I think it would be well not to speak of the first orchestral performances of this work, for two very good friends of mine—Dr. Hanson and Eugene Goossens—played it in their respective cities within a few weeks of each other, and each claimed credit for a first performance. So, in order not to hurt either of these men whom I admire so much, perhaps it would be as well not to mention either performance as being the *first* orchestral one. Since then, of course, I have conducted it on several occasions with Miss Arvey as soloist.

"Three Visions" has no dedication, though I have mentally dedicated it to my friends who have departed this life. It is a group of three compositions for piano in the modern (not ultra-modern) idiom. First played in concert in Los Angeles in the Spring of 1936 by Verna Arvey. I have since made an arrangement of the second one, "Summerland", for small radio orchestra. The first one is called "Dark Horsemen" and the third "Radiant Pinnacle".

"Dismal Swamp" is a poem for orchestra with piano solos, and is largely built on a single theme. It is sombre, for the most part, and moves slowly. (Didn't I send you a score of this? If so, the poem at the beginning will express what I was trying to say musically.)

"Lenox Avenue" is a series of ten episodes and Finale for orchestra, chorus and announcer, with a short piano solo. It was especially designed for radio performance and was first performed over the Columbia Network on May 23, 1937 with Howard Barlow conducting. The continuity for this performance was by Verna Arvey, as is the scenario for the ballet version that was made of it later and will soon be produced in Los Angeles. The whole thing is a musician's view of Lenox Avenue, the street that cuts through Harlem, and all the events seen there.

"Great Day" was changed by the publisher into the book of Spirituals I sent you.

"Deserted Plantation" has no dedication and was first performed by Paul Whiteman at the Metropolitan Operahouse in N.Y. in 1933. I do not consider this work representative enough to require a complete analysis.

Now, you ask about songs, piano pieces and violin pieces, etc. I've already described the three piano pieces. There are no pieces for violin, although my arrangement of "Summerland" for radio orchestra is fixed so that a violin and piano might play it. There are two songs, both published by Schirmer. One is "Winter's Approach", a humorous song to words of Paul Lawrence [*sic*] Dunbar, and the other is "Breath of a Rose" to words of Langston Hughes. The first is rollicking, the second pensive and more or less ultra-modern in style.

I think I've covered everything you asked for now. Please forgive this very careless typing. I became enthusiastic over getting details correct, and perhaps started going too fast. And please let me know if there is anything else I can do.

Always, gratefully—

Sincerely,

Still

Early in 1939 Verna Arvey's monograph "William Grant Still," a volume in the series Studies of Contemporary American Composers, was published by J. Fischer & Bro. Irving Schwerké thanked Arvey for his copy on February 28. Schwerké's own "comprehensive article" was never finished: probably he came to the conclusion that a genial correspondence with a composer and a deep involvement with a few pieces was not a sufficient substitute for the personal contact that had informed his other large-scale articles on composers.

Schwerké left Paris in mid-1940—his last dispatches to the *Musical Courier* were published in their issue of June 15. When he left Paris he put his material in storage; by the end of the war, when he could retrieve it, Still's career had moved substantially past what Schwerké's material documented. Schwerké never again raised the possibility of collaborating on a detailed article on Still: his postwar life was that of a teacher, not of a journalist.

One incident of Schwerké's flight prompted an entertaining response from Still. While Schwerké was in Lisbon he was interviewed by a local music critic, and declared that Still and Roger Vuataz were "duas maiores revelaçoes da vanguarda." [62] Schwerké enclosed a clipping of the interview in his letter to Still announcing his arrival in America ("Just a word to say, here I am!"). Still replied:

> March 25, 1941
>
> Dear Irving:
>
> Many thanks for your note, and for sending me the clipping from Portugal. I hope you meant for me to keep it, as it made me very proud and I've already pasted it into my scrapbook. Incidentally, if you really do consider me America's outstanding composer, you might find yourself very unpopular with a few other American creators who have settled it in their own minds and among their friends that they and they alone deserve that honor!!!!
>
> [. . .]

The Still-Schwerké correspondence for the years after 1941 is pleasant and enjoyable—if this were a Complete Correspondence it could be reprinted without apology—but it is not particularly revealing. Composer and writer say hello, apologize for the amount of time it has been since they have written each other, congratulate each other on triumphs (Schwerké is particularly happy to hear of the success of *Troubled Island*), and in general write like old friends who cannot think of anything particular to say.

What, finally, was Schwerké's significance to Still's career? It was chiefly as Still's European representative in the early 1930s, securing performances of Still's orchestral works—notably of *Africa,* which as a shorter work than the *Afro-American Symphony* had more appeal to a European conductor looking for a single American work. We should not exaggerate the importance of these performances. Schwerké, a single person with single copies of two works (and those in versions that by 1937 had been superseded), could do only a limited amount for the composer: only a publisher with good European connections could have done much to establish Still in Europe in the 1930s.[63] Still's European reputation had to be built afresh in the 1940s—largely by conductor Rudolph Dunbar; it must be built again today.

But we should not underestimate the value of Schwerké's work for Still either. The performances Schwerké arranged—coming at a time when nonexpatriate Americans had few opportunities for European performance—must have seemed to the young composer like a voice ratifying his importance as a composer and his ability to speak to a general audience of the cultured. And when the conductors to whom Schwerké showed Still's work in the early 1930s came to America in later years, Still's name was already familiar to them. Nor should we underestimate the value of Schwerké's "sympathetic ear": here was a man on another continent, knowing and known to Still only by words and notes on paper, willing to believe in the importance of his music. Nor, finally, should we see Schwerké entirely in terms of Still: the article on Schwerké in *Amerigrove*, a just if brief summary of his importance, makes do without mentioning Still at all.

For the Still scholar the letters are extremely valuable. We tend to see Still principally from the Arvey years, when he had a skilled journalist, publicist, and organizer as his helpmeet. It is valuable for us to hear his voice in his earlier years: already confident of his musical ability, but less sure in his dealings with others. The Still-Arvey collections in Fayetteville and Flagstaff are rich in letters to Still of this period,[64] but Still's own letters, save for the few represented by carbons, must be looked for elsewhere. We have only begun to look beyond the Still collections for Still letters: perhaps this sample from what can be found in a single collection will inspire researchers to look further.

We can even be grateful to Schwerké for being available as a dedicatee for the *Afro-American Symphony*. What would we make of an *Afro-American Symphony* dedicated to Hanson or Varèse? Even a dedication to a major black cultural figure such as Alain Locke would tempt listeners to hear the *Afro-American Symphony* in the light of that figure's ideas of Afro-American culture. Dedicated to someone whom Still knew only as a disembodied "sympathetic ear," the *Afro-American Symphony* stands splendidly on its own, a work that helps to define American culture rather than a work defined by it.

NOTES

Letters of William Grant Still are in the Irving Schwerké Collection, LC, unless otherwise noted.

Letters of Irving Schwerké to Still are in the William Grant Still–Verna Arvey Collection, University of Arkansas, Fayetteville, unless otherwise noted. Some are present in Fayetteville only as Xeroxes.

The letters have been edited gently, with a minimum of editorial intrusion; footnotes, however, have been given their head. Obvious typos have been silently corrected, but Still's accentless "Schwerke" and "Varese" have been allowed to stand, as has "Lawrence" for Paul Laurence Dunbar's middle name in Still's letter dated "[Spring 1938]." I have noted the one misspelling in a letter written by hand. (Still's first two letters are in his flowing hand; all other correspondence is typescript.)

Both Still and Schwerké indulged in an occasional fit of ellipsis marks. Editorial ellipses are distinguished from these by being put in brackets, thus: [. . .].

1. Arvey to Schwerké, [1937 May].
2. Or rather "To my friend, Irving Schwerke." Still never did quite believe in the accent on the final letter of Schwerké's name.
3. Ramona H. Matthews, "Schwerké, Irving."
4. I was assured of this fact by Verna Arvey when I interviewed her in February 1982.
5. I was given photocopies of Schwerké's letters to Still by Verna Arvey in 1981; this paper represents a very belated acknowledgment of my debt to her.
6. Still's first two letters have the added use to the researcher of giving a sample of Still's longhand writing style. (The remainder of Still's side of the correspondence is typescript.) Still, who in fact wrote a beautiful longhand, seems to have been ashamed of it: what little of his later correspondence is not in typescript is in his idiosyncratic (and also handsome) print hand. He did occasionally rely on longhand in informal situations: these letters give us one of our most extensive samples of that hand.
7. Dated from Schwerké's reply of October 9. Still's letter is undated: Schwerké may have gotten the date from the postmark.
8. Still, whose spelling is generally impeccable (though without accents), writes here—and only here—"sincerly."
9. The version published in this volume, dated October 1930, is too late to be the precise text Schwerké saw.

10. Schwerké is thinking in French (as, later in this letter, "dedicace"), not forgetting his plurals.

11. The two songs were doubtless "Winter's Approach" and "Death of a Rose," published by G. Schirmer in 1928. Neither the "snapshot" nor the manuscript is now in the Schwerké Collection.

12. If Still had written Schwerké about *Sahdji,* the letter is lost. This remark does suggest that we are missing some of the early letters of Still to Schwerké: surely Still would have remembered if he had written Schwerké a letter containing a works list.

13. *Deo volente*—"God willing."

14. Still to Schwerké [1931 March? (letter beginning "On presenting the scores. . .")].

15. Undated letter [March 1931?] beginning "I am sending you scores . . ."

16. This letter is not in the correspondence as we now have it. (Perhaps Still put it in a scrapbook?)

17. Dated in pencil by Schwerké.

18. "The beginnings of American music are not to be found in the lore of the American Indians or Negroes, or in the hybrid jazz. Its origin must be sought in quite another field, that is, the psalm-singing of Colonial New England. . . . [T]he psalm-singing of New England became the starting point of the musical art of America." "American Music 1579–1931: A Brief Sketch." *American Music Festival in Bad Homburg, July 6 to 8, 1931* [program book], 45–46.

19. The footnote (on page 52 of the copy of the program book in the Schwerké Collection) reads in part: "Our book *Kings Jazz and David,* published in 1927, gives a reprint of data on jazz which was published some years before the War, and in which the word *jazz* is seen to be a direct descendant of the French verb *jaser,* nothing more nor less."

20. The shipping of the score of *Africa* had involved similar problems: Schwerké probably felt that Still should have learned from that experience.

21. We do not have the original of this letter. (Perhaps Schwerké framed it.) A typed transcript—presumably by Schwerké—is fastened onto the dedication page of the 1931 manuscript of the *Afro-American Symphony.*

22. Still's first Guggenheim opera would finally be *Blue Steel.* That he here describes the opera he intends to do as "African" is evidence that he is still contemplating an operatic version of *The Sorcerer.* See "Finding His Voice" above.

23. Furtwängler to Schwerké, July 24, 1931.

24. Letter dated March 29, 1932. Still's letter to Schwerké of February 28, 1932 ("won't it be great if Mr. Furtwangler decides to perform the symphony?") establishes that it was the *Afro-American,* not *Africa,* that Furtwängler was examining.

25. Rhené-Baton to Schwerké, September 21, 1932.

26. I am assuming that Still's letter given below—a letter inconveniently undated—precedes that of February 28, 1932, and replies to a previous letter of Schwerké. This is done partly to preserve the flow of narrative, for which it is important that Still's letter of February 28 be followed immediately by Schwerké's letter of March 7. But it is most likely that each of the two letters is written in response to a different letter, and it seems unlikely that the undated

letter, with its immediate exclamation "AFRICA to be performed in Paris . . . ," would postdate the much more elaborate letter of February 28.

27. *La Guiablesse* was in fact performed at Eastman on May 5, 1933.

28. The work was the job of arranging for and conducting Willard Robison's radio program, the "Deep River Hour."

29. The "in" in this sentence has been added in ink.

30. Still's letter is dated by Schwerké as "20-IV-32"—probably from postmark, not from date of receipt. The photographs are no longer with the letter.

31. Arranging for the "Deep River Hour."

32. Presumably the program books from the Bad Homburg festival.

33. Dated by Schwerké.

34. Only the first and third movements were performed at this concert. The performance was billed as a "première audition," which it was not.

35. Still replied, on receipt of the package: "My dear Irving: You certainly do things well. I was amazed to see so many things concerning AFRICA. Back of the many kind things you said I could read your desire to help me, regardless of how helping me would affect you. That's true friendship. And I'm thankful for it. I pray that God will bless you, Irving. [signed] Still."

36. Letter dated March 2, 1933, by Schwerké.

37. Later than October 10, the first New York performance of *Porgy and Bess;* a few days earlier than October 28.

38. Irving Schwerké, *Views and Interviews* (Paris: Les Orphelins-apprentis d'Auteuil, 1936). Probably Schwerké gave Still's letter to whoever was taking care of orders for the book (though note that Schwerké autographed Still's copy).

39. In March 1934 Still had signed a contract with Robbins Music Corporation, giving them "permanent ownership" of everything he was to write for the next two years, and to *Africa* and *A Deserted Plantation*. It was a disastrous contract: in the end Robbins published nothing of Still's but a butchered version of *A Deserted Plantation* and an arrangement of Foster's "Old Folks at Home."

40. The underlinings in this paragraph are in pencil. They may well be Schwerké's rather than Still's.

41. The notes are no longer with the correspondence.

42. Leonard Liebling was editor-in-chief of the *Musical Courier.* "Variations" was its column of miscellanea, which mixed comments by Liebling with items sent in by correspondents (Arvey sent in one for the November 28, 1936, issue).

43. Schwerké, after quoting an unnamed writer as saying, "Music is the mirror which most perfectly reflects man's inner being," had written: "Some recent concerts submitted Parisians to an almost indecent amount of new music . . . and I regret to report that none of it revealed the kind of 'inner being' that I, a simple mortal, should like to go after." *Views and Interviews,* 46.

44. No extant letter of Stokowski to Still suggests "this view of modern music."

45. Schwerké and Hughes did not meet. [Schwerké to Still, January 11, 1938: "The young writer with whom you are collaborating 'phoned me yesterday evening, and as he is leaving tomorrow for America, I shall not have the pleasure of seeing him."]

46. The G minor.

47. *Views and Interviews* contains no substantial material on any twentieth-century American composer, though it does quote Alexander Steinert and Edgard Varèse entertainingly on the subject of "wicked Paris" and the innocent American music student (153–154).

48. *Alexandre Tansman, compositeur polonais* (Paris: M. Eschig, 1931). (An English-language version, listed at the front of the book, never appeared.)

49. The article on deFalla in *Views and Interviews* is in fact brief and may not reflect an interview.

50. There is no Still Third String Quartet (he once wrote to Alain Locke saying that he disliked the form): this is an abstract example.

51. The articles are "Italian Piano Music, Contemporary and Past," *Musical Courier* 108, no. 22 (June 2, 1934): 6 ff.; and "Musical Potentialities in Cuba and South America," *Musical Courier* 113, no. 11 (March 14, 1936): 6 ff.

52. This material is no longer with the correspondence.

53. In fact *Central Avenue* was not "completely destroyed"; the first half of it, given a substantially new libretto, forms the first half of *Lenox Avenue*. There is a complete piano reduction, with stage directions, of *Central Avenue* in the Still-Arvey Collection in Fayetteville. Still may have worried that *Central Avenue*, written while under contract to Robbins Music Corp., might be invoked by that publisher to get rights for *Lenox Avenue*. (Apologies to Jeffrey Magee, who cited an earlier version of this footnote in the periodical *Lenox Avenue* [2 (1966): 5–6].)

54. Schwerké dates in pencil "May 1937." June—after Schwerké's letter of June 12—seems more likely.

55. J. Fischer and Bro., Inc.

56. Dedications are, in fact, particularly vulnerable. A story may help here. In the early 1980s I edited Charles Ives's *The Fourth of July* for the Charles Ives Society. I had done all of the work on the music when I decided to look at Ives's letters to Henry Cowell, whose New Music Editions published the first edition. Ives's letter on the receipt of the published score mentioned only one of the many mistakes in the engraving—some of them rather important—but complained bitterly that the dedication, to Ives's business partner Julian Myrick, had been omitted. In several years of intense work on the musical substance of the work I had seen no sign of a dedication: had I not read these letters the new edition, like the old, would have lacked a dedication.

57. Still's answer is undated. "Spring 1938" can serve as a brief identification.

58. For works through 1931, compare with the "Personal Notes" above and with descriptions in Arvey's essay.

59. I have assumed that "at D" is a slip of the typewriter in my reconstruction of the musical examples.

60. In fact, a full score of *Puritan Epic,* retitled *From the Heart of a Believer,* is in the possession of Judith Anne Still.

61. This interpretation of the hero's motives is not clear from the libretto. In any case, it is seduction and elopement, rather than kidnapping, that he plans.

62. *Diario de Lisbòa,* December 24, 1940. The critic who interviewed

Schwerké was Francine Benoit. Roger Vuataz is a Swiss composer and organist, born 1898.

63. Of American publishers of the period perhaps only G. Schirmer, against which Still nursed an obscure but powerful grudge, had the power to promote an American composer's career in Europe. J. Fischer and Bro., Still's helpful and cooperative publisher from 1935 to 1942, was influential in America but not in Europe.

64. Though they, too, tend to represent Still's California years much more thoroughly than earlier periods. This represents partly Arvey's talents as an organizer, but more the universal human tendency to accumulate things when you stay in one place and to throw them out when you move.

William Grant Still

A Study in Contradictions

Harold Bruce Forsythe

This is the earliest-known commentary on Still's work that extends beyond the a few sentences to be found in reviews of concerts at which his music was performed. It is also the only extended contemporary explication of Still's music from a New Negro, Africanist position. Both because of its specificity and because of the positions its author takes, it is far from the generalized New Negro positions on the music of African Americans taken by W. E. B. Du Bois or Alain Locke, described by Gayle Murchison in her chapter, above. Forsythe, who was twenty-two when he wrote this essay, drew on his training as a pianist and composer in the European and jazz traditions as well as his familiarity with the writers of the New Negro movement and the issues that occupied them. Both because he had long been aware of Still's work—ironic that he, raised in Los Angeles, knew more about the concert works of a composer who was based in New York than did eastern critics—and because of his own involvement as a composer who aspired to write concert music that honored his racial and national inheritance, his insights are compelling.

Forsythe's sweeping judgments about Still and his work were made on the basis of music now thought of as Still's "early" work, very little of it known today except by name. At the time Forsythe wrote the first surviving draft of this essay (February 1930), Still was just completing the score of *Africa*. It appears that Forsythe saw the score to *From the Land of Dreams,* but it has since been listed as lost and, though recently located, has yet to be heard a second time. *Portraits* is entirely unknown except for its mention here. The two ballets, *La Guiablesse* and *Sahdji*, were still unfulfilled dreams, although a version of the former existed. The *Afro-American Symphony*, the *Songs of Separation,* the opera *Troubled Island,* and the choral ballad *And They Lynched Him on a Tree* all lay in the future. By the time of the final draft (October), Forsythe had obtained the score to *Darker America,* but the newly completed *Sahdji* was out of reach in New York, as were the first performances of *Africa.* The virtual abandonment of this part of Still's production along with the vicissitudes of his later career (including Forsythe's estrangement from both Still and Verna Arvey and Still's changed position on *Darker America*) at least raise the question of whether Forsythe's judgments are valid for Still's later career. That they will remain stimulating and germane to discussions of Still's work seems certain. Forsythe's passionate interest in Still's work to 1930 strongly suggests that a real reexamination of Still's music should include these now-forgotten works.[1]

After a short preface and a rather pompous opening paragraph suggesting that most composers are misunderstood in their lifetimes, Forsythe launches into the meat of his essay. He offers a description of Still's unique talent and of Still's physical appearance, conversational manner, and pronouncements on other composers. A great deal of this detail is unique to this essay. After some discussion of earlier works, he then addresses the one substantial Still score to which Forsythe had access at that time, *Darker America,* composed in 1924 and published in 1928.

Still's *Darker America* has a large role in this essay and is discussed in the other sources published here as well. Therefore, some information about it is given here. Still provided this program note for the 1928 performance:

> *Darker America,* as its title suggests, is representative of the American Negro. His serious side is presented and is intended to suggest the triumph of a people over their sorrows through fervent prayer. At the beginning the theme of the American Negro is announced by the strings in unison. Following a short development of this, the English horn announces the sorrow theme which is followed immediately by the theme of hope, given to muted brass accompanied by strings and woodwind. The sorrow theme returns treated differently, indicative of more intense sorrow as contrasted to passive sorrow indicated at the initial appearance of the theme. Again hope appears and the people seem about to rise above their troubles. But sorrow triumphs. Then the prayer is heard (given to oboe); the prayer of numbed rather than anguished

souls. Strongly contrasted moods follow, leading up to the triumph of the people near the end, at which point the three principal themes are combined.[2]

Carol Oja describes the work as one "that synthesized black idioms with areas of intense chromaticism . . . by employing planes—or whole areas—that evoked African-American traditions and juxtaposing them, either vertically or horizontally, with a dissonant fabric." She points out his use of call-and-response technique: "The music for the 'call' imitates black vernacular idioms of uptown New York, and that for the 'response' is a dissonant crash from downtown."

Forsythe's judgment of the work is substantially different from that given later by Still in his "Personal Notes," his letters to Schwerké, and in Arvey's monograph, "William Grant Still." By the time Forsythe wrote about it so eloquently, Still had become dissatisfied with *Darker America*. "My opinion: Darker America has quite a few faults, viz. lack of consistency in form; too much material for such a short composition; faulty harmonization in places."[3] Oja observes a similarity between the sectional structure of *Darker America* and that of "the potpourri of hit tunes that make up the overture to a musical comedy." Although the critics admired its energy and originality, they also commented on its "lack of development." Thus they "ignored the possibility that this kind of discontinuous formal structure might have grown out of Still's work as an arranger and that such a source could be credible."[4] Still himself would likely have rejected the overture-medley structure of *Darker America* on the grounds that in practice it did not work as well as he wanted; he needed the broader symphonic structure to allow his themes enough space to speak effectively.

This is the second and later version of the manuscript, located in the Still-Arvey Papers; Judith Anne Still called my attention to it. Another, earlier version is now in the Forsythe Papers at The Huntington Library.[5]

1930

. . . For there is music wherever there is harmony, order, or proportion . . .
Sir Thomas Browne, *Religio Medici*[6]
To M. Edgard Varèse & Mr. Charles E. Pemberton:[7]

Without the one, there would
Perhaps have been no necessity

For this book; and without the
Other, it could never have
Been written . . .

PREFACE . . .

This little book does not pretend to be a full appreciation or even a
just criticism of the man with whom it is concerned. It no doubt suf-
fers all the faults and disadvantages of a pioneer work, since it is, to
my knowledge, the first that has yet been written concerning the peculiar gifts of Mr. Still. Biographical details are necessarily fragmentary and *Darker America* is the only work discussed at great length,
for the reason that space prohibited discussion of but one work, and
that composition seems to be the most representative production of
the composer.

Holding no exemption from the common infirmities of human nature, I have fallen into the customary deceptions and errors, but possessed of an opinion, not rapidly or carefully nourished, but an opinion that burst forth surreptitiously and slowly spread its foliage until
it became an obsession, it has seemed necessary to parade that
thought before the world, and to listen with interest to the conflicting echoes that ring in answer. . . .

Bruce Forsythe '30

I

A few years ago, in a letter to Katherine Ruth Willoughby Heyman, I
poured another decanter into the distilled ocean of tears already shed
over the senile fact that the artist is doomed to years of misunderstanding, even from the otherwise judicious, and to eternal damnation as far
as the masses are concerned.[8] After lavishing the customary compli-
mentary adjectives upon the Yahoos, I proceeded to lament that the only
recourse the harassed artist has at his command is to make himself so
incomprehensible that all and sundry will let him severely alone. Afflicted
at that time with the seriousness of youth, it seemed very strange that
many of our major critical voices were so bound in traditional techni-
calities and dogmas that they were, (and still are), unable to see that one
may love the clear daylight of Mozart and at the same time intelligently
appreciate the significance of Debussy, Stravinsky, Varèse, and all the
other men who have had something to say but have confounded the un-
imaginative by saying it in voices that sing somewhat out of tune with

the accepted Bibles of theory. Whereupon, the author of *The Relation of Ultra-Modern to Archaic Music,* wisely realizing all the unpleasant truths unseen by my optimistic eyes, answered that the artist is nothing more or less than a sort of glorified radio broadcasting station, sending out his "message" to all those who have receiving sets capable of "tuning in." It is apparent, even to a musician, that if a man followed Mrs. Heyman's advice, he would automatically make himself a disciple of my somewhat ancient suggestion.

This is the tragedy of the man whom nature has graced with ideas, and who has taken the trouble to equip himself with the mechanical means necessary for their logical development. Such a man is far removed from his immediate surroundings and from his friends. Physically he is among them. He eats, drinks, talks, rides or sleeps with them, but his feet at times trudge gingerly up steep precipices that are glass hills to them, broad fields that to them are barren he finds arable, his eyes are on dim and distant horizons that are mere strips of froth to them, ideas that to them are dead he flings into the marmoreal catafalque of his consciousness where, phoenix-like, they spring to life dripping with the yeasty beauties of his soul, he hears soundless sounds, sees with blinding clarity invisible patterns, his hands are up to the elbows in effervescent urns from which his friends "flee howling in terror." Even when this man of talent sees an equal in a friend, or when he is working seemingly in the company of disinterested people, the wall is still existent. He will, perhaps, enthusiastically discuss his art. But when he feels the mysterious ferments working deep within him, and realizes that an idea is about to burst like a bud into a full blown rose, he flees man as he would flee the plague. Not for fear of bees that might suck from the rose its perfumes, but from plebeian nostrils without the delicacy necessary for the appreciation of its scent, and hands that might sully the flower with careless handling. When the first flush has gone he will share it. Jealously, and with perhaps no little suspicion and caution. He then feels a bit like "broadcasting," partly out of pride, partly from the urges of an inferiority complex, partly from healthy egotism, but no doubt largely from a profound conviction that he has said something worth saying and that someone else might benefit from the hearing of it. This, upon a high plane, is called talent. Upon an infinitely higher perch, so lofty at times that it is not clearly visible, it is called genius.

It is increasingly difficult to write of a Negro of talent. The Negro press itself is impossible. Each day there appears in its columns lengthy accounts of tea-party musicales at which "Prof." J. Wilson Holmes presented an "original composition which was a great delight to the audience," and Evelyn Mae Smith "charmed the audience with a beautiful trombone solo." These quite dreadful lucubrations are the work either of dunces, or of clever journalists out for larger circulations and advertising sections. Another class of writers, however, has done even greater damage. An intensely serious class of musician, functioning "critically" on weekly sheets, has overworked the words "beautiful," "talent," "genius," and "wonderful" until they have little meaning. Of course all sober men know that this is so much whim-wham. The Negro is not the prodigiously talented individual his sheets assure him that he is, as he is not so downtrodden and forlorn as these same rags contend. Quite to the contrary he seems to be a race of harmless and polite mediocrities. In every field he has practitioners, but the best of these men would be forced to accept third or fourth place on an interracial list. Some men, Cullen, Hughes, Thurman, McKay, Walrond, Douglass; have done excellent work.[9] Perhaps in Jean Toomer he has a genius, as in Walrond, Hayes and Robeson he has men of very exceptional talent; but in the art with which we have to deal, he has very little to offer on the creative side.[10] Mr. Burleigh has written some polite and polished things, and gained a reputation quite out of proportion with his artistic output.[11] Dett, Diton, R. Johnson, Hall Johnson and many others have done good work.[12] The latter has done some exquisite things in arranging spiritual melodies for his inimitable choir, and he has made some striking songs, notably his vigorous and resonant setting of Langston Hughes' "Fyah Lawd!" Freeman and others have written very dreadful things, even more dreadful than certain of Mr. Burleigh's songs.[13] But these men for the most part have remained safely and sanely academic: their personalities are without color, and their occasional dabblings into intellectual seas have not been happy.

The intelligent white press is of course suspicious of Aframerican composers. They suspect, and rightly, that each new name ballyhooed will turn out to be a new conductor of spiritual arrangements, vocal confectionery and dishwatery compositions for the piano. They perhaps suspect what has long been a patent fact, that the Negro has little inclination or aptitude for music. A facile and fundamental sense of rhythm and harmony, and a group of excellent folk songs have given rise to the absurd nonsense about the Aframerican's "inherent musical genius." Of course it will be understood that what is meant by music is the ebb and flow of the polyphony of Bach and the cosmic sweep of Wagner's instrumentation and not the weeping of blues singers or the croon of plantation darkies. In Los Angeles, my home city, the situation is grotesque. Among the Aframericans there is a handful of honest and serious students, but they are overwhelmed by the most complete, ambidextrous and pyrotechnical mob of charlatans ever created.

But for the inevitable exception. As usual, he is the least known, and, if we except a small and select circle, the least honored. His name is ignored on the lists of Negro artists, issued in the press during the past year. The Journal of the fraternity of which he is a member ignores him in a long lucubration on contemporary Negro composers. Dr. Moton has evidently never heard of him and Carl Diton has recently printed a longwinded essay in which my subject does not receive the insult of bare mention, among men who are by no means his equals.[14] This man of whom I speak is a wildly colored flower, headily perfumed and exotic in contour, blooming alone but without loneliness in a vast and uncompromising desert. There is something poisonous about this perfume, to be true, but that has only tended to destroy the banalities of the common run of Negro composers. And to chuck their musty souls into the academic barrels where they belong. This man, William Grant Still, is without doubt the most talented Negro ever to compose music in America, and the only man of his race to abandon the past on one hand, to cling to it successfully on the other, and to make a successful and original artistic cohesion of the two. He has his hands in assorted dishes. He has written *From the Land of Dreams,* a strange, inchoate but brilliant fantasy, in which he takes the hand of that modern intellectual circle to which no other Negro, save only Jean Toomer has ever been admitted; he can write *Levee Land,* in which he brews the familiar racial stews in exotic kettles; he arranges American jazz well enough to work as running mate with Ferde Grofé;[15] and he has written *Darker America,* the most significant and thoroughly artistic tonal work ever written by a man of African descent. These are unusual feats, suggesting a plastic intelligence and a sound education, to say nothing of a singularly resilient talent.

He has hidden behind his position as an arranger of popular music. Most of his closest associates receive with surprise the news that he is an artist. A lady once made a remark that instantly recalled the cry of Heine's inamorata: "They tell me my Heinrich is a great poet. Is it true?" Having suffered all the neglect and misunderstanding that inflicts such exquisite pain upon the man of talent, and having in his hide the pointed barbs of narrow-visioned critics, to say nothing of the even more painful arrows of patronization, he has constructed about himself that fortress erected by all men who have something new to say and have had trouble in saying it to people who are incapable or unwilling to understand it. I knew him for months before I had the first inkling of his significance and before he showed me one of his orchestral scores.

Still is handsome in a languid Latin manner, inclined to portliness, and with eyes that glow with an unholy and unhealthy light when working, or when a beautiful woman interests him. It is curious that the flash is identical. The most revolutionary Negro composer ever heard of, and seemingly the quintessence of Paganism, he exhibits an outward display of religious devotion that is nothing so much as amusing. He has repeatedly warned me that unless I recant, repent, and mend my ways, I shall wake up one day in hell. To which I retorted that if he said verbally what he wrote in *Darker America,* he would be kicked out of Church. I am not here interested in religious discussions; there exists a vast literature of criticism to which I can add nothing. I note these facts because they are simply manifestations of the bundle of contradictory elements in this man's personality. He is singularly charming. It is significant that a sophisticated lady once remarked that he resembles a "bad little boy who has been caught stealing jam." He is equally at home in the company of jazz piano players, lady nondescripts, seers, bores, cabaret entertainers and society matrons. It is only when he is assailed by Intellectuals that he begins to fidget. However, I have seen him sit unmoved and without facial expression while intellectual imbeciles grew misty-eyed over the beauties of Bizet, and endure without facial expression the ordeal of a discourse on Beethoven by a local attorney. These feats at first greatly puzzled me. I soon found that he is the least intellectual of artists. He has little reverence for the very large men of his craft. He remarks without passion that *Tristan* is not so good, and that he prefers Italian opera; a moment later sneers at Mozart in such a manner that my ears fairly burn with anger; and causes one to fairly howl for his blood by refusing to be moved by Beethoven, Scriabin or anyone else, save only Bach. Sebastian he deems the greatest of composers, a fact for which we may pardon him his other sins. Since he has admitted that Bach has for him almost a purely intellectual appeal, it is perhaps logical that the mighty emotional storms of the Master [i.e., Beethoven] escape him. This seeming insensitiveness is very misleading, and will create a paradox when we come to consider his extraordinary feeling for orchestral color. Then too, we always take these opinions with a grain of salt. I for one, think Still is spoofing, and refuse to believe that he sees beauties in Leoncavallo, Mascagni and Verdi that he cannot see in Beethoven,

Mozart and Wagner.[16] He does not know himself as yet, and it is a credit to his honesty that he does not pose.

His ideas on music are terse and brief. He believes that music is "primarily an appeal to the ear," and that the composer "who attempts to offer concrete theories" is posing, and that "the theories of certain composers, notably Rebikov,[17] are nothing but attempts to explain away their musical shortcomings." He believes in tossing Jadassohn, Prout, Goetschius, and Richter into the desk drawer forevermore.[18] (Always granting that one knows their contents, of course!) The only text he keeps at hand is Cecil Forsyth's splendid treatise on orchestration.[19] He is pointed in his opinions, very honest, and cares little for justice where his own prejudices are concerned. He denounces other men's work without giving them any examination whatever, possibly because he has suffered the same fate.[20]

He is a connoisseur in liqueurs, an epicure, and is fond of clothing. He is not interested in the world of ideas, outside of music, reads only time killing fiction, but betrays little of this one-sidedness in his compositions.

He has a gift of attraction that makes it impossible to regard him with indifference; you either like him immensely or dislike him. He has uncritically and with no examination, disparaged my own work, my "not much praised but altogether satisfactory lady" has become sweet on him, and I feel but a mild if slightly bitter amusement.[21] The voice of the soothsayer has for him great truth.[22] I would hate for a haruspice to tell him that I was hatching a foul plot against his life. He is not interested in the fact that he is a Republican, a Kappa Alpha Psi and a Negro, and I wish he would lose interest in the fact that he is a Presbyterian. He carries large tone cathedrals behind a skull embellished by raven-black locks and masked by a face radiating "good fellowship," artlessness and a baffling lack of profundity.

But underneath there is a nervous sensuality, a psychic unscrupulousness, a fitful spurting of moods that is like a vast fingerprint in his works. We shall see how Paul Rosenfeld, with his customary insight, saw this in Still's very first work to receive performance, and how it follows in nearly all his subsequent compositions. It is not altogether a physical sensuality, though that plays a large part, but a certain androgyne-like conception of creation dwelling in a man who is at once normal and devout. He is a perfect model of a pagan consciousness, a nihilistic entity without regard for the troubles and aspirations of other men, completely smothered under a mass of traditional hocus-pocus that refuses to allow him a moment of rational concrete speculation. His music, as usual, is the safety valve. There his nervous energy and his unconscious revolt against the false mass of dogma under which his true person sleeps takes expression. Great slabs of sound in *Darker America* spit forth the sincerity of spirit many do not believe him to possess.[23] He notes that it is his intention in this work to suggest the "triumph of a people over their sorrow through intense prayer," and that "The Backslider" is not a parody on religion. The exalted recesses of his unconscious spirit, immune from dogma and the pettiness so characteristic of artists, as well as conscience, flutter like an orchid hued but tinged with sable out of the dank cellars of apparent paradox.

He is not without sadism; a mental pleasure in mentally inflicting pain upon those who are fond of him. It is not the gross gloating of a successful suitor over a vanquished rival. He is harsh at times, as his music is harsh, for the pleasure received in rubbing the bruises with a disarming balsam. Sometimes it is with an innocent chord of the ninth, again it is with a "wisecrack." Sincerity at times hangs in the balance, but we cannot say that he is excused on artistic grounds, for he is forgiven by those for whom his music cannot possibly have any appeal or meaning. Such a man is a living argument both for and against himself. As mentioned above, he is not full of windy ideas that he is incapable of putting into practice. He is the only Negro composer with the instincts and heart of the artist (though totally devoid of any outward marks), a wealth of genuinely new and arresting ideas, and the technical training necessary to present them logically. He spurts out his compositions as abstract manifestations of feelings he cannot express concretely and proofs of an innate nobility of spirit that outwardly some would deny him. This is the dominant characteristic of genuine musical genius.

II

William Grant Still was born at Woodville, Mississippi, on May 11, 1895, but much of his early life was spent in Little Rock, Arkansas. Those who knew him as a child remark concerning the exceptional shyness and reserve of his manner, and his stubborn resolution. He was fortunate in having a mother of exceptional culture who wished to see him well educated. A monkey wrench was thrown in the family machinery, however, when the young William announced that he had decided to study music. The highly respectable family was scandalized. Perhaps it is necessary to explain that better-class Negro families of the very adjacent past lifted their skirts in holy horror of music as a profession (of course they had no conception of it as an art), listing it with the theatre and with bank-robbery as snares set by a wily and ever alert devil to ensnare the young, lead astray the middle aged, and charm the footsteps of centenarians from the grave. The family pooh-poohed the boy's declaration and decided that he should become a doctor. Still laughs ironically at the very imagined picture of himself cutting out tonsils or prescribing for the baby's colic.

Openly defying parental authority, as he now defies the musty authority of textbook compilers, he followed his general studies at Wilberforce University with serious musical courses at Oberlin and at the New England Conservatory, where he had Mr. Chadwick as professor in composition. It is significant of his nervous haste that he completed a year's course in harmony in three months or less.[24] About this time the most important event in Still's artistic development took place. Edgard Varèse, the brilliant French-American whose audacious compositions have been so deeply damned and highly praised, saw a potential anarch in young Still. Varèse is a very vivid personality, even to one who has never heard his works. Still has explained them to me so vividly that it seems that the shivering of percussion instruments has assailed my own ears. There are those who have tried to sneer at the composer of *Octandre, Integrales* and *Hyperprism* with the characteristic charge that the composer thinks "he can express the fourth dimension and the Einstein theory in music." Well, for all we know, perhaps it can be done! On the other hand M. Varèse has been called "the man destined to lead the art of music onward from Stravinsky's fresh virgin realms of sound." The remark of the Parisian newspaper, *Comoedie* that "Sa personalite lui vaut des admirateurs enthousiastes et des adversaires acharnes. C'est l'indice certain d'une force creatrice," is the best summary of the matter for one as unfamiliar with his scores as I am.[25]

Still has been criticized for submitting himself to the influence of Varèse; well-meaning critics asserting that his virgin talent has been perverted by the revolutionary doctrines of the Frenchman. This, I think, is so much buncombe. It is possible that Still *might* have followed the same paths had he never met M. Varèse, but it is not likely that he would have followed them so well. Quite to the contrary of many critics of *Levee Land,* Varèse has put Still in possession of the materials that he needed. From him Still has learned how to be individual and free of the academic remnants of the New England Conservatory. I shudder to think of the young Negro writing consonant barcaroles for the pianoforte and Burleighesque songs. Examination of some choruses written during student days makes the shudder more pronounced. Varèse has been the guide into uncharted paths of modern music, and after all influence has been shaken off and his spiritual forces thoroughly orientated to his method, the composer may express himself in a work of major consideration.[26] It is perhaps regrettable that Still has not interested himself in literature, for the unconscious influence of some modern poet would undoubtedly have been of great inspiration, and not without a power of liberation from the astringency of his subjects and the unpoetic quality of his titles and programs.

In October, 1915, Still married Grace Bundy,[27] and since has become the father of four children, to whom he is sentimentally attached. This streak of sentiment is perhaps the greatest handicap he has to overcome if he would become a major composer. It sticks to his fingers like soft taffy in the *Portraits,* one of his latest works; and a composition that notwithstanding is beautiful and imaginative. It is not always a dishwatery sentimentality, however, but has savage and even vicious undercurrents. I have spoken of the unholy flash of his eye, and immediately after the short indulgence in confection, he writes an atavistic sketch above a pounding ground bass that ends in a thrilling crash.

With his unusual success as an arranger of jazz I do not intend to dwell here, save to note that his arrangements for *Runnin' Wild, Earl Carroll's Vanities, Shuffle Along, Dixie to Broadway,* Don Voorhees and Paul Whiteman's orchestra stamp him with Grofé and Challis as a leader in the field, helped him to useful publicity and colored to a large extent his serious composition.[28] Whether he has been more successful than Gershwin in utilizing jazz motives I will not opine, but it seems that the *Rhapsody in Blue* is a failure in that it is either one thing or the other successively, while Still has succeeded in writing, in *Darker America,* jazz rhythms that seem a logical and smooth part of the whole.[29]

From the Land of Dreams, the first serious work of Still to receive public performance, (though *Three Fantastic Dances* for chamber orchestra, and *From the Black Belt,* for full orchestra as well as numerous songs, were already in manuscript,) was played at a concert given by the now defunct International Composers' Guild, an organization founded by Edgard Varèse for the advancement and presentation of new music, on February 8, 1925. The work appeared in company with Bartok's *Sonatina,* the *Three Preludes* of Acario Cotapos, and works by Carlos Chavez, the young Mexican who directs the National Conservatory at Mexico City, and who has lately received much recognition for his ballets, *Four Suns* and *New Fire,* Carlos Salzedo and Anton von Webern, the protege of Schoenberg.[30] The concert was conducted by Vladimir Shavitch.

From the Land of Dreams is scored for flute, oboe, clarinet, bassoon, horn, viola, cello, double-bass, bells, triangle and three voices (high soprano, soprano and mezzo soprano), used instrumentally. It is in three movements, Lento, Allegretto, Allegro moderato. The composer excuses his introduction of jazz motives in the last movement on the ground that "there are dreams with clearly defined and very vivid outlines." The composition seems to have astonished the critics, although it is well known that most metropolitan writers carry an attitude with them to such concerts. One reviewer called forth the gods of tradition to witness that "William Grant Still . . . tried the instrumental use of human voices in an incoherent fantasy . . . and succeeded once or twice in making them sound like Wagner's Rhine Maidens." A clever phrase signifying nothing.

Olin Downes wrote: "One hoped for better things from Mr. Still . . . for he knows the rollicking and often original and entertaining music performed in Negro reviews. But Mr. Varèse, Mr. Still's teacher, has driven all of that out of him. Is Mr. Still aware that the cheapest music in the reviews that he has orchestrated has more reality and inspiration than the curious noises he has manufactured?"[31] Mr. Downes proceeded to announce that the three voices did little but howl, and wound up with the remark that "this is music unprofitable to compose or listen to." It will seem that Mr. Downes has added his name to the long list of well-meaning but patronizing Nordics who have kindly taken it upon themselves to attempt to guide young Negroes out of forbidden territories. He is absurd in saying that there is more "inspiration" in burlesque-show music than in the shattering dissonances of this strange composition, although he is perhaps right about the "reality." He seems to expect Still to write like Walter Donaldson or Harry Burleigh, as others expect Roland Hayes to sing like Al Jolson.[32] M. Varèse has by no means driven the jazz spirit away, or so far as I can make out, ever tried. Mr. Downes should have listened a bit more attentively to the last movement, and to the *Fantasy on the St. Louis Blues,* of which the New Yorker said: "The composer has prodigious gifts. The *Fantasy* . . . is the best blues transcription that we have ever heard. . . . " The Jungle episode since written for Whiteman indicates that jazz is still very much with our composer. If the voices in the *Dream* "howl," so does the voice in Medtner's *Vocal Sonata,* and most of the coloratura soprano solos I have yet heard.[33] No genuine idea of a sensuous and iridescent character such as Still's is either unprofitable to compose or, indeed, to listen to. The half forgotten radio-leitmotif re-enters.

Among American critics, aside from James Huneker, Paul Rosenfeld, with his sympathetic insight, his broad catholicity of taste, and his breadth of knowledge, speaks with the greatest authority on musical subjects.[34] Van Vechten is a mere surface polisher and wise-cracker, Mencken (the greatest of American men of letters and a profound music lover) is hopelessly archaic in his musical tastes and opinions, and most of the others, especially the academics, are negligible.[35] Some are scared to death of a chord of the thirteenth, and some of a Mozart sonata. Edgard Varèse has written of Rosenfeld in the same French newspaper already quoted: "Cette vie Americaine a crée pareillement une litterature nationale. Celle-ci se divise en deux groupes: a la tete, du premier sont Paul Rosenfeld, le plus brillant essayiste Americain, remarquable par sa largeur de vues, par l'interet qu'il porte a tout ce qui est nouveau et par la generosite de sa pensee. . . . "[36] What he goes [on] to say about Kreymborg is not important.[37] But it is of great importance that this same Paul Rosenfeld wrote in the *Musical Chronicle* of *From the Land of Dreams:*

> W.G.S . . . adds another member to the growing company of American musical embryonics. Still has learned a great deal from Edgard Varèse . . . although he has not yet quite learned to speak out freely: a certain absence of freedom in the use of his ideas limit one's enjoyment, and the material of the first two sections of his composition is insufficiently contrasted. But Mr. Still has a very *sensuous* (italics mine) approach to music. His employment of his instruments is at once rich and nude and decided. The upper ranges of his high soprano have an original penetrating color. *And the use of jazz motives in the last movement of his work is more genuinely musical than any to which they have been put, by Milhaud, Gershwin, or any one else . . .* (italics mine).

Aside from the interesting circumstance that Mr. Rosenfeld pricked the Gershwinian bubble just when it seemed to be the thing to blow, it is remarkable how one of the dominant traits of Still's work struck him at this single hearing. The composer admits that *From the Land of Dreams* was little more than a tentative experiment in harmonic and orchestral color, and that in the writing of it his own personality was colored in a large manner by that of Varèse, but he violently denies that he is simply indulging here in strange noises for the mere sake of appearing ultra-modern. It is pleasing that one man saw the germ in this first offering, and that man was Paul Rosenfeld himself. Alain Locke wrote the composer in compliment, and noted the work in his *The New Negro,* a fact that deserves mention because other than this, and letters from Charles S. Johnson, Still has been either abused or ignored by the intellectuals of his race.

Levee Land, a group of four songs with orchestral accompaniment, was performed at an I.C.G. concert at Aeolian Hall on January 24, 1926. The late Florence Mills sang them in an inimitable manner and a great deal of the applause went to the little entertainer. The performance was no mean feat for her since she read no music, and had to be taught the difficult scores entirely by ear. The first song, "Levee Song," is a blues poem in the Langston Hughes manner, treated modernistically, while the second, "Hey Hey," is broadly humorous and without words, as is the third, "Oroon." The composer, with rather comical care, has noted that the fourth number, "The Backslider," is not a satire on religion, as one would naturally think, from the words and music. It tells the old tale of the good sister who means well but:

> "Wen dat banjo go plunk-plunk
> An' foller up wid brrrunk
> Ah felt religion goin'" . . .

Still has further proved his skill in writing richly humorous music in his setting of Dunbar's quaint little poem, "Winter's Approach," that has a droll hum that brings a contagious smile to the lips, and a highly characteristic rhythm. Of course there were the customary smart-alecky, superficial press comments on *Levee Land.* One writer, borrowing the ancient platitude concerning Varèse, said that *Levee Land* sounded like the Einstein theory and the fourth dimension applied to the blues. A compliment, perhaps. One may read, in Osgood's *So this is Jazz,*[38] intelligent and favorable remarks on the work, and the *Musical Courier,* after digging up dry bones long enough to again denounce *From the Land of Dreams* as a "slavish imitation of the noises that Edgard Varèse calls compositions," admitted that the *Levee* songs are "good, healthy and sane," and that the composer belongs on a high plane of the super jazz fiend. It is not at all curious, but noteworthy that the Nordic is so willing to grant recognition to a Negro in this particular field, but denounces him as an invader the moment he feels himself too broad for confining racial fetters. Nobody complains when Julia Peterkin, Waldo Frank, Haldane McFall, W. B. Seabrook, Covarrubias and Du Bose Heyward take Negroid material and do vastly more with it than Negroes themselves, but the moment a Negro steps nakedly into the symphonic field and speaks as a pure artist, howls of protest are heard.[39]

Still's career has not been without either encouragement or rebuke. *Black Bottom* and *Three Negro Songs for Orchestra* were returned to him by Stokowski with the excuse that he had no time for their examination, and with a promise of future consideration that has never been kept.[40] Still once high-handedly set about orchestrating Norman Peterkin's *Dreamer's Tales,* because both Dunsany and the little piano pieces appealed to him, and was severely reprimanded by Gustave Schirmer, whose firm owned the copyright.[41] The group of symphonic sketches, *From the Journal of a Wanderer,* was submitted to a contest conducted in 1926 by the Chicago North Shore Festival Association, and although attaining to the distinction of being one of the five compositions selected for public rehearsal by the Chicago Symphony Orchestra, under Frederick Stock, the contest was won by a *Tragic Overture* by Edward Collins. Maurice Rosenfeld wrote of the *Journal* that it was a series of five pieces "without rime or reason." In the spring of 1929, however, it was played by Dr. Howard Hanson and the Rochester Symphony with great success. The five pieces in the suite are: "Phantom Trail," "Magic Bells," "The Valley of Echoes," "Mystic Moon," and "Devil's Hollow." They display without doubt Still's consummate skill in instrumentation, and his knowledge of the resources of the orchestra, and are of astonishing rhythmic interest and harmonic ingenuity. One misses in this work the stark directness of *Darker America,* or the mysticism of *Africa,* but when considering the diverse subjects, it is perhaps a compliment to the composer's versatility. The Eastman School of Music has added a copy of the score to their library.

Of great interest is the ballet Still next undertook to write, at the instigation of Adolph Bolm, the distinguished dancer of the Russian Imperial Ballet, Diaghilev Ballet Russe, and the Chicago and Metropolitan grand opera companies. It was to have appeared on a series of ballets and music for small orchestra presented by the Chicago Allied Arts, Inc., in company with new compositions by Carpenter, Milhaud, Williams, and Alexander Tansman.[42] Something happened, and the work was never produced. Bolm, to judge from his letters, had much praise and much censure for Still's score, and after a somewhat lengthy correspondence it was finally decided to dispense with the ballet, although it had been extensively advertised. The music was written to a legend of the isle of Martinique, *La Guiablesse* adapted by Ruth Page. There is much that is beautiful in the musical score. "The Dance of the Yzore" is particularly delicate. This exquisitely fragile little piece offers another paradox in the work of a man who is a bundle of contradictions.[43]

Shortly after the performance of *From the Land of Dreams,* Alain Locke had written to Still suggesting Richard Bruce's libretto for an African ballet "Sahdji" as a subject. Bruce's work had grown out of a very good sketch of the same name, printed in *The New Negro.* One wishes for time to dwell on this vivid personality, for of the myriad of young Negro "intellectuals," he is the most interesting, and has accomplished many beauties both with the pen and the brush. Still became interested in "Sahdji" but soon found that the poetry found little response in his own nature, and abandoned the project entirely. Bruce told me that he was rather pleased at this, since he would prefer to have his verse set by a "more modern" composer. "Sahdji" may be read in Locke's collection of *Plays of Negro Life.*

From the Black Belt, in six orchestral sketches, "Dance," "Honeysuckle," "Dance," "Des' Keep on Shovin'," "Blue," and "Serenade" was played by Georges Barrère's Little Symphony, and later, at one of John Murray Anderson's Sunday Nights at the Park Avenue Theatre, by a Negro orchestra conducted by Mr. Still himself. *Log Cabin Ballads* was played by the same organization. The witty Barrère has been very sympathetic to the composer, and the several letters, which Still treasures, are of a blunt kindliness, and show admiration for the gifts of the young Negro. O. G. Sonneck would not publish the *Log Cabin Ballads* in the orchestral version, although he seems to have liked them.[44]

Jesse Zachary sang the three *Dialect Songs* at a concert at the New School for Social Research auditorium in 1927, during the same season, I believe, that Gorham Munson gave his lectures that have culminated in his splendid book *Style and Form in American Prose.*[45] The concert was arranged by Paul Rosenfeld. One of the numbers, "Winter's Approach," has already been mentioned.[46] The "Breath of a Rose" is a setting of a sentimental poem of Langston Hughes and bears the same relation to Still's best work that Debussy's banal and lovely "Romance" bears to his best songs. It is better than most of the songs of Negro composers, but it is by no means so good as the songs in the same idiom written by Frenchmen. The vague melodic outlines and the harmonic style seems affected with the little poem. On paper it looks positively rococo, when sung it is not without loveliness, which is a quite different thing from beauty. All of Still's work for piano, that is, songs with pianoforte accompaniment (he writes no piano solos) seem like diminutions of orchestral scores. Keith Corelli and other pianists have expressed willingness to play the compositions of Still, and many believe that with effort, he could produce not inconsiderable work for that instrument. The piano plays a prominent part in the scores of *Darker America* and in *Africa*.

Darker America, the finest of Still's works to date, (*Africa*, completed a few days before this was written, will not as yet be considered) received its debut in 1926 under the auspices of the same association that has been so consistently kind to new composers. Of this extraordinary composition, Olin Downes, writing in the New York Times, said "The best music last night was that of *Darker America* . . . the polyharmonic treatment of the theme in the opening and closing measures is more than ingenious. In communicates an atmosphere. . . . This music . . . has direction and feeling in it, qualities usually lacking in contemporaneous music." Samuel Chotzinoff and others were too busy with their flippant attitude to give an adequate review, but both the *Musical Courier* and *Musical America* saw that a great development had taken place in the composer since *From the Land of Dreams*, and that *Darker America* is something more than a groping but a broad free and logical form. The writer in the *Musical Courier* was bold enough to declare that Still is destined to "blossom forth as one of America's really great composers." (!) Far back, commenting on the *Dreams*, Still had warned that he was not trying to depict, uplift, or glorify anything, and when referring to *Darker America*, always uses the word "suggest." This did not stop a number of critics from denouncing him for not simply and straightforwardly expressing the life of the Negro. The composer explains that it was part of his intention to "suggest the triumph of a people over their sorrows through intense prayer." But the material got out of his control, stuffs get into it unawares, and Mr. Downes was right, but very incomplete.

Darker America is music devoid of sentimentality and attitudinizing. It is direct, vigorous, decided, at times harsh and rugged; with edges sharply out and with no rounded contours. Its formlessness is its form. It is the formlessness of the chaotic impulses and desires and rebellions of all of us. There is no French fluidity, no Debussian revelry in silken sensuousness, no dreamlike fantasy, no American chauvinism, blowing of racial trumpets, glorification of concrete ideals. It is music that awakens an indefinable thrill of recognition of some spiritual battle we have fought with ourselves, and from which we have emerged with our faith in the gods a bit shattered. It is the battle of a man with himself; the rebellion not against man-created prejudices, but an unconscious revolt against the unseen forces that dog our footsteps from cradle to grave.

There are three themes in the work, two of which are of major importance.[47] Mr. Downes was quite right in speaking of the theme that appears at the opening and closing. He might have added that it appears, in some guise or other, all the way through the work, and that it is intensely interesting to follow it as it serpentines its way along, changing hue with the versatility of the chameleon and disguising itself behind ingenious developments. This theme, of a bald nudity, and of great simplicity and directness, is announced in unison by the violins, viola and cello in G minor. It comprises simply the G minor triad, with a curt upbeat at the close. It is followed immediately by a unison passage in the woodwinds that accentuates the cutting rising inflection. A muffled pizzicato in the strings supported by the piano ushers in a plaintive answering motif in the flutes. The generative theme is then repeated, as decidedly as before, but this time the upbeat is replaced by a sinister drop of an augmented fourth. The ensuing development, intensification and colouring of these ideas, with the masterly and economical introduction of new material is more than remarkable. One is astonished, after study of the score, to read criticisms in which men charge that it is fragmentary, chaotic, pointless and other nonsensical things. Blocklike slabs of sound are sometimes vomited from the orchestra. There are no pretty patterns, neat little furbelows of harmonic or contrapuntal cleverness. The work has about it an elemental roughness and vigour. It is the work of a potential master of musical architectonics. There are spurts of nervousness, as the passage that ushers in the jazz theme; in quite Dettesque fourths. The rhythm, however, is not ordinary, nor is the colouring. Against this jazz motif, the woodwinds sing one of the three principal motifs of the piece. The composition is not without beauty. The passage in which the opening theme is sung in A-flat minor, below a sustained sixth in the horn and trombone, and a plaintive downbeat in the English horn, while the piano, with dampers against the strings, plucks sonorous chords of the ninth, is beautiful, if somewhat grotesque.

On page 41 of the printed score, the opening theme reappears FFF in the pianoforte, reinforced by the basses, cellos and bassoons, with the second subject appearing polyharmonically against it. This example of Still's polytonality is particularly biting and has an almost mystic modal flavour. The pompous inexorability of the principal theme is broken by a nervous ascending passage in the piano and flutes that is nothing so much as the harassed gesture of a man feverishly trying to wipe away unpleasant thoughts with the back of his hand. But the gesture is fruitless. The bald, naked theme crashes forth again—again the flickering wave of the hand—but now more brutally than ever the uncompromising figure returns, this time in B-flat minor, where it is greatly intensified. Quickly it makes a final, irrefutable statement in the original key, where, as if nature has said the last, pitiless word, the spirit, with a rattling sigh accepts the final edict and is quiet. Whispers in the woodwinds, held up by a quietly tense pulse in the cymbal, close the composition.

Darker America was later awarded second prize in a contest conducted by the Eastman Foundation in Rochester, where Dr. Hanson played it with the Rochester orchestra. Dr. Hanson has been more than generous with young Still. The jury that awarded the prizes was composed of Olin Downes, Eugene Goossens, Howard Hanson, Edward Royce, Bernard Kaun and Stuart Sabin, who has written as favorably of the *Journal of a Wanderer*.

III

Still definitely severed the already strained lines uniting him with racial classification when the Pan-American Association of Composers, at their second meeting, held at Birchard Hall February 9th, 1928, voted him a member. Those present were Edgard Varèse, Henry Cowell, Emerson Whithorne, Carlos Chavez, Adolph Weiss, Miss Armitage and Louis Mesam. Most of the representative modern composers were invited to join, Chavez wiring invitations to Cubans and F. F. Fabini to composers in South America.

Between Still and the other Aframerican composers no possible comparison can be made. He overtops them too simply and completely. He is, of course, a rank modernist, in the purest sense of that much abused word. As stated above, he is quite without windy theories concerning modernity, or anything else, though one may receive with surprise his spoken word that: "Music is nothing more than an appeal to the ear." But it is important that he does not make noise for the mere sake of causing vibrations. The same is true of many so-called "cacophonous" composers. They are called "crazy" by the same class that held Mr. Joyce thought it "was smart" to drop punctuation marks in the final chapter of *Ulysses*. Inherently sincere, Still writes nothing that does not sound well to his own extraordinarily sensitized ears. He pretends to dislike Scriabin, Mozart and Wagner, attitudes that are of no importance. He has not entirely escaped Debussy, as the first of the three *Portraits* affirms.

Although *Darker America* and other works are largely polytonal, Still is gradually falling into atonality. The first of the *Portraits* is supposedly in B flat, although that tonality scarcely appears in it from stem to stern. Rhythmically as above stated, he is astonishingly fertile. He flings out sprays of notes as a cowboy flings a lasso, coils them about an idea, and yanks them into the consciousness of the auditor, and (granting the commensurate radio set) makes it simmer and glisten in brilliant flickers of orchestral colour. In *Darker America* he hammers the eternal hopelessness of mankind into us and adds an ironically pious footnote. Pessimism with overtones of jazz and with a dogmatic tag! Looking at some of his scores, one seems to feel the rhythms tripping over one another, and laughing heartily as they fall into a crotchet, bruising their glittering backsides.

The newly completed *Africa* is claimed by the composer to be his major work. It is an imposing work, growing out of a later and arresting generative motif into a vast architecture. Space makes it impossible to discuss it in this little paper. No doubt it has by now been performed by Georges Barrère's orchestra, as has been planned.

In December, 1926, *Comoedia* noted that "William Grant Still, orchestrateur prestigeux, qui vient d'ecrire un opera, dont le livret fut connu par un poète de sa race, Countee Cullen."[48] This opera, "Rashana," a fantastic story well suited to the gifts of the composer, has not yet been written, and bids fair never to be. Countee Cullen did not finish the libretto. In 1929 it passed into the hands of the writer, and my efforts have met with no musical response from the composer. It is possible that "Rashana" may go the way of *La Guiablesse* and *Sadhji,* which would be a pity, considering the beauty of the story and the abundant sketches he has made for it.

With the *Journal of a Wanderer* recently played, *Three Portraits* and *Africa* completed, and "Rashana" an unknown quantity, there can be no question as to whether or not Still is industrious, or whether or not he is written out. He is the contented and doting father of four children, and the sympathetic cousin of Charles Lawrence, whom I believe will be heard from musically in the future, since he complements his coldly searching intelligence with a genuine harmonic sense.[49]

William Grant Still is, with Jean Toomer, one of the very first artists of his group. Both of these men have a touch of the divine spark, and are no more to be classed as Negro artists than as Eskimos. Each time I read "Kabnis" or the scores of *Darker America, Africa,* or the sketchbooks of "Rashana," I am more convinced of it.[50] Despite Still's name, he is destined to make a great noise in the world, when he has completely oriented himself, and when the spiritual stuffs, already sending out incipient flashes of smoke and flame, burst forth in a fiery efflorescence. . . .

Bruce Forsythe
Los Angeles
October, 1930

NOTES

1. For Forsythe's off-the-cuff later response to the *Afro-American Symphony,* see p. 144.

2. Program notes, International Composers' Guild Concert, November 28 [1926], ICG Programs, Music Division, New York Public Library, New York City. Quoted in Carol J. Oja, " 'New Music' and the 'New Negro': The Background of William Grant Still's *Afro-American Symphony,*" BMRJ 12, no. 2 (Fall 1992): 145–169. Oja reads the program note to suggest four themes, although Still lists six in his letter to Schwerké describing the piece. (See the music examples in "William Grant Still and Irving Schwerké," above.)

3. "Personal Notes," 1933. The "faults" Still found with this work are amplified along these same lines in Arvey's "William Grant Still," below.

4. Oja, " 'New Music' and the 'New Negro.' "

5. Later in 1930, Still forwarded what was presumably a copy of this essay to Irving Schwerké in Paris. Schwerké was to forward it to Varèse. This copy remains unlocated.

6. *Religio Medici,* ca. 1635, published 1643. Browne was a physician, but the book is a profession of faith rather than a medical treatise.

7. Edgard Varèse (1883–1965) was a prominent member of the avant-garde in New York City in the 1920s. He was Still's teacher for a time. Forsythe claimed to have studied with him as well, though this has not been confirmed. Charles E. Pemberton, with whom Forsythe studied composition, taught at the University of Southern California.

8. Katherine Ruth Willoughby Heyman (1877–1944) made her debut as a pianist with the Boston Symphony Orchestra in 1899 and concertized widely thereafter. A champion of Scriabin's music, she wrote *The Relation of Ultra-Modern to Archaic Music* (Boston, 1921) from which Forsythe quotes below. Scriabin's music and his thought were of considerable interest to musical modernists in the 1920s.

9. Except for Frederick Douglass (1817–1895), a sometime slave who became a major advocate of abolition, these are writers of the Harlem Renaissance, most of whom were known to Still and probably to Forsythe as well.

Countee Cullen (1903–1946) began an opera project with Still. Langston Hughes (1902–1967) authored the libretto to Still's opera *Troubled Island*. Wallace Henry Thurman (1902–1934), like Forsythe a westerner, attended the University of Southern California and edited the journal *Outlet*, to which Forsythe contributed, in 1924. Thurman left Los Angeles in May 1934, the month of Still's arrival there. The associations with Claude McKay (1889–1948) and Eric Walrond (1898–1966) are not so clear.

10. Jean Toomer's first novel, *Cane*, published in 1923, had a major impact on readers of both races, although Toomer (1894–1967) did not produce other work of comparable quality. Toomer, who was raised as a white and later lived as an African American, chose eventually to identify as "American" rather than with either race. Ralph Kabnis (see text, below), a principal figure in *Cane*, is portrayed as a black northerner who experiences a nightmare of race relations as a schoolteacher in the South. *Cane*, with its focus on mysticism, and Toomer's later advocacy of Gurdjieff and his cult, may have been a source for some of Still's ideas, such as his symphony, *Song of a New Race*, his view of his role as a composer, and his interest in the occult.

Roland Hayes (1887–1977) was a tenor who toured widely, singing both the Western European repertoire and spirituals before largely white audiences. In 1948 he published *My Songs*, his editions of his repertoire of spirituals.

Paul Robeson (1898–1987), earned the LL.B. but became a bass singer and actor. His radical politics interfered with his artistic career in the United States; he lived abroad for some years starting in the 1950s. His book, *Here I Stand*, was published in London in 1958.

11. Henry Thacker Burleigh (1866–1949), baritone, composer-arranger of spirituals, sang for Dvořák during his famous stay in the United States. See Jean E. Snyder, "Harry T. Burleigh and the Creative Expression of Bi-Musicality: A Study of an African-American Composer and the American Art Song" (Ph.D. dissertation, University of Pittsburgh, 1992); and Anne Key Simpson, *Hard Trials: The Life and Music of Harry T. Burleigh* (Metuchen, N.J.: Scarecrow Press, 1990).

Considering Still's reported aversion to Wagner's *Tristan*, it is interesting that Burleigh said he had seen this drama more than sixty-six times.

12. All African American composers who, among other things, arranged spirituals.

13. Harry Lawrence Freeman (1869–1954) composed several operas and was probably the first African American to conduct a symphony orchestra in his own works (Minneapolis, 1907). Still may have heard his opera *Voodoo* in New York City in 1927, produced by Freeman's Negro Opera Company.

14. Robert Russa Moton (1867–1940), founder of the National Negro Business League and principal of the Tuskegee Institute, was viewed as very conservative on race relations. In *What the Negro Thinks* (Garden City, N.Y.: Doubleday Doran, 1929), Moton lists as model composers Burleigh, Dett, and Coleridge-Taylor, an Englishman. Carl Diton published a collection of spirituals from South Carolina in 1925.

15. Ferde Grofé (1892–1972) began as a symphony musician on the West Coast but joined Paul Whiteman in 1920 as an arranger.

16. Contrary to Forsythe's expectation, Still remained consistent in these judgments, which may be generalized as a lack of interest in the German classical and romantic composers such as Mozart, Beethoven, and Wagner and an enthusiasm (not characteristic of modernists) for nineteenth-century Italian opera, including such composers as Leoncavallo, Mascagni, and Verdi. His interest in Bizet's very popular opera, *Carmen* (1875), and his indifference to *Tristan und Isolde* (1865), the first of Wagner's music dramas, follows this pattern. Likewise, Still was uninterested in Scriabin's musical mysticism but found Johann Sebastian Bach's logical approach to composition a useful model.

17. Vladimir Rebikov, 1866–1920.

18. Salomon Jadassohn (1831–1902), Ebenezer Prout (1835–1909), Percy Goetchius (1853–1943), and Ernst Friedrich Richter (1808–1879) were nineteenth-century pedagogues of music theory whose textbooks were still widely used in the United States when Forsythe was writing.

19. Cecil Forsyth (1870–1941), *Orchestration* (New York, 1914; 2d ed., 1935).

20. The first version adds: "He offers insults so affably that they seem like compliments. He is the only man who ever disliked my music and made me like the way he disliked it."

21. Forsythe is probably referring to Verna Arvey. The source of the quotation remains unlocated.

22. In "William Grant Still: Eclectic Religionist," *Theomusicology: A Special Issue of Black Sacred Music: A Journal of Theomusicology* 3, no. 1 (Spring 1994): 135–156, Jon Michael Spencer makes the case that Arvey introduced Still to spiritualism. Spencer's hypothesis is contradicted by this sentence, by Arvey's statement in *In One Lifetime,* and by other evidence. Still kept track of his visions in the few pre-1930 (and therefore pre-Arvey) diaries that survive; he also noted visits to psychics in Los Angeles before his marriage to Arvey.

23. This sentence and the next are connected. The original reads " . . . possess, and although he notes . . . ," probably a typing error.

24. George Whitefield Chadwick (1854–1931), composer, was then director of the New England Conservatory. He took Still, who was in Boston for an indefinite period as a member of the *Shuffle Along* orchestra, as a private student.

25. "His personality earns him enthusiastic admirers and hostile adversaries. It is a sure indication of his creative power."

26. "Guide": appears in the original as "guiding" without a noun to modify. The student choruses to which Forsythe refers are unlocated.

27. Still met Grace Bundy when both were students at Wilberforce University. They separated in 1932 and divorced in 1939.

28. Donald Voorhees (1903–1989) had a long career (1925–1959) as a conductor on radio and conducted on Broadway from the 1920s.

Paul Whiteman (1890–1967) began as a symphony musician on the West Coast and later achieved fame with his own band. He conducted the premiere of Gershwin's *Rhapsody in Blue* at Carnegie Hall in 1924. Still arranged for his "Old Gold Hour" broadcasts in 1930.

William H. Challis (b. 1904) orchestrated for Whiteman from 1927 to 1930.

29. See the headnote for Still's program note on *Darker America* and excerpts from other commentary on it. In the early draft, Forsythe calls Gershwin's *Rhapsody in Blue* "almost sophomoric" in comparison to *Darker America*.

30. All modernists, most of European or Latin American nationalities.

31. Olin Downes (1886–1955) wrote music criticism for the *Boston Post* before joining the *New York Times* in 1924. Compare with discussions of *From Land of Dreams* in the introduction and in Still's "Personal Notes."

32. Walter Donaldson (1893–1947), a white songwriter, composed "My Blue Heaven" and "Making Whoopee." Al Jolson (1886–1950) was a white actor and singer well known for performing in blackface.

33. Forsythe is referring to the *Sonata-Vocalise* by Nicolai Medtner.

34. American music critics. Forsythe's writing shows the influence of Rosenfeld, an advocate of contemporary composers.

35. Carl Van Vechten was a white enthusiast and an influential patron of the Harlem Renaissance. H. L. Mencken (1880–1956) was an influential literary and music critic of the 1920s and 1930s.

36. "Likewise, this American culture has created a national literature. It divides itself into two groups; at the head of the first group is Paul Rosenfeld, the most brilliant American essayist, remarkable for the breadth of his views, by his interest in all that is new, supported by the generosity of his thought."

37. Along with Lewis Mumford and Paul Rosenfeld, Alfred Kreymborg edited *New American Caravan* (1929).

38. Henry Osborne Osgood, *So This Is Jazz* (Boston: Little, Brown, 1926).

39. Waldo Frank (1889–1967). All were writers of European extraction who used African or African American materials in their work. Heyward (1885–1940) later used his novel and play *Porgy* (1924) as the source for the libretto to Gershwin's *Porgy and Bess*.

40. Stokowski later conducted Still's music frequently.

41. Gustave Schirmer (1890–1967), the third family member to be involved in the business, ran the music publishing house G. Schirmer during the years 1907–1921 and 1944–1957.

42. All contemporary composers, but about a generation older than Still. Given this pattern, "Williams" might be Ralph Vaughan Williams.

43. The scenario is described by Arvey in her "William Grant Still," below.

44. Oscar Sonneck was president of G. Schirmer at the time. Forsythe did not know that Still had finally composed *Sahdji* in summer 1930.

45. Gorham Munson, *Style and Form in American Prose* (Garden City, N.Y.: Doubleday Doran, 1929).

46. The third song, "Mandy Lou," was not published by G. Schirmer, as the other two were. See Arvey, "William Grant Still," below.

47. See "William Grant Still and Irving Schwerké," above, for a reconstruction of the six themes Still writes of in a letter to Schwerké.

48. "Still, the prestigious orchestrator, has just written an opera whose libretto is by a poet of his race, Countee Cullen."

49. Lawrence, whose family was Forsythe's landlord and who was a cousin of Still's, was one of the pianists who appeared on a concert of music composed by Forsythe, given in Los Angeles in 1931.

50. "Kabnis" refers to the hero of Jean Toomer's novel *Cane* (1923). A letter from Forsythe to Toomer in JWJ, dated August 29, 1934, expresses Forsythe's extravagant admiration for Toomer's *Cane:*

> Since those earliest days, when I was a pale-yellow youth in short trousers, and "Kabnis" boomed through my brain with such force that I felt carried forward by it, my conception of the genius of Jean Toomer has never faltered. . . . [I]n public "lectures" and private conversation, I have doggedly insisted that you are not so much the finest but the *only* writer partaking of the Blood, in this country. . . .
>
> An impassioned, solitary worker, . . . I feel that my works, both in music and literature, have been largely influenced by the clear and rich aesthetic vision which as a youth I saw in "Cane."

Forsythe asks Toomer's permission to quote from Toomer's "Balo" in order to "clarify an aesthetic and psychological *figure,* too complex to describe in a short letter. . . . Also, in the course of the book which is somewhat concerned with the Root-heart of the Spiritual and a clearer valuation of the ethnic-influence in music, it has been found necessary to say some true things about Jean Toomer." JWJ.

No response from Toomer has been found. Toomer later dramatized part 4 of *Cane,* in which Kabnis appears. "Rashana" was the name of an opera Still planned but never completed. Countee Cullen was to write the libretto, based on a novel by Grace Bundy, then Still's wife. Cullen did not complete the libretto; Bundy's manuscript is unlocated.

Plan for a Biography of Still

Harold Bruce Forsythe

In answer to this letter, Still provided Forsythe with twelve single-spaced pages of notes on his life and works, reproduced in this volume as "Personal Notes." Forsythe did not produce the projected four-volume work, but the questions he raises as essential to a biography of Still remain relevant. Ellipses are Forsythe's.

1432 West 36th Street
Los Angeles, Cal.

[1933]

Dear Billy:

I cannot tell you how much I appreciate your letters, and assure you that procrastination is the only reason for my tardy answer. I was a bit piqued, naturally when no response greeted my frantic appeals for co-operation on the Biography. I have always been more or less intense, and at that time was passionately interested in doing this work, but I could do nothing without an enormous amount of information concerning you . . . dates, facts of residence, crucial periods of your life, little human-interest stories of childhood and youth, accounts of your school days, teachers, letters . . . also some atmospheric snapshots, early programs . . . and MOST ESPECIALLY, THE SCORES OF *FROM THE LAND OF DREAMS, AFRO-AMERICAN SYMPHONY*, . . . etc.

. . . this is a great deal, but this book IS A GREAT DEAL. I want it to really amount to something. IT WILL NOT BE A GREAT BOOK, but IT WILL BE A GOOD BOOK. You will absolutely be a historical character. After long seances over the scores I have, due consideration, fasting and prayer, I am persuaded of that. Future and more able biographers will find themselves materially aided by my book for material and facts. They will be compelled to continually quote it.

Having now written about six books, the last *Blue Brooms,* composed of critical essays, I feel a slight preparation for this task. *William Grant Still: A Study* will not be completed for a few years, for it is rounding out in my mind as a very hefty volume, and not the short one. I am going to completely canvass the history of American Music and also give much study to the sociological aspects of the Negro, as well as aesthetics, for I shall seek to rationalize your position in American music as well as your peculiar isolation from your Race. I will attempt to show that this isolation is only apparent, but that underneath there are significant ties. I am sending you my essay, "Basalt," which I shall ask you to read carefully and return, as it contains the kernel of a thought I shall develop at great length in the book. Or, frankly, if, with your wider acquaintance, and position in the big city, you could suggest a possible publisher for the essay, you know my appreciation would be enormous.

For myself, I am still combatting ill health and poverty, with glittering periods of exhilaration and fervent happiness. Have been passionately in love with an extraordinarily charming woman, the gift of whose body at first amazed and then utterly delighted me. To hear that you have not always been happy in the immediate past has not contributed to my serenity, to be sure.

. . . I am continuing, of course, my study of counterpoint and the song. Last week made settings of Thoreau's "Smoke" and "Mist" . . . cannot get in the proper frame of mind to revise and complete my strangest and most original work, a long monody to be called "Garden Magic" . . . for one figure, and a very small orchestra . . . My long Symphonic Poem, finished last July, has been read by Leonard Walker [an English-born conductor then in Los Angeles] and Pemberton . . . my old teacher was astonished for the song has for years been my love . . . neither of us could understand the sudden coruscation that made this work imperative . . . for myself, I can only say that during the months of its composition I lived in a sort of trance, and as I read it over now, I almost believe in God, for I cannot imagine how the devil the stuff got down on the paper . . . The orchestra is a somewhat heavy one, but its full strength utilized only a few climactic moments.

I know you will survive any seemingly important minor troubles. For Billy, I must tell you that to you only music is important, and anything that interferes with the unfolding of your talents should and must be ruthlessly cast aside. Life is strange and has no meaning. We only know that some of us are somehow different from others in that we MUST DO SOMETHING. You must compose . . . At your age you are just rounding out and your future work is to be watched with great attention.

My only regret is that I cannot live close to you, for I really believe that I see deeper into you than most others, and have not yet seen anybody else who sees as clearly as I the beauty of the music on your pages of paper . . . not having yet heard a note of your music. How wonderful it would be to live in New York now, near you and Reginald, of whom I am extremely fond.

. . . By the way Eugene Page is on the way to N.Y. and will no doubt call on you. He is a terrible ass, but be kind to him.

. . . The old gang has drifted apart and my associates are mostly people you do not know. Verna Arvey, the girl who played for us that time, frequently asks about you. I seem to go to more Ofay affairs now than ever before, and never fail, at these intellectual gatherings, to expound to them the music of W.G.S.

. . . Please do not hold against me my procrastination, and write at once.

Harold

Now Billy, this is serious business, son. I am really begging, that now, when the wind is in the sails, and all seems fair, you in turn will not be angry and refuse the help that is absolutely necessary for the writing of this book. This letter was written some time ago . . . a good month . . . but I too have had a slightly stony time, and wished to wait, before beginning serious work on this great matter.

I am sure you will understand, and be guided entirely by your own conscience. I believe you are a great musician, and that book should be written. I believe I am the man to write it. Already plans are laid. The books I must read for a general historical and chronological background are decided upon. I will not list them, but believe me boy, I have mapped out one helluva list.

I will explain the form of the book. The first part will follow somewhat the outline of the present little essay; that is become a broad discussion on you as a whole . . . as a composite personality. By this means, the reader early in this book will get a general idea of the man with whom they have to deal.

Part Two will be biographical, containing all the material you send me, plus the good old "fillers in" that good journalists can add to even a small amount of actual facts. But boy, we want a LARGE AMOUNT OF ACTUAL FACTS!

Part Three will be a very serious and learned section, embracing historical, philosophical, sociological aspects of genius in general and in America in particular. I intend a profound analysis of Negro Folk material, as well as the pure African folk materials. This part, largely based on the essay "Basalt," before referred to, may be termed a digression by the unintelligent, but the careful reader will see that the gist of the book will be here. I AM HERE TRYING TO ACCOUNT FOR THIS PHENOMENON, W.G.S. WHAT HE IS, HOW HE GOT THERE, HIS RELATIONS TO HIS BLOOD ROOTS, AND HIS HISTORICAL AND FOLK HERITAGE.

The concluding section will be devoted to a discussion of the music itself. Read over what I said of *Darker America,* years ago, after a superficial reading of it. I honestly think I came near to the heart of this music, even then, and like the little paragraphs written upon it.

Now Billy, as I said before, I don't know how this book will come out, but passionately wish to work on it, and sincerely ask that you cooperate. Read over the little one, allow for maturing and further study, and if you think my intellect is equal to my love and understanding, please answer by return mail with as much stuff as you can send.

Above all, please tell me if you are still willing to cooperate, for already I have digested several source books, and you can see that the book has not taken complete form in my mind, and I am impatient to begin.

And so, not only for the profound admiration I have for you as an artist, but despite your sometime brusqueness, I have always felt affection for you as a man, I ask that you aid a brother in distress with this biography, and even if the book is never "published," we will have it for our own possession. And we will make it beautiful.

Sincerely in great haste, H

William Grant Still

by Verna Arvey

The following essay on Still, with an introduction by John Tasker Howard, was published as a brochure by J. Fischer and Bro., in 1939, as part of its promotional effort on behalf of Still's music. Its source is very likely an early, incomplete biography whose remnants arc at WGSM, very severely cut and edited to fit the publisher's needs. Long out of print, its usefulness in reflecting Still's thoughts about his own compositions and in reporting some recollections about his early career is evident. In particular, its information about the *Afro-American Symphony* and *Darker America* should be compared with other discussions of the same works elsewhere in the Sources section of this volume and in "The *Afro-American Symphony* and Its Scherzo," above.

The sectional subdivisions that are present in the initial publication have been assigned titles. The music examples, taken from works published by Fischer, remain unchanged. Capitalizations, spelling, and punctuation are unchanged except to correct obvious errors.[1] The use of italics and quotation marks for titles is changed to conform with standard current practice.

INTRODUCTION

The music of William Grant Still has commanded attention in recent years as one of the truly significant contributions to our native music.

Embodying some of the raciest elements of our current music of the people, as well as a background of the southern Negro, it has been elevated by its composer to a dignity that renders it of lasting value.

It is interesting to read, in the following pages, of the successive steps which led to the ultimate flowering of Still's extraordinary talent. Verna Arvey treats her subject with discernment, and her enthusiasm is infectious because of its sincerity. She has made an important addition to the literature on American music: one which may well have a place in the library of every music lover and student.

It is therefore a pleasure to welcome Miss Arvey's interesting addition to the series of Studies of Contemporary American Composers.

John Tasker Howard
January 2nd, 1939

I. THE ELEMENTS THAT GO TO MAKE UP A REAL AMERICAN

The America of tomorrow will be even more of a mixture of races, of creeds and of ideals than the America of today. Moreover, because they will have progressed so far in each other's company, they will have lost some of their identities. Just such a person is William Grant Still: a product of so many different phases of American life that each separate phase is now unrecognizable. It follows that his music is a more accurate expression of that life than any yet conceived.

Speaking on American music over a national broadcast on October 17, 1937 (when the Columbia Broadcasting System held a resumé of its first American Composers' Commission), Still said: "This music should speak to the hearts of every one of you, for it comes from the hearts of the men who wrote it." He meant that. His own music is sincere; he concludes that the music of other American composers is also sincere. More than that, he meant that every American should be as he is: passionately fond of all things American. Other music is lovely: but an American creation—even a Blues song, if it is a good one—thrills him to the core. He expects all Americans to be like that.

Officially, William Grant Still is reckoned a Negro composer, because the laws of the United States say that anyone with a drop of Negro blood in his veins is a Negro, and because some of his ancestors came from Africa where their rhythmic tom-tom beating may have been a forerunner of the primitive simplicity and powerful rhythmic impulse in Still's music today. Many of his ancestors, however, were already on the North American continent when the Negroes arrived. They were Indians, and it may be from them that Still inherited his bizarre harmonies and his almost oriental love of subtlety. There is still another group of ancestors: the European immigrants (mostly Irish) who danced old-world dances and sang the folk songs that had been theirs for generations. Thus, in Still's heritage we find almost all the elements that go to make up a real American.

Musically, he has all the requisites too. A thorough grounding in harmony and theory (the late George W. Chadwick was one of his teachers; he also studied at Oberlin) combined with the freedom that only ultra-modernism can give (the generous but revolutionary Edgar Varese, who taught him, once wittily remarked "You know, some critics think one is writing music only to annoy them!") as well as the determination and will to strike out for himself into new and individual paths, have made him unique in the field of modern music.

II.   EARLY LIFE AND STUDY

Born in 1895 (May 11th) in Woodville, Mississippi, William Grant Still had for parents two people who would be ranked as intellectuals even today, when standards are more exacting. Both were accredited teachers; both were musicians; both were talented, brilliant and versatile. The father's musical education was gained at the cost of great effort. Every cornet lesson he took cost him a seventy-five mile trip. Once he had acquired musical knowledge, he started a brass band—the only one in town—and thus became the idol of Woodville. He died when his son was but three months of age. After his death they found scraps of paper on which he'd tried his hand at musical composition! Had he had then the opportunities accorded his son many years later, he might have become equally famed. But he was the product of a different era; the inhabitant of a different, narrower world; the unwilling participant of an entirely different mode of thought.

His wife took the baby son to Little Rock, Arkansas, where she was to teach school until the end of her life, in 1927. It wasn't strange that, as soon as the child realized what music was, his thoughts turned toward it so unerringly that no scoldings, no arguments nor pleadings could shake his desire to be a composer, although on several occasions he indulged in the popular pastime of most young boys, the idea that the most thrilling thing in life was to be a street car conductor, or to raise chickens for a living.

Often, when the boy wished to amuse himself, he made toy violins to play upon. They were varnished and equipped with strings. They even succeeded in producing tones! Later, it was decided that he must have violin lessons. No sooner did he learn to read notes than he wanted to write them. Lacking manuscript paper, he made his own. Immediately, he jotted down little melodies, and even took his new enthusiasm to school. When other students were scratching aimlessly on paper in their spare moments, he scribbled notes.

While his grandmother worked about their house, she sang hymns and spirituals. "Little David, Play on Yo' Harp" was one of her favorites. Thus he grew up with the songs of his people, and grew to love the old hymns, which he plays today with the addition of such exquisite harmonies that they assume unsuspected beauty. A communal habit of the childhood days was that of serenading. It was pleasant to be awakened from slumber by such sweet sounds. He has always deplored the passing of that custom.

He learned to sing, and did not confine his singing to the immediate family. The aisles of trains made a splendid setting for his youthful vocal efforts. He quickly noticed that people gave him money and candy in return, so thenceforth he sang to everybody.

When young Still was about nine or ten years of age, his mother married Charles B. Shepperson, a postal employee who was a lover of operatic music and who spent a large share of his salary to buy a phonograph and the best of the red-seal records that were then on the market. This gave the boy an opportunity to hear music that pleased him more than any he had ever heard before: music that he had thought existed only in his wildest dreams. He used to play each record over and over again, to the utter neglect of whatever work there was to do. Mr. Shepperson also took him to good musical shows and told him stirring stories that fired his romantic imagination. At home, they sang duets together and discussed the plays they had seen and the music they had heard.

His mother's determination, good sense, talent and high moral character influenced his life strongly. She was the sort of vital personality who could command attention merely by entering a room. Her students adored her, and learned more from her than from anyone else; so did her young son, for he too was in her classes at school. Here she was stricter with him than with anyone else, for she did not want to be accused of favoritism.

William Grant Still was graduated from high school at sixteen. He was first honor bearer and class valedictorian.

Although she was at heart in sympathy with his desire to become a composer, his mother openly avowed her disapproval, simply because she felt that there was then no future for a musician, especially for a colored one. Thus, when he enrolled at Wilberforce University, he worked for a Bachelor of Science degree. Wilberforce statistics today show that he maintained a slightly above average scholastic record.

The mere fact that his mother had insisted that he work for a Bachelor of Science degree did not dampen Still's musical ardor in the least. Wilberforce had a string quartet, which occasioned the first arrangements he ever made. From that, he went on to making arrangements for the Wilberforce band of which he was first a member, then a bandleader. These arrangements were perhaps not perfect, but they had fewer defects than one would expect from a beginner. He made these because he didn't like the instrumental ensembles he heard. Therefore, he automatically set about to remedy their faults, just as the dancer La Argentina once set out to make a beautiful instrument from the castanets she so abhorred.

Every month before his allowance came, the music books he wanted were checked off and as a result, music publishers and dealers practically confiscated all his spending money. When he started to buy opera scores, his first acquisition was Weber's *Oberon*. The second was Wagner's *Flying Dutchman*. His French class was enlivened and made more interesting for him when he took into it a music book containing stories of all the famous Symphonies and read it while class was progressing. The teacher never discovered the substitution.

Some of the teachers went with him to operas and concerts in Dayton, Ohio. Other teachers encouraged his efforts at composition, and it was at Wilberforce that his first complete recital of his own compositions (some songs, some band numbers) was given. The approbation accorded him meant much at that time.

In addition to his playing of the violin, he learned how to play the oboe and clarinet. The latter he played in the choir and thus learned to transpose easily, for then no separate parts were written out. Everyone had to read from the same sheet. In his capacity as bandleader, he had to learn to play different instruments such as the piccolo and saxophone so that he could teach them to other players. The intimate knowledge of all instruments gained in this fashion has meant much to him in later years, and to his career as an orchestrator.

At Wilberforce, Still decided that he wished to emulate Coleridge-Taylor in every way, and spent many months in a fruitless attempt to make his hair grow straight upward, as did that of his hero. That failing, he made a new and important decision: some day he would be greater than Coleridge-Taylor and wear his hair in his own way!

On his summer vacations at home, Still entered several national contests for composers. To avoid his mother's scorn, he used to compose his entries at night, and would beg those who discovered him not to tell his mother. He entered a contest for a three-act opera (and ambitiously mailed out a score totaling twenty pages in length!) and another contest in which the judges wrote to tell him that his music had merit, but that they were afraid they didn't completely understand it!

Within two months of graduation, Still left Wilberforce. However, in 1936, Wilberforce awarded him a diploma of honor and the honorary degree of Master of Music, in recognition of his erudition, usefulness and eminent character.

Lean years followed the Wilberforce days, years in which he married, worked at odd jobs for little money, played oboe and 'cello with various orchestras, starved, froze, joined the U.S. Navy and nearly always wondered how he could crash the business of making music and getting paid for it. It was during those years also that he received a legacy from his father and promptly put it to good use studying privately at Oberlin. When it was exhausted, he worked and made enough money to return for the regular session. He completed one semester's work in theory and violin. Professor Lehmann, impressed by his talent and sincerity, asked him then why he did not go on to study composition. Still replied frankly that it was because he had no money. A few days later, Lehmann informed him that in a meeting of the Theory Committee it had been decided that he was to be given free tuition, and that Dr. George W. Andrews was to teach him composition.[2] Thus a scholarship was created for him where none had existed before.

III.   WORK WITH HANDY; NEW YORK

W. C. Handy, Father of the Blues, offered him his first job in New York City as an arranger, and as a musician on the road, traveling through large and small Southern towns with Handy's Band. Later he accepted a job with Eubie Blake's orchestra for the epoch-making *Shuffle Along*. While *Shuffle Along* was playing in Boston, Still became aware that he now could afford to pay for musical instruction, and filed his application at the New England Conservatory of Music. When he returned for his answer, he was told that George W. Chadwick would teach him free of charge. He protested that he could afford to pay, but generous Chadwick refused to take his money.

Back in New York, Still accepted the position of Recording Director for the Black Swan Phonograph Company. There he found a man preparing to write to Edgar Varese to tell him that, in response for his request for a talented young Negro composer to whom he could offer a scholarship in musical composition, he knew of no one suitable. Still said, "I want that scholarship. You can just tear up that letter!" Thus came about his introduction to Edgar Varese, and modernism. Later, Still often declared, "When I was groping blindly in my efforts to compose, it was Varese who pointed out to me the way to individual expression and who gave me the opportunity to hear my music played. I shall never forget his kindness, nor that of George W. Chadwick and the instructors at Oberlin."

For many months, he played in vaudeville and in the pit for many musical shows. He played banjo in the orchestra of the Plantation, a New York night club at Broadway and 50th. When the conductor of this orchestra left, Still advanced to its conductorship.[3] He went into business as an arranger, and made arrangements for such people as Sophie Tucker, Don Voorhees. He orchestrated several editions of *Earl Carroll's Vanities,* one edition of J. P. McEvoy's *Americana,* and *Runnin' Wild* and *Rain or Shine.* Later he arranged for Paul Whiteman, who was to play some of his compositions for the first time in public and to commission several notable works from him.

He was the first to arrange and record (with Don Voorhees) a fantasy on the famous "St. Louis Blues." This was in 1927, on a Columbia disc.

The last orchestra with which he ever played professionally was that of LeRoy Smith. So much work as arranger and orchestrator came his way that he was no longer in need of such work to make a living.

When CBS first started, Still was arranging Don Voorhees' music for the network broadcasts. Somewhat later, he was arranging at NBC when Willard Robison was singing on the Maxwell House Hour. Soon Still was making arrangements for Robison's "Deep River" program and (at WOR) some of the orchestra men quietly suggested to Robison that Still be allowed to conduct their organization. The management agreed, as long as the men were satisfied. In that way, he became the first American colored man to lead a radio orchestra of white men in New York City, and he held the post for many months.

In this way he became intimately acquainted with Jazz, the American musical idiom that has been damned by so many, and praised by so many more. He, too, realizes that Jazz has many faults, but he also realizes that it has many fine points, and he believes that from its *elements* a great musical form can be built. Today he points out the many things Jazz has given to music as a whole: rhythm, new tone colors, interesting orchestral devices, and a greater fluency in playing almost all of the orchestral instruments. He mentions the amazing things a modern player can do—things that would have caught an old-time symphony man napping. He believes that every composer, to deserve the name of "American", should be thoroughly acquainted with Jazz, no matter whether he uses it much or little in his work. It is one of the few musical idioms developed by America that can be said to belong to no other people on earth!

IV. SOME POPULAR SONGS AND EARLY CONCERT MUSIC

Still's first published composition is lost today, even the title forgotten. It was published by one of those fly-by-night concerns that will print anything for a monetary consideration. The second published work was a bit more fortunate. It was a popular song called "No Matter What You Do", His wife was the lyricist; W. C. Handy the publisher. Two popular songs by Still were published by the Edward B. Marks Music Corporation under the pseudonym of Willy M. Grant. Their titles were "Brown Baby" and "Memphis Man."

Several of his pieces were played many times on the air and found great favor with the musicians because they were catchy and were saddled with dubious titles. The composer laments today that he has lost the music for these, but is happy over the fact that they were never published and distributed over a wider area.

Three Fantastic Dances for chamber orchestra he never finished; his *Death,* a choral work for mixed voices a cappella on a Dunbar poem was completed and deliberately thrown away. He also wrote *Three Ne-*

gro Songs for orchestra (i.e. "Negro Love Song," "Death Song," "Song of the Backwoods") as well as an orchestral composition called *Black Bottom* which he described as follows: "A swamp where, between the hours of four A.M. and six A.M., Death and the fiends of darkness revel. Death, disguised as a siren, dances and sings a song which is repeated by the fiends. All join in the revelry which is interrupted at its height by a distant clock striking the hour of six." This work is cast in a decidedly ultra-modern idiom.

There were also several songs. One entitled "Good Night," to words of Dunbar, was dedicated to William Service Bell, baritone. "Mandy Lou" belonged to but did not appear with the set of two songs later published by G. Schirmer, Inc. At last, all these early efforts and smaller compositions were scrapped. Whatever was good in them was incorporated into a larger work. For instance, the "Dance of Love" (played over the radio many times) was put into *The Sorcerer* ballet which has itself been scrapped and its themes used in other compositions, and the "Dance of the Carnal Flowers" was inserted, with few changes, into the ballet *La Guiablesse*.

From the Land of Dreams was his first major work to be subjected to critical comment when it was performed by the Composers' Guild in New York February 8, 1925. It was scored for three voices and chamber orchestra, the voices treated as instruments. It occasioned a storm of protest. In it, the composer simply tried to suggest the flimsiness of dreams which fade before they have taken definite form, but Olin Downes wrote sharply: "Is Mr. Still unaware that the cheapest melody in the revues he has orchestrated has more reality and inspiration in it than the curious noises he has manufactured? Mr. Varese has driven his original and entertaining music out of him." On the other hand, Paul Rosenfeld, while admitting Still's limitations at this period of his life and work, spoke more kindly of this composition.

The score of *From the Land of Dreams* is now lost, much to the composer's delight. He fervently hopes it will never again be played, and now jokingly refers to it as a musical portrait of an owl with a headache. It was, indeed, ultra-modern in style: pure cacophony throughout.[4] It was not until the moment of performance that Still realized that he was dabbling in an idiom unsuited to him, one that robbed his music of its character, for a harmonic scheme can make or mar the feeling of the music. He thereupon determined to find an idiom of his own, and made known his decision to M. Varese.

Should Varese have felt badly over this decision so flatly announced, it doubtless comforts him today to realize that the fruits of his teaching are evident in Still's music in far more subtle, more logical ways than if the young composer had merely adopted Varese's own individual idiom without question.

Today, from the lesson he learned in his attempts at cacophony, Still will occasionally emit remarks like these: "When a person sets out to write music on the basis of a preconceived scientific idea, something invariably goes wrong. If the counterpoint is smooth, the melody will be imperfect, and so on. The result may be correct, but be entirely lacking in spiritual content. In music, one must think more of what is to be said than how it is to be said."

From the Journal of a Wanderer (written in 1925, performed by the North Shore Festival Orchestra in Evanston, Ill., with Frederick Stock conducting in 1926 and by the Rochester Philharmonic Orchestra in 1929) is important in this period as a lesson in "what not to do," according to its composer, in spite of the fact that at the time of its performance, it seemed to be a decided step in advance of *Darker America* (to be discussed later). In a sense, it was more versatilely written, more spectacularly conceived. On this point, critics agreed, though one of them did admit that it savored of stunt writing. The reason Still was personally disappointed in it was simply that the result of his planning (in performance) was quite different than what he expected. Into the score he had written a great many clever orchestral effects. He had gone the limit in the division of his string. It all looked very well on paper. His surprise at the difference in sound can well be imagined. *From the Journal of a Wanderer* comprised extracts from the musical diary of a globe trotter who had visited far lands and viewed strange scenes. It was in five parts: "Phantom Trail," "Magic Bells," "The Valley of Echoes," "Mystic Moon," "Devil's Hollow." The original manuscript of this score is now in the Sibley Musical Library at the University of Rochester, gift of the composer.

Two comparatively unimportant works may be mentioned here, out of their chronological order: *Log Cabin Ballads,* consisting of three parts, "Long To'ds Night," "Beneaf de Willers," "Miss Malindy" (written in 1927 and performed by the Barrère Ensemble in New York on March 25, 1928); and *Puritan Epic* (written in 1928). Both of these are orchestral works.

At the time of their creation or performance (1928), Still was receiving the second Harmon Award, granted annually by the Harmon Foundation, for the most significant contribution during the year to Negro culture in the United States.

V.   "NEGROID" COMPOSITIONS TO 1930

After much thought, Still decided to adopt a Negroid idiom; to use Negroid titles for his compositions. Since that decision, his departures from his original resolve have been rare.

Levee Land was written for the singer, Florence Mills. It consisted of four robust, jazzy, Negroid songs. Critics joyfully lauded his farewell from the peculiar noises comprising Varese's musical idiom when it was performed by the International Composers' Guild at Aeolian Hall on January 24, 1926. The *Musical Courier* called it "Four foolish jazz jokes: good, healthy, sane music." And the incomparable Florence Mills, veteran of many stage and floor shows, was unreasoningly nervous at this, her first concert venture. She sang beautifully, however. Her vibrant personality was a vital part of the songs. Yet *Levee Land* was not even perfect of its kind. It simply marked a step toward the goal the composer wished to reach. With the exception of the spontaneous first song, there were many things in *Levee Land* that were creations of the brain, not of the heart.

At the time it was written (1924) *Darker America* was his strongest work. The program for it was compiled after the creation of the music. It received an enthusiastic reception on its performances (by the International Composers' Guild at Aeolian Hall in New York on November 28, 1926, by the Rochester Philharmonic Orchestra in 1927 and in 1930, and for broadcasting by John Tasker Howard in New York in 1933), and was later published by the Eastman School of Music through C. C. Birchard Co., in Boston. The *Musical Courier* averred that he was less under the influence of Varese than he was a year before, and that the less that influence was felt, the better for his music. It prophesied that on his full liberation, he would blossom forth as one of America's truly great composers. "There is no doubting the man's power!" Another metropolitan periodical remarked that, despite Varese, Mr. Still had been "unable to suppress that rhythmic ingenuity and naive melodic atmosphere which are inherently of the American Negro." But how fortunate for Still that he had the assistance of a man like Varese! Without that, he might still be groping among unexciting, academic methods of writing music. He might never have had the courage to strike out for himself!

Nevertheless, Still himself does not consider *Darker America* a good example of his work. It is, he declares, fragmentary. It contains too much material. At the time it was written, he was struggling with musical form. His conception of it was rather hazy. He had not yet learned how to do a great deal with a few themes. He was obsessed with the beginner's idea of using a great deal of material, whether or not it was related.

Darker America was intended to suggest the triumph of a people over their sorrows through fervent prayer. At the outset, the strong theme of the American Negro is announced by the strings in unison. Following a short development of this, the English Horn announces the Sorrow theme which is followed by the theme of Hope, given to muted brass, accompanied by strings and woodwinds. The Sorrow and Hope themes appear intensified, and the prayer is heard, stated by the oboe. Strongly contrasted moods follow. At the end, the three principal themes are combined in triumphant music.

After the performance it was evident that Still's advance as a composer had been tremendous, for the ugly discords were conspicuously absent and the thematic material of *Darker America* was rich, potent, and served to characterize him as a composer of definite individuality and power.

About 1926, when *From the Black Belt* was written, Still conceived an idea which has ever since been evident in his works. He began to base each composition on a different harmonic scheme: a scheme that would be an essential part of his own musical individuality, but which would differentiate each composition from the other. He began also to try to express moods, story, even thoughts by means of harmonies.

The same vigorous sense of humor that led the youth to play pranks on other people in College is shown in many of his compositions, especially in *From the Black Belt* (easily the most racial of all) written for small orchestra, and composed admittedly to please those who hear it. The first section "Lil' Scamp" lasts for eight measures only. It was expected to provoke laughter and it always does, whenever it is performed. Says the composer: "If one were to base his judgment on the volume of sound he would think this little fellow, who delights in playing childish pranks, a big scamp. But the aptness of the title is not determined by volume for it is the brevity of the piece which tells us that he is a 'little scamp.'" The other sections are entitled: "Honeysuckle" (a musical suggestion of the saccharine odor of the honeysuckle), "Dance, Mah Bones Is Creakin'" (An old man, afflicted with rheumatism, complains loudly of his creaking bones), "Blue" (a plaintive melody which suggests the "blues" songs of the southern Negro), "Brown Girl" (a tone picture of a lovely mulatto girl), "Clap Yo' Han's" (the participants in a dancing game for children clap their hands). It was performed by the Barrère Ensemble in New York on March 20, 1927 and by the Eastman School Little Symphony in Rochester in 1933 and 1934. On one of the latter occasions, a Rochester critic wrote: "This genial, soft-spoken Negro has proved himself a leader in the movement to write music that is not merely cerebral, that has no fear of melody, that begins with the definite intention of pleasing his hearers. His suite was of seven short movements, but their ingratiating tunes and rhythms had the audience asking for a repetition, and that at the end of a long concert." This was later arranged by the modernist, Nicholas Slonimsky, for clarinet, violin, 'cello and piano.

Two works of beauty which emerged from this particular period were the songs "Winter's Approach" to words by Paul Laurence Dunbar, and "Breath of a Rose" to a poem by Langston Hughes. The former was written for Marya Freund, the latter for a stage production in which Paul Robeson was to have been featured, though the song was not intended for Robeson to sing. In these two simple songs (published by G. Schirmer, Inc.) Still's scope as a composer and his distinction are evident. Both are unmistakably his own, yet are entirely different in character, their ultimate form having been dictated by the subject. They show the sharp individuality of the music, the lack of monotony, and give evidence that, though he is decidedly a modernist, he is not an ultra-modernist. His writing for the voice is sympathetic, vocally grateful and facile. Throughout both songs, the piano accompaniment plays an important part, for it expresses mood and meaning.

VI.   THE TRILOGY: *AFRICA,* THE *AFRO-AMERICAN SYMPHONY,* AND *SYMPHONY IN G MINOR*

Africa, the *Afro-American Symphony* and the *Symphony in G Minor* comprise a trilogy of works whose composition occupied their creator over a period of years, during which time other works were also written and played.

Perhaps most intellectual young American Negroes think much about their African background. William Grant Still's meditations on this subject took a musical form. It was in 1930 that he wrote *Africa,* a symphonic poem in three movements, designed as an American Negro's wholly fanciful concept of the cradle of his Race, formed on the folklore of generations. Because the movements have descriptive titles, one might call *Africa* a suite, but the composer prefers to describe it as a poem, believing that the unity of the idea justifies it.

Africa, which critics said was "not as inchoate or as desultory as his *Darker America* and *Journal of a Wanderer,*" quickly became one of his most highly praised compositions. During five years, four different versions of *Africa* were scored, three of which were performed. In January of 1933 appeared the fifth and supposedly last version. But in 1935 Still noted a flaw, and a sixth version came into being. This constant revision is not unusual with him. Many things he destroyed completely because, in his own judgment, they "weren't good enough." He constantly criticizes his own work and constantly revises. This results in much extra labor, but he feels that final perfection justifies it.

The three movements of *Africa* are titled: "Land of Peace," "Land of Romance," "Land of Superstition." [5] In the first movement, two kinds of peace are portrayed, the first pastoral, the second spiritual. It is an active peace and quietude, not a lethargic slumber. "Land of Romance" is tinged with sadness, intensified by the orchestral treatment of the first part of the movement. It ends on a note of passionate longing. In the final movement, two forms of superstition appear: that of the pagan African and that of the followers of Mohammed. The music abounds in the suggestion of startling unspoken fears, lurking terrors. It subtly conveys the idea that the race has not yet shaken off primitive beliefs, despite the influence of civilization. The opening theme later proceeds into a rather Oriental motif, by which the composer intended to depict the arid Northern part of Africa. *Africa* places the listener instantly on the soil of the Dark Continent; it is not merely a picture of abstract beauty.

Africa was dedicated to the eminent flautist, Georges Barrère, and was performed by the Barrère ensemble in New York in 1930, by the Rochester Philharmonic Orchestra in Rochester in 1930, at the Festival of American Music in Bad Homburg in 1931, in Paris by the Pasdeloup Orchestra in 1933, in Rome under the leadership of Werner Janssen, and in part by Paul Whiteman's Orchestra in New York in 1933, by the New York Sinfonietta in 1933, and under the composer's direction by the Hollywood Bowl Orchestra in 1936.

The second composition in the trilogy, the *Afro-American Symphony,* was composed in 1930, dedicated to Irving Schwerké and performed by

the Rochester Philharmonic Orchestra in Rochester in 1931 and 1932
and in part under the direction of Dr. Howard Hanson (who introduced
it) in Berlin, Stuttgart and Leipzig in 1933. These dates show conclusively that Still's work preceded that of another Negro composer who in
1934 was heralded as having written the first Negro symphony.

This *Afro-American Symphony* really became widely known through
the energy of its publishers who were canny enough not to allow important publications to gather dust on their shelves. From the date the
symphony was accepted for publication, and since its performance under Hans Lange and the New York Philharmonic Orchestra, this symphony has had many performances. Leopold Stokowski played its last
movement in many American cities on his nationwide tour with the Philadelphia Orchestra, thus bringing it to the attention of many American
music-lovers.

A reviewer said, "There is not a cheap or banal passage in the entire
composition." A Rochester critic opined that it was "by far the most
direct in appeal to a general audience than any of his music heard
here, and it has a greater technical finish. To some extent he has replaced
that arresting vigor one has admired by deft sophistication." Another
Rochester critic dubbed it "honest, sincere music . . . developed without
recourse to theatrical invention." David Kessler said it "seemed a much
more important work on second hearing than it did the first time it
was played"—genuine praise, indeed. An audience in Berlin broke a
twenty-year tradition to encore the Scherzo from this Symphony when
Dr. Howard Hanson conducted it there; several years later, when Karl
Krueger conducted it in Budapest, his audience did the same thing.

Of this symphony, Still wrote:

At the time it was written, no thought was given to a program for the *Afro-
American Symphony,* the program being added after the completion of the
work. I have regretted this step because in this particular instance a program
is decidedly inadequate. The program devised at that time stated that the music portrayed the "sons of the soil," that is that it offered a composite musical portrait of those Afro-Americans who have not responded completely to
the cultural influences of today. It is true that an interpretation of that sort
may be read into the music. Nevertheless, one who hears it is quite sure to
discover other meanings which are probably broader in their scope. He may
find that the piece portrays four distinct types of Afro-Americans whose sole
relationship is the physical one of dark skins. On the other hand, he may find
that the music offers the sorrows and joys, the struggles and achievements of
an individual Afro-American. Also it is quite probable that the music will

Example 8. Principal theme, first movement, *Afro-American Symphony*. Used by permission.

speak to him of moods peculiar to colored Americans. Unquestionably, various other interpretations may be read into the music.

Each movement of this Symphony presents a definite emotion, excerpts from poems of Paul Laurence Dunbar being included in the score for the purpose of explaining these emotions. Each movement has a suggestive title: the first is Longing, the second Sorrow, the third (or the Scherzo) Humor, and the fourth Sincerity. In it, I have stressed an original motif in the blues idiom, employed as the principal theme of the first movement, and appearing in various forms in the succeeding movements, where I have tried to present it in a characteristic manner.

When judged by the laws of musical form the Symphony is somewhat irregular. This irregularity is in my estimation justified since it has no ill effect on the proportional balance of the composition. Moreover, when one considers that an architect is free to design new forms of buildings, and bears in mind the freedom permitted creators in other fields of art, he can hardly deny a composer the privilege of altering established forms as long as the sense of proportion is justified.

The Moderato Assai, the first movement, departs to an extent from the Sonata Allegro form. The first division might be called the Exposition. This begins with an introduction in A flat Major, derived from the principal theme, and is followed by the principal theme (example 8). Following this, the principal theme reappears in a new treatment, and with a rhythmic counterpoint, which is extended to form a bridge between the repetition of the principal theme and a transition that strongly resembles a development of the principal theme. The subordinate theme is in G Major (the fact that the keys are here unrelated is a departure) and is in the style of a Spiritual (example 9). Then, instead of a Codetta, there is a transitional passage, starting in G Minor and leading to the Development in Division Two, in A Flat Major, the material here derived from the principal theme. Division Three is a Recapitulation,

Example 9. Subordinate theme, first movement, *Afro-American Symphony*. Used by permission.

Example 10. Principal theme, second movement, *Afro-American Symphony*. Used by permission.

Example 11. Secondary theme, second movement, *Afro-American Symphony*. Used by permission.

in which there is a radical departure. The subordinate theme reappears in A Flat Major, instead of a repetition of the principal theme. There is a re-transition before the final appearance of the principal theme in A Flat Major in a new and rhythmic treatment. The movement ends with a coda.

The second movement is short. There is a six measure introduction, scored entirely for strings and muffled tympani. The material of this introduction is derived from the principal (blues) theme of the first movement. The principal theme of the second movement, however, is played by oboe alone, accompanied by violas and 'celli divisi and by a flute obligato. It is eight measures in length (example 10). This theme is repeated, then extended slightly. The gap between the principal theme of the second movement and its subordinate theme is bridged by four measures of material taken from the introduction to the second movement, and used in transitional fashion. The subordinate theme is given to the flute at the outset, and is derived from the principal theme of the first movement (example 11). Thereafter, appear four-measure blocks of this same melody treated in different ways, a development of an individual sort. This lasts for thirty measures and leads to a repetition of the movement's principal theme, extended and working up to a fermata, and a pause. The movement ends with the introductory material given to muted strings and muffled tympani, here extended to eight measures.

Example 12. Principal theme, third movement (Scherzo), *Afro-American Symphony*. Used by permission.

Example 13. Transformation of the symphony's main theme, Coda of third movement. Used by permission.

Example 14. Principal theme, fourth movement, *Afro-American Symphony*. Used by permission.

The form of the third movement, or Scherzo (the humorous aspect of religious fervor) is also unusual. The Introduction, in E Flat Minor, is derived from the principal theme, yet resembles in a general way the episodic material. The principal theme is in A Flat Major (example 12). Just before the Coda there appears a transformation of the blues theme of the first movement, as an accompanying figure (example 13).

The fourth movement, Lento con Risoluzione, has a decidedly free form. The principal theme is announced at the outset by strings accompanied by clarinets, trombones and tuba (example 14). The subordinate theme in A Major is derived from the blues theme (example 15). This theme is presented again in C Major and is then developed, the development being extended and presenting, during its course, the blues theme in a different form. Much later in the score, there is a new development in 6/8 time which enters abruptly. In

Example 15. Subordinate theme, fourth movement, *Afro-American Symphony*. Used by permission.

this, the blues theme reappears in still another form. Just before the coda brings the movement to its close, the principal theme of the movement is re-stated.

The harmonies employed in the Symphony are quite conventional except in a few places. The use of this style of harmonization was necessary in order to attain simplicity and to intensify in the music those qualities which enable the hearers to recognize it as Negro music. The orchestration was planned with a view to the attainment of effective simplicity.[6]

Third in the trilogy is the *Symphony in G Minor* which, at the earnest request of Dr. Leopold Stokowski, who introduced it with the Philadelphia Orchestra in Philadelphia in December of 1937 and then played it twice in New York City a few days later, was subtitled *Song of a New Race*. This music, too, was composed as abstract music, with no thought of a program. Its creation occupied the composer for more than a year. Measure by measure, phrase by phrase, the work grew slowly, until it became one of the finest of his symphonic works to date. The theme of the second movement alone is masterly in its inspiration (example 16).

Of this Symphony (dedicated to Isabel Morse Jones), the composer has written the following:

This Symphony in G Minor is related to my *Afro-American Symphony* being, in fact, a sort of extension or evolution of the latter. This relationship is implied musically through the affinity of the principal theme of the first movement of the *Symphony in G Minor* to the principal theme of the fourth, or last, movement of the *Afro-American*.

It may be said that the purpose of the *Symphony in G Minor* is to point musically to changes wrought in a people through the progressive and transmuting spirit of America. I prefer to think of it as an abstract piece of music, but, for the benefit of those who like interpretations of their music, I have written the following notes:

The *Afro-American Symphony* represented the Negro of days not far removed from the Civil War. The *Symphony in G Minor* represents the

Example 16. *Symphony in G Minor* (No. 2), "Song of a New Race," second movement, opening. Used by permission.

American colored man of today, in so many instances a totally new individual produced through the fusion of White, Indian and Negro bloods.

The four movements in the *Afro-American Symphony* were subtitled "Longing," "Sorrow," "Humor" (expressed through religious fervor) and "Sincerity," or "Aspiration." In the *Symphony in G Minor,* longing has progressed beyond a passive state and has been converted into active effort; sorrow has given way to a more philosophic attitude in which the individual has ceased pitying himself, knowing that he can advance only through a desire for spiritual growth and by nobility of purpose; religious fervor and the rough humor of the folk have been replaced by a more mundane form of emotional release that is more closely allied to that of other peoples; and aspiration is now tempered with the desire to give to humanity the best that their African Heritage has given them.

Linton Martin, writing in the Philadelphia Inquirer for December 11, 1937, said "*Song of a New Race* by the Negro composer, William Grant Still, was of absorbing interest, unmistakably racial in thematic material and rhythms, and triumphantly articulate in expression of moods, ranging from the exuberance of jazz to brooding wistfulness." A few days later, Olin Downes wrote: "It is interesting to perceive how far Mr. Still can go in a purely melodic manner, without resort to many of the traditional symphonic devices to fill out his tonal design." Leopold Stokowski, however, wrote to the composer that the new work was a

Example 17. *Symphony in G Minor,* page from the composer's score. Used by permission.

tremendous advance over the former symphony, beautiful and vital though that was.

VII.   BALLET MUSIC

Choreographic music has always held a fascination for William Grant Still, and dancers have not failed to take advantage of his willingness to write for them, and to perform his works accordingly. *La Guiablesse* was begun before *Sahdji,* but was completed later. Both of these are ballets, with a woman dancer as the central character.

La Guiablesse (a patois word meaning female devil) is based on a scenario by Ruth Page which in turn was based on a legend of Martinique. It was produced in 1933 at the Eastman School in Rochester, also in Chicago; later it was produced thrice in a single season (1934) by the Chicago Grand Opera Company. In later years, Rochester also revived it several times.

This ballet music is not at all superficial, as is most created dance music. Before writing it, Still studied West Indian and Creole musical material, but finally determined to create his own themes as being truer to scene and mood. The scene is laid on the Island of Martinique. The opening theme is that of La Guiablesse. This appears throughout the score, and finally in the funeral march at the end. The she-devil herself is introduced by an offstage contralto solo, a haunting, wordless melody. Sensuous beauty and dramatic intensity mark the music. It progresses from a fairly quiet and atmospheric beginning to a thrilling climax. The story concerns two young lovers, Adou and Yzore, whose tender love is interrupted by the appearance of the greedily sensuous she-devil. She lures Adou away from his village sweetheart. Then, just as he is past returning, the music assumes a horrible tinge as the beautiful woman turns into a demon, and like demoniac laughter it continues as she insists on claiming her prey. Adou, unconscious, falls from her embrace into the pit below.

Herman Devries, writing in the Chicago American, said of it: "It is far above the average ballet music . . . both in quality of invention and in the value of its themes and imagination. It is a highly-colored, vivid, evocative, gorgeous score." Stuart R. Sabin in Rochester wrote: "The music is charming, picturesque and dramatically suggestive, never padded, never divorced from the action, yet with an individual appeal of its own."

The ballet *Sahdji,* dedicated to Dr. Howard Hanson, is significant for two reasons: it is more important musically than choreographically; it marked the turning point in the regard of critics such as Olin Downes. Downes came to Rochester for the performance (it was done in Rochester in 1931 and in 1934) and wrote at length about it. Other ballets were on the same program, but Downes concentrated his remarks on *Sahdji.* He commented on the unusual form in which the work was cast, said "Still harks back to more primitive sources (i.e. than Harlem jazz) for brutal, persistent and barbaric rhythms," and acknowledged him as one of America's finest, most promising composers.

Sahdji is elemental: fine music, significant drama. It is a ballet for chorus (singing a text connoting incidents in the action) and bass chanter, interpreting the ballet by reciting African proverbs. A psychological effect is produced by drums. The story is told in pantomime and is built around the faithless favorite wife of the African chieftain Konumbju. The scene is laid in ancestral, central Africa. It is a hunting feast of the Azande tribe. Librettists were Richard Bruce and Alain Locke.

William Grant Still spent about a year and a half preparing to write *Sahdji,* absorbing African atmosphere so as to be able to write in that idiom without resorting to authentic folk material. The so-called "Invitation Dance," when Sahdji lures Mrabo into the hut, came to him first and around it he built the rest of the ballet. Once begun, his eagerness to complete it knew no bounds. In its form, the old Greek dramatic model is approximated.

In 1936 *Sahdji* was revised, several minor changes being made, and a prologue to be sung by the Chanter was added. The ballet has never yet been performed in its revised version.

VIII. WORKS FROM THE GUGGENHEIM PERIOD AND FOR PAUL WHITEMAN

Both *Ebon Chronicle* and *A Deserted Plantation* were commissioned by Paul Whiteman and were scored for Whiteman's instrumental combination, so that when the former was played by Whiteman with a large symphony orchestra it was termed "dull and pretentious" by a critic. With this statement, the composer disagreed slightly, for he had never written it with the idea that it was a major work of art, nor did it pretend to a distinction that was not intended for it. *A Deserted Plantation,* excerpts from which were later arranged for piano and published by Robbins

Music Corporation, was once recommended to diversion seekers by Walter Winchell. Its prologue is played separately, and the succeeding four movements continue without a break, being linked by interludes for solo piano. It is a musical picture of the meditations of Uncle Josh, an old colored man who is the sole occupant of the dying plantation and who delights in dreaming of its past glory. The music is nostalgic in mood. Every movement has a motto, taken from Dunbar's poem, "The Deserted Plantation." The Spiritual in the (third movement) is an adaptation of the well-known "I Want Jesus to Walk With Me"—the exception to his rigid rule about employing alien themes in his serious works. On its performance in 1933, the critics came out with an interesting disagreement. One said it was not Mr. Still at his best, while another characterized it as "skillfully constructed music" and lauded it from many different standpoints.

Two other symphonic works, written during the period of his Guggenheim Fellowship, and more worthy of serious consideration, are the poems *Dismal Swamp* (which employs a solo piano at intervals) and *Beyond Tomorrow*—the latter unperformed as yet.

Beyond Tomorrow is dedicated to Still's four children. It is melodic throughout, and hauntingly beautiful. When it is played in public, Paul Whiteman may be the first to introduce it, for it was written on a commission from him, though it is entirely different in treatment, thought and scope from anything Still had ever done for him before.

Dismal Swamp is a musical portrait of a dreary swampland that assumes a strange wild beauty as the visitor progresses farther into it. It is based on a single theme, moves slowly, and rises to a tremendous climax. This was played by the Orquesta Sinfonica de Yucatan under the direction of Samuel Marti three times in 1938; Dr. Hanson has also programmed it in Rochester. It was dedicated to Quinto Maganini.

IX.   PIANO MUSIC

Until 1934, almost all of Still's works were for orchestra, for that was his field. He felt at home in it as he did in no other. True, some piano reductions of his orchestral works had been made, and he had used the piano as a unique addition to the orchestra in several of his symphonic works. *The Black Man Dances* for piano chiefly, with orchestral accompaniment, came suddenly and was the forerunner of many more interesting and lovely works for that instrument. This suite of dances represents four characteristic phases in the life of the Race. The first is an African flute serenade. After a short introduction, the flute has the principal and sole theme, which is thereafter embellished with little piano cadenzas. The second is a tribal dance, in which the entire ensemble is used more rhythmically than melodically. The third section is a Barrelhouse episode, reminiscent of the blues and of old-time ragtime piano players and player pianos. The last is a Shout, expressing the religious ecstasy of the Negro in rather free and joyous style. It is much fuller for piano than either of the three preceding dances. This suite was commissioned by Paul Whiteman and is as yet unperformed.[7]

It would be incorrect to class this suite as "great" music, or even to say that it fully utilizes the possibilities of the piano as a solo instrument. However, it is important because it served as a prelude to other piano works by Still that are truly inspired and that not only display a more intimate knowledge of the infinite possibilities of the piano, but utilize those possibilities in hitherto unsuspected ways. For that reason, Still's piano music is difficult for the contemporary pianist to grasp.

Kaintuck', for piano and orchestra, is short and poetic, but equally as strong as Still's previous works. As a matter of fact, a careful study reveals it to be by far the finest work for piano to date of any Negro composer. Its creation came easily. It was written to express musically his inner reactions to the peaceful, shimmering, misty sunlight on the blue grass of Kentucky. It is a subjective not an objective picture, however. *Kaintuck'* is built chiefly on two themes: everything else grows out of them. The piano opens the poem quietly, then runs into a rhythmic accompaniment to the orchestral statement of the themes. Both the piano and the orchestra are heard in huge, authoritative chords just before the cadenza by the solo instrument. This cadenza, unlike most, does not aim toward the exploitation of the interpreter, but simply and colorfully enhances the thematic and harmonic material that has preceded it. The theme is re-stated, and the piano closes the poem as quietly as it opened it. It is haunting, memorable. It was first played on two pianos at a Los Angeles Pro Musica concert, with Verna Arvey, to whom the work is dedicated, at the solo piano. Since then, Dr. Hanson has played it in Rochester and Eugene Goossens in Cincinnati. The composer has also conducted it in his own orchestral concerts in Northern and Southern California, with Verna Arvey as soloist.

One of the finest groups of piano compositions to be written by any American composer is the *Three Visions* by William Grant Still, published by J. Fischer and Bro. The harmonies in these *Visions* are strange.

Example 18. "Dark Horseman," from *Three Visions* for piano. Courtesy of William Grant Still Music.

Example 19. "Summerland," from *Three Visions*. Courtesy of William Grant Still Music.

By them, the listener is aware that the "visions" are real only to the dreamer. As music, they exemplify the scope of Still's musical individuality. Once again, he has given us strongly contrasted moods, unified by his own personal idiom and by his spiritual concept of the music he creates. The first *Vision* is one of horror. It is entitled "Dark Horsemen," and in it the hoof beats of the horses alternate with the shrieks of anguish they cause by their very presence (example 18). The second *Vision* is a portrait of promised beauty in the afterlife. It is called "Summerland," after the peaceful Heaven of the Spiritualists (example 19). It has been arranged by the composer for small orchestra, and published. The last *Vision* is of the radiant future, a vision of aspiration that is ever-climbing, never-ending. It is called "Radiant Pinnacle" (example 20). Its continual rhythmic flow and its final, deceptive cadence leave one with the feeling that there is more to come: that the last word has not been said.

"Quit Dat Fool'nish" was composed as a little encore piece for *Kaintuck'*. It is for piano alone, as are the *Visions*. So joyous and effervescent is it that, when played as an encore, it has often been known to be encored on its own account!

Example 20. "Radiant Pinnacle," from *Three Visions*. Courtesy of William Grant Still Music.

X.   SPIRITUAL ARRANGEMENTS

Perhaps because, until his time, most Negro composers had won fame purely as arrangers of Spirituals and not on creative efforts, and because a great many people harbored the delusion that their work should stop there, Still made it a point not to arrange Spirituals (except when he was required to do so, in his commercial arranging) for many years. However, during the period of his Guggenheim Fellowship, the talented writer, Ruby Berkeley Goodwin, approached him with several short stories she had built around familiar and unfamiliar Spirituals. She needed new and distinctive arrangements, so Still agreed to make them. He arranged twelve for solo voice and piano; and these, along with the accompanying stories, are now published in two volumes by the Handy Brothers Music Publishing Company. Three of these ("Gwinter Sing All Along de Way," "Keep Me F'om Sinkin' Down" and "Lawd, Ah Wants To Be a Christian") have recently been arranged for chorus by the composer. Others in the group are "All God's Chillun Got Shoes," "Lis'en To De Lam's," "Great Camp Meeting," "Great Day," "Good News," "Peter, Go Ring Dem Bells," "Got a Home in Dat Rock," "Mah Lawd's Gonna Rain down Fire" and "Didn't Mah Lawd Deliver Daniel?"

There is one thing that makes these arrangements unique among Spiritual arrangements: they are as characteristic as the spirituals themselves. Through long years of visiting small Negro churches in search of little-known Spirituals, of hearing groups of people sing them spontaneously in revivals or shouting in ecstasy at basket meetings, Still learned that the usual, conventional arrangement robs the Spiritual of its folk flavor. No wonder people discover Caucasian influences in them, thought he, when often their whole characters are altered by the foreign quality of their arrangements!

If there is a trace of Caucasian influence in the Spirituals themselves, it resolves itself into a case of the music of the white emerging transformed form the soul of the colored man. However, the rhythmic, stirring, emotional Spirituals are purely African in essence. The secular folk music of the American Negro is the Blues, and these are far more Negroid than the Spirituals, on the whole. Still has no delusions as to the triviality of Blues, despite their origin and the homely sentiments of their texts. The pathos of their melodic contents bespeaks the anguish of human hearts and belies the banality of their lyrics. They generally conform to a definite pattern that affects lyrics, form and mood of the music.

Still's high regard for the Blues is shown by the fact that he based his *Afro-American Symphony* entirely on a blues theme—an original one, not borrowed from an anonymous day-laborer or field-hand, nor yet from any published composition—and made it into a creation of haunting beauty and noble sentiment.

XI. *BLUE STEEL*

By far his most powerful completed work to date is *Blue Steel,* an opera on a plot by Carlton Moss and libretto by Bruce Forsythe. The subject is Negroid. The scene is a mythical swamp. The protagonists are a Negro from Birmingham (Blue Steel), a young girl of a voodoo cult (Neola), a high priestess of the cult (Doshy), and a high priest (Father Venable), Neola's father. Inevitably there is a conflict between black magic and materialism. Black magic, with the aid of the faith of centuries, is the victor. Musically, Still has used every element possible to bring about a powerful and compelling climax, from the moment the arresting "Blue Steel" motif introduces the opera, to the final chords. His choruses and drum rhythms are thrilling; his melodies unforgettable. The entire first act is made up of lovely arias, melodies that are emotional, facile and even psychological. The second act is made up mainly of exciting rhythmic choruses and a characteristic ballet dancing the sacred rites for the ceremony of renewal. At the end of the act, Blue Steel shoots the high priest who has attempted to dissuade Neola from eloping with the luring stranger. In the last act, Blue Steel and Neola try to escape, but the voodoo chants and drums have their effect on him, and he leaps madly to his death in the quicksands of the river.

Throughout the opera, Still has employed the logical, but seldom as dexterously-used device of indicating musically the mood of the moment. That is, when Blue Steel tells of the bright lights and glories of the cities, the music assumes a jazz form, harmonically and rhythmically seeking, while the melody remains true to the whole outline of the opera. When Blue Steel becomes terrified and looks toward his own God for aid, the music assumes the outward characteristics of a Negro Spiritual.

Blue Steel was not only the climax to years of study and effort, but the beginning of broader creative conceptions, for since its composition, Still has begun work on a new opera that bids fair to surpass the first one in dramatic intensity and genuine beauty. This one will be called *Troubled Island.* Its libretto is by the famed Afro-American poet, Langston Hughes, and its plot was taken from Haitian history: the short but tragic career of the ill-fated Emperor Dessalines.

Needless to say, this vehicle is more logical than the preceding, since it is founded on fact, not fantasy. The poet has created lines of great beauty to which the composer has responded with all the intensity of his creative nature.

There may be a little authentic Haitian musical material in it when it is finished, especially in the market scene, but for the most part, the composer will do as he has always done in the past: create his own themes and treatments as being truer to the story.

Troubled Island, like *Blue Steel,* is built around a baritone soloist in the leading role. Here, too, the music assumes the character of the actors' thoughts, for when Paris is mentioned, the music becomes light, gay and sophisticated. Brutally ugly is the theme for Dessaline's scars; portentous is the revolutionary theme; strongly Negroid and dignified is the theme for Martel, the aged advisor who speaks of the kingly pride of their African forebears.

XII. *LENOX AVENUE* AND RADIO MUSIC

William Grant Still often mentions the similarity of the theme of his *Lenox Avenue* to that of *Blue Steel,* and insists that he did it on purpose, to ally the voodoo story with the raucous and tender rhythms of modern Negroid life. In fun, he says it happened because Blue Steel used to live on Lenox Avenue and liked it there.

Lenox Avenue is a series of ten orchestral episodes and finale, built on scenes the composer had witnessed in Harlem, for orchestra, chorus and announcer, the narration being written by Verna Arvey. This was commissioned by the Columbia Broadcasting System on the first American Composers' Commission. It received its first performance over a national broadcast under the baton of Howard Barlow on May 23, 1937 and was repeated on October 17, 1937. The composer has since conducted it on many occasions in concert.

The themes had been gathering for many years, and Still had even made a tentative effort to shape them into a composition.[8] When the commission for CBS, in the shape of a telegram from Deems Taylor, arrived, Still realized that the perfect form for this musical material was at hand, in a symphonic work to be built directly for a radio audience. Still has never asserted that in *Lenox Avenue* he created a new form. After all, on the Deep River programs long before, the announcer had spoken over musical interludes. Thus Still simply took something old and applied it in a very special way: made a coherent fusion of all the elements. It was, indeed, the first time such a thing had been done in a single musical work.

Out of one hundred and seventeen letters received directly concerning *Lenox Avenue* after its initial broadcast, not more than six were unfavorable. Those were not all unqualified disapprovals. Some were emphatic in their disapprovals, however, and asked for more nineteenth century music instead. Many of them said they were writing for the first time. One listener wrote: "I tuned in as usual, expecting nothing more than an hour of interesting music, competently played. And then the opening bars of *Lenox Avenue!* I can only describe the impression it created in me by saying that I felt the same emotion as when for the first time, thirty-seven years ago, I heard Charpentier's *Louise.* . . . If Charpentier has described in sound the magic of Montmartre, the brief glimpse of happiness love can give to a Parisian coquette before she once more disappears into the anonymous sea of mediocrity, *Lenox Avenue* has done much the same thing for another type of humanity." Wrote another: "If anything, *Lenox Avenue* is a bit too authentic. It is truly everybody's music." Another: "I have a difficult time enjoying or understanding most of the modern compositions of our day, but this music impressed me differently . . . from the depth and warmth of the music emerged a soul."

Lenox Avenue was later converted into a ballet, and in this version was introduced by the Dance Theatre Group in Los Angeles in May of 1938, with choreography by Norma Gould and with Charles Teske dancing the leading role of "The Man From Down South."

One of the best liked of all the sections in *Lenox Avenue* was that of the Philosopher, although, strangely enough, this melody did not come to the composer during the actual creation of the work. It was after he had finished it and had composed an entirely different section that this

Example 21. "The Philosopher," from *Lenox Avenue*. Courtesy of William Grant Still Music.

Example 22. "Blues," from *Lenox Avenue*. Courtesy of William Grant Still Music.

bit of inspiration came (example 21). In sharp contrast is the Blues in the House Rent Party Scene, reminiscent of barrel-house piano players (example 22).

When the Theme Committee for the New York World's Fair of 1939 wished to find a truly American composer to write the Theme music for the Fair, it heard records of the works of many American composers without the names of those composers being revealed. Among those records were *A Deserted Plantation* and *Lenox Avenue*. On hearing these, the Committee decided that this composer was the man needed to write the six-minute musical background for the City of Tomorrow in the Theme Center. He was, of course, William Grant Still.

On a description by Henry Dreyfuss, designer of the Theme Center, and by Kay Swift, Still set out to compose this music with stopwatch, much as he would have composed film music (for among his many experiences has been that of working in the music departments of Hollywood's studios) although this music was necessarily more inspired than film music could ever be. It is also unique, unlike anything Still has ever written before, for its idiom is more or less universal. There is nothing Negroid about it. It contains two memorable, rhythmic melodies. On its completion, Henry Dreyfuss wrote enthusiastically to Still to thank him for all of his "self" that had gone into the music.

XIII.   STILL'S ORCHESTRATION

It has been justly said of some composers that they are merely skillful orchestrators but are barren creatively, as is shown when their works are
reduced to a minimum. This is not true of Still. Though his orchestral
works are not as effective in a piano reduction as in the original scoring,
they yet retain that harmonic piquancy and thematic originality that are
distinctly his own.

Dr. Hanson wrote to him, "I heard a part of some charming selec-
tions from your pen over the radio last night. As usual, I was impressed
with the highly colorful and original type of orchestration you have developed. Even over the radio it sounds very convincing."

Some people moan that orchestral resources have been exhausted.
Still disagrees with that belief. His trouble lies in making a decision between so many fascinating orchestral possibilities.

When he first began to orchestrate, he imitated others, but always
tried to choose the best to imitate, not those who were too individual,
so that he would not acquire mannerisms. As soon as possible he broke
away and began to experiment with different orchestral effects by himself, so that he would have a greater fund of knowledge at his command.
To his amazement, he found that many effects which were strictly forbidden were really quite effective and were, when used with modifica-
tions and with regard to the limitations of the various instruments, most
fascinating. He thus learned that everything is possible when approached
in the right way. Now he never accepts statements about impossible instrumental combinations without first trying them out.

The more he scores, the more convinced he becomes that the simplest
style gets the best results and is the most effective in the end. Nevertheless, in the art of orchestration, he found that he must include many
things that are not actually heard during the performance, but which are
absolutely necessary to the general effect. His orchestrations are so carefully worked out that if the exact combination for which he has scored
is not available, the music sounds wrong. Similarly if the balance is bad
in a broadcast or a recording, and a single instrument is missing or out
of proportion, everything is thrown out of line. This sometimes results
in the music sounding like Jazz, when it was not intended to sound that
way at all.

Copyists comment on the many rests in his scores. He believes that
one of the secrets of good orchestration is to know what to leave out,

and when. Only the beginner uses *all* the instruments *constantly,* just because they are available.

"In orchestration, art and science must work together," declares Still.

> Often a tone color in one's mind will defy actual reproduction through physi-
> cal means, but it can be approximated. The proper choice of instruments de-
> pends on the orchestrator's ability to hear at will the tone of any instrument
> in any register. In scoring, a tasteful variety of tone-color is necessary. One
> may define that as "pleasing contrasts that are related," and the relationship
> should be one of mood. One must choose the instrument that best portrays
> the desired mood. It follows that one must have an intimate acquaintance
> with all the instruments. They must assume the importance of personalities
> to the orchestrator.
>
> The use of certain instruments may entirely change the character of vari-
> ous themes or melodies.
>
> Clarity (where each voice is proportionately distinct) is necessary, and is
> gained by not over-orchestrating. It is worse to over-orchestrate than to or-
> chestrate thinly, for the ear has limitations. The melody should always stand
> out. This is what I call a "nude" style of orchestrating. Balance is also neces-
> sary, and is gained more by cold calculation than by artistic sensibilities. It
> has to do with instrumental combinations. Clarity often depends on balance,
> for a badly balanced orchestration can never be clear.

XIV.   STILL'S IMAGE AND STYLE

In the musical world of today, Still is a dignified, sophisticated figure. He
is far from exemplifying the popular conception of a Negro composer.
One recalls the mistaken, but well-meaning lady who scanned a copy of
Still's *Kaintuck'* and asked at what point precisely did the saxophones
enter, and who seemed alarmed when the colored composer (who by all
rights should have had a battery of saxophones in his score) responded
that there were no saxophones in *Kaintuck'*. "No saxophones?" she
queried, in dazed fashion. And then one cannot avoid mentioning the
people who have been told that all colored people are imitators and
who therefore search Still's music diligently for *some* evidence of imitation, be it ever so small. Still has been accused of imitating composers
who were known plagiarists; he has been accused of imitating men who
openly avowed their indebtedness to Negro music; he has also been accused of imitating composers he never heard of. As a matter of fact, his
style is so individual and so fascinating, once one is really acquainted
with it, that it is as recognizable as Bach's, or as Brahms'.

Still has few recreations. He is not a "social" person. Almost all of his
time is spent in steady, feverish work, in an effort to get everything done,

to say all he must say before it is too late. One afternoon a visitor entered. "It's so warm today!" he remarked.

Still looked up from his composing. "Is it?" he asked.

"Yes."

"Then I guess I'd better take off my coat."

It wasn't a pose, that absorption in work. Nor is his modesty a pose. Whenever he feels that he has done something worthwhile, whenever something pleases him, or whenever a new honor is accorded him, he sits down and humbly gives thanks to God, the Source of Inspiration. That is the real clue to his personality: his profound reverence.

People are already beginning to regard him as a great man. He hears the things they say and is grateful for them, but he is never impressed with his own importance. At a meeting of the NAACP, after the speeches had been unusually long, someone noticed that the renowned composer, Mr. William Grant Still, was in the audience. Would Mr. Still consent to speak to them on some matter of moment? The famed Mr. Still arose in an impressive silence. Then, with all eyes focused on him: "I wonder," said he quietly, "whether everyone is as hungry as I am?" Then he sat down, and the meeting was dismissed.

William Grant Still, a genuine American composer, will become world famous. When he does, he will be the last person in the world to know it, or to believe it if the knowledge is thrust upon him!

XV. CONCLUSION

As Still made history for the Afro-American when he was first to conduct a white radio orchestra in New York City and first to write a symphony, he also made history when he conducted the Los Angeles Philharmonic Orchestra in two of his own compositions at a Hollywood Bowl summer concert in 1936, for it was the first time in the history of the country that a colored man had ever led a major symphony orchestra.

He is a member of the Pan American Association of Composers and of the American Society of Composers, Authors and Publishers (ASCAP). He is also the recipient of a 1934 Guggenheim Fellowship which was twice renewed for periods of six months each.

He is mentioned in the following books, among others: *Composers in America* by Claire Reis; *Complete Book of Ballets* by Cyril W. Beaumont; *Ballet Profile* by Irving Deakin; *Composers of Today* by David Ewen; *Negro Musicians and Their Music* by Maude Cuney-Hare; *So This Is Jazz* by Henry Osgood; *The Negro and His Music* by Alain

Locke; *American Composers on American Music* by Henry Cowell; *The Negro Genius* by Benjamin Brawley, and in the Fall (1937) issue of the *New Challenge,* a literary quarterly published in New York City.

PUBLICATIONS [through 1937][5]

Darker America. C. C. Birchard Co. for the Eastman School of Music at the University of Rochester, 1928.
"Winter's Approach" and "Breath of a Rose" (songs). G. Schirmer, Inc., 1928.
Afro-American Symphony. J. Fischer and Bro., 1935.
Deserted Plantation, piano arrangement of three sections. Robbins Music Corp., 1936.
Three Visions, for piano solo. J. Fischer and Bro., 1936.
Dismal Swamp. San Francisco: New Music Society of California, January 1937.
Scherzo, from *Afro-American Symphony,* arranged for small orchestra. J. Fischer and Bro., 1937.
"Summerland," from *Three Visions,* for small orchestra. J. Fischer and Bro., 1937.
Twelve Negro Spirituals, for solo voice and piano, three of them arranged and published for chorus. New York: Handy Bros. Music Co., Inc., 1937.
"Blues," from *Lenox Avenue* orchestral score. J. Fischer and Bro., 1938.
Lenox Avenue, piano score. J. Fischer and Bro., 1938.
Quit dat Fool'nish, piano solo. J. Fischer and Bro., 1938.
"Rising Tide," theme song commissioned by the New York World's Fair during 1938. Arrangements (a) for orchestra, (b) for piano solo. J. Fischer and Bro., 1938.

PERFORMANCES [through 1937][10]

From the Land of Dreams, for 3 voices and chamber orchestra, performed by the International Composers' Guild, Inc., in New York on February 8, 1925, under the direction of Vladimir Shavitch.
Levee Land, performed in New York on January 24, 1926, by the International Composers' Guild, Inc., with Florence Mills as soloist and Eugene Goossens conducting.
Darker America, performed by the International Composers' Guild, Inc., in New York on November 28, 1926, with Eugene Goossens conducting.
From the Journal of a Wanderer, played by the Chicago Symphony Orchestra under Frederick Stock at the Chicago North Shore Festival Association in 1926.
From the Black Belt, for chamber orchestra, played by Georges Barrère and the Barrère Little Symphony at the Henry Miller Theatre in New York on March 20, 1927.
Log Cabin Ballads, played by Georges Barrère and the Barrère Little Symphony at the Booth Theatre in New York on March 25, 1928.
Africa, a symphonic suite, performed by Georges Barrère and the Barrère Little Symphony at the Guild Theatre in New York on April 6, 1930.

Afro-American Symphony, performed at an American Composers' Concert at the Eastman School in Rochester, New York, in 1931 under the direction of Dr. Howard Hanson.

Sahdji, ballet for chorus, orchestra and bass soloist, performed at the Eastman Theatre in Rochester, New York, on May 22, 1931, with Dr. Howard Hanson conducting.

Deserted Plantation, played by Paul Whiteman and Orchestra at the Metropolitan Opera House in New York on December 15, 1933.

La Guiablesse, ballet, performed at the Eastman Theatre in Rochester, New York, on May 5, 1933, with Dr. Howard Hanson conducting.

Blue Steel, excerpts from this opera presented at the Eastman School of Music in Rochester, New York, on April 3, 1935, with Karl Van Hoesen conducting.

Kaintuck', commissioned by the League of Composers and first performed on two pianos, though scored for piano soloist and symphony orchestra, at a Pro Musica concert in Los Angeles on October 28, 1935, with Verna Arvey as soloist.

Dismal Swamp, played at the Eastman School of Music in Rochester, New York, on October 30, 1936, conducted by Dr. Howard Hanson.

Ebon Chronicle, played on November 3, 1936, by Paul Whiteman and the Fort Worth (Texas) Symphony Orchestra.

Lenox Avenue, played over CBS on May 23, 1937, with Howard Barlow conducting.

Symphony in G Minor, played by Leopold Stokowski and the Philadelphia Orchestra in Philadelphia, Pennsylvania, on December 10, 1937.

NOTES

1. "Edgar Varese" is not changed to "Edgard Varèse," but "Marya" is corrected from "Mayra," and the spelling of other names is silently corrected.

2. Friedrich J. Lehmann (1866–1950) published a treatise on the violin (1899) and several textbooks on harmony, counterpoint, and form. Still's copy of his harmony text is heavily marked. George W. Andrews (1861–1932) published songs, music for piano and organ, and choral works.

3. The conductor was probably Will Vodery.

4. Compare with discussions of this piece in the Introduction and in Forsythe's "A Study in Contradictions."

5. "Land of Enchantment" in some versions.

6. Compare with the analysis in the Still-Schwerké correspondence.

7. The first performance was June 26, 1998, by the Centennial Celebration Orchestra, Ronnie Wooten, conductor. Richard Fields was the pianist.

8. This was *Cental Avenue,* which was actually completed.

9. The format of this list is slightly changed. For fuller lists that extend beyond the date of publication of Arvey's monograph, consult both *Fusion 2* and the *Bio-Bibliography.* Dates of publication, not composition, are given. Commercial arrangements are not listed.

10. Rearranged in chronological order.

Major Sources on Still

William Grant Still and Verna Arvey gave their papers to the University of Arkansas, Fayetteville, where they are catalogued as Manuscript Collection 1125 (126 boxes, 84 volumes) in the Department of Special Collections, Fulbright Library. This remains the largest and by far the most important source for materials on the Stills. Its finding aid is available in photocopy from the Department of Special Collections. The scrapbooks, an important component of the collection, are available on microfilm through William Grant Still Music, Flagstaff, Arizona. Still Music publishes and holds performing rights to Still's music that was not published elsewhere in his lifetime; in addition, it retains certain items not at the University of Arkansas.

Harold Bruce Forsythe's surviving papers, long in the possession of his son, are now the Forsythe Papers at The Huntington Library, San Marino, California. Much of his output is lost, however. The Forsythe Papers include Still's "Personal Notes" and an early draft of "A Study in Contradictions." There is much else of interest to Still scholars and students of African American music and culture: a lengthy monograph on the ballet *Sahdji,* a report of an interview with Still on music for radio, a lengthy novel on the New Negro culture of Los Angeles (alternately "Frailest Leaves" and "Masks"), and more. The Forsythe Papers include Forsythe's own list of his literary and music manuscripts, some of which are noted as lost. The surviving music manuscripts are mainly youthful songs, along with some piano music. The most important of the surviving manuscripts, in addition to an earlier draft of the monograph published here, are "The Rising Sun: A Biography of the Sahdji of William Grant Still, with a note on the Choreography by Thelma Biracree" (128+22 pp., music examples, October, 1934); "Some Meanings in the Drama of *Blue Steel*" (4 pp.); and "Frailest Leaves," a novel (600+ pp.). The collection also contains a handful of Forsythe's later letters to Arvey and his mother's letters to him while he was in New York City. In addition to the collection at The Huntington Library, the Still-Arvey Collection contains part of a published article on Still by Forsythe, two letters (one each to Still and Arvey), and four short compositions for piano. Four more short manuscript compositions for piano are at WGSM. "A Study in Contradictions," a mimeographed typescript dated October 1930 (the version published here), is in both places. Several letters from Forsythe are in the James Weldon Johnson Collection, Beinecke Library, Yale University.

The Still-Schwerké correspondence was assembled mainly from the Still-Arvey Papers and holdings in the Library of Congress, which also has a number of Still's scores. The papers of Alain Locke in the Moorland-Spingarn Library at Howard University also contain correspondence with Still. The Performing Arts Division of the New York Public Library contains materials on the New York City Center for Music and Drama (particularly the Hedi Baum Papers) and program books from theatrical productions for which Still made arrangements, among other things. An undetermined number of Still arrangements, most not clearly identified, and some other useful materials are in the Eubie Blake Papers, Maryland Historical Society, Baltimore, as well as in the Ellington Collection, the Smithsonian Institution, the Hogan Jazz Archive, Tulane University, and private collections.

Scores of articles on Still, including many written by Still or Arvey, were published in Still's lifetime. A number of them are cited in the notes here. A fuller but incomplete (particularly with reference to Arvey's writings not directly related to Still) list appears in Judith Anne Still, Michael J. Dabrishus, and Carolyn L. Quin, eds., *William Grant Still: A Bio-Bibliography* (Westport, Conn.: Greenwood Press, 1996). This essential if imperfect volume lists 173 concert works by Still with performance and publication information and cites numerous reviews as well. Its general bibliography on Still contains more than four hundred entries. Unfortunately, its discography, list of Still's commercial arrangements, and index are not complete and cannot be until much more research is done on popular music in the 1920s.

The most important of Still and Arvey's publications have been reprinted in various collections, some of them more than once. Among volumes devoted entirely to Still, Verna Arvey's memoir, *In One Lifetime* (Fayetteville: University of Arkansas Press, 1984), is essential if quirky reading. "The Life of William Grant Still," Benjamin Griffith Edwards's Ph.D. dissertation (Harvard University, 1987), is a biography that addresses cultural issues in Still's career from a different point of view. Though now outdated, it was the first to construct a narrative of Still's life on the basis of the primary sources, especially the scrapbooks, and therefore remains useful. Eileen Southern edited *A Birthday Offering to William Grant Still,* a special issue of *The Black Perspective in Music,* vol. 3 (May 1975), one of several useful collections of essays, in honor of the composer's eightieth birthday. *William Grant Still and the Fusion of Cultures in American Music,* edited by Robert B. Haas (Los Angeles: Black Sparrow Press, 1972), is a collection of several of Still's most important essays. Judith Anne Still, in collaboration with Celeste Anne Headlee and Lisa M. Headlee-Huffman, has edited a revised and much enlarged version of Haas's collection, *William Grant Still and the Fusion of Cultures in American Music* (Flagstaff: Master-Player Library, 1995), especially valuable for its reprint of Still's (incomplete) thematic catalog as it was edited by Arvey. Some of the same essays are also anthologized in Jon Michael Spencer's *The William Grant Still Reader,* a special issue of *Black Sacred Music: A Journal of Theomusicology* 6, no. 2 (Fall 1992), which also contains a lengthy and interesting introduction by the editor. Gayle Murchison, "Nationalism in William Grant Still and Aaron Copeland between the Wars: Style and Ideology" (Ph.D. dissertation, Yale University, 1998) contrasts the work of Still and Copeland in limited areas, contributing substantial new material in the process. For a general overview of the work of African Americans in music, Eileen Southern's *The Music of Black Americans: A History,* 3d ed. (New York: Norton, 1997), remains the standard. More scattered but valuable commentary on Still by Samuel S. Floyd, Jr., Gayle Murchison, Carol J. Oja, Wayne D. Shirley, Jon Michael Spencer, Judith Anne Still, and many others is cited in the notes in this volume.

Note on Recordings

As yet there is no thorough discography of Still's music that includes all of his numerous commercial and concert titles. A thorough search has yet to be made for recordings of Still's commercial arrangements, even among such obvious sources as the numerous recordings made by Paul Whiteman. Since Still (like other arrangers) is not identified as the arranger in many instances, this is no easy task. Very limited experience to date suggests that although some recordings credit his work, other cuts must be recognized solely by Still's autograph stylistic features. The list in the *Bio-Bibliography,* therefore, cannot be considered complete, nor is the list in the second edition (1995) of *Fusion 2.* Moreover, the reel-to-reel tapes in the Still-Arvey Papers remain unsorted, untransferred, and uncataloged. Their content is uncertain because of Still's late practice of recording over older material and possibly also because of their deteriorated state. We may hope that developing technology, interest, and funding will allow their recovery. For historical recordings, William Grant Still Music is at this writing the more accessible source. This collection includes acetate recordings of performances conducted by Hanson, Stokowski, and others (the CBS broadcast of *Lenox Avenue,* for example); six sides of the "Deep River Hour," Arvey's recordings for the short-lived Co-Art Turntable label; broadcast and taped interviews with Still over several decades; along with other items, about eighty-five records in all. Many of these have been transferred to tape and are available by special order as archival recordings from WGSM. What is listed in the next paragraph is selected from CDs available as of August 1999, including reissues.

The *Afro-American Symphony* (1931), Still's best-known work, is available in three versions, all with features to commend them: Cincinnati Philharmonia

Orchestra, Jindong Cai, conductor (Centaur CRC 2331, 1997); Detroit Symphony Orchestra, Neeme Jarvi, conductor (Chandos CHAN 9154, 1993); and a historic recording in stereophonic sound (1965) by the Royal Philharmonic Orchestra, Karl Krueger, conductor, reissued by the Library of Congress (OMP-106; also available on Bridge 9086). The Cincinnati CD includes two other works by Still not otherwise available, in excellent performances: *Kaintuck'* and *Dismal Swamp*, both with Richard Fields as the sensitive and brilliant piano soloist. The ballet *Sahdji*, a major work from the same year as the *Afro-American Symphony*, is available in a reissue of a fine stereo recording by the Eastman-Rochester Orchestra and Chorus, Howard Hanson, conductor (Mercury Living Presence MM 434 324–2, 1992), as part of a collection of American ballet music. *Symphony No. 2 (Song of a New Race) in G Minor*, has been released by the Detroit Symphony Orchestra with Neeme Jarvi (Chandos CHAN 9226, 1993). One hopes that the Detroit Symphony will continue to issue CDs with Still's large symphonic works. *Symphony #3* is also available, performed with less polish than the others by the North Arkansas Symphony, along with several smaller works (*Festive Overture; Romance;* excerpts from the *Folk Suites* and *Spirituals*), on Cambria Master Recordings (CD 1060, 1996). *Darker America,* the subject of so much discussion in the sources, and the witty suite *From the Black Belt,* both recorded in 1973 by the Music for Westchester Symphony Orchestra under Siegfried Landau, have been remastered and reissued, revealing their brilliant use of orchestral color and Still's unique brand of modernism ("The Incredible Flutist," American Composers Series, VOX CDX5157, 1996). The excellent ballet *Le Guiablesse, Danzas de Panama,* and two shorter pieces are available as well (Berlin Symphoniker, Isaiah Jackson, Koch 3-7154-2H1, 1993).

Witness Volume II: William Grant Still (Collins Classics 14542, 1996), by the Leigh Morris Chorale and Ensemble Singers, in the Chorus and Orchestra of the Plymouth Music Series, Philip Brunelle, conductor, and William Warfield, narrator, is a collection of newly recorded choral and choral-orchestral works. The most important of these, the choral ballad *And They Lynched Him on a Tree,* rather misses the mark stylistically, though the other works (*Wailing Woman, Swanee River, Miss Sally's Party, Reverie, Elegy)* are admirably performed.

There are several successful collections of smaller works, both instrumental and vocal. *Works by William Grant Still* (New World Records CD 80390–2, 1990) includes excellent recordings by the group Videmus of the *Suite for Violin and Piano; Songs of Separation; Incantation and Dance; Here's One; Summerland; Citadel; Song for the Lonely; Out of the Silence; Ennanga;* and *Lift Every Voice and Sing. Remembrance: African-American Songs,* with Dina Cameryn Foy, soprano, and Polly Brecht, piano, includes Still's best-known cycle, the five *Songs of Separation* and three others (DCR-MTSU, 1996). *Get on Board: Music of William Grant Still,* recorded by the Sierra Winds and supporting artists, contains nearly flawless performances of *Miniatures; Folk Suites No. 2, 3, 4; Incantation and Dance; Quit dat Fool'nish; Summerland; Romance; Vignettes; Get on Board* (Cambria Master Recordings CD 1083, 1994). (*Miniatures for Flute, Oboe, and Piano* is available in another fine performance on Crystal CD 321, reissued 1986.) The Manhattan Chamber Orchestra, Richard Auldon Clark, conductor, and Margaret Astrup, soprano, has recorded *The*

American Scene: The Southwest; The American Scene: The Far West; The American Scene: The East; From the Hearts of Women; Mother and Child; The Citadel; Phantom Chapel; "Golden Days" (aria from the opera *Costaso*); and *Serenade* (Newport Classic LC 8554, 1995) with a little less panache but still very well. On *Here's One* (4-TAY Inc., CD4005, 1997) Zina Schiff, violin, and Cameron Grant, piano, perform several items, some arranged for violin and piano by Still's friend Louis Kaufman, with polished elegance.

Louis Kaufman, violinist, long a champion of Still's music, is heard in *Ennanga* and *Danzas de Panama* on Music and Arts CD 638, a reissue.

Althea Waites gives a fine performance of *Three Visions* ("Dark Horseman," "Summerland," "Radiant Pinnacle") on Cambria Master Recordings CD 1097, 1993. A poorly edited and not well performed piano version of the suite for orchestra *Africa,* a major work, along with other piano music, is available on Koch CD 3–7084–2H1, by Denver Oldham, mentioned here only because there currently is no other recording of *Africa.* The Berliner Symphoniker performs Still's revised, complete version of the ballet *La Guiablesse* and *Danzas de Panama* on Koch CD 3–7154–2 H1, 1993; these are paired with Still's arrangements for flute and piano of "Quit Dat Fool'nish" and "Summerland." The flutist is Alexa Still, no relation to the composer. Alexa Still performs other Still numbers in her own arrangements (not nearly so interesting as Still's own) with the New Zealand String Quartet on another Koch CD.

Still's arrangements for Artie Shaw (*Frenesi; Gloomy Sunday; Adios, Mariquita Linda; Marinella; Don't Fall Asleep; Chantez-les bas*) have been reissued on Pavilion Records (CD 9779).

Index

Text: 10/13 Sabon
Display: Sabon
Composition: G&S Typesetters
Printing and binding: Thomson-Shore
Index: Barbara Roos